Brief
Counselling
in Schools

Brief
Counselling
in Schools

Brief
Counselling
in Schools

Dennis Lines

Los Angeles | London | New Delhi
Singapore | Washington DC

First edition published in 2002. Reprinted 2003, 2005.
Second edition published 2006. Reprinted 2007, 2008, 2010.
This third edition published 2011.

SAGE Publications Ltd
1 Oliver's Yard
55 City Road
London EC1Y 1SP

SAGE Publications Inc.
2455 Teller Road
Thousand Oaks, California 91320

SAGE Publications India Pvt Ltd
B 1/I 1 Mohan Cooperative Industrial Area
Mathura Road
New Delhi 110 044

SAGE Publications Asia-Pacific Pte Ltd
33 Pekin Street #02-01
Far East Square
Singapore 048763

Library of Congress Control Number: 2011927006

British Library Cataloguing in Publication data

A catalogue record for this book is available from the British Library

ISBN 978-0-85702-511-1
ISBN 978-0-85702-512-8 (pbk)

Typeset by C&M Digitals (P) Ltd, Chennai, India
Printed and bound in Great Britain by CPI Group (UK) Ltd, Croydon, CR0 4YY
Printed on paper from sustainable resources

Contents

About the Author

Born in 1947 to a Birmingham factory worker and Staffordshire nurse, Dennis Lines was educated in Birmingham. Leaving school at 15, he became an apprentice toolmaker and spent the first 12 years of his working life in engineering. A change in career occurred when Dennis was 30 after training at Newman Teacher Training College. He became a teacher in religious education, science, and physical education at Shenley Court School. This was not his first engagement with young people. From the age of 18 onwards he ran youth clubs in the local area where he lived and took many young people on camping expeditions. He managed a children's home in Bromsgrove for a short while and has fostered many young people. He is an approved Foster Carer of the Birmingham Teenage Fostering Team.

A tragic accident occurred in 1986 when Dennis sustained a broken neck and spent the 10 months in Oswestry Spinal Injury Unit. Having become a tetraplegic, he was now dependent on the support of others, and notably the young people in school who enthusiastically rally to his aid in routine support. Dennis studied under Bill O'Connell, a Solution-Focused practitioner, and Windy Dryden, a therapist-trainer in REBT.

Following his broad experience in youth work, and formal education in engineering, teacher training and counselling theory and practice, Dennis has gained insight over adolescent difficulties as they arise in school, and has found that intergrative and pluralistic approaches applied briefly to be highly effective in educational setting. He has published widely in academic journals on various topics of teenage difficulties, as well as writing four books: *Brief Counselling in School*, now into its third edition, a personal biography following his accident called *Coming through the Tunnel*, another book published by *Sage entitled Spirituality in Counselling and Psychotherapy*, and *The Bullies*, by Jessica Kingsley Publishers, which examines the dominant-submissive dynamics within close-knit relationships.

Preface to the Second Edition

My thanks are extended to the team at SAGE for giving me an opportunity to write this second edition. Apart from more up-to-date referencing, this edition reflects current British law on child protection and new legislation that applies to counselling in school, together with the BACP *Ethical Framework for Good Practice in Counselling and Psychotherapy* (2002). A broader perspective on adolescent development arising from social constructionist thinking is given in this edition to give the book a more universal feel. The text is laid out differently, with boxed case examples and key points at the end of each chapter, for quick reference. I am grateful to Nathan Marsh for his illustrations.

One major criticism of the first edition was that it was too Eurocentric, and I have attempted to rectify this in order to make the work more accessible to a multicultural audience. A further shortcoming was the absence of attention to violence and aggression in school, as pointed out by an American reviewer. Coincidently, I was working with one youngster who was unable to stop fighting in school, and so much additional material in the new chapter is indebted to what was learned from that experience. The closing chapter prompted an encouraging review from one journal where the different emphasis of brief counselling from task-centred working towards being-psychology was welcomed. I particularly enjoyed composing this chapter and was very pleased that SAGE gave me the opportunity of expanding these therapeutic insights in a much fuller treatment.

Dennis Lines
January 2006

Preface to the Third Edition

When first asked to produce a third edition, I had presumed this would be a light task, a mere updating of referencing and perhaps a slight re-editing of the text to accommodate new findings in neuroscience. After rereading each chapter, however, it became apparent that the whole book had to be recomposed in order to be up to date. Whereas the second edition was a slight modification, with an additional chapter on violence and aggression in schools, this edition is virtually a new book, with a much more inclusive stance, a challenge I have enjoyed immensely.

At the time this book is published, the UK will be undergoing a period of austerity that has not occurred for a considerable time, and this will result in yet another challenge for school counselling. Indeed, my own post may be under threat of government cutbacks and redundancy. Such changing times endorse the need for the practitioner to be adaptive.

Counselling and psychotherapy has attempted in recent times to have a greater foothold in research validation, and the professional bodies have had to adjust to changing needs and requirements. There have been in-house tensions within the profession between research-informed and intuitive practice, and the requirement for accreditation. For nearly a decade, there have been strides to regulate the profession, even though the pace of regulation slowed down under a different government administration. Academies are likely to become a more popular means of delivering education at the secondary level, where private–public partnerships take over from local authority control. All such changes will have implications for practitioners. Counselling in schools and colleges will need to be flexible and adaptive, then, if it is to survive. This third edition is an attempt to support the practitioner and trainee therapist in becoming better equipped in finding a niche within the rapidly altering therapeutic marketplace. The particular emphasis of this book in regard to adaptation is to promote the merits of practising briefly.

One factor is certainly constant and no less pressing in this than at any other time of social change. It is that teenagers – in their inner emotional being and social relationships – are struggling no less today to meet the challenges of independent and fulfilled living. Making the most of educational opportunities in preparation for adulthood is an essential task that counselling has an important part to play in, not only for disadvantaged pupils but for others experiencing occasional difficulties.

I am grateful to the publishing team at SAGE for giving me the opportunity to produce yet another edition of *Brief Counselling in Schools*. I extend my gratitude also to those who have critically appraised and reviewed former editions and who have helped anonymously to steer this project. As ever, I am grateful to those students who have enriched my practice and to two particular students – Connor Tierney and Ellie Gibbs – and their parents for granting permission for the front cover photograph. Thanks also to Charlotte Hessey, who provided the sketch of the human brain, and to Teresa Hotchkiss who drew the cartoon figures for the chapter on school bullying.

Dennis Lines

April 2011

Acknowledgements from the First Edition

Without the sharing of minds, the individual's thought becomes sterile and unimaginative: I have benefited enormously from theoreticians and practitioners whom I have consulted. A number of colleagues have supported me in the composition of this book. First, I am grateful to Janet Bellamy and Bill O'Connell, my tutors in training, for their insistence on academic rigour and for their patience and imagination when nurturing my counselling skills; particularly Bill in pointing me forward to where brief counselling was moving. I acknowledge also the inspiration and encouragement of Ron Best, an academic I have never met personally, but with whom I have corresponded frequently. I am grateful also to Alison Poyner, Commissioning Editor, and the rest of the team at SAGE, for their encouragement in steering me through this project and for giving me an opportunity to put into writing all that I have learned in brief school-based counselling. To all my teacher colleagues who have taught me so much in adjusting my idealism to the practicalities and constraints of a school-based setting, I remain grateful. I especially acknowledge Marie Woods and Wendy Oldfield-Austin for their suggestions on early drafts of chapters. I acknowledge also my former headteacher and current headteacher who, along with the Birmingham LEA, have supported the provision of counselling in school and who thereby have given weight to the need to support the emotional literacy of pupils. I thank also Deirdre Barber for her painstaking work in correcting proofs.

Finally, and more importantly, I express my gratitude to my daily tutors of life's rich experience: the pupil-clients who come forward for counselling. I have learned from them more than I can express, and every problem presented in the counselling room has been a means of developing my practice and refining my technique. One 15-year-old pupil once presented a series of paintings through which she articulated her stormy relationship with her father. Through brief art therapy, we explored her world, and this was one of the most poignant contacts I have ever made with a young client. Regretfully, she would not grant me permission to publish her story or reproduce her paintings. I remember feeling sad about this because the material would have contributed something to this book, but obviously I have respected her wish. It struck me afterwards that the learning I had acquired was being absorbed in my practice almost imperceptibly with further clients. It seems that each client adds something to the counsellor that has the potential to develop practice if the practitioner can remain intuitive to what the client is saying and feeling on different levels.

Dennis Lines
August 2001

Introduction

The initial impetus to write *Brief Counselling in Schools* was to campaign for the cause of more effective in-house school counselling, and secondly to reason that most school counsellors, from whatever persuasion and background, practise briefly or in a time-limited manner. This third edition addresses similar objectives, but in a new educational context of financial constraint and political change.

Counselling in school settings has undergone many changes, largely because it principally serves as an adjunct to the educational enterprise of most institutions. In the ever-increasing competition to raise educational attainment figures, the provision of therapy for pupils and students in schools and colleges has had to compete for resources with more conventional pedagogical priorities. But raised educational attainment figures and improved emotional and social well-being are not mutually exclusive objectives – they are interdependent. There is a strong case for arguing that the former is contingent upon the latter. This book serves to make the case.

School Counselling and Learning

It is broadly accepted that pupils who are anxious about being bullied, or who are facing an impending separation of parents, or who have become obsessed about their body image or sexual development, or who are worried about a personal illness, a family bereavement, or a fallout with their best friend, with the possibility of public ridicule on a social networking site, cannot learn effectively or make full use of even the most riveting curriculum stimuli.

I was delighted to write this third edition, and to present research on the effectiveness of school counselling for emotional and social obstacles to learning. Among typical adolescent problems that previous editions covered, this edition includes interventions for pupils who self-harm or who become involved in internet bullying, both of which disrupt the learning process.

School Counselling and Research

Another primary focus of this book has been to acknowledge the growing body of evidence coming to light from studies of neuroscience and the mapping of the teenage brain. This third edition collates current research that is relevant to adolescent development, along with the social and emotional responses that pastoral teams have to manage which arise from neurological factors.

Counsellors have tended to become polarised into two nominal groups: those pressing for more evidence-based therapy and cost-effectiveness, and others of a more humanistic persuasion reasoning that such evidence cannot be found. But for fundholders, principals, headteachers and governors, the argument is largely academic. Unless they are presented with evidence-based therapy relating to the particular cohort of the educational establishment, it is not likely that time and money will be allocated for school counselling. Evidence-based research on the effectiveness of school counselling is beginning to emerge and this edition foreshadows this promising trend.

Research on the effectiveness of brief therapy is presented, along with those approaches that lend themselves to time-limited school counselling. As the book will argue, most counselling in school tends in practice to be brief. Many education-based practitioners work eclectically or would describe their work as integrative. Along with a resurgence of interest in school-based counselling research, there has been much attention of late given to pluralistic counselling. In some cases, the model of brief counselling demonstrated is integrative and, in others, the therapy stems from a pluralistic perspective.

School Counselling and Reflection

One valid criticism of early editions has been the absence of the moral and ethical tensions that regularly confront youth therapists working in educational settings. I have attempted to redress this imbalance in this edition, to reflect more accurately what takes place at the coalface of the therapeutic encounter with young people when addressing their various dilemmas. I have found this reflective presentation a valid addition in conveying that counselling teenagers is no easy engagement within a culture of safeguarding standards and child protection legislation. The reflective questions also serve as a means for students on counselling courses to examine their own views and values when undertaking training in this most exciting form of support.

Intended Readership

This book is written primarily for counsellors who wish to take up a post in a secondary school or college of further education. It will also be of interest to stakeholders, headteachers and governors, who may be considering setting up or maintaining a counselling service in school, particularly the material covered in Chapters 1, 3 and 4. A range of practitioners – including clinical or educational psychologists, teacher-counsellors, mentors, careers advisers or connexions practitioners, pastoral staff, social workers and educational social workers – who may be considering briefer ways of supporting young people therapeutically, may find the theoretical and practical material offered over a range of teenage difficulties beneficial.

Lecturers involved in counsellor training and modular courses of counselling skills will find the references, boxed layout and reflective assignments instrumental in teaching, and in giving students an insight into evidenced-based brief therapy for adolescents.

Anti-discriminatory Practice, Case Vignettes and Safeguarding

Throughout the book, the terms counselling, psychotherapy and therapy are used interchangeably for variation of written style, with no implicit intention to denote any hierarchy by use of terminology. Clients in therapy are referred to as 'pupils' in the lower part of school, i.e. those in (UK) Years 7 to 9 (aged 11–14 years), and 'students' in the upper part of school or college, i.e. those in Years 10 to 13 (aged 15–18 years). Occasionally, they are referred to collectively as 'young people', or 'adolescents', again for variety of style. Clients' names are pseudonyms or invented characters to protect identity, since I consider most are not able to give consent which is 'informed'. Nevertheless, the case material reflects real practice of my own work.

All attempts at anti-discriminatory practice have been the aim, in terms of ethnicity, gender, social class and sexual orientation, and I apologise in advance for any unintended oversight of prejudicial terminology or practice. Although I am a full-time practitioner in a UK school, which recently became an Academy, I am aware of an international audience and have selected suitable research data accordingly. Some of the practice recommendations, particularly regarding self-referral and working collaboratively with other staff, may be considered too ambitious for the part-time practitioner. Nevertheless, they are presented as the ideal.

Safeguarding and child protection legislation is principally written for practitioners in the UK, and the reader will need to translate such requirements in accordance with their own state or country, since most western democracies have similar procedures in place to safeguard the welfare of children and vulnerable adults.

Chapter Contents

The book is composed in two parts. Chapters 1–5 cover research, theoretical, psychological and legal matters appertaining to the client group in the particular setting when engaging in brief therapy. Chapters 6–13 demonstrate principles and insights put into practice over the whole range of teenage difficulties in school or college.

Chapter 1 considers evidence-based practice and research on the effectiveness of brief therapy, as applied in school, with the following chapter looking at the particular approaches applied briefly or which readily lend themselves to time-limited practice. Advice and guidance on setting up a counselling service is covered in Chapter 3. Chapter 4 considers legal and ethical issues surrounding client status in an educational setting. This is followed in Chapter 5 by an attempt to define 'adolescence' from a multicultural perspective.

Casework in brief therapy begins in Chapter 6, addressing low self-esteem through depression, anxiety and reaction to abuse. Chapter 7 examines self-harm and suicidal ideation, which is followed by a range of brief approaches in response to school bullying in Chapter 8. Anger, aggression and violence are covered in Chapter 9, and loss and bereavement are taken up in Chapter 10. The particular trials encountered by young people when their parents or carers separate is the topic of Chapter 11, while smoking, drugs and alcohol misuse are covered in Chapter 12, and in Chapter 13 the delicate area of teenage sexuality closes the book.

Key Features

The practice section of the book is specifically designed for the school counsellor to dip in and out of when counselling has reached an impasse. This third edition is written in such a way that the time-pressured practitioner can grasp the essence of brief styles and approaches to school counselling, and the particular techniques that I and other practitioners have found effective in a quick and readily accessible manner. The text is presented concisely with suitable headings of the various themes and approaches contained in each chapter.

For those who wish to explore the research data more extensively, I have referenced the material in boxed sections. Case vignettes are also boxed for easy identification for those readers who like to explore the process of therapy through the narrative of the presented problem, the context and the ensuing discourse. At the close of each chapter, there are key points to assist in scanning the material each chapter covers. Moral and ethical issues arising from each chapter are presented for argument and personal reflection, and also to serve as suitable essay questions in youth counsellor training courses.

1 Brief Counselling

This chapter covers:

- Evidence-based counselling
- Brief therapy – what the research shows
- A definition of brief therapy
- Is counselling cost-effective?
- School counselling research
- Is brief counselling in school cost-effective?

Introduction

The effectiveness of therapy is first considered by examining counselling research generally, and then we take a look at the particular contribution of brief therapy. Finally, research on school counselling is reviewed. Headteachers and governors have a difficult task when deciding whether to finance a counselling provision in school or college. Their primary interest is in raising achievement, measured by examination results, and a principal concern will be whether or not counselling serves this purpose. If it is accepted that contented pupils learn better than when they are stressed, then the question is a case of whether counselling in school reduces anxiety.

Counselling is a costly provision, and although students consistently say through self-reporting surveys that they find therapy in school helpful, some stakeholders may require more objective evidence than subjective surveys. Objective research is beginning to show that school counselling is effective in reducing student anxiety.

Evidence-based Counselling

The massive research project carried out by Smith, Glass and Miller (1980) concluded that all psychotherapies – verbal or behavioural, psychodynamic, person-centred or systemic – were beneficial to clients, and were consistently effective. Mick Cooper's (Cooper, 2008) survey endorses earlier studies. In spite of this, counsellors are sometimes reluctant to consider the implications of research.

An American study showed that only 4 per cent of psychotherapists ranked research literature as the most useful source of information on how to practise compared with 48 per cent opting for 'ongoing experiences with clients', 10 per cent for 'theoretical literature' and 8 per cent for 'their own experiences as clients in therapy' (Morrow-Bradley and Elliott, 1986).

Pitfalls in Counselling Research

While stakeholders and funding managers may be wary of this reluctance when considering whether to resource counselling, there may be some partial justification for counsellors to dismiss research. Counselling informed by sound research, and no less school counselling, is imperative in these days of accountability, but research-based therapy is not as easy to achieve as might be imagined. There are systemic difficulties. For example, by its very nature research talks in generalities rather than specifics (Cooper and McLeod, 2011), and considers average outcomes for given approaches or techniques; it doesn't mean that one particular client will definitely improve with a given approach or technique (Cooper, 2008: 4). In addition, all research is essentially influenced by the researcher's assumptions and agendas.

It is known in the pharmaceutical industry that when research is commissioned by a particular drug company, it yields better results for its own product than for those of its competitors – what is 'found' is what has been 'looked for'. If cognitive behaviour therapy (CBT) researchers are testing their treatment programme for a given problem, say a panic disorder, and have found it objectively effective, they may claim success for an average number of clients with this difficulty but they cannot claim it to be better than other treatments if they have not conducted comparative tests (Cooper and McLeod, 2011).

Another limitation centres upon the particular tool a researcher is using to measure outcome. Researchers can come up with different conclusions when analysing the same data. If a therapist is seeking to reduce a physical symptom by a chosen intervention and this proves to be successful, the intervention may not be the best for producing other improvements, such as social well-being or alleviating stress. And, finally, approaches favouring some cultural groups may not be as effective with others (Cooper, 2008: 3–4).

In spite of these limitations, meta-analyses substantiate the claim that most counselling and psychotherapy is effective (Cooper, 2008, 2010), and that all counsellors and psychotherapists should have confidence in Carl Rogers' sentiment that *the facts are always friendly* (Rogers, 1961: 24). Cooper states that whether a client's feelings (i.e. their inner-subjective states) or more measurable behaviour changes (The Clinical Outcome in Routine Evaluation Outcome Measure (CORE-OM) scores, for example) are assessed, the 'findings from such studies show that participation in counselling and psychotherapy is associated with positive changes ...' (2008: 16).

Even randomised controlled trials (RCTs) – where subjects are unwittingly selected and compared with a 'control group' (i.e. those receiving no intervention) – the facts do show that those who receive therapy tend to improve more than a control group over time (Lambert and Ogles, 2004). And even with clinical trials, which attempt to rule out the *expectancy* factor, known as the placebo effect, counsellors have every reason to celebrate that although the placebo effect does make a difference, the change is not as great as therapeutic interventions are (Cooper, 2008: 16–20).

Meta-analysis also demonstrates that therapeutic improvements continue to remain for periods of reasonable timescales for clients living in the real world outside therapy. Further, counselling and psychotherapy compares favourably with pharmacological treatments. There is evidence to substantiate the notion that many psychological therapies have a more enduring effect in time after treatment than drugs alone (Gould et al., 1995), but in respect of combined treatments of drugs and talking cures for particular conditions 'immediately after therapy', there is less certainty (Cooper, 2008: 33–4).

Pre-eminence of Approaches or Pluralism

From such findings, many counsellors reason that 'all are winners', following what has been termed as 'the dodo effect', from the dodo bird in *Alice in Wonderland* who declares that every competitor in the race should have a prize because everyone has won. But other psychotherapists contest this, arguing for the pre-eminence of particular approaches over others, and this has divided the world of psychological research.

Combined research shows that CBT has proved to be the most effective over a wide range of psychological difficulties, particularly anxiety disorders and depression, bulimia nervosa and sexual dysfunctions, and some researchers argue that resources should be put into 'what we know works'. On the other hand, if there is evidence from RCTs, even if it is limited, to show that non-CBT therapies – psychodynamic therapy, experiential therapy, family therapy and interpersonal therapy – have been effective for some problems, they can be supported if 'the ongoing experience' of practitioners, supported by 'client feedback', claims they have been beneficial (Cooper, 2008).

From the accumulation of evidence-based therapy, the National Institute of Health and Clinical Excellence (NICE) has supported the superiority of CBT and has recommended from research (Shapiro and Shapiro, 1982) that

(Continued)

(Continued)

decisions over resources should favour this approach. Opposition from other theorists follows the reasoning that CBT – which lends itself more readily to objective measurement and which is privileged in receiving generous funding for clinical trials – is bound to come out on top, and, further, that just because there is no *evidence* to support an alternative therapy for a given problem, that does not mean that the particular approach does not work in practice (Cooper, 2008: 36–59).

In consequence, any given approach should not be ruled out on the basis of there being no extant evidence to support its efficacy, but then again neither should sound research be ignored which may indicate that, on average, a particular approach or technique has proven effective with a particular problem. Perhaps there is a balance to be struck where counsellors should recognise the common ground and be less concerned with promoting their own brand. Further opposition to 'brand promotion' has been voiced by advocates of pluralistic counselling, in light of psychological research that shows that 'human functioning is multifaceted, multidetermined and multilayered' (Cooper and McLeod, 2011: 153).

Common Factors with all Counselling

Given the biases and prejudices that are bound to exist (Cooper, 2010), purists should not dismiss the fact that common factors underlie most approaches to counselling, such as client variables and extra therapeutic events, expectancy and placebo effects, and the all-important therapeutic relationship, rather than place an over-reliance on an approach or techniques belonging to a particular psychotherapy.

With regard to 'extra therapeutic events', Lambert's findings (Asay and Lambert, 1999; Lambert, 1992; see Figure 1.1), which several authors and practitioners draw upon (Cooper, 2008; Davis and Osborn, 2000), highlight the importance of factors outside of counselling that contribute towards a successful outcome. These personal and environmental resources for young people include friendships, family support and fortuitous events. They represent the largest influence for improvement (40 per cent), followed by psychotherapeutic factors, such as the therapist–client relationship (30 per cent),[1] expectancy of positive change (15 per cent) and the specific techniques employed (15 per cent).

The position adopted in this book is to favour those integrative approaches which have CBT leanings with regards to adolescent stress and social problems, and to give due credence to those non-directive and interpersonal approaches to problems that centre upon personal trauma and loss.

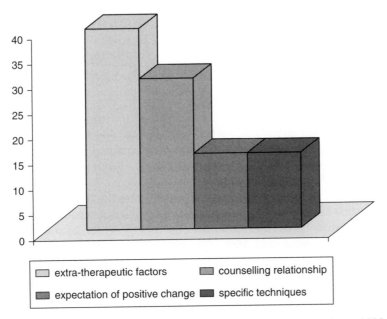

Figure 1.1   Factors influencing improvement (%) (Asay and Lambert, 1999; Lambert, 1992)

Brief Therapy – What the Research Shows

However counsellors view themselves, what is crystal clear is that a radical change is taking place through the changing requirements of the counselling profession and the pressing demand for brief methods that can be shown to work. Short-term counselling has developed in the public service institutions because of the pressure to become cost-effective and to reduce long waiting lists (Butler and Low, 1994).

A comprehensive review of brief therapy outcome research can be found in the literature for practitioners and teachers (Davis and Osborn, 2000; Feltham, 1997; O'Connell, 2005), with research regularly pointing to the preference of brief interventions for a particular problem range (Curwen et al., 2000).

The last decade saw a proliferation of research on the efficacy of brief therapy generally (Lambert and Bergin, 1994), particularly for less severe difficulties such as job-related stress, anxiety disorders, mild depression and grief reactions, and for incident stress situations, such as PTSD, earthquake experience and rape. Improvement through brief therapy for clients having poor interpersonal relations is also supported by research (Koss and Shiang, 1994).

Single Session Therapy

Moshe Talmon's (1990) study of the significance of 'one session' remains highly influential. He studied 10,000 outpatients of a psychiatric hospital over a period of

five years and found that the most common number of appointments for any orientation of psychotherapy was one. He found this the case for 30 per cent of
patients for a given year, and that the majority of clients dropped out of counselling
because they felt sufficiently helped and had no need of further support.

> Two hundred clients of Talmon's were followed up and it was found that 78 per
> cent said they had got what they had wanted after one session, and that for
> those receiving planned single-treatment programmes, 88 per cent felt they
> had improved and had no need of further work – 79 per cent said that one
> session was sufficient (O'Connell, 2005).
>
> Other research on short-term counselling indicates positive outcomes. Meta-
> analysis shows a 15 per cent improvement before the first session began, 50 per
> cent improvement after eight sessions, 75 per cent by session 26 and 83 per cent
> by session 52 (Howard et al., 1986). An early large percentage rise in improve-
> ment, therefore, is followed by a slower rate as the number of sessions increases.
>
> Meta-analyses of the most rigorously controlled studies indicate that short-
> term psychodynamic psychotherapy appears moderately effective over a
> period of time for a broad range of common mental disorders (Abbass et al.,
> 2006: 10), particularly for clients with depression (Leichsenring, 2001), which
> compares well with CBT. Clients suffering from anorexia nervosa have been
> shown to benefit from short-term psychodynamic therapies (Fonagy et al.,
> 2005; The Sainsbury Centre for Mental Health, 2006), as well as cognitive analytic
> therapy (Treasure et al., 1995). There is also some evidence that short-term psy-
> chodynamic psychotherapy has benefited clients who misuse opiates, with the
> exception of cocaine (Fonagy et al., 2005), but there is no evidence to suggest
> that short-term psychodynamic therapy helps clients with anxiety difficulties
> (Cooper, 2008: 164).

Single sessions and short-term psychotherapy are not to be seen as failure, therefore,
but as success. Some have pressed counsellors to assume that short-term counselling should be suitable for everyone until there is strong evidence to show that brief
therapy simply does not work (Wolberg, 1968). When a client is aware of a time-
limited period of counselling, she may better handle the disclosure of deeper feelings (Thorne, 1999). She may also cope with frequent and more intense sessions,
knowing the time limitations of the work and her right to decide what to disclose
and what to withhold. But what is meant by *brief* therapy?

A Definition of Brief Therapy

Brief therapy is not a specific approach, or model of distinctive theory and practice,
but a descriptor of time-pressured counselling which utilises strengths, sees
problems in context and concentrates on the future (McLeod, 2003: 435–7). It is a
foreshortened practice of mother models (Feltham, 1997; Talmon, 1990; Thorne,

1994). Freud practised brief therapy when 'curing' Maler with only one session while walking in the woods. Although Freud was proud of his analysis of the psyche, he was disappointed that the process of therapy was so lengthy.

Time-limited Therapy

Brief therapy has a certain kinship with time-limited psychotherapy. Working briefly can mean anything up to 40 or 50 sessions, whereas time-limited counselling is not usually more than 20 at most, and can include single session therapy. Brief counselling may occur by design or by default, as determined by outside pressure rather than a planned meeting of a desired outcome (Feltham, 1997: 1).

For many practitioners, any contract of less than 25 sessions is brief therapy. Colin Feltham (1997) has worked in a number of counselling agencies, including some which had no time limit imposed. In one agency offering up to an initial contract of six sessions, the mean number actually used was 3.5–3.75. Feltham also found that many clients dropped out of therapy after the first session, not necessarily due to dissatisfaction or defensiveness, as is often assumed, but because 'they had not expected to attend longer and do not feel a need to' (Feltham, 1997: 22). He says we have to give consideration to client preferences.

In addressing the move towards brief therapy, Brian Thorne recognises a tension within himself between the person-centred virtue of establishing the time-essential counselling relationship as the process for change, and his feelings about the success of an experiment he carried out when offering early-morning, three-session focused work to university students (Thorne, 1999). The short-term counselling achieved a bonding with clients and a genuine commitment on their part to attend.

In consequence, given the priorities and pressures of time and resources in educational settings, all counselling in schools is likely to be brief.

Is Counselling Cost-effective?

At some point, the question has to be asked: *is counselling cost-effective?* The most influential report produced in the UK on mental health and counselling was the Layard Report (2004), which declared that mental illness costs the UK some 2 per cent of its gross domestic product, or around £25 billion per year, through time off work for depression, anxiety and stress, reduced opportunities for employment due to poor health, caring for the mentally ill and the costs of GP surgery time, drugs and social services support (Cooper, 2008: 34). The Report calculates that a saving of as much as £2000 per individual can be made if a patient is offered 16 sessions of CBT for depression, quite apart from increased happiness and social well-being.

The same applies in the USA, where compared to the costs of hospitalisation, lost days at work and other more tangible factors, counselling and psychotherapy research establishes that psychological treatments over a non-therapy control can produce savings of $10,000 a year for every individual (Cooper, 2008: 32–3).

School Counselling Research

A large-scale review of research on effective therapy with young people was commissioned by BACP (Harris and Pattison, 2004), and Cooper's project (2009) has contributed to the growing evidence supporting the efficacy of school counselling (Cooper and McLeod, 2011: 125). Although some research evidence applies to younger children, we shall have cause to draw on this material for our client group in the pages that follow.

The systematic scoping review commissioned by BACP asked the question: *is counselling effective for children and young people?* The review covered behaviour and conduct problems, emotional problems, medical illness, school-related issues, self-harm and sexual abuse. Cooper's survey established that 88 per cent of participants wrote that they were 'satisfied' or 'very satisfied' with the counselling services, 74 per cent said that counselling had helped them 'a lot' or 'quite a lot', and 91 per cent said that they would 'definitely' or 'probably' use the counselling service again (Cooper, 2006; Cooper and McLeod, 2011: 125).

An earlier review of school counselling outcome research carried out between 1988 and 1995 showed that there was tentative support for career planning, group counselling, social skills training and peer counselling (Whiston and Sexton, 1998). Although the study focused more upon remediation activities than preventative interventions, the research validated peer counselling as being particularly cost-effective (Geldard, 2009). Skills learnt in peer mediation programmes assist in resolving conflicts at home, particularly for students facing family disruption (Whiston and Sexton, 1998: 424).

Four of the reviewed studies indicated that social skills training programmes were beneficial to students. Although it was claimed that students' self-esteem or self-concept had improved through counselling interventions, it was not clear how such a nebulous concept as self-esteem could be measured, and various studies used different measures which meant that no clear conclusions could be drawn.

One primary interest to stakeholders and fund managers is the relationship of school counselling to academic achievement, and again no fixed conclusions could be drawn owing to the complexities involved in designing a research programme to measure the 'counselling intervention' in isolation of other social and institutional factors surrounding students' lives in school. A study in Malta showed that school counselling using CBT helped dyslexic students progress through raised self-esteem (Falzon and Camilleri, 2010).

Random Control Trials in School Counselling Research

There has been a drive to conduct research into the effectiveness of school-based counselling using RCTs in the UK, as reported at the BACP Research Conference in 2010 (Hanley, 2010). This resurgence of interest follows Cooper's (2009) comprehensive review of evaluation and audit findings from 30 studies, involving 10,830 clients, which brought together quantitative and qualitative outcome papers to give clear evidence of the effectiveness of school-based counselling according to self-evaluation reporting. In setting a platform for comprehensive research, Cooper et al. (2010) carried out a feasibility study, and although the findings consistently reported beneficial outcome through self-reporting, there was found to be little difference between the reduction in distress reported by those receiving humanistic counselling and those awaiting therapeutic intervention. It is possible, of course, that those on counselling waiting lists may have been anticipating recovery through the motivational power of hope, as Lambert's (1992) study, highlighted above, indicated, which is that hope represents 15 per cent of improvement for clients.

Hanley (2010) recognises that quantitative data using RCTs are required by fundholders, since qualitative research on client feedback, although consistently positive, is prone to bias in the sense that most clients tend to report favourably on their therapy. There is a need to know, for example:

- that reported change would not have occurred anyway, or through other means than therapy
- that change is the result of counselling provided
- that those other than clients recognise change
- that change is sustainable over time.

Research-informed Counselling

Cooper and McLeod (2011: 117–33) press for counselling to be research-informed, rather than research-driven, and argue for a need to establish 'potential pathways of change rather than universal laws', to focus on 'micro-processes rather than global relationships' of factors. The question to ask is *what treatment* works, for *whom* is it effective and for *what* specific problem is it effective (Paul, 1967)? Sometimes the same clients, particularly in school, may need *different things* at *different times*. Such questions are beginning to be addressed in school counselling research through more comprehensive and objective measures than merely self-reporting questionnaires (Hanley, 2010).

In sum, the efficacy of school-based counselling remains largely dependent on self-reporting, not that this is insignificant. Brief therapy has proved beneficial for adults in many settings, and research using RCTs is currently under way to establish its benefits for teenagers in school settings for any approach, including those advocated in this book (see Appendix I).

Is Brief Counselling in School Cost-effective?

In spite of outcome studies and client-feedback surveys indicating favourable results, there is no research on the effectiveness of *brief counselling in school* using RCTs at this time. There is, however, anecdotal and inferential evidence. Although no systematic study has been carried out to estimate the cost savings of putting a counsellor in every school or college, it stands to reason that any form of learning that draws heavily on focused cognitive attention will be impaired through stress, worry or social upheaval, whether or not it results in absent days.

The cost-effectiveness of school-based counselling is not easy to assess because decisions centre on values and on the role of education, values such as the importance of emotional literacy and personal well-being, and the educative role of developing the *whole person* in place of passing examinations (DfES, 2001, 2004). However, as mentioned earlier, the Layard Report (2004) validates the cost-effectiveness of counselling in terms of lost days from work, among other indicators. Student attendance figures are examined by Ofsted. Pupils absent from school because of emotional troubles cannot learn, and neither can those who though attending may be silently suffering. This rather suggests the question of cost-effectiveness answers itself.

Conclusion

This chapter has examined research on the effectiveness of brief therapy as an approach in school or college. Outcome research for briefer ways of working is fairly sound, and findings gathered through client feedback demonstrate the effectiveness of school-based counselling. Research using RCTs is currently being planned to establish unequivocally the benefits of counselling in educational settings, and I remain confident that continuing evaluation will carry the argument for school-based therapy.

Brief therapy appears to be supported by consumer choice, and by extension it does not seem unreasonable to conclude that if this is the case for adults it can equally apply for adolescents, even though their problems will be different.

Reflective Exercise

1. In reading this book, you must be considering using briefer ways of working in school or college, whatever your training has been. Suppose your agency manager, or the senior pastoral teacher in school or college who is managing you, had instructed you that owing to the rising demand of referrals you had no choice but to work with teenagers in a maximum of three sessions:

    • What would be your initial thoughts and feelings over such pressure?
    • How would it alter your practice?
    • What would have to be cut out or foreshortened?

(Continued)

(Continued)

2. How would briefer ways of working influence your ability to form a therapeutic relationship with your young student-client?

3. How would you argue the case for more provision of counselling in school? Present a bullet point list for the headteacher from research outlined above to argue the need for an extra day of counselling in school, supposing he has asked you to present a case for cost-effectiveness in learning outcomes to take to the governors for funding.

Key Points

- Outcome studies utilising randomised control trials (RCTs) support the claim that psychotherapy is effective for a range of social and emotional difficulties.

- CBT and non-directive therapies have been shown to be cost-effective in the UK and the USA. NICE supports therapy (principally CBT) in UK clinical settings.

- There is evidence to show that clients improve with brief therapy, that in practice most counselling is brief, and that in general time-limited support is what clients prefer.

- Brief therapy is not a particular model but a descriptor of a certain time-limited stance which utilises strengths, sees problems in context and concentrates on the future.

- Most school counselling is brief – there are fewer sessions than might occur in other settings.

- Evidence-based school counselling is beginning to show promise, and students in self-reporting surveys consistently claim they find it helpful, saying that it is a source of help to which they would return.

- Besides in-house testing and client feedback, RCTs are currently being planned to demonstrate the efficacy of school-based counselling.

- The cost-effectiveness of school counselling is through raised attendance, improved socialisation, reduced anxiety, less maladaptive behaviour and a higher focused attention to learning: although a direct link of school counselling and attainment would be difficult to establish, common sense suggests they are related.

2 Brief Counselling Approaches

This chapter covers:

- Counselling approaches applied briefly in school
- Time-limited, goal-centred counselling
- Focusing on solutions
- Collaborative therapy
- Coaching skills

Introduction

This chapter outlines a range of interventions for school counsellors to consider within a brief pluralistic perspective. Apart from supporting traditional counselling approaches applied briefly, this book will promote elements of Egan's three-stage model, solution-focused therapy, neuro-linguistic programming, motivational interviewing, narrative therapy and a range of social and coaching skills as utilised in cognitive-humanistic therapy. Outcome evidence in support of the efficacy of brief therapy is impressive, even though RCTs have not as yet validated all brief models. The rationale for those approaches and models drawn upon in this book is based primarily on the experience of practitioners and client satisfaction feedback.

Counselling Approaches Applied Briefly in School

A number of integrative models lend themselves naturally for brief therapy. In addition, traditional individual and family therapy approaches (Dryden, 2002; Street, 1994) that are cost-effective (Cooper, 2008) and research informed (Bergin and Garfield, 2004; Cooper, 2008; Elliott and Zucconi, 2010) have been adapted within the time-pressured setting of school or college (Lines, 2000). Many school counsellors practise eclectically by utilising a range of techniques belonging to different models than those they customarily work under, and some work from a pluralistic perspective (Cooper and McLeod, 2011).

Psychodynamic counselling, Gestalt therapy and transactional analysis have been applied briefly (Mander, 2000; Houston, 2003; Tudor, 2001, respectively), along with CBT (Curwen et al., 2000), solution-focused therapy (O'Connell, 2005) and neuro-linguistic therapy (McDermott and Jago, 2001).

In addition, Feltham identifies behaviour therapy, rational emotive behaviour therapy (REBT), multimodal therapy, reality therapy, Egan's three-stage approach, cognitive-analytic therapy (CAT), single session therapy, the two-plus-one model and contextual modular therapy as lending themselves to short-term and time-limited counselling (Feltham, 1997: 29–44).

Psychodynamic theories of adolescent development offer a framework for understanding young people's difficulties, which can enlighten many forms of brief therapy. These insights, when combined with the person-centred notion of the client in a state of 'becoming' (Rogers, 1967), have appeal as a conceptualisation of adolescent development (see Chapter 5).

Adjusting Traditional Psychotherapy for School

According to some psychoanalytical theorists, the dynamics of transference and the insight triangle are essentially timely (Lilliengren and Werbart, 2005; Orlinsky et al., 2004); others contend a degree of transference occurs the minute a person enters a room, or as Molnos (1995: 47) puts it, 'transference needs no time' (Feltham, 1997: 30). After engaging with teenagers as early as the second session, transference occurs and a pattern becomes evident between the attachments formed in child rearing, the current relationships among peers and teachers, and the therapeutic alliance. The setting of boundaries can occur in the first session, but the counsellor's role in being passive and non-disclosing may have to be modified, or even discarded, in view of limited time. Young people live in an internal and external world, and the internal world substantially determines feelings and actions in ongoing external relationships (Jacobs, 2010), including that formed with a counsellor.

Brief humanistic approaches (notably, person-centred) are popular in education (McGuiness, 1998; Prever, 2010a), along with integrative cognitive-behavioural counselling (Geldard and Geldard, 2010). CBT supports an image of the person that makes sense for the pragmatic, scientific mind (McLeod, 2003). Its transparent outcomes lend an air of validation when dealing with youngsters in school who have been tutored to accept empirical forms of reality (Lines, 2000). The practical experimental-type methods and techniques of observation, measurement and evaluation mark CBT as 'the most overtly "scientific" of all major therapy orientations' (McLeod, 1993: 45). The strong emphasis upon action makes brief CBT and related therapies popular in educational settings.

Finally, there are brief approaches that have emerged from family therapy which embrace social construction theory – such as solution-focused therapy (Davis and

Osborn, 2000), solution-focused systemic counselling (Bor et al., 2002) and narrative therapy (Winslade and Monk, 1999), all of which this book draws upon. Accountability has also led to the integration movement in psychotherapy (Nelson-Jones, 1999a; Norcross and Grencavage, 1989; Ryle, 1990) and to the demand for cost-effective brief methods of counselling that freely utilise techniques in an eclectic manner (Egan, 1990; Lazarus, 1990).

> In this book, I use the term 'integration' to cover an informed combination of theoretical models and practical interventions from different schools of psychotherapy. 'Pluralistic school counselling' refers to the collaborative style of assessing which goals, tasks and methods suit the specific problem for the particular client in therapy.

Time-limited, Goal-centred Counselling

Egan's Three-Stage Model

One popular model for counsellors working with young people is Egan's three-stage model (Egan, 1990; Mabey and Sorensen, 1995). Egan's three-stage model is built upon the core counselling skills of congruence, unconditional positive regard and empathy. However, this approach gives more attention to directing clients in the creation of goals and tasks to bring about change. It is a practical, short-term method of working which is centred on problem solving. The process is first an assessment of where clients are, then where they want to get and finally how they may be helped to get there (Figure 2.1).

Stage 1 is the introductory phase of discussing the client's current scenario, and is not very different from the introductory sessions of most approaches. The person's present predicament and those problems that are standing in the way of healthy functioning are explored, but the style is optimistic. The counsellor will help the pupil-client to see clearly that the presented problem need not be a permanent condition. The pupil will be asked to articulate a story while an assessment is made in an attempt to bring blind spots to the surface that are a cause of malfunctioning. The emphasis is on achievement as problems are outlined in an order of importance so that only those that are solvable will be selected. The aim is to help the pupil *manage a current situation better.*

Stage 2 covers the ideal situation in which a youngster wishes to be. It involves setting goals and objectives, and this exercise fits neatly within modern educational methods of achievement. The pragmatic course of conduct screening (arranging difficulties in order of priority) and the setting of down-to-earth, specific and realisable goals which are right for *this person* – changes in lifestyle, associations with different friends, doing things differently or changing routinely established patterns of behaviour – helps youths to see where the counselling is going and what its purpose is from the outset. The approach recognises that the more the pupil frames the situation, the more she owns the means of remedy and the more she is committed.

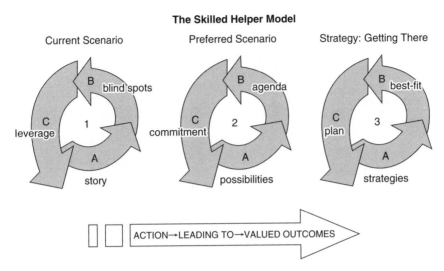

Figure 2.1   Egan's three-stage model

The practical nature of Stage 3 is equally attractive to young people in that it encourages collaboration between counsellor and client in devising an action plan to attain the specified goals, largely through behaviour techniques. It may reach outside the counselling room in calling upon agents of support, which include people, places, things and organisations as well as the youngster's personal resources. This method has the attraction of being short term, so that counselling closes when the plan has been executed. Evaluation is not left until the end, but takes place regularly – *Is this helping? Is that making sense?* It is in keeping with learning measures of continual assessment. Working collaboratively on clients' goals is known to have positive outcomes (Maluccio, 1979; Tryon and Winograd, 2002).

Motivational Interviewing

Motivational interviewing (Miller and Rollnick, 1991) is a brief goal-centred style that helps people suffering from addictive or habit-formed behaviour to bring change through insight and active behaviour management. Motivational interviewing (MI) has been applied to drug and alcohol misuse, offending behaviour, smoking, eating habits, relational difficulties, sexuality (Devere, 2000) and poor academic performance (McNamara and Atkinson, 2010). The teenager is first encouraged to address ambivalent views of continuing or ceasing the habit-formed behaviour, and then to enter the Cycle of Change (Prochaska and DiClemente, 1982) through free will and self-regulation. The student will be shown a diagram by way of explanation (Devere, 2000).

The Cycle of Change represents progress from 'contemplation' to 'permanent exit', or 'relapse' in the case of breakdown (see Figure 2.2). The teenager suffering from addictive behaviour may enter or exit the circle at any time. After relapse, for example, the client may return to the cyclic process with higher motivation to tackle the addiction again. Alternatively, he can internalise the model so as to serve as a future

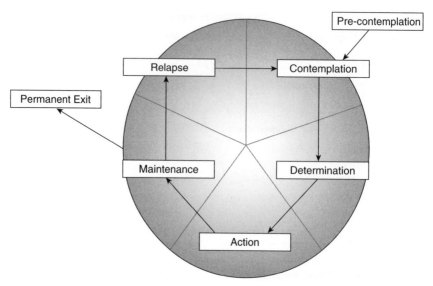

Figure 2.2 Cycle of change

Source: This diagram format was published in 'New models: the counselling of change' by Merav Devere, which appeared in the August 2000 issue of the *Counselling* journal, previously published by the British Association for Counselling. This diagram is reproduced with the kind permission of the author and publisher.

tool of recovery outside the counselling session, and this instils hope for long-term possibilities. MI has been intensively evaluated using RCTs to positive effect.

> MI has been shown to be effective particularly for alcohol, substance misuse, and diet and exercise problems (Cooper, 2008: 172–3), with evidence of being on average three hours briefer than alternative approaches such as CBT and 12-step programmes.

Focusing on Solutions

Solution Focused Therapy

A number of brief therapies have evolved in recent years that are sensitive to the power of language in socially constructing people's lives. These include solution-focused therapy (SFT), narrative therapy, collaborative language systems and neuro-linguistic programming.

The pragmatic, future-orientated style of SFT works step by step, encouraging clients to put into practice their self-selected goals. Advocates of SFT claim the approach has proved effective with as few as three sessions, the average being from four to six. The emphasis moves from 'problem deliberation' towards a 'future pictorial' focus, to viewing life without 'the problem'.

The 'miracle question', devised by de Shazer (1988; O'Connell, 2005), is enticing to a youngster's imagination:

> Imagine you woke up one morning and a miracle had occurred and everything you had wanted to change had taken place:
>
> > How would you know the miracle had taken place?
> > What would be different?
> > What would be happening that has not been happening before?
> > What would you be doing that you're not doing at the moment?
> > What else ...?

The co-constructed engagement with the therapist offers the client self-respect in the mutual entertainment of small changes of mental outlook to improve mood, communication or behaviour that is in line with the goal. A number of principles or assumptions guide SFT and highlight its empirical attraction (O'Connell, 2005):

- fix only that which is broken
- look for small change to bring about bigger change
- keep doing that which is working
- stop that which is not working
- keep therapy as simple as possible.

The future orientation encourages the pupil to move hastily from counsellor dependence towards managing alone: When will you know when you're ready to leave counselling? What will have happened so that you no longer need my support?

The technique of scaling helps the pupil to maintain a true sense of objectivity and a means of measuring improvement that does not rely on inaccurate recall. The feedback at the close of the session assimilates the client's deliberations and the counsellor's perceptions in shared discourse. This positive, non-critical and non-patronising feedback motivates the youngster towards a successful outcome by praising successes and validating personal resources (Claiborn et al., 2002; Finn and Tonsager, 1997; Goodyear, 1990).

Neuro-linguistic Programming

Neuro-linguistic programming (NLP) has become popular in recent times in contexts including counselling, management training and sports coaching. Many therapists will have practised unconsciously elements and techniques of NLP – styles of questioning and visual techniques – to positive effect. NLP is the practice of understanding how people organise their thinking, feeling, language and behaviour to produce positive results.

> A key element of NLP is that human beings form internal maps (Neuro) of the world as a product of the way data are filtered and perceived through the senses – known as 'first access'. When personal meaning is assigned, the brain forms a second map of the data through language (Linguistic) and thereby gives the experience meaning – the 'linguistic map'. The emerging behaviour is the product of neurological filtering to fit the linguistic map (Richard Bandler and John Grinder founded NLP from observing the communication skills of Erickson, Perls and Satir: see www.pe2000.com/nlp-history.htm).

NLP is a brief method of encouraging clients to restructure their thinking in positive ways to achieve a desired outcome, recognising that people 'cannot not communicate', and that 'actions result from choices'. Clients often resort to labouring their difficulties, which becomes disempowering, as though they require the therapist to understand fully the extent of what they are going through before they can be helped, as though their problems define who they are – a well-rehearsed script of self-identity. Consequently, NLP therapists are not overly concerned with content but with removing the mental blocks that impede progress. The therapist will gently divert clients from overstating their difficulties and ask: *What do you want to happen?* (An exercise is presented at the close of the chapter to demonstrate how powerful NLP can be in its form of questioning.)

Many NLP techniques have developed from other models, sometimes with different terminology. 'Realistic goal setting', 'reframing' and 'anchoring', for example, have developed from Egan, family therapy and CBT. NLP therapists are keen observers of the rolling of clients' eyes, whether they glance to the right or left, look straight forward, upwards or downwards, since these and other facial expressions indicate how information is being processed.

> Commonly observed eye-accessing cues are:
>
> - eyes up to right = processing through visualisation
> - eyes up to left = visual recall
> - eyes straight to right = auditory processing
> - eyes straight to left = auditory recall
> - eyes down to right = kinaesthetic
> - eyes down to left = auditory internal dialogue (McDermott and Jago, 2001:96).

A counsellor may ask a student to recall a childhood scene when his father and mother got along and then notice their eyes rolling upward to the left before saying, 'I can't – there was never a time'. After pausing for reflection, the eyes roll to the right, they smile and lighten up and say, 'Well, there was one Christmas when …'.

Through imaginative restructuring, clients are helped to review from where strong feelings may have originated, by such techniques as rewinding the film strip of early life to a past event, or by encouraging a client to step off a timeline (a piece of string stretched along the floor) at various stages of their life and to recall and replay particular feeling states (see the two case studies in McDermott and Jago, 2001: 145–69). The NLP therapist attempts briefly to sequence improved feeling states from positive questioning and to reframe current events and experiences more positively (McDermott, 2008a: 16):

1   How do you feel now? **Anxious**
2   What would feel half way between feeling anxious and happy? **Feeling on track**
3   What would feel half way between feeling anxious and confident? **Happy**
4   What would feel half way between feeling happy and confident? **Looking forward**
5   How would you like to feel? **Confident**

In spite of the growing evidence for the efficacy of brief therapy, and despite the growing popularity of approaches supported in this book, it has to be acknowledged that there is little systematic research evidence employing RCTs that validates SFT and NLP at this point.

Although SFT has been applied extensively in education (Ajmal and Rees, 2001; Bor et al., 2002; Davis and Osborn, 2000; Durrant, 1993; Lethem, 1994; Rhodes and Ajmal, 1995) for empowering pupils to use their own resources to resolve conflicts within a non-blaming framework, Cooper (2008: 172) can find only moderate support of SFT and no substantial evidence in support of NLP, which is in line with other problem-oriented approaches.

SFT has been shown to be as effective as more traditional psychotherapies in less time in some research but in others has proved to be comparable (Cooper, 2008: 173). Gingerich and Eisengart (2000) reviewed 15 controlled outcome studies of solution-focused brief therapy (SFBT) and found positive outcomes of five 'well-controlled' studies: four better than none or standard treatment and one comparable to interpersonal therapy for depression. 'Existing outcome research, therefore, is less than adequate and must be interpreted cautiously', declare advocates of this approach (Davis and Osborne, 2000: 20), largely because most of the reports have been made by the founders of SFT at the Brief Family Therapy Centre in Milwaukee, and with poorly designed methodologies.

Collaborative Therapy

Narrative Therapy

The validating of subjective experience in narrative therapy fits the philosophical climate of the postmodern world, and the telling of stories to make sense of personal experience is also compelling for young people (Epston et al., 1992).

Narrative therapy relies heavily upon social interrelatedness and dialogue. Through collaborative dialogue, teenagers experience the counsellor both as neutral and equal, with none of the disciplinary distancing that normally characterises pupil–teacher relations.

The intervention of 'externalising the problem' (White, 1989) encourages the youngster to separate problems from the self, and to minimise unproductive conflict between people, particularly disputes over who is responsible. It undermines the sense of failure and paves the way for individuals to cooperate with each other. It opens up new possibilities for teenagers to take action to retrieve their lives, and it enables them to take a lighter, more effective approach to 'deadly serious' problems. Finally, it presents options for dialogue rather than monologue.

Many young pupils have a story to tell: a story of hurt, bewilderment, anger or disappointment; a story of an opportunity lost or of a relationship broken down. Often the main account is a 'problem-saturated' deliberation (White later preferred 'thin description'). The therapist adopts a pose of 'interested inquiry' as she confronts a narrative that is persuasive and compelling. This stance of respectful curiosity communicates high esteem for troubled adolescents, since the therapist looks continually for areas of competence to combat the effects of the problem on the client.

The 'plot of the alternative story' invites the pupil to give explanations for those unique experiences that hint at more positive aspects of the personality, and this stimulates a search for personal resources to achieve pro-social outcomes. Through the therapeutic process, the counsellor helps the client to see where the alternative story may have begun and where it may be developing.

The closing techniques of what is termed 're-authored lives' in written narrative (Epston et al., 1992; White and Epston, 1990) may have limited value for some young people, and the technique of enlisting an 'outside witness group' or 'audience' to consolidate the new narrative may not be practical. But documents of change (certificates etc.) have undoubted merit in strengthening the significance of improvement for young people (Winslade and Monk, 1999).

Research on the effectiveness of narrative therapy is limited, but then there are authors who reason that all therapies are narrative therapies, and that the counselling experience can be understood in terms of telling and retelling stories (McLeod, 1998).

A study assessing the effectiveness of narrative therapy in reducing parent/child conflicts was carried out by David Besa (1994). Parents measured their child's progress by counting the frequency of specific behaviours during baseline and intervention phases. Six families were treated using several narrative therapy techniques. The results were evaluated using three multiple baseline designs and the findings were then compared to baseline rates. Five of six families showed improvements in parent/child conflict, ranging from an 88–98 per cent decrease in conflict. Improvements occurred only when narrative therapy was applied and were not observed in its absence.

Pluralistic Counselling

Cooper and McLeod (2011) commend the collaborative stance of 'pluralistic counselling'. Pluralistic therapy is an integrative approach that builds upon the ideas of existing models of therapy integration (McLeod, 2009), but which avoids privileging single orientation schools of practice. It embraces the philosophical construct of pluralism rather than psychological constructs, and it commits the practitioner to sustained engagement with the client's view of what will be helpful for them (Cooper and McLeod, 2011: 8).

The pluralistic counsellor begins each session with an assumption that *different clients are likely to benefit from different therapeutic methods at different points in time and that therapists should work collaboratively with clients to help them identify what they want from therapy and how they might achieve it.* It is pointless to say what is best; we have to ask what may be best for this person in this situation: it argues that many different things can be helpful to clients, and to find out what they need requires collaborative conversation in place of fitting the client into a preconceived model of practice from a predetermined theory of problem acquisition.

Pluralistic counselling has similarities with Lazarus' (1981, 2005) multimodal therapy and Egan's (1990) three-stage model, but with different terminology (see Figure 2.3). The authors, however, are keen to point out the differences. Both Egan's and Lazarus' models are located within a specific theoretical framework, and have highly specified forms of assessment; they are 'problem management' approaches which advocate highly specified sets of procedures for helping clients overcome their difficulties. They are not pluralistic but remain consistently within 'social-cognitive learning' theory. Lazarus sees the polar opposite of the multimodal approach as the Rogerian person-centred orientation, which is entirely conversational. With integrative and eclectic approaches, there is still a tendency to be tied down to specific methods and specific theories relating to the aetiology of problems and their resolution. Through regular collaborative discourse, the counsellor assists the client to articulate a *life goal*, to plan a *series of tasks* to meet that goal, and for each task to devise *particular* methods that might best meet the overall goal.

However, while adults may have sufficient independence of mind to discuss life goals in therapy, it cannot be assumed that all students in school have the capacity to see that far ahead; they may need more direction in goal setting, which is the antithesis of the pluralistic perspective. Youngsters do not always know what is best for them; they just know what they don't like, or what they want or don't want to happen! Adults, however, when referring students for therapy normally have a very clear idea of what *they want* their charge to change, even though it may not agree with their child's/student's views and concerns – hence the need for collaborative conversations.

Coaching Skills

In addition to brief cognitive-behavioural counselling, another brief approach that has merit in school settings is Nelson-Jones' cognitive-humanistic counselling – a

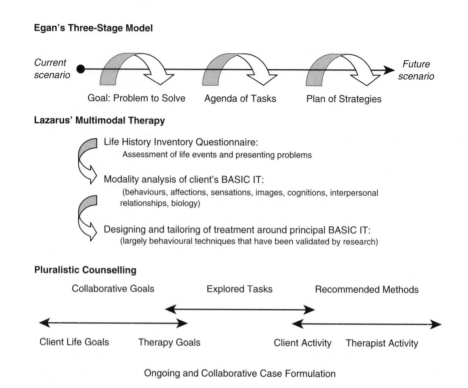

Figure 2.3 A comparison of goal-centred, integrative and eclectic approaches

cognitive way of working that espouses the values of humanistic psychology and person-centred counselling (Nelson-Jones, 1999b). The emphasis on the primacy of mind underlying all affective states, which are not autonomic responses, resonates with the way that many teenagers function. Young people can develop 'self-talk' to acknowledge the importance of listening to and understanding their feelings. They use their minds to manage unwanted feelings like anxiety, to question the reality of anxiety-evoking perceptions and to see how closely they match the facts (Nelson-Jones, 1999b).

'The life skills counselling approach' (Nelson-Jones, 1997) encourages youngsters to take a pride in shared secular values through daily attendance to, say, altruism and compassion, rather than ignorance and selfishness. Socially ill-equipped youngsters benefit enormously from relational skills training with not just practitioner observations but sound research to support the utilisation of such coaching in secondary and primary education (Whiston and Sexton, 1998).

(Continued)

(Continued)

There is evidence to support 'social skills' and 'coping skills' training with psychotic patients and with those suffering from schizophrenia (Cooper, 2008: 166–7), but little to no systematic research done with lesser adult difficulties or with teenagers generally.

Assertiveness training with adults has been shown to be effective (Dilk and Bond, 1995), particularly for those who are socially phobic, but it is not always clear whether improvement comes through skills acquisition or through *in vivo* exposure (i.e. practising certain behaviours in social settings to the point that anxiety subsides [Emmelkemp, 2004; Woody and Ollendick, 2006, cited in Cooper, 2008: 167]).

The teaching of partner skills in developmental education (Nelson-Jones, 1999a) must be sensitive to the different 'family' compositions comprising British society, and the need to plant 'seeds for future generations to possess better mind and communication skills' has obvious merit (Nelson-Jones, 1999b: 52–3).

The 'mind skills' techniques of creating 'rules for governing', and the offering of perceptions, explanations and expectations, are powerful in regulating affective states and in shaping more productive lives.

The particular skills of 'self-talk' and 'visual-imaging' are applicable to young people in school in anger management and self-control when they have felt ridiculed and wound up and when they believe their peers are making fun of them.

Conclusion

In spite of compelling evidence for the efficacy of brief therapy, no one approach or model can claim to be 'the most beneficial therapy' to be used in school or college – the evidence for superiority is too reliant on subjective evidence of practitioner reports. However, many traditional approaches – including psychodynamic, cognitive, humanistic (person-centred, Gestalt) – can be adapted in educational settings to meet the requirements of such time-pressured locations, and a number of approaches can be applied briefly in education without violating their theoretical principles on how clients improve.

Effective techniques deriving from other models are commended under a pluralistic perspective, particularly those of Egan's three-stage model, SFT, NLP, narrative therapy and cognitive-humanistic therapy. Techniques, such as collaborative goal setting, scaling, form of questioning, relaxation exercises and coaching, will be illustrated and applied for a range of teenage difficulties as commonly surface in school. In the next chapter, we consider the practicalities of brief counselling in an educational setting for meeting the emotional and social needs of young people.

Reflective Exercise

1. Jot down a series of questions that you customarily ask with each new client after initial introductions. Now reflect on a particular problem in your life, great or small. Covering with a piece of paper the questions in the right-hand column in Figure 2.4, compare your questions with those in the left-hand column. As a mental exercise, answer the questions in the left-hand column relating to your own problem.

   Now answer for yourself the questions in the right-hand column relating to your problem. What differences did you find in resolving your difficulty?

Problem frame	Outcome frame
What is your problem?	What do you want?
How did it begin?	How will you know when you have got this?
How long have you had it?	What else in your life will improve when you get this?
Who is to blame?	What resources do you already have that can help you achieve this outcome?
What is your worst experience of this problem?	What is something similar that you did succeed in doing?
Why haven't you solved it yet?	What is the next step?

Figure 2.4   Problem and outcome frames (McDermott, 2008b: 13–14)

2. Consider a past case of a student in therapy, preferably one that had been written up as a learning exercise, and review how much time was spent in deliberating on 'the problem' as opposed to reaching 'a solution'.
   a. What does this teach you about a client's tendency to dwell on difficulties they are having?
   b. What are the risks in 'steering' students towards solutions that may leave them feeling they were 'not heard'?

3. In your ongoing work, take note of clients' eye-directional movements in an unobtrusive way and attend to what your clients are saying shortly afterwards.
   a. Do you agree with those NLP theorists who claim that eye positioning, facial expression and tone indicate particular features of mental processing?
   b. Discuss the pros and cons of reading too much into interpreting body language and facial expression.

Key Points

- Traditional counselling approaches can be adapted to work briefly in educational settings.

- Egan's three-stage-model, with its emphasis on only those goals and tasks that are achievable, is a suitable scheme of therapeutic progress.

- Solution-focused therapy has become popular in contexts which include schools; it avoids the tendency of problem-saturation talk and draws clients towards future possibilities.

- NLP offers a particularly effective range of future-oriented questioning.

- Motivational interviewing is effective with addictive behaviour.

- Narrative therapy assists those adolescents who feel labelled or disempowered by overarching attitudes to locate new resources within themselves for change.

- Mind skills, coaching and assertiveness training skills, as featured in cognitive-humanistic counselling, are fitting techniques for students in educational settings.

- A pluralist perspective to brief counselling in school can be summarised as being goal-centred and focused on a fully collaborative planning of tasks and methods for change.

3 Counselling in School

This chapter covers:

- The development of school counselling
- Planning a counselling service
- Working collaboratively in teams
- The counsellor role
- Practice issues
- Ethical issues arising from collaborative practice
- Developing a personal style
- Counselling notes
- Counselling evaluation

Introduction

Counselling provision in education is varied, though generally on the increase, with most establishments financing therapy from their own budgets. This chapter looks at the planning stage of setting up and maintaining a counselling service in school. Practical matters, such as a suitable location for counselling, referral policies, role and collaborative working, note-taking, auditing and evaluating the service, are discussed, together with the contractual details of employment. The premise of these considerations is that brief counselling in school will need to evolve with the altering requirements of the educational institution.

The Development of School Counselling

The development of school counselling in Britain, and to a lesser extent in Australia, can be traced from the social changes occurring in the industrial revolution (McLeod, 2003), the rise of youth culture in the 1960s (Jayasinghe, 2001), the changed emphasis in education (Milner, 1980), the proliferation of counselling courses in the 1970s (Mabey and Sorensen, 1995), and an expanse of provision in schools (Lines, 2002a; 2006b; Prever, 2010a). A review of counselling in schools in

England, Wales and Northern Ireland has been commissioned by the NSPCC and Keele University (Baginsky, 2004). One survey established that 75 per cent of a sample of schools in England and Wales had a counsellor in 2005, with a current move to have a school counsellor in every school in Northern Ireland, Scotland and Wales (Hanley, 2010). Therapy for children and young people in the USA has had a much longer history (Capey, 1998; Reid, 1996).

Counselling in the UK has been consistently highlighted as helpful for children and young people with emotional and behavioural difficulties in school (DfES, 2001, 2004), and the Layard Report (2004) promoting an increase in CBT for adults has been influential – not that this resulted in extra funding in education (*Therapy Today*, 21 March 2010: 6).

In the West Midlands, school counselling is as diverse as full-time practitioner support (my own practice), local authority services (as occurs in Dudley), outside agency contracts (such as Open Door) and freelance provision (McGinnis and Jenkins, 2009). Most counsellor contracts are for one to three days a week paid from local budgets. In addition, counselling for students in education is not the exclusive role of a trained therapist. Different personnel are engaged nationally in providing counselling skills, such as pastoral teachers and support staff, psychologists, careers advisers, nurses, health workers, language instructors for overseas students and educational social workers.

Practitioners based at a school or college work under a system orientation, while those visiting therapists on a part-time basis will be open-orientated, having their codes and practices determined by the organisation offering a service rather than by the host institution employing them (Mabey and Sorensen, 1995). Each orientation has inherent advantages and disadvantages in terms of offered level of confidentially, safeguarding restrictions and the granting of rights to children to receive counselling without parental foreknowledge or consent (McGinnis and Jenkins, 2009).

Planning a Counselling Service

The BACP sub-division, CCYP, has produced guidance on setting up a counselling service in schools (McGinnis and Jenkins, 2009), along with a toolkit (referred to as *Toolkit*) which can be found on the website (www.ccyp.co.uk), the former offering a comprehensive guide for the non-specialist manager who has to consider such issues as legal matters and contractual details. The *Toolkit* offers checklists and exemplar documents of good practice and terms of counsellor employment. Other authors (Bor et al., 2002; Lines, 2006b) advise on a range of practice issues.

One major consideration in planning will be around the extent of therapy being offered in school or college, and the freelance counsellor setting up a counselling service will need to reflect on whether therapy is solely for students, or also for their parents and carers, or for others of the establishment, including teachers and lecturers. There are questions to consider within the time-allotted and contractual agreements discussed beforehand, such as whether to:

- offer group therapy as well as individual counselling
- engage in couple work or family therapy
- organise and manage a peer counselling service
- teach relationship skills to younger pupils
- run modular courses on counselling skills with older students
- publicise the service in assemblies and staff briefings
- consider how information might be disseminated with key personnel.

In my experience, it is best to consider these practice issues at the outset when negotiating the contract with managers and fundholders, rather than let them emerge when time becomes pressing and role conflict problematic. As a full-time school counsellor, I have carried out all the above, but then I am not pressured by time as much as a teacher-counsellor or part-time therapist might be.

Experienced school counsellors deliver a diverse practice, engage in family work and undergo training to extend their role, learn how the teenage brain develops and have a proactive role in pupil monitoring systems in school (Fallon, 2010). Apart from the particular approach and model with which the brief counsellor feels competent, some thought may need to be given to extra training if the work requires:

- a different approach than trained for
- Gestalt empty chair work
- psychodynamic in-depth therapy
- couple counselling, mediation or systemic family therapy
- managing, training and supervising peer counsellors
- CBT techniques, assertiveness training and social skills teaching, etc.

It should be borne in mind, however, that being too adventurous in offering an eclectic service for a broad range of clientele may over-stretch a part-time practitioner with only a contract of a day a week.

Embedding the Practice

It is imperative that school counselling is embedded within the culture and systems of the particular school or college, not only to secure a practitioner's long-term employment but in order for collaborative work to take place among other professionals who are working towards similar ends – namely, student well-being. Authors Bor et al. (2002) also stress the importance of working collaboratively, particularly within the school pastoral system so as to dispel the myth that the counsellor has secret agendas not akin to those of other professionals. They suggest that the new appointee should learn how the school functions in order to tailor practice within existing pastoral and organisational cultures and to avoid perceptions of the counsellor wishing to work in isolation.

They commend the idea of consulting regularly with the head and promoting the service to senior staff and the governing body through presentations and staff briefings so that all personnel are aware of how the therapist intends to work. In my experience, most headteachers are too busy for regular communications, and tend to delegate such management to other senior teachers who have a pastoral role or the responsibility for *Every Child Matters.*

Working Collaboratively in Teams

Whatever training a youth counsellor may have received, the therapist working in school or college is required to be a member of a team, normally a pastoral team (Lines, 2003). As such, the brief counsellor may be expected to receive and give information to other personnel within the institution, and this may present an ethical dilemma for many counsellors not used to working in this setting. It is not as though the code of confidentiality is not recognised within school or college, or as though privileged information shared in counselling is expected to be casually passed on to third parties, but it is because all practitioners work together for the well-being of students, and this requires information sharing; it is conventional practice in education.

> I am part of a 'Filter Group' that regularly meets to discuss the needs of pupils failing in mainstream education and, although I am not expected to provide detailed information disclosed in counselling, my opinion informs the collective decision-making process. Some school counsellors may be based in a Special Needs department, may work among others involved in mentoring, may manage peer counsellors, may run anger-management groups or provide social skills training, or may take part in classroom-based activities and the like, and, as such, the therapist naturally is part of a collegiate team.

Being part of a team does not infer, however, that the school counsellor will always see eye to eye with other key personnel – no team functions this way, even though members work together for the common good.

CAF Meetings and Case Conferences

Common Assessment Framework (CAF) meetings are convened in England when youngsters are not having their social and emotional needs met within the family. The case may not be as great as to require social services input, and so any professional (including a counsellor) may be asked to call together a team of health visitors, the GP for the family, family support workers, probation officers, educational psychologists, housing officials and drug workers, along with parents or carers and school staff, to identify and meet particular needs for the targeted child – at the very least, a counsellor may be nominated a particular role in such a meeting.

CAF meetings are prescriptive and have set procedures, schedules and documentation, and are in place as a preliminary before social work intervention. CAF meetings are part of the *Every Child Matters* agenda, but their merit at the time of writing is a controversial topic in secondary schools, and there are many professionals in education who are ambivalent about their value, and who are certainly reluctant to call a CAF meeting, seeing it as a means to obfuscate social work involvement. General experience of CAF meetings throughout the country is varied, as one CAMHS practitioner has said: 'the promise inherent in the CAF for much-needed, joined-up early intervention has only partially materialised, and it seems to be a postcode lottery in my county' (Catchpole, 2010: 11). However, calling CAF meetings for children in need is a legal requirement, but who should be expected to take a leading role is a debatable question.

> It is not advisable in my judgement for counsellors to lead in CAF meetings unless they have other roles in school. The planning and convening of successive meetings and the administrative duty to distribute minutes to involved parties makes this labour-intensive, not to mention the perceptive risk of role confusion for the student-client.

Combined Roles

Some schools may have a teacher-counsellor, while others have mentors and teaching assistants using counselling skills, yet all effective pastoral staff will engage with troubled teenagers (Prever, 2010b), alongside or without the involvement of parents and carers. Dual roles can be problematic and seldom preserve 'neutrality' (Prever, 2010a: 39), particularly when the counselling role is subsidiary to other responsibilities. Teaching commitments will invariably take precedence over therapeutic engagements, and, as such, the perceptions of the school populace will be that counselling has marginal importance to other priorities.

Teacher-counsellors having departmental management briefs, such as organising the moral and health curriculum, or coordinating careers, Special Needs, or 'looked after children' (those in care), in addition to classroom work, are likely to experience boundary conflicts when disciplining pupils. I manage the School Reception Service, but experience no role conflict in doing so, certainly not as when I taught my specialist subject combined with counselling. Even if a counsellor has no conflicting role, she is still expected to operate wholly within the ethos, aims and objectives of the particular educational establishment, since to work otherwise could leave youngsters and carers confused over conflicting expectations of the institution.

The Counsellor Role

The brief school counsellor will soon become aware that she is not the only practitioner in school or college providing counselling or practising counselling skills. Youngsters are frequently counselled and guided on a daily basis within all educational institutions, and research has shown that there is no direct evidence to support the view that the more qualified the therapist the better the therapy (Bratton et al., 2005; Cooper, 2010). 'Studies comparing professionals and paraprofessionals have not found substantial differences in the effectiveness of these two groups of therapists' (Berman and Norton, 1985: 405), particularly with younger clients and in briefer forms of therapy. Most other personnel, however, are not likely to have the time, the skills or the aptitude to work at depth with youngsters over feelings of despair and loss (McGuiness, 1998).

Establishing the Role

I would advise that the brief counsellor takes active steps to write up the distinctive role and job description, and have it broadly published around the school, in the prospectus, on the website, in the staff handbook, in leaflets and pamphlets for parents and students in accessible language (bearing in mind those having special needs or English as their second language), or anywhere else that gives all members of the community an informed understanding of what is on offer for the range of difficulties that commonly occur for teenagers in school. Not to have a job description and clear outline of the role and responsibility of the school counsellor is a serious shortcoming that leads to confusion, role conflict, occasional power games and unproductive alliances. This often makes mediation work between student and teacher virtually impossible.

If not in place, the counsellor and line manager could work together and write a specific counselling role and job description. The *Toolkit* provides sample documents, which serve as a useful starting point, but I would commend that practitioners modify such templates so as to match the job with the requirements of the particular establishment. The job description and therapeutic policy of the counsellor will be framed within the institutional ethos, the aims of the establishment and the *Ethical Framework for Good Practice in Counselling and Psychotherapy* (2002) published by BACP (hereafter referred to as the BACP *Ethical Framework*), or other such ethical framework.

The job description will cover working practices, including:

- the referral procedure
- the extent of offered confidentiality
- safeguarding and child protection protocols
- supervision
- membership or accreditation with an official body (BACP)
- auditing and recording.

Line Management

Some heads and principals have not given much thought to the line management of a counsellor in education – whether they are from an outside agency, are a commissioned freelance therapist, or, again, as in my case, are a full-time counsellor in permanent post (I have had six different personnel as line managers in school over the period). For some schools, the Special Needs teacher will assume responsibility, but for others a senior teacher responsible for misbehaviour, or pastoral matters, or *Every Child Matters*, will take the lead. A few years back when learning mentors were brought into my school, the headteacher was initially their line manager and there was no job description for any of us, which resulted in much confusion and an unnecessary duplication of work – targeted youngsters were removed from class and spoken with by up to three professionals at a time, sometimes receiving contradictory advice.

The Contract of Employment

There should never be any confusion over a school counsellor's contract of employment (legal and ethical issues are considered in Chapter 4). I have consulted local school counsellors and not everyone has a written contract specifying the scope of their work, suggesting that although the school or college is showing a commitment to provide therapy for students on the campus, the service has not been thought through or is embryonic and evolving. I am not saying the service should be fixed and static, far from it, but some thought should be given to how counselling is to be aligned with the existing pastoral system, the teams of operation and the particular management roles already in place. The contract will specify the working terms and conditions, pay, qualification requirements, hours of work, holidays and sickness, indemnity insurance, complaints procedure and other details that apply to all, such as a criminal records bureau (CRB) check. Contract exemplar documents can be found in the *Toolkit* (2010: Part 2).

The Perspectives of the Counsellor

Being visible during assemblies and at parents' evenings and other social functions will help the therapist become fully integrated within the school community, so that any visit to the counsellor will not be viewed as a stigma, as though the youngster has a *'serious problem' that requires in-depth analysis by the shrink!* Perceptions among teachers and students are crucial. I know of school counsellors who run youth clubs and discos in school, go on school camps and various social engagements. How a school counsellor is viewed is important, and practitioners are advised to canvas those who will give a frank assessment on the matter.

Practice Issues

It is as well to consider a range of practicalities when negotiating a counselling service in school or college, and in earlier editions of this book these were considered in the light of school counselling having a weaker foothold than is the case generally today.

Location for Therapy – Accessibility and Autonomy

Of principal concern is the location of the room used for therapy. There is a need to balance two opposing requirements: room accessibility – so that any youngster can approach the counsellor and self-refer without being reprimanded for being 'out of bounds' – and anonymity – so that any cautious pupil may confidently approach the therapist for help without it being too public, bearing in mind that complete anonymity is unrealistic in school. In many cases, however, the counsellor has little choice but to utilise what is available, particularly when working part-time.

Commonly, the counsellor will have to share a room with a pastoral teacher, or may even have to find a suitable corner behind a screen in the Special Needs room. Once a school counsellor has become established, and perhaps offered more time, it may not be considered unreasonable to request better conditions – in promoting the essential requirements for containment and confidentiality. Being too demanding early on though will not foster good and collaborative relations. Whatever room is used, attention must be given to safeguarding – such as a window to avoid suspicion of abuse in closed and secluded rooms. Therapists, just like teachers who work alone with pupils, are potentially in a risky situation, and all negative perceptions must be guarded against with good planning and forethought.

The Therapy Room

If the school counsellor is lucky enough to have a choice in such matters – and has a budget with which to organise a specialist room – there are matters to consider when planning an appropriate arena for therapy. Given that teenagers are wholly preoccupied with image and status, I think it is well to project a certain persona of being in touch with youth so as to avoid perspectives of being odd and out-of-the-ordinary – the counsellor should not be unpopular. The success of self-referral is solely dependent upon perspectives, and such will be thwarted or reinforced the first time a youngster enters the room.

A brief school counsellor will need to consider how much 'personal self' they wish to reveal through pictures and posters on walls and notice boards. This is a controversial issue for practitioners, as discussed in *Therapy Today* (22 January 2011: 35–7), and will depend on whether a counsellor views revealing their 'humanity' as being instrumental in therapy or considers a plain, opaque environment better serves the purpose – I favour the former (see below).

Revealing of Self – Making Connections

As Robert sat in the waiting room before his first session, he glanced at some of the pictures on my wall. 'I see you like classic cars. My dad has an old Sunbeam … He's teaching me to do up a Mini Cooper.' As I was making a drink, he began to tell me how far he was into his restoration project. Almost immediately, a bond was formed over a mutual interest and, after telling me that I had once worked with his father when he was at school, it seemed as though a counselling relationship was established before we had begun our session.

A welcoming environment is created with illustrations that are stimulating and thought-provoking, immediately communicative and enticingly attractive, ideally in sync with teenage issues and fashion so as to provoke curiosity. Within the room, there will be artefacts and items of what might be termed 'the therapeutic tools of the trade': perhaps a sand tray, puppets, visual aids for engaging inarticulate youngsters; artistic materials for those who wish to explore inner-depths without verbal deliberation; books, articles and self-help manuals for teaching and training staff and sixth formers; together with leaflets and information of referral to sexual health clinics and other such services. In my room, I have eye-catching, reflective and humorous poetry, proverbs and sayings to stimulate thought and perhaps a smile for pupils in waiting.

The sort of ambience counsellors wish to create will depend upon taste and personal interest. Should there be a scented aroma and soft music in the waiting area? And, if so, what? What subliminal messages will particular fragrance and melody give? Music eases tension for angry pupils, but it can also draw an unwanted audience and prove a distraction from business to hand. Subtly selected music may calm fermenting fury for those who have been 'marched to the counsellor' for behavioural reasons, or those on the brink of a fight, but it will also polarise individuals into already formed cliques defined by musical tastes.

Working Around Interruptions

It is unrealistic for any therapist working in school or college to have the same expectations of peace and non-interruption as occurs in outside agency therapy centres, whether engaged in individual or group therapy, particularly if the room is shared and if there are regular comings and goings of pupils seeking teachers who are normally found in the same office. If it is possible, without offending other personnel, it is best to temporarily disconnect the telephone and put a sign of engagement on the door. These arrangements should be discussed and planned well before engaging in in-depth work.

The therapist is advised to set his watch to lesson changeovers, and to plan sessions in light of when the bell will ring. I do not think the brief school counsellor should be highly principled over occasional interruptions. In my experience, although there are occasions when naturally a highly traumatised client will be distracted, in the majority of cases youngsters are quite used to people popping in and out of rooms, however disturbing this may be for the newly qualified therapist. School counsellors simply have to work around interruptions and see them as being part of working in school.

Managing Interruptions

We were midway through a heavy-going session, as I engaged with Lauren over the death of her mother, when a Year 9 pupil opened the door and said, 'Sorry to disturb you, but have you seen Mr Johnston?' After seeing young Lauren in floods of tears, the pupil looked somewhat embarrassed, and apologised for bursting in. He did not notice the illuminated sign: ENGAGED – DO NOT ENTER

Referral Procedures

At the early stages of planning a school counselling service, it is essential to decide on how referrals are made, whether through a pastoral teacher, the form or subject teacher, an outside agency, a parent or carer, students presenting themselves, or all of these. If self-referral is offered to students – and I think it should in a caring institution – it is imperative to plan a discrete system of communication. All affected staff need to be informed of the referral procedure and the means of communicating each and every session. I work in an academy where many clients self-refer and where every age group, ethnic background and both genders alike make liberal use of counselling support. I work within a team of referring professionals – a nurse, the pupil welfare manager, the behaviour coordinator, an attendance worker, heads of college, pastoral support managers, the Special Needs coordinator and all senior and junior staff (see Appendix II).

Consulting other school counsellors working part-time in schools and colleges, there appears to be a low take-up of self-referral generally, compared with teacher referral. Inevitably, when budgetary factors are borne in mind, the school or college will aim to get the maximum service for the money, and this means that the counsellor's line manager will aim to fill every session in advance. If a pre-planned session does not occur because the pupil is absent, or has forgotten their pre-arranged appointment, then there is some scope for others to refer themselves immediately for counselling – that is if there is a system in place.

Bor et al. (2002) suggest that a postbox could be fixed in a suitable place for students to place a request for a counselling session. The *Toolkit* presents exemplar referral sheets. However self-referral takes place, the practitioner will need to ask the all-important question of how a pre-arranged appointment is to be communicated to teaching staff.

McGinnis and Jenkins (2009: 16) recommend that an appointment slip marked 'pastoral care appointment', put in an envelope, could be passed on discretely by teacher and/or pupil to preserve anonymity, but this would not work in my school. I favour openness and the need to remove any stigma involved in seeking and attending counselling – complete anonymity is unrealistic in school during lesson time. In my practice, a new referral is contacted by the pupil receptionist, but for pre-arranged appointments I use permission pro forma slips of request for a pupil to be excused part of their lesson.

However communications occur, appointment making poses particular problems in school. Although my principal grants self-referral, she also places a high priority on every pupil being in lesson on time, engaging in learning and receiving their full curriculum entitlement, and having to register each pupil electronically in every lesson will lead to unnecessary and unhelpful disagreement between the teacher and counsellor if a pupil fails to turn up at the start of the lesson for reason of making an appointment or seeing the counsellor.

A Not Untypical Case

Kieran approached me at the beginning of period 3, asking if I could 'get him out of his lesson'. 'Why do you not wish to go to your lesson, Kieran?' I asked. 'Because Jamie and Delroy keep taking the mickey.' 'I'm afraid I cannot see you now', I replied. 'I have to attend a meeting, and, besides, I cannot authorise you not to be in your lesson. Perhaps, if you had seen me beforehand to discuss the matter, say, during your break or lunch, we could have explored a way round the problem. If it becomes impossible for you to go, then you will have to speak with your pastoral support manager. Come and see me tomorrow during your break and let me know how you got on.'

Cavalier practice fails to distinguish a genuine need for counselling from a lesson-avoidance strategy (perhaps the student has not completed their homework); these are tendencies which occur in school and can undermine the counselling service if not guarded against with proper planning.

I am conscious that when students have begun their examination courses, I have to try to negotiate with their teachers beforehand – through a note or via email – whether it is convenient to speak with the pupil in a particular lesson, sometimes giving way and usually respecting the teacher's wish. This is a policy decision that is not without logistic and ethical problems – I will, with the principal's blessing, override the teacher if I judge it to be a crisis situation that cannot wait.

Customarily, I tend to plan later sessions in the second half of the lesson, so as to enable the student to receive the input of the planned lesson and not get too far behind, this being communicated through a permission or appointment slip that the pupil is expected to hand in to the teacher. Inevitably, this means that complete anonymity cannot be preserved, but I have to consider the fact that the institution where I work is a learning environment where the raison d'être is not therapy but conventional learning. Therapy is an adjunct to the learning process, and this is where I have learnt to fit into the ethos and working practices of my educational institution

Ethical Issues Arising from Collaborative Practice

A range of issues emerge from collaborative practice, such as the passing on of information entrusted to the therapist, the particular role of confidante in group meetings when discussing pupil welfare, permitting access to counselling files, composing reports for the headteacher who is deciding whether or not to exclude a pupil, and the like. As said above, the school counsellor is well advised to plan these matters before commencing therapy in school or college so that the distinctive role of counselling is understood by all parties.

Some school counsellors may be required to attend case conferences on particular clients they have counselled, write a report in cases of child protection conferences or even be part of a core group meeting when a care plan has been drawn up, and, again, there are ethical questions to consider which are best dealt with by prior consultation with the clients themselves and sharing with them the reasons for their attendance. If a written assessment is required, or a report about their client is requested, the counsellor has to consider the ethics and whether the document should be composed collaboratively, where appropriate. There is no doubt that professionals convening statutory meetings value the input of counsellors, but such contributions have to be balanced by ethical considerations of how the therapist is viewed by the student-client.

The therapist may be asked to attend a meeting convened by CAMHS, or psychiatric nurses, or other mental health practitioners, to make a contribution to discussion on the mental functioning of their particular student-client, and although collaborative practice in teams is becoming the norm in educational institutions, the school counsellor cannot neglect the ethical complications that may arise from such inputs.

Naturally, sensitive material, and particularly narratives which are shared in confidence, are not expected to be passed on needlessly and unprofessionally, but there are occasions when opinion is sought of the therapist that may inform decisions taken by others. Confidentiality, as we shall see in Chapter 4, is the recognised code between therapist and client, as conforming to the body in which the practitioner belongs, such as the BACP *Ethical Framework*, but the brief therapist will form a judgement and may indeed be required to make an assessment of one of their clients after a few sessions of engagement that provides for a team a particular insight as to how best a student may be managed, or guided in the furtherance of their educational career in school or college.

Developing a Personal Style

All school counsellors will have favoured ways of working and predispositions (Cooper, 2010), and it is well to be aware of these and bring them up in supervision or personal therapy. But they will also have biases. I regard my practice as integrationist with CBT leanings while preserving a pluralistic perspective (Cooper and McLeod, 2011).

An approach is selected *intuitively* and *collaboratively* after listening to the referral data and the client's story, revising decisions regularly as work progresses through reciprocal 'talking about talking' (metacommunication) – *Is this helping? Are we on track here?* Contracts and programmes of work are modified at significant stages when the focus is altered or through review and supervision.

As the young student sits before me and describes the problem, it is not given as raw data without context. The problem is presented within a narrative, a narrative that is supported by a range of stories that represent my student-client's reality. Whether the problem is considered as residing within her head or located in her relational world, there will emerge a narrative that depicts a perspective, or range of perspectives, on how she sees the world or how she perceives the world treats her.

Therapy Screening

When implementing a referral screening methodology during the introductory phase, I ask 'What is going on in my head?', for while I cannot know what is in my client's mind at this point, I know what is in mine. In my mind, I rapidly run through a catalogue of styles and approaches that are filed away through learning, practice and experience. As we negotiate collaboratively each of the tasks and methods of therapy, my initial activity and contribution involves a sifting and selective process through a range of questions that require answering:

- Is counselling indicated for the problem outlined?
- Is there a need for in-depth work, or merely the passing on of information?
- Should the counselling be directive and have a pedagogical emphasis?
- Is there a precise problem that can be addressed with solution-focused approaches, or is there a need to explore deeper and unclear levels of what to this point has not been articulated?
- Is the problem merely about solving a dispute between peers or between child and adult that might indicate a referral to a pastoral teacher or other agency, or is there a more comprehensive requirement to help my client with adaptive social skills because of more general communication difficulties?
- What particular intervention is likely to result in a positive outcome?
- Is there a need to facilitate the expression of my client's sadness and validate her sense of loss through humanistic counselling, or is cognitive therapy indicated to help her rise above a depressive state or, alternatively, to combine the best in each with cognitive-humanistic counselling?
- Should we engage in existential therapy to explore her sense of being and philosophical outlook?
- What is my client's principal mode of functioning (feelings, cognition, behaviour)?

The Counselling Process

All clients have a dominant mode of functioning (Lazarus, 1981, 2005); some are intuitive and others pragmatic. Some prefer to engage in a practical task, while others benefit from a cathartic expression of feelings – cognitive therapy is favoured for those who function cerebrally, while Gestalt therapy has tended to appeal to those operating in an imaginative and expressive mode.

I learn as much from *how something is said* as from what is said; as much from how my client *presents himself* as from the words that make up the sentences; as much from the *hesitancy* and *pausing*, the *holding back*, the *momentary reflection*, the *intensity* of displayed emotion and the *energy* in delivery. I might take up briefly a psychodynamic opaque style and allow for unconscious processes to emerge. Then again, I might engage in micro-skills – listening, non-verbal communication, observing, reflecting back, questioning and challenging (Hill, 1999) – and elect to become entirely conversational and take up a person-centred stance and follow where my client may lead towards self-actualisation. Or, again, I may become more proactive and consider from our collaborative discourse that a social skills programme is preferred, or a specific social problem has to be resolved through CBT or SFT, in order for the student-client to make changes.

Counselling Resources for Change

One research factor cited earlier has particular relevance for students in educational settings. It is Lambert's findings (Asay and Lambert, 1999; Lambert, 1992) on the significance of 'extra-therapeutic' factors influencing successful outcome, such as changing friends, family dynamics, change of teacher or natural events. Frequently, I become aware of such extra-therapeutic details through finely tuned questioning and interested inquiry, even though assessing the relevance of merging factors is not easy. In the process, however, I must not become too obsessed with facts about my client's life, for the *counselling relationship* (the second influencing factor for change), which is measurable (Cooper, 2008), is critical for adolescents to improve. Any façade of caring will soon become evident, and when appropriate, and with necessary caution, I may *self-disclose* to serve as an offering for mutual consideration (Cooper and McLeod, 2011: 106–7).

> Self-disclosure can impede therapeutic progress (Truax, 1971), particularly for emotionally unstable young people, but in proactive styles of therapy it can help in normalising experience (Geldard and Geldard, 2010) so long as the 'use of self' is not superimposed by 'talk of self' as a pseudo form of genuineness (Prever, 2010a).
>
> Regarding touch in counselling, I feel generally that, although many youngsters are deprived of warmth and affection, touch is not necessary for 'emotional holding' and is prone to be misinterpreted as potentially abusive (Tolan, 2003). It may also encourage an unhelpful counsellor-dependence. I will, however, on occasion, hug a past client at the time of them leaving school.

Whether timely interventions are made, or I sit in silent attention, my client is weighing me up and testing out the fantasy:

Can this counsellor be trusted? Does my direct experience today confirm what I have heard within the home–school community?

Whether I steer or facilitate my client's feelings, my counselling merit can only be evident for *this* person, addressing *this* specific problem, within *this* particular context (Cooper and McLeod, 2011). Regarding the therapeutic relationship, I have to ask myself:

- Will the relationship itself be the catalyst for change, or will it serve as the conduit through which to deliver an intervention for progress?
- Is it the means of awareness-raising and empowerment, the process through which inner resources are discovered, or the means of instilling a degree of commitment to alter thinking and behaving for things to happen?

Counselling Notes

There is no consensus among counsellors in Britain on keeping files or on the nature of content within them. Tim Bond (2010) articulates the arguments for and against record-keeping, and for me – in favouring the disadvantages, in spite of the increasing demand for accountability – the most compelling factor is around 'informed consent'. 'Both the law and professional ethics require that clients have consented to records being kept' (Bond, 2010: 198), and I do not consider that most teenagers can give consent which is *informed*. Even though they know that in school files are kept on them, which is lawful, they are never consulted on the matter, and counselling is different.

McGinnis and Jenkins (2009) outline the legal implications for school counsellors when recording confidential information on students (Chapter 4). The issue is whether personal information constitutes an 'educational record', where the legal rights of students and/or parents (with or without their child's consent) have a right of access.

> A parent or carer can be denied access to confidential counselling material if this was against a client's (and, presumably, counsellor's) wishes, particularly if it does not form part of the 'educational record' of their child (McGinnis and Jenkins, 2009).
>
> Legally, it is a case of balancing 'parental rights' of the Data Protection Act (DPA, 1998, SI 2000/297) with the rights of the 'data subject', i.e. the child. Denial of parental access can also be supported under Article 8 of the Human Rights Act 1998 (DPA, 1998, Schedule 2, Section 4(3) 6(1)), whereby a child's right to privacy is being undermined.

As the authors state, the guidelines are not clear, but the practitioner, nevertheless, must keep up to date with current legislation appertaining to education law (CCYP has useful contact details on its website: www.ccyp.co.uk; Julie.camfield@bacp.co.uk.).

All counsellors and psychotherapists will have developed their own style of making notes and aide memoires of counselling sessions, whether or not they keep an individual file on each and every client – a file in school would be classified as an 'educational record'. Being disabled and unable to write with a pen, I am restricted from taking notes in session, but should I not be in this situation I still would not make notes in session while engaging teenagers in therapy. Particularly in the first or early sessions, clients will be apprehensive and unclear about what is taking place in the therapy situation. They may be unsure about what counselling is or where it may lead. Until the full nature of the process has been experienced, they may be suspicious as to why the therapist is recording what they say, as though it is an oral examination for which they have not prepared.

And, further, when interviewed by a senior teacher who is taking notes, most students in school will customarily experience this as a consequence of misconduct, a breach in school or social rules, or being accused of bullying – where witness statements are required, or an incident log is completed that may prove them culpable or party to an offence. They will anticipate their parents being contacted. The brief school counsellor does not wish to give any such impression. To avoid this misapprehension, I would suggest that the therapist does not take notes in session, particularly early on, until it is transparently clear why the notes are being taken and for what particular purpose a record is stored. Obviously, this will mean an increase in workload in having to record whatever is necessary after every session.

> Each practitioner will need to consider how much recording is needed to serve as an aide memoire particularly in brief counselling where repeated sessions after long intervals of engagement are not uncommon. Although it is conventional practice and an administrative necessity (*Toolkit*), there is no legal requirement or prescription to compile counselling notes (Bond, 2010) or to have therapy files, unless the particular institution makes such a requirement of the therapist.

In all cases, I consider it ethical to give clients an understanding of why information about them is being stored, remembering that a copy of an 'educational record' of a student in school cannot be withheld after request by a student or parent (DPA, 1998), or a court on demand (McGinnis and Jenkins, 2009). Obviously, all confidential records must be stored in a lockable cabinet and destroyed after a prescribed period of time (Bond, 2010).

Counselling Evaluation

As with all current therapy, school counselling must be informed. Research issues were covered previously, where attention was drawn to Cooper's (2008) work, particularly the project on the effectiveness of school counselling conducted in Strathclyde (Cooper, 2006) and the scoping review commissioned by BACP (Harris and Pattison, 2004). A special edition of *Counselling and Psychotherapy Research* (Cooper and Richards, 2009) is worth consulting.

There are two very good reasons why a counsellor must carry out an audit and evaluate the therapy provided in school or college, at least once a year. Headteachers and governing bodies require a regular review of the effectiveness of therapy before deciding on whether to allocate or maintain continued funding. In addition, it is an indicator of professional practice (Bor et al., 2002). Gaining feedback from clients and from other interested parties assists the counsellor in modifying the practice so that the work undertaken continues from an informed stance.

> When two researchers (Naylor and Cowie, 1999; see also Lines, 2005) approached the school where I work a few years back to pilot peer counselling in education, they carried out a systematic assessment of the current counselling service and provided for myself and line manager valuable feedback. Being a school counsellor for the past 25 years, I had assumed that I was so well known that there was no need to advertise the provision, and while the questionnaire results proved this to be the case generally, it was not the case for incoming pupils in Year 7 or for new staff of the school.
>
> As a result, I made myself more fully known through assemblies and year team meetings, through the school website and through posters liberally displayed in the corridors. Having this debrief helped to improve my practice; my assumptions needed examining. In modifying my practice from this feedback, incoming pupils were given more access to counselling.

Outcome research suggests the need for careful screening in the introductory session and such data should inform counselling choice and preference. Miller et al. (1997) recommend that outcome research should enlighten practice rather than press for new models of counselling, but practitioner bias will nevertheless assert itself, often unconsciously. However, brief goal-centred counselling offers more scope in outcome analysis. Having collaboratively devised a task, it should not be too difficult to devise instruments to measure whether or not that task has been achieved.

Composing a Research Report

Counsellors who have studied formally at diploma or degree level will not be unfamiliar with research methodology: collecting quantitative or qualitative data, composing a narrowly focused research question, recording results, framing discussion and writing conclusions that outline the territory for further work. Perhaps the most fundamental question to ask prior to the research project is what precisely the researcher is attempting to discover. And this is crucial for formulating the research question. It is wise to consult others, particularly the line manager, when planning the scope of investigation, when composing the research question and electing which form the evaluation should take. There is much guidance on this in the literature (Gardner and Coombs, 2009; McLeod, 2010, 2011a, 2011b).

Apart from questions that evaluate performance (such as *Did the therapeutic intervention bring improvement for the particular student-client?*), a range of further questions come to mind when considering an annual audit in school or college (Bor et al., 2002):

- Who are the principal clients – in terms of age group – making use of the service?
- How long does therapy customarily take?
- What predominant racial or ethnic group takes up counselling, or conversely never comes forward?
- How long does it take from referral to first session?
- Who are the principal referrers for counselling?

- What types of problems are brought to therapy?
- In cases of self-referral, how did the clients find out about the counselling service?

These and many other practice questions will assist the counsellor in improving the service offered, and will provide valuable data when making a report for the principal and governing body. However counselling assessment and evaluation are carried out, perhaps, as Bor et al. (2002) suggest, an audit should be 'simple' and targeted towards 'one specific area' at a time, leaving other information gathering to a later stage. It should not become so muddled and multi-factual that it makes the exercise confusing and unhelpful.

Client Satisfaction Questionnaires

Client feedback through questionnaires and self-evaluation forms are one means of information gathering, in spite of their inherent limitations of subjectivity. Authors on school counselling have offered questionnaire samples for practitioners to utilise, or to modify, largely from NHS 'client satisfaction' questionnaires (samples can be found in Bor et al., 2002 and the *Toolkit*). It must be faced, however, that measuring 'client satisfaction' is not without its difficulties. It is recognised that health service surveys illustrate that obtaining client satisfaction is notoriously difficult (Bor et al., 2002: 113).

> NHS 'client satisfaction' questionnaire answers are so influenced by a sense of loyalty and appreciation for treatment that getting a truly objective response is virtually impossible. I have found this continually to be the case in school practice. Methodologically, managing 'client satisfaction' questionnaires myself – where I have a vested interest in what is reported and where my clients *like me* or may *wish to return* for sessions later on – will result in favourable and less objective responses.

And, further, how is it possible to isolate the *particular intervention* of the therapist from other factors that may frequently change in a young client's life, such as a change in circumstances at home, a move to another class, a change in friendships, and so on? In short, how is it possible to isolate and measure a *therapeutic factor for change*, in a systemic way, from other changes frequently occurring in a teenager's life?

In Appendix I, I present my own counselling evaluation report for education-based therapists to consider modelling for their own annual audit. It comprises a client-feedback, scaling questionnaire and a demographic study, with an evaluative write-up. The questions are simple, measurable and quick to complete (in piloting my questionnaires [essential in any such exercise], a few modifications were made because some of my clients found a few questions too intrusive of family matters). When I give my clients this, or a similar evaluation task, I am aware of the subjective nature of the exercise, that it would be better if another person – senior manager, governor, parent or sixth-former – carried out the survey, but I have found it virtually impossible to arrange for another manager to conduct the questionnaire, particularly if they have no interest in the outcome and if, as is likely, they have other priorities.

Conclusion

In this chapter, I have been mindful of three stakeholders having a vested interest in school counselling: students, and by extension their parents and carers; newly trained counsellors who have a particular interest in working in education; and fundholders who have to decide on whether or not to put resources into school counselling.

The major emphasis of this chapter has centred on the practicalities of setting up, or maintaining, a school counselling service. The chapter has considered the particular role of the counsellor and a range of practical issues, such as room layout and referral procedures. There is a need to embed therapy within existing pastoral systems and to engage in teamwork practice. We have discussed the composition of counselling files and note-making, and the requirement to audit and evaluate work annually.

Each school or college has different pastoral systems and staffing structures, different clientele to serve and a variety of ways of addressing teenage difficulties. Writing such a chapter as this, therefore, cannot be prescriptive, but can only offer guidelines on practice that are likely to be common in most educational establishments with counselling provision. The experience of the author, as a full-time school counsellor of many years, is limited to experience in a comprehensive school in England that has recently become an academy.

Reflective Exercise

1. Should you be given an opportunity to plan a school counselling service, and a modest budget to support the work:
   a. What type of chairs and furnishing would you consider essential?
   b. What posters and pictorial images would be placed on walls that you consider to be helpful for teenagers who were waiting to speak with you?

2. Discuss the merits and pitfalls in having background music in the waiting area, and the particular type of music appropriate for the ambience you wish to create.

3. What ethical dilemmas would be posed if you were asked by the head-teacher to write a counselling report on a student she was considering permanently excluding from school? How would you resolve this issue?

4. Consider for a moment your preferred theoretical model. Suppose you are asked by your line manager to run a youth club, or to go on a residential trip with a group of students, some of whom have been your clients in therapy. What ethical problems would this create for you?

5. With regard to Lambert's (1992) widely acknowledged findings, select a particular case study from your work and consider what precisely

(Continued)

(Continued)

happened to bring improvement for your client, particularly those 'extra therapeutic factors'.

6. Discuss your dilemma of being asked by your line manager during a CAF meeting to divulge 'confidential information' about your client's parenthood to present family members who are not privy to the information:'Has Sarah discussed with you who she thinks her father is?'

7. Is there a moral imperative for you to question a particular decision that would seriously undermine the progress of your client? Discuss the tensions of working collaboratively in a school setting where beliefs of discipline are particularly punitive.

Key Points

- Counselling in an educational establishment is not only the preserve of a trained therapist, as many other practitioners provide similar support.

- School counsellors may be employed by the school on a full-time basis, but by far the majority are freelance therapists working part-time. Some local authorities employ a team of counsellors to serve a local group of schools.

- A full-time resident school counsellor will work on a system-orientation basis, being part of a team, whereas a part-time therapist will be self- or agency-oriented and will function under external regulation; each has merits and limitations with regard to confidentiality.

- There is advice available on the planning and setting up of a school counselling service, but the therapist should tailor the service around existing pastoral systems.

- There is a need to also consider a range of practice issues, such as line management, communication, and terms and conditions of employment. The practitioner must also design the service in line with ethical considerations, such as those of the BACP *Ethical Framework*.

- The school counsellor must consider the scope of counselling, location for therapy, referral policy, communicating sessions to teachers and the predominant model to use, whether to work eclectically, to be integrative or to work from a pluralistic perspective.

- Being part of a team presents ethical dilemmas like passing on and sharing confidential information, and composing counselling reports for official purposes, such as CAF meetings and child protection case conferences, may result in breaching the code of confidentiality.

- The school counsellor should conduct an annual audit and compile a report for the governing body in the interests of professional practice and for personal feedback on the quality of service at the point of delivery.

4 Legal and Ethical Codes in School Counselling

Excuse me a moment while I check with my solicitor whether I can keep confidential what you've just told me!

This chapter covers:

- Confidentiality
- Confidentiality and child protection
- Managing disclosures of abuse
- The duty to report and confidentiality
- Safeguarding
- Supervision

Introduction

There are particular legal and ethical issues to consider when counselling in school or college, issues which arise when working with this specific age group in educational settings. As outlined in Chapter 3, each institution will prescribe its own codes of working, but there will be laws and regulations of the state that apply to everyone. Although this chapter focuses primarily on UK legislation, there will be common injunctions of all educational institutions in western democracies.

Chapter 3 covered the need to have a working contract and a written job description for the role of the counsellor to be clear for all students, parents and professional colleagues working in the same institution. In this chapter, the code of confidentiality as can be applied in an educational setting is discussed. The legal framework of child protection – which in England and Wales is termed Safeguarding – is then considered before addressing a range of ethical dilemmas surrounding the duty to report abuse. The dilemma of a duty to report a client's offending and self-harming is then examined. Finally, safeguarding regulations applying to therapists are raised and the requirement of counsellors to receive regular and ongoing supervision closes the chapter.

Confidentiality

In spite of the recognised need for confidentiality to make therapy effective (Bond, 2010), there is no law that guarantees that information shared in counselling can never be disclosed (Casemore, 1995; Hamilton, 2004). Although the police have a right to seize files as 'relevant evidence' (PACE, 1984), counselling notes are generally exempt from this statute (section 11), apart from where terrorism is suspected. The BACP *Ethical Framework* outlines in clear detail the code of confidentiality:

> Respecting client confidentiality is a fundamental requirement for keeping trust. (2002: 16)

Although children and young people have a right to receive counselling (Hamilton, 2004), 'complete confidentiality' cannot be offered in an educational establishment (DfEE, 2000). Students in school are not in such a privileged position as adults are in therapy centres. Their legal status is that of a minor, being accountable to their parent or carer. Teachers and managers in school or college are acting as parents in absentia and therefore their primary duty and legal accountability is to those who manage their students at home. The school counsellor, however, can offer the student a high degree of confidentiality; he or she is not required to report information shared in therapy to the parent or carer (McGinnis and Jenkins, 2009). To practise otherwise would invalidate the principles of counselling and lead to an ineffective service. There is a balance to be struck, therefore, and the BACP *Ethical Framework* recognises this:

> Working with young people requires specific ethical awareness and competence. The practitioner is required to consider and assess the balance between young people's dependence on adults and carers and their progressive development towards acting independently. Working with children and young people requires careful consideration of issues concerning their capacity to give consent to receiving any service independently of someone with parental responsibility and the management of confidences disclosed by clients. (BACP, 2002: 15)

Ofsted inspectors will evaluate a counselling provision as part of the *Every Child Matters* agenda, and to satisfy themselves that safeguarding principles have been met, but they are not permitted to sit in session against the wishes of the client or practitioner.

Confidentiality and Child Protection

Child Protection Law

Although there is no mandatory duty under British law to report child abuse (Jenkins, 2010), there is an ethical and organisational duty for all personnel working in schools and colleges to report to the appropriate services, customarily social service departments, any disclosures of a child protection nature. If a child discloses to a teacher, for example, an incident where their welfare is judged to be at risk in the categories of neglect, physical, sexual or emotional abuse, there is no alternative for them but to report the matter to the appropriate senior teacher or manager of the school, normally the Designated Senior Teacher/ Person (DST).

> Section 47 of the Children Acts 1989 and 2004 makes it a duty for a local authority in the UK to make enquiries if they have reasonable cause to suspect that a child is suffering significant harm. Other operative legal codes in England and Wales include *Working Together to Safeguard Children (2010)*.

However, current safeguarding procedures require all local authority employees not to be reactive but *proactive*, and to report to social services any concern before waiting for a disclosure. School nurses have some leeway in this requirement – depending on the terms and conditions of their employment – but school counsellors are in a particularly difficult position in this area, since the requirement raises ethical dilemmas in regard to codes of confidentiality. Nevertheless, counselling young people in school is viewed in current legislation as a 'controlled activity' (Safeguarding Vulnerable Groups Act 2006), and is therefore regulated under safeguarding procedures.

Child Protection Law in Practice

In cases where the student discloses that an abuse has taken place, where the youngster says they have been physically maltreated or sexually violated – particularly if they say they are in fear of returning home that day – then there is no option but to report the matter immediately. Child protection takes precedence over all other concerns. All personnel, including the school counsellor, should not take detailed evidence but merely gather information of a factual nature, an overview so to speak, of what has taken place, the frequency, times and places, etc. of the abuse. It is helpful to record briefly the student's feelings concerning what has happened, together with a word on what they feel about the person having to pass on the disclosure to the DST. I think, also, it is imperative to inform the victim what is likely to take place after reporting and the likely times-cales involved. If the young person is happy for this to happen, then there is no boundary conflict or ethical dilemma for a school counsellor. In this instance, the therapist can support the student, as appropriate, while the procedures take their course.

There are many cases, however, where the decision is not so clear-cut, where the duty to report matters on may be in conflict with the client's wishes and the counsellor's code of confidentiality. According to the Sexual Offences Act 2003, for example, no child under the age of 13 is capable of giving *informed consent* for a sexual act, and therefore sexual intercourse involving an adult or older teenager with a child under 13 is defined clearly in law as illegal. There is no defence under the 'Gillick competence' principle.

The Fraser Guidelines (Gillick, 1986, 3 All ER 402) gave general practitioners the right to give contraceptive advice to young people under the age of 16 without parental permission if the child so wished, and the only stipulation was that consent should be *informed* – measured by the age, intelligence and maturity of the individual. This assessment was endorsed after Victoria Gillick unsuccessfully attempted to override a decision for her daughter to receive confidential advice from her general practitioner relating to contra-ception without her mother being informed. The ruling came to be known as 'Gillick competence'. This meant, in practice, that there was no offence committed, and therefore no need to report the matter to social services, if a young person engaged in sexual intercourse so long as the counsellor (doctor or sexual health nurse) could ascertain that they were 'Gillick competent'.

The right to give individual contraceptive advice without parental permis-sion has been extended to counselling. 'Gillick competent' young people have a right to confidential counselling with or without their parent's or carer's per-mission, as confirmed by recent case law (*Axon* v. *Secretary of State for Health* [2006] – see McGinnis and Jenkins, 2009: 19).

The Sexual Offences Act 2003 in respect of sexual behaviour below the age of 13 then is one example where a statute overrides a principle of personal judgement. Sex with a child under 13 is classified as 'statutory rape'. More problematic is the course of action for two young people below the age of 13 known to be having consensual sexual intercourse.

Sexual Relations Before 13

Jessica in Year 8, aged 12, had been going out with another pupil in her year group, who was also under the age of 13. They were always together during non-contact time, never with others of their peer group. The school nurse had voiced concerns over the intensity of their relationship. They would often be seen together in passionate embrace, kissing and occasionally fondling each other, in the corridor and on the playground, to such an extent that a pastoral support manager cautioned them about inappropriate behaviour.

I had counselled Jessica previously, and it became clear during our sessions that sexual attitudes were relaxed within the family, that her mother had frequent partners during the day and that their brazen lovemaking could be heard by Jessica and her brother in a downstairs bedroom – they would bang with their fists on the wall telling the adults to shut up! When it became public through the internet that she and her boyfriend had engaged in sexual intercourse, it posed a dilemma for the counsellor and pastoral staff.

McGinnis and Jenkins (2009) note that professional opinion is currently divided in the UK on whether to report all known sexual activity – some child protection policies require automatic referral, while others (guided by sexual health workers) advise the use of discretion, preferring to preserve confidentiality and offer education instead of criminalising the behaviour. In general, however, the Gillick principle still applies where it does not conflict with other statutes, and counsellors have a right to exercise their judgement on whether they feel their student-client is sufficiently informed and mature to make the decision to engage in a sexual act. The ruling applies to gay and lesbian sexual relations as to heterosexuality in the UK, but it may not be as yet the case in every country or state.

Ethical Decisions within a 'Reporting Culture'

There will be occasions where the threat to a student's well-being becomes evident to the counsellor through information which is purposefully or incidentally shared in session, and which poses a particular ethical dilemma for the practitioner. A child may disclose that they have been hit, beaten or sexually touched, or that they have suffered neglect or emotional abuse. School counsellors have been well trained to anticipate and deal with such disclosures, and in the past have exercised their own judgement on whether to keep the matter confidential or to pass it on to the parent or carer, or another party who has a statutory duty to protect the young person. There is not as much latitude currently for school counsellors in the UK to exercise exclusively their own judgement in face of the 'reporting culture' as was formerly the case, and this poses particular ethical dilemmas. Child welfare is of paramount

importance, but making an assessment of what particular course of action constitutes *child welfare* is not always easy.

Peter Jenkins (2010) has reminded counsellors of their duty to clients to preserve
their *right of confidentiality* in light of the prevalent 'reporting culture'. A number of
high-profile media cases, where children have been tragically abused and killed
(sometimes by their carers), have resulted in an increase in reporting to social services every suspicion of unusual and secretive behaviour. There has been a call for
better communication between agencies after a few controversial 'Serious Case
Reviews' of children's deaths at the hands of their parents or carers. There has also
been more legislation and a general tightening up of procedures owing to greater
public awareness of paedophiles living within communities where children often
play. Once, practitioners in school exercised discretion, but now they are reluctant
to do so. In consequence, there has grown a tendency to 'cover one's back' through
automatic and unreflective referral.

In the wake of the 'reporting culture', Jenkins (2010) promotes the need for
'confidential space' where children can work on their problems without the
'immediate threat of child protection procedures', following The Laming
Report and in support of the NSPCC's calling for a 'mixed economy' of services
(2010: 18–19). Jenkins asserts that therapists should not rush into reporting
matters to avoid personal culpability.

I wrote a response to this article (Lines, 2010) to seek the views of practising
youth therapists in post, offering them five hypothetical cases and inviting an
individual response. All respondents acknowledged the increased tension they
felt from an 'expectation to report'. All experienced inner conflict when striving
to preserve confidentiality and autonomy against mounting regulation. Some
had to face a dilemma where senior managers put pressure on them to
respond in the same way as teachers should within the institution. One counsellor said that she was instructed to report any information where it was
learnt that teenagers were sexually active, and another had threatened to
resign when instructed by the headteacher to report every hint of disclosure
without question. All responses to the case examples were different, indicating
how diverse the practice is among professional counsellors in school (the exercise is presented below – see Appendix III).

The BACP *Ethical Framework* outlines the code of confidentiality, but interpreting
ethical codes in each case of disclosure is where the difficulty lies. Frameworks are
not prescriptive, and each counsellor must make a judgement and therefore be
accountable for their actions, remembering that they could be subpoenaed to
appear before a court of law, or at least be required to make a statement to the
police, to justify an earlier decision not to report.

It is not unknown for a youth counsellor to be called into question in a case of historical abuse for not reporting a previous disclosure because their client did not want this to happen at the time. There are many cases where abuse occurs during childhood where the student is not prepared to make a disclosure until they have become an adult, at a time when they feel safe to do so and where the perpetrator is no longer a threat to them. In the current climate, it is not easy for a school counsellor in the UK to justify a decision not to report a case purely on the grounds of their client's wishes. Needless to say, each therapist is advised to make full use of supervision in this respect, and should liaise frequently with their line manager and with those responsible in school or college for safeguarding. Cases will be presented throughout this book where decisions of a safeguarding nature have had to be made in preserving the welfare of students in school.

Managing Disclosures of Abuse

The school counsellor is advised to publicise the limits of confidentiality that can be extended to pupils and students in school (see Chapter 3). Some authors have suggested that when a child protection disclosure occurs in therapy, and the school counsellor is obliged to halt the session and pass on information to the DST, the contract and 'confidentiality can usually be satisfactorily renegotiated with a young person if there is time and if a good relationship has been built with the child protection team' (Mabey and Sorensen, 1995: 97–8). Personally, I favour anticipating the problem beforehand. In my judgement, every client (where it is suspected that abuse has occurred) should be informed of what the practitioner must do with the information at the outset. Practice in such matters should be transparent. In consequence, with older students where suspicions are held in school, I tend to begin the session with something like:

Dennis: I feel it's necessary before we begin to explain what you can say that's confidential. Although I work in school, I don't have to share with your parents what you say to me, as teachers might have to. I will not speak with anyone unless you agree it would help. But if you tell me you've been abused, I have to pass that on – it cannot be kept confidential. I'm sorry to begin this way, but I feel it's necessary to be clear. I wonder if you'd like to respond to anything I've said before we start …

Such an introduction may be entirely unsuitable for a younger pupil, however, for, while it may be assumed that an older student would understand what child abuse is, this cannot be taken for granted with pre-pubescent children. A simplified vocabulary and explanation are called for. Taking the precaution to avoid leading questions for legal and therapeutic reasons, the whole issue would need a fuller introduction that might follow this form:

Dennis:	I'd like to explain to you, Sara, that counselling is a choice. If you would like us to talk about your difficulties that's okay, and you can end counselling whenever you want. What we speak about is confidential, and I will not be speaking with your parents unless you want me to, or to any teacher. What is said is confidential, but I wonder what you understand by confidential?
Sara:	Does it mean keeping secrets?
Dennis:	In a sense it does, but it's more like an agreement. It's like trusting me not to tell other people your problems. Is that clear?
Sara:	Yeah.
Dennis:	There's one exception to this that I'd like you to understand before we start speaking. I can't promise you that I can keep absolutely everything confidential. Say, for example, you told me you were being hurt in some way. If someone was hitting you, or if someone was doing things to you sexually, then I couldn't keep that confidential. I would have to stop counselling and tell someone. I would still support you, but I feel you should have a clear understanding of what would happen. Do you know what I mean by sexual?
Sara:	Yeah.

With such approaches, the pupil-client is left with no confusion over what will happen should she choose to reveal details of significant harm. For clients who have been abused, the issue over such an introduction may well be when to disclose rather than whether to open up. For the client who is nursing no secrets of painful abuse, this will seem superfluous and irrelevant, but the legal and professional standing of the practitioner working in school makes this the most prudent course. On balance, then, the pupil-client will have confidence through being spoken with directly, with no hidden agendas or surprises at the point at which the contract has been entered.

The Duty to Report and Confidentiality

Students in school may occasionally disclose to their therapist incidents of themselves or friends being in breach of the law, particularly if they put great trust in the school counsellor. This can pose an ethical dilemma for the therapist on whether such information should be reported to a senior teacher, a student's parents or carers, or indeed to the police. A youth counsellor, generally, would keep minor infringements like smoking, drinking, truancy, riding a motorbike on the fields, or lying to parents, etc., confidential if such behaviour was not having dire consequences for them or others, but preserving such confidences is not so straightforward for the counsellor in school.

Delinquency, Vandalism and Drugs Misuse

Does the counsellor have a legal responsibility to report a client's criminal offending? For McGinnis and Jenkins (2009: 25), confidentiality does not preclude the right to report crime or intended crime, but it is more a case of common law than criminal law and the wider public interest that overrides. It is not strictly illegal not to report crime. A question to bear in mind, apart from the degree of offending, is whether any other party is being, or has been, injured. In the case of vandalism, for example, a shopkeeper, or the owner of a vehicle, will have suffered financially if property has been defaced or damaged.

> ### Balancing Confidentiality and Law
>
> During a counselling session with Colin, he began to scribble with pen on paper, quite unconsciously, as he related his difficulty. It was apparent to me that the pattern he drew was his tag (a recognisable signature of an artist's graffiti). This posed a moral dilemma. Throughout the school, this particular tag had been distributed to all staff because there had appeared an excessive amount of graffiti on shop windows and shutters in the vicinity. The issue was whether or not I, as his therapist, should keep this confidential or report it to another party.

Theft and burglary is another example of behaviour having consequences for others, and the therapist will have to consider the cost to other parties when electing not to report a matter to the authorities. School counsellors come across clients who have committed physical assaults in the community, and in cases where an 'offence' has been undetected by the authorities there will be difficult decisions to make in regard to whether to withhold information or report an incident to the police. The level of seriousness will usually determine the decision.

A second consideration is whether or not a young person is being unduly influenced by older unemployed youths in the area, and whether by continuing to offend the behaviour is being reinforced, with the risk of this leading to a life of crime. In such situations, the counsellor has to weigh up the right of confidentiality – together with the trust that might be jeopardised throughout the school for successive clients – and the right of other parties, including clients themselves, by choosing to withhold such information at an early stage. The impressionable nature of young people, particularly boys (see Chapter 5), is a serious question the counsellor has to address when balancing confidentiality with an ethical responsibility to pass on information to other parties.

In questions of drug misuse, school counsellors, while addressing the particular needs of their clients, will have to consider the wider public – including those potential victims of drug misuse – when considering whether to keep information confidential or to report intelligence to the authorities. It is a case of waving individual interests to prevent injury to innocent parties. Although it is not unlawful in the UK not to report an offence, save in the case of terrorism (the Prevention of Terrorism Act 2005) and drug money laundering (McGinnis and Jenkins, 2009), the Children's Legal Centre has pointed out that professionals working with young offenders should be careful to avoid doing something that might constitute aiding and abetting the committing of an offence (Hamilton, 2004: 5), and the decision to withhold information on grounds of preserving confidentiality does not make the decision ethical.

Self-harm

Cases where young clients threaten to harm themselves put considerable pressure on school counsellors working with students under the age of 18 (see Chapter 7). If policies are clear, ethical dilemmas may be partially resolved. Counsellors generally fall into two groups; there are those that hold dearly the sanctity of all life and the preservation of health at all costs, and there are others that respect personal autonomy and the rights of an individual to determine their own fate, including the right to harm themselves. Continued English case law, from the Magna Carta onwards, has supported personal liberty and autonomy, so that if an adult wished to self-harm or take their life it is not unlawful.

Cases will be presented in Chapter 7 where students have disclosed that they have self-harmed, and some discretion may be called for in deciding whether to inform the parent or carer. As will be illustrated later, many teenagers adopt copycat behaviour, influenced by friends, or, in modern times, by the internet and social networking sites ('You Tube' and 'Facebook'), and in such cases the behaviour may not be judged as being serious. However, there are other students who harm themselves by repeated cutting, amateur tattooing, removing hair, starving and self-purging, etc., who use such means to relieve themselves of stress, where forming a habit through repeated behaviour could be injurious and potentially life-threatening. There may be cases of excessive obesity where a parent may be prosecuted on grounds of neglect for not providing an appropriate diet and exercise for their child. The rights of student autonomy have to be balanced with the counsellor's responsibility to safeguard the young person from harm, and in extreme cases of injury, or loss of life, no grounds of confidentiality can be used as a defence against culpability (Bond, 1994: 4). As the BACP *Ethical Framework* states:

> Situations in which clients pose a risk of causing serious harm to themselves or others are particularly challenging for the practitioner. (BACP, 2002: 14)

Suicidal Ideation

In British law, it is a criminal offence to assist an individual in commiting suicide, even if it was their expressed wish and even to prevent suffering in terminal cases – this is not the case in Holland or Switzerland. Although high-profile media cases frequently challenge the law, such is the fear that supported euthanasia might lead to exploitation of vulnerable people that it does not look as though there is likely to be a change in British law in the foreseeable future.

Adults have a legal right to take their lives, and to refuse life-saving medical treatment, but they cannot depend on assistance from others and be certain that they may not avoid prosecution by so doing. Apart from cases where mental health issues are prevalent, support through counselling would not normally constitute as assisting in the termination of life. The liberty to keep suicidal intent confidential is not extended for counsellors working with clients between the ages of 16 and 18 – even more so for those under 16. The balance of public interest switches in favour of seeking assistance in such cases, and the 'Gillick competence' principle in such matters carries little weight. There is a general acceptance that a school counsellor employed by the local authority should not keep confidential a student's intention to commit suicide owing to their 'duty of care' (McGinnis and Jenkins, 2009). In most USA states, counsellors are required to breach confidentiality and report all clients' suicidal intentions (Bond, 2010).

Mental health professionals recognise that suicide ideation is often a temporary phase, where such feelings are short-lived (Bond, 2010), and young people have insufficient life experience to make such fatal decisions. When counselling students over 18, more latitude in decisions to report their client's suicidal tendencies is called for. Decisions will be based upon the following principles:

- the degree of risk of suicide
- the decision being rational and autonomous, and well planned out rather than prompted by mental illness or drugs
- a realistic means of prevention
- the legal issues centring upon breaches of confidentiality (Bond, 1994: 4).

As Bond (2010) asserts, the law regarding a young person's right to receive or refuse medical treatment between the ages of 16 and 18 is complicated if the decision is contrary to that of the parent or carer – say, in a case of a young person whose parents are Jehovah's Witness being refused a blood transfusion, or an anorexic youngster rejecting medical treatment to restore health. The High Court may override the wishes of parents or young people in such cases.

There is no fixed point through adolescence where childhood becomes adulthood, where the responsibility of a carer shifts to that of the individual, and the therapist must consider how her client's best interests are served in the long term, how ethical decisions comply with the *Every Child Matters* agenda, and how actions conform to agency and child protection protocols. There will be ethical dilemmas arising in therapy that are not informed by law which test codes of confidentiality. Counsellors, generally, support adults' right to make their own decisions, but such a privilege cannot be granted to young people in school or college. Although a counsellor would not be prosecuted for withholding information over an adult's intention to take their life – unless the means of suicide could injure other parties, such as crashing a car on the motorway – it may not be regarded as ethical in all cases, and certainly not the case for students in school.

Safeguarding

Safeguarding Children Boards have a regional responsibility to secure that all training is carried out, that all agencies have reporting systems in place, and that procedures are there to check all employees working with children (Safe Network, 2011). These organisation and institutional requirements have placed new demands upon school counsellors.

All counsellors working in schools and colleges, whether employed by the institution under its own terms and conditions or being managed by an outside agency or local authority, will be expected to have a criminal record check on their eligibility to practice. In the UK, the employing organisation will apply for a document from the criminal records bureau (CRB) before enrolling a counsellor in school or college, since counselling in school is regarded as a 'controlled activity' (Safeguarding Vulnerable Groups Act 2006). To employ personnel without a CRB check renders the agency culpable in law and liable for prosecution. All therapists in schools and colleges are required to be cleared of criminal offences against children and vulnerable adults, to have no convictions of offences against children, and therefore to pose no risk to them in school or in the wider community. Each individual will have been cleared in order to preserve safeguarding requirements necessary for the protection and welfare of children and vulnerable adults.

One of the major new requirements of Ofsted inspectors is to carry out a comprehensive review of the school's policy to safeguard each and every student. This requirement has placed extra demands on educational institutions, ranging from guaranteeing pupil safety to vetting adults coming onto the campus, such as peripatetic music teachers, inspectors and advisers, etc., governors, parents of pupils and even past students, and providing them with an escort to the appropriate person they wish to see with a badge of identification. Accounting for each and every pupil on roll who is present each day is also a strict requirement, including whether they have turned up on placement for work experience, and if they have transferred to other areas of the country – their tracking procedures, etc.

Supervision

The school counsellor is accountable to the headteacher, but is also accountable to her professional body (BPS, BACP, BAP, UKCP, etc.) to practise at the highest possible level, both professionally and ethically, and to comply with the require-ment of supervision. Regular and ongoing supervision is expected of all counsellors, customarily 1.5 hours for every month's work (BACP *Ethical Framework*).

If the particular school or college elects to budget for counselling supervision from a separate fund then the counsellor is spared the expense. Some agencies man-age their own supervision, operating in a team at the agency centre and away from the particular school or college, while other freelance youth therapists have to arrange their own supervision, and in this case it is advisable to seek out a supervi-sor who has had experience with adolescence, one who is conversant with the trials and developmental issues of teenagers, and, ideally, one who has some awareness of educational pressures and the manner in which schools and colleges function gen-erally. The BACP journal, *Therapy Today*, advertises available supervisors, but can-not be held responsible for the quality of supervision given, since this is a personal matter – school counsellors in post can be useful guides on who might be available in a given area (Bor et al., 2002).

I personally supervise two school counsellors, and in turn am supervised by another freelance youth counsellor. Some school and college counsellors have grouped together in a given area to arrange group supervision on a rotational basis from one centre of operation to another, or from a suitably convenient location, and in such cases are required to plan a longer session to cover the self-evaluation and casework of every participant.

Given that teachers generally undergo performance management rather than individual supervision (unlike social workers, for example), it may be advisable to outline why supervision is judged to be so necessary. Supervisors assist counsellors through their casework to examine their technique (*is what I'm doing the best way of helping this student?*), to explore ethical issues (*can I keep this confidential for a minor in school?*) and to review how the material is affecting them personally (*what powerful feelings has my client's narrative awakened in me?*) (McGuiness, 1998). A supervisor will also monitor casework, help improve the supervisee's skills, validate their practice, assist them when reaching an impasse, offer alternative perspectives on cases and provide evidence, where required, for continuing professional registra-tion (Bor et al., 2002). Paradoxically, in supervising the counsellor, the supervisor is attempting to guarantee that the student-client receives the best possible support.

Conclusion

This chapter has considered the legal and ethical codes centring on school counsel-ling. The law of the land, together with the rules and requirements of the organisa-tion, have to be honoured, but there will always be ethical issues where decisions have to be made that present a dilemma for the practitioner. It is impossible to be prescriptive over such decisions as to whether or not to involve parents or carers, other staff of the school or college, the general practitioner, or the police or social services, where young pupils and students have revealed information that could be injurious to themselves or to other parties. It is a question of balance. No school counsellor will pass on information of minor indiscretions and breaches of rules, or even of the law, indiscriminately and without forethought of the consequences by so doing. If confidentiality is to mean anything at all, it must mean that young people can expect that most things shared in confidence will not be discussed outside the therapeutic relationship. How else can counselling be beneficial?

The guiding principles of confidentiality in school and college – as outlined in the BACP *Ethical Framework* – have been discussed with relevance to child abuse, offending behaviour, self-harm and suicidal ideation, and in matters of disclosed sexual relations of young people the 'Gillick principle' still overrides where this does not conflict with legal statutes. In the case studies which follow, there will be examples of the application of codes and first principles. It is in such matters where judgements and decisions are not so clear-cut that the school counsellor makes full use of personal supervision, liaises frequently with their line manager or the DST and takes every opportunity to become conversant with changing policy and legislation that is likely to affect their daily practice.

Reflective Exercise

1. What are the merits and disadvantages in publicising to every new client the extent and limits of confidentiality that can be granted in school counselling? Discuss.

2. What criteria would you use – in balancing personal autonomy with a duty to protect the welfare of the client – in a case where a student of 16 years had disclosed to you that they were in a homosexual relationship with a partner five years their senior?

3. Take a look at the following five hypothetical case examples, and attempt to answer the questions before sharing your responses with a colleague (Appendix III):

    a. The Sex Offences Act 2003 declared that on developmental grounds no child is able to give consent to an intimate sexual act below the age of 13. What would you as a school counsellor do in the following case? A child of 12 years 11 months is known by you to be having sex with a 13-year-old partner. Should this younger person be your client who had disclosed this, would you pass on the information to the child's parent, the DST for child protection or to Children's Services as a referral?

(Continued)

(Continued)

Contain the client	Inform parent	Refer to DST	Refer to Children's Services
Rationale:			

b. How different would your course of action be if your client's partner was known to be 14 or 15, and in your judgement you felt your young client was 'Gillick competent'?

Contain the client	Inform parent	Refer to DST	Refer to Children's Services
Rationale:			

c. Suppose your client is a boy of 14 years (quite mature in your judgement and quite able to give consent, again in your judgement) who is engaged in intimate sexual relations with a girl of 17 years at the same school. Supposing you could determine no power differential, and it was a question of different levels of maturity, would you feel compelled to inform the parent, the DST for child protection, or Children's Services (assuming, that the contractual arrangements of the school or therapy agency permits engagement with young clients without, of necessity, involving parents or carers)?

Contain the clients	Inform parent	Refer to DST	Refer to Children's Services
Rationale:			

d. Two young clients approach you who are involved in a gay or lesbian relationship with each other. They are 14 and 15 years of age and

(Continued)

(Continued)

there is no power differential but a fully consenting engagement. They approach you because they are afraid of homophobic taunting from peers in school and also because of what their parents might say should they find out – they have not come out publicly within their families. Would you as a counsellor 'contain' these two young clients or feel compelled to pass on this information to a third party?

Contain the clients	Inform parent	Refer to DST or pastoral teacher	Refer to other parties
Rationale:			

e. A youth of 14 years shares information about an argument at home the previous evening whereby his stepfather (with whom he had been living with his mother since he was 3) had hit him across the mouth with the back of his hand for 'swearing at his mother', she had challenged him over 'theft of money and drinking alcohol in the park in the evening hours'. He had a red mark showing on his face and he was still angry. He said in counselling that he had never been hit like this before and that his stepfather had no history of being abusive. The pupil was known to be challenging in school. What course of action would you take?

Contain the client	Inform parent	Refer to DST	Refer to Children's Services
Rationale:			

Key Points

- Offering young people 'complete confidentiality' is unrealistic in school or college.

- The BACP *Ethical Framework* outlines the principles of confidentiality and its application in educational institutions.

- In cases of child protection, where a young person's welfare is at stake, the school counsellor has no option but to report the matter to the Designated Senior Teacher or appropriate body.

- Particular issues, such as suicide ideation, self-harm, teenage delinquency and illicit drugs misuse, pose particular difficulties for school counsellors when deciding whether to preserve confidentiality or to pass on such information to carers and/or official safeguarding parties.

- In cases of sexual behaviour of young people, the school counsellor may apply the 'Gillick principle' to ascertain the client's level of maturity to give consent before breaching confidentiality, unless such a decision would be unlawful, as in the case of a child under 13 in the UK who is judged as being incapable of giving *informed* consent.

- Safeguarding regulations govern all activities designed to preserve the welfare of all students in school or college, and one stipulation is that all therapists have to be cleared of any offences against children and vulnerable adults by the Criminal Records Bureau (CRB).

- All school counsellors are expected to receive regular and ongoing supervision, customarily 1.5 hours for each month's counselling work, in conformity with the requirement of BACP or another official body.

5 Adolescence

Your children are not your children.

They are the sons and daughters of Life's longing for itself.

They come through you but not from you.

And though they are with you yet they belong not to you.

You may give them your love but not their thoughts, for they have their own thoughts.

You may house their bodies but not their souls, for their souls dwell in the house of tomorrow,

which you cannot visit, not even in your dreams.

(Gibran, 1972 [1923])

Introduction

Passing through the later years of education, pupils undergo a developmental transition from child to adult, from dependence to autonomy, and this transition in western society is termed 'adolescence'. This chapter attempts to portray this period of development as it impacts within school and on into college, since brief counselling cannot suitably address teenage difficulties without an understanding of their internal and external world. These characteristic transitions of body and mind are systematically discussed in this chapter.

Sexual growth from puberty to late adolescence involves physical and hormonal changes which have relational and social consequences. Emotional development is influenced by early attachments and these have implications for the school counsellor. As young people encounter larger social contexts, different demands are made of them to achieve a range of tasks, which can pose particular tensions for ethnic minority teenagers.

Cognitive development is discussed through psychological research and the recent findings in neuroscience, which has widened our understanding of a teenager's growing mental aptitude and temporary deficit in functioning. The school counsellor is advised to consider this research and attune interventions in light of the client's altering cognitive abilities. Finally, attention is given to parenting qualities which assist in supporting children to come through adolescence relatively unscathed.

Puberty

Adolescence is marked by the onset of puberty. Physiological growth spurts take place concurrently with cognitive development, social pressures and educational expectations during adolescence. Hormonal changes happen within the bodies of adolescents that affect the way they look and feel about themselves. With the onset of puberty, there occurs physical maturation: menstruation in girls and nocturnal emissions in boys. The hormone oestrogen causes menstruation for girls between the ages of 10 and 16 (the average being 13). The ovaries produce an egg each month, the hips begin to widen and breasts form. Puberty in boys, between 11 and 16 (the average being 14), is triggered by testosterone which results in the testicles producing sperm, the chest getting larger, the voice deepening and a growth in facial and pubic hair. Although in recent decades puberty has occurred earlier, the onset is variable at a time when adolescents are preoccupied with 'normality', and those who are outside the perceived 'norms' experience anxiety (Geldard and Geldard, 2010; Thomas, 1990).

Increased Sensitivity

Hormonal changes and bodily alterations create deep emotional feelings that can result in precociousness, confusion, embarrassment, self-consciousness or a lowering in self-esteem for those who mature later than the majority. Younger adolescents (aged 11–14) are trying to come to terms with new feelings of attraction and sexual urges, and may undergo mood swings, touchiness and irritability. Name-calling and mickey-taking is a common defence as sensitivity is masked through humour – boys frequently call their friends 'gay', sometimes in fun but on other occasions to disguise their same-sex attraction.

The school counsellor needs to understand this sensitive stage of development and synchronise the counselling process with adolescent experiences,
remembering that humour and a sense of light-heartedness can sometimes
diffuse the intensity of heightened emotions. Needless to say, interventions of
humour have to be measured.

Sexual Development

Teenagers are developing sexual interests, but in the early stages they will form close
relationships with friends of the same sex because they lack confidence (Blos, 1979).
They will fantasise and boast about opposite-sex encounters. Sex play and experimentation without intimacy occur much earlier than at adolescence (Bancroft,
2009), often harmlessly, among siblings within the family and among friends during
sleepovers (Finkelhor, 1980). Making sense of personal sensations is not the need for
intimacy at this point, but more a curiosity over each other's 'private equipment' –
pupils stare at others in the shower and at various stages of undress, comparing the
growth of sexual organs and pubic hair (Bancroft, 2009; Thomas, 1990).

Personal masturbating, both for boys and girls, is the means by which sexual
urges are satisfied until later on. A spirit of innocence and coyness checks such feelings for some, but for others there may be talk and boasting. But, for all, the body
has become a spring of sensations. It is a time for fantasising of 'trial runs for actions
and feelings which are strange and frightening' and for ironing out mistakes before
they happen (Noonan, 1983: 24).

Experimentation

Sex drives become more pronounced during later adolescence (aged 15–18) and a
strong desire to have sex develops. It is a time for experimentation and daring
(Conger, 1975), and peer-group pressure to compete requires psychological adjustment. There is a delicate balance between being viewed as too 'prudish' and too
'promiscuous'; being sexually stigmatised is more common for girls than for boys
(Lees, 1993). Powerful sexual feelings can lead to obsessions about personal appearance and altering images of self. Such obsessions can result in oversensitive reactions
to expressed opinions and to criticism. There is broad diversity in sexual attitudes and
behaviours (petting and coitus) across gender, age and demographic, socio-economic
and social class boundaries, together with a general trend towards greater frequency
and earlier experience in a cultural change of increased 'openness' (Bancroft, 2009).

Intimacy

At late adolescence for western youth, many form intimate relations with those of the
same or the opposite sex. Decisions about sexual preference take precedence and

inclinations towards gay and lesbian sex bring tension in a society where many are homophobic. For some adolescents, the satisfying of sex drives is deferred for reasons of inhibition, social convention, internalised value systems, or simply for lack of opportunity, and for these sexual fantasy lingers within the imagination for longer periods than might be the case if they lived in a society with no sexual taboo, or where parenthood occurred relatively early. From the late 1970s onwards, however, evidence of earlier sex among the majority of western adolescents has been accumulating.

> 30 per cent of boys perceive that sex is the most important thing in a relationship compared to 13 per cent of girls, and one report found that the first experience of penetrative intercourse occurred on average at 16 years for girls and at 18 years for boys (Sherratt et al., 1998). Brook reports a quarter of girls having had intercourse before 16 (Jenkins, 2005), but other data suggests 37 per cent for boys and 40 per cent for girls (Mosher et al., 2005). Gathering data on such a topic is notoriously difficult and some findings are contradictory, perhaps showing varied experience from one geographical area to another and across different cultures.

In spite of the risks of HIV infection and AIDS, casual sexual relations among the young are not uncommon and, in most cases, first intercourse involves no use of a condom.

A Not Untypical Case

Erica came for counselling after losing her virginity one evening. At 14, she was keen to keep her first experience of sexual intercourse for 'that special time when it felt right'. One evening, when sitting in the back of a car with a 19-year-old male acquaintance (a person she knew had fancied her for some time), she became so engrossed in conversation that she was unaware of what was happening. They kissed for a while, and then it happened. She came for counselling the next day with a range of feelings. Apart from being angry, there was regret over her lost virginity – this was not 'that special time when it felt right', that moment she could treasure.

Emotional Development

Adolescence is recognised in western thinking as a transitional journey towards autonomy, the pulling away from parental dependence to a growing reliance upon friendships. It is a period which is both exciting and scary. The western understanding of adolescent development takes, as a starting point, the upsurge of instincts that take place at puberty. At this point, argued Freud (1937), a number of internal emotional changes occur: the personality becomes more vulnerable than at any other time since the end of childhood and this is evidenced by an upset in psychic balance (Coleman, 1987). Teenagers have to navigate a variety of internal and external stimuli during their development. Internally, apart from hormonal and physical changes coming into effect, psychological needs of attachment have been recognised as being highly significant.

Attachment

The 'ideal mother–child relationship' has been the subject of psychological papers for some time. It has been established that a *secure attachment* has enormous consequences for adolescents completing the task of separation and autonomy (Bowlby, 1952). A piece of research relevant to insecurity in children is Ainsworth's Strange Situation experiment (Ainsworth et al., 1978), which involved a mother and her 1-year-old infant during a 20-minute playroom session.

The mother was first asked to leave her child with a researcher, after which the child was left alone for three minutes. Mother and child were then brought together. The whole sequence was recorded and analysed, focusing primarily on the responses of the child to separation and reunion. It was found that:

- If the child is *securely attached*, she will feel slight distress when separated but then when reunited receive comfort and begin to play again.
- If there is an *insecure-avoidant attachment*, the child will show few overt signs of distress when separated and will ignore her mother when she returns, remaining watchful but inhibited in play.
- With an *insecure-ambivalent attachment*, the child will be highly distressed when alone and will not easily be pacified when joined with the mother. The infant will seek contact but then resist by kicking, turning away and squirming, refusing offered toys for play.
- An *insecure-disorganised attachment* relates to a small group of children who illustrate a diverse range of confused behaviours including 'freezing' or stereotypical movements when reunited with the parent (Holmes, 1993: 15).

Psychoanalytical therapists reason that challenging behaviour in the neighbourhood and school is probably due to unresolved attachment issues where youngsters unconsciously seek out in their streets and schools 'transitional attachment figures', but find in reality the same projected 'insecure', 'anxious', 'avoidant' or 'resistant' attachments' experienced in the home (Bowlby, 1969, 1973, 1980). Many squabbles among younger pupils in school may reveal an unconscious psychological need to experiment with *attachment* and *separation* (Geddes, 2006; Luxmoore, 2000). Luxmoore (2006) presents a pertinent case of an altercation between pupil and teacher. Attachment needs can also be detected among violent street youths (Batmanghelidjh, 2009).

Unresolved attachment needs are judged to be a predictor of strained adult relationships, where individuals unconsciously seek out substitute carers, often placing unrealistic demands on partners. Attachment theory describes the way in which individuals instinctively seek to attach themselves to someone to keep them safe, since without attachments people struggle to survive socially. Babies instinctively attach to their carer, normally the mother, but as they venture into a world from the safety of first attachments, they seek other figures for comfort, stimulation and safety. Attachment theory proposes that the quality of new and different attachments will relate directly to the quality of earlier ones.

> The counsellor will be all-too-aware of a tendency to become an *attachment figure* for neglected pupils. The care and attention rarely given in any other context than counselling in school is likely to be unconsciously interpreted for both as a 'mother–child' substitute, and this needs to be guarded against in a sensitive manner.

Socialisation

Pressures within a youngster's social milieu also have an effect upon their thinking and feeling. Psychologists have constructed various theories and terms to describe the process of adolescent autonomy, and a major factor is the growing sense of 'I-ness' or individuality that they experience, which is conventionally referred to as 'individuation'.

Individuation and Identity

Western psychologists describe adolescent transition as 'individuation' – a term used by Jung to describe the lifetime process of becoming whole, indivisible and uniquely that person the self 'was meant to be'. The adolescent begins to sever powerful emotional bonds with parents and becomes more sexually aware and drawn to look for 'love objects' outside the family. Inevitably, this instinctive breaking away results in tensions of loyalty. The personality is fickle and fragile at this point and the adolescent learns to cope with this feeling of tug-of-war tension by employing defence mechanisms, unconscious devices that may be maladaptive. Maladaptive behaviour stems from the inadequacy of psychological defences to cope with inner conflicts due to thwarting the individuation process. The process is similar to that occurring at the end of the third year, where the self-reliant toddler behaves regressively with infantile sulking and tantrums (Mabey and Sorensen, 1995).

Erikson (1968) viewed adolescent development as the completion of tasks. In his classic studies, he saw adolescent life as an 'identity crisis', as a series of stages during which the young person must establish a coherent identity and overcome a sense of *identity diffusion*. The adolescent must make major decisions at this time in almost every area of life, and each task involves a crisis and a need to defeat identity diffusion.

The first task is to overcome a *fear of intimacy*, to commit and engage in a close personal relationship, involving a surrender of self and a loss of personal identity. Many adolescents require a long period of dating and testing out of relationships before they will fully entrust themselves in intimacy. Adolescents lacking a strong identity of trust from early positive childhood attachments are prone to form formal relationships or unsuitable partnerships.

The second is the need to combat what Erikson calls *diffusion in time perspective*. This is where the adolescent finds it difficult to plan for the future. There is ambivalence over the possibility of a promising future: on the one hand, a disbelief that time will bring change and, on the other, an anxiety that change might indeed come with time.

Third, there is *diffusion of industry*, in which the adolescent finds it difficult to harness resources in a realistic way, either in practical work or in study. It is a paralysed condition of lethargy, an inability to concentrate or a preoccupation with one activity to the exclusion of others.

Finally, there is the appeal of forming a *negative identity*, one that is contrary to that which is preferred by the parent or carer. The wish to oppose is a process of finding a true identity. It is expressed as a scornful rebuttal of the role that is considered respectable and proper by the family or community. Erikson also speaks of a period of *psychosocial moratorium*, a time when decisions can be left in abeyance.

Western society encourages the decision to delay major choices. Adolescents find space to experiment with roles in order to discover the sort of person they wish to be, which, for Erikson, is healthy and provides an opportunity for social play.

Autonomy or Integration

The Eriksonian model of adolescent development has been criticised for reflecting western experience. In the context of cultural diversity, other accounts of human transition are credible, such as those arising from social construction theory. The emotional and psychological traits associated with 'adolescence' arise from a social expectation for the individual to become autonomous and independent, but other social groups require their aspiring young adults to become integrated and to conform to set roles – as outlined in the influential work of Margaret Mead (1928, 1930, 1949). The phenomena of 'childhood' and 'adolescence' did not exist for the majority of the labouring poor until late into the nineteenth century (Muncie et al., 1995), and the 'rights of children' have only been the focus of political and social change in relatively recent times (Daniels and Jenkins, 2000). 'Adolescence' may not be a biological programme that all have to pass through, then, but a socially constructed narrative.

Two studies of adolescence (Chatterjee et al., 2001; Galatzer-Levi, 2002) have challenged the western paradigm.

Teenagers brought up within non-industrialised and less technological societies – where the economy is not dependent on extended youth training and where marriage and sexual unions are entered into early – are found to have higher self-esteem by comparison to those from more sophisticated societies (Chatterjee et al., 2001). In addition, marginalised ethnic groups of young people within industrialised societies who 'have lesser knowledge requirements' tend not to fare well (Chatterjee et al., 2001: 11). In traditional, low-industrialised societies, marriage for girls comes soon after reaching reproductive capacity, and boys marry soon after acquiring the capacity to support a household – men only marry late if economics determines the decision (Galatzer-Levi, 2002).

A qualitative study of two adolescents illustrates how experience can be shaped by overriding narratives (Galatzer-Levi, 2002). Two young men were undergoing an 'identity crisis' measured against conceptions of 'normality'. One dropped out of a career training programme and felt guilty, until reading Erikson's theory of *psychosocial moratorium*, which inferred that his behaviour was 'normal'. The other was a 14-year-old leader of a gang who was arrested for murder. Having felt let down, he aligned himself with a group of 'trustworthy friends'. All the messages coming to him from family, friends, counsellors and professionals were that he lived 'as a soldier'. Having internalised a 'soldier identity', he rose to the rank of 'general' and killed 'an enemy' to protect 'his army'.

Both adolescents lived out stories 'told about them', and assumed identities that appeared to them as 'normal', but which were social constructs: 'they created themselves in others' eyes' (Galatzer-Levi, 2002: 46). Adolescents create their sense of 'self' from others' perspectives.

Many are dissonant about their own desires and the expectations others have of them. There are expectations of parents and carers, and expectations of school and peers, that leave young people in a quandary over what *they* want and who *they* are. Perhaps the greatest influence during this phase is friends.

Peer Influence

Adults largely prescribe roles for young people, but dominant teenagers in school can sometimes take up powerful roles as all are drawn to integrate within different cultural compositions. Schools are great social mixers. The insecurity of becoming less dependent on parents and carers has the effect of making young people depend more upon a peer group for reassurance in supporting the self-concept (Geldard, 2009). Role change, then, is an integral feature of western adolescent development (Coleman, 1987).

Each school is likely to have a hierarchy of social communities, and the dominant cultural group tends to determine conceptions of 'normality'. For example, in the school where I counsel, there is an anti-work ethic among a dominant white 'working-class' peer group, where the risk of attaining high grades and being called 'a boffin' is as risky as the opposite of being called 'thick'. A dominant group of attractive white female pupils achieve status from dating black (westernised) boys, which leaves their white male counterparts feeling lesser sexually attractive beings – an observation that marks black boys as being at the pinnacle of the sexual hierarchy (Youdell, 2003). The music of black American culture, rapping and street dancing determine the dominant identity of being. The dress to which each youngster 'must aspire' is designer-labelled clothes:

Dennis:	Do we know why Shiraz is away again?
Zoe:	He had a mega bust-up at home for not coming to school in freaky shoes and black trousers on non-uniform day. And I don't blame him; I'd stay away.
Dennis:	And that stops him coming?
Jazmin:	I wouldn't be seen dead in anything he wears!

Geldard and Geldard (2010) cite the work of Waterman (1984) to describe ethnic identity tensions. Ethnic identity goes through transition where individuals belonging to minority groups accept the values and attitudes of the majority culture, internalising negative views of their own group. But in the later stages of adolescence, there is an awareness of the need to learn more of one's origins, to carry out an ethnic identity search, which ultimately brings them to engage with their own culture. This can be highly emotional as they adjust to the norms of their own ethnic group, sometimes becoming quite hostile to the majority society. If peer influence is recognised as being significant, it seems highly appropriate to utilise pupils in programmes of peer support.

> Research supports the effectiveness of peer-support programmes (Geldard, 2009; Naylor and Cowie, 1999; Whiston and Sexton, 1998; Wilson and Deane, 2001). It is known that pupils in secondary school are *less likely to tell a teacher if they are being bullied* than when they were in primary school (Smith and Sharp, 1994), that they will become *more reluctant to speak with anyone at home as they grow older* (Whitney and Smith, 1993), and that they *only report when matters become extreme* (Besag, 1989; Olweus, 1993).
>
> Young people across all socio-economic groups *prefer the support of their friends* for their problems than their parents and teachers (Gibson-Cline, 1996), and such observations have led to the creation of many novel systems and training programmes (Cowie and Sharp, 1996; Smith and Sharp, 1994). There is also guidance on the setting up of peer-support systems and pupil mentoring in school (Lines, 2005).

> Much self-referral is over peer-group disputes arising from division and clan-like conflict, and the school counsellor will become acquainted with the clichés and fashions of rival groups. Dress and image become important for all teenagers. For those youngsters coming from families of low income and unemployment, the therapist may have to address low self-esteem issues, particularly for those not belonging to the 'in-crowd'.
>
> *(Continued)*

(Continued)

Imaginative therapists utilise pupils in mutually supporting their friends, indirectly through group work, and systemically through peer-support programmes on a drop-in or matched counsellor–client basis.

Cognitive Development

While the social environment is a major influence on development, the complex internal context of cognition has a bearing on identity and behaviour. The two go hand in hand and are complementary. Along with significant growth spurts and hormonal changes, the stage of adolescence is a transition from 'egocentrism' to higher cognitive abilities (Geldard and Geldard, 2010; Thomas, 1990). It is a time of inner conflict as youngsters seek to define their identity and begin to relinquish their 'dreamlike', playful consciousness for focused attention. But they are moving towards a stage of responsibility and personal accounting in a social flux of paradox and mixed messages. Adolescents become inconsistent as they pass through this crucial phase. They are idealistic and yet unrealistic. Eventually, they move towards a more moderate phase of self-acceptance and integration, a stage that is only fully reached in adulthood. There will be the *need* for some adolescents to rebel, which, while difficult to manage and live with at times, should be viewed as a natural process in securing ego strength and identity.

Increased Cognitive Ability

Around puberty, there is a significant development from a form of thinking that Jean Piaget described as 'concrete operations' to higher forms of reasoning and abstract thinking – *formal operational thought* (Inhelder and Piaget, 1958). Earlier adolescent behaviour was determined largely by social learning through reward and reinforcement. If a child experienced a favourable outcome for a particular behaviour, she would tend to repeat it to get rewarded, and the more consistently the conditions applied the more reinforced became the behaviour. At adolescence, a fundamental shift occurs in cognition. The teenager becomes capable of forming propositions from abstract ideas, of forming hypotheses around possibilities and of reasoning in deductive logic. Not all behaviour is reward-induced.

Adolescents' abilities in formal operational thought allow for the possibility to think not only about their own opinions, but also the opinions of others (Geldard and Geldard, 2010). To see the perspective of others while not necessarily agreeing with them brings about a different form of egocentrism, an egocentrism that is, paradoxically, different in character from that of childhood. Adolescent egocentrism is conditioned by will in an awareness of others, whereas childhood egocentrism is more an instinctive impulse (Coleman, 1987). Thus, teenagers are quick to perceive an adult's inconsistencies and contradictions, and just as quick to point them out. On the receiving end, they understandably become sensitive to criticism and ridicule. These complex cognitive changes make identity formation quite confusing. Examples are given throughout this book where trials resulting from cognitive development have led to social upheaval in respect of both family and friends.

A 'Need' to Rebel

Although a moderate degree of resistance and rebellion should be anticipated and, indeed, expected in healthy adolescent individuation, there are cases where this goes disastrously wrong. Unstable family factors, indiscipline, loose boundaries and socialising with offending role models can lead an adolescent into trouble (Geldard and Geldard, 2010).

Kieran's attendance waned in Year 10 (to 35 per cent) as he began to link up with a group of unemployed youths in the neighbourhood. Although his parents had split up, his father was involved until an overnight stay. Kieran crept downstairs early in the morning while his father was asleep, took his bank card and withdrew £200 over the day in two withdrawals. Slipping it back into his wallet, his father didn't initially know of the theft. The money was squandered on alcohol with his 'friends'. He stayed away that night and, in an intoxicated state, broke into his school, causing serious criminal damage. He now has a criminal record.

Maturing Humour

One final and, I think, very important factor of adolescent development is the altering capacity for fun and joviality, and I consider that this area is insufficiently recognised in the literature. Teenagers enjoy a good laugh and are known to smile and laugh in general much more regularly than adults do throughout the day. The topics of humour vary throughout development, from 11–13-year-olds being amused by bodily sensations (such as farting) and pulling silly faces, tripping and pushing friends in the mud, etc., to the more sophisticated comedy of 14-year-olds who find humour in innuendo, subtlety, irony and characterisation, as befits their higher cognitive ability.

Humour bonds people together and the therapist can utilise humour in counselling so long as it is not interpreted as ridicule. Being aware of cognitive improvements during adolescence, the school counsellor will draw on metaphor and abstract concepts more fittingly, and will assist collaboratively in shaping goals for each client that are in tandem with their cognitive abilities. One useful intervention I customarily make is to ask clients in the second session to relay for me what they had 'heard' from our previous meeting. This not only tests their memory but their understanding and the effectiveness of my communication – it can reveal startling information and provide valuable feedback.

Neuroscience: The Teenage Brain

Major developments in neuroscience and the mapping of the teenage brain have greatly improved our understanding of adolescent mental development, and this research has significant implications for counselling in school and college. Advances in MRI scans of teenage brains combined with in-vivo experiments have considerably shifted our understanding in at least two areas. It was once thought that the major wiring of the brain was completed by as early as 3 years of age and reached maturity at puberty, at around 10 to 12 years of age. It was also assumed that brain development was a one-way linear process.

We now know that the teenage brain is radically different from that of a child or adult and that fundamental alterations are occurring at puberty and on into late adolescence, to the extent that along with improved conceptual reasoning there is also a deficit in tasking functionality and interpretation of body language during this critical period. This has implications for counselling adolescents. Studies have revealed that teenagers are prone to make poor choices and misread situations (see Chapter 9) owing to the fact that, in certain situations, the amygdala (a structure in the temporal lobe that discriminates fear and other emotions) is more active than the frontal lobes (the seat of goal-oriented, rational thinking). There also appears to be a temporary reversal in progress through puberty.

Shaping the Brain

Emotional states, like falling in love or being in shock, can be mapped with computer-generated images in intricate detail as connections between neurons are occurring, and different mental tasking results in different adult brains (a taxi driver's brain is different from that of a musician). While it is evident that poor attachments in early infancy will not foster rich neuronal interconnections (Gerhardt, 2004; Kuhl, 2004), it is also true that both nature *and* nurture are in a 'perpetual dance', so that 'neither genetics nor environment nor individual agency can ever be independent of each other. The nature *versus* nurture argument is obsolete' (Sercombe, 2010: 22). It is now known that environmental factors affect the health of cells under investigation (Lipton, 2009), and that the nervous system is responsible for 'reading' the environment to select appropriate genes that the organism uses to build a structure, or form a behaviour, to enable it to survive in that environment (Cox, 2010; Lipton, 2009).

Synaptic Changes

Scans of teenage brains show altering ratios of white and grey matter (the tissue surrounding the brain) throughout puberty. It has been suggested that this might indicate that a rapid increase in neuron connections, or synapses, is taking place at this time, as though the organism is being prepared for a new environmental challenge (i.e. moving away from home). White matter is called myelin which provides insulation for brain circuitry, which massively increases the speed and efficiency of message transmission.

The increasing grey matter apparent at the onset of puberty begins to fade away after puberty in certain brain regions, and this process has been attributed to post-pubescent synaptic pruning, a process which selects and strengthens only those connections necessary for the organism to function efficiently (Giedd et al., 1999).

Neuron activity occurs in the brain of infants during the first 12 months of life. Babies are able to distinguish between all speech sounds to which they are exposed. They have a propensity to acquire any language and become multilingual. By the end of the first year, they lose this ability so that only those phonetic properties of the mother tongue are strengthened (Kuhl, 2004). This pruning process permits the strengthening of only those connections necessary for survival, resulting in an inability to learn a second language with age (Hakuta et al., 2003).

It is thought that the second wave of neuron activity, followed by selective pruning, serves to strengthen the principal connections necessary for survival in an altering social environment (Blakemore and Chaudhury, 2006). Until pruning occurs after puberty, synaptic connections in the frontal cortex generate low signal-to-noise ratios due to an excess of synapses, and this renders cognitive performance initially less efficient. One author has likened the process to the many dirt tracks formed en route to the Australian goldfields, tracks which became covered through lack of use and which were replaced with major highways – fewer in number but more efficient (Sercombe, 2010).

During early puberty, young people are learning fast and inventing a hundred ways of doing things. They are developing brains which are a vast repository of information and stored experience. Through routine and habit, many of these varied neuron pathways become obsolete and therefore the circuitry fades into non-use, under the principle of *use it or lose it* (Sercombe, 2010).

The school counsellor has a significant role in helping young clients to explore their creative capacities to solve the fundamental problems of social survival, to utilise imaginative skills and to explore the potential made available through synaptic proliferation.

Skill Deficit and Development during Adolescence

Images of teenage brain scans have been matched with behavioural studies of executive function, which is a range of skills that include selective attention, decision making, voluntary response inhibition and working memory, skills which can be traced through functioning magnetic resonance imaging (fMRI). It is known that, through adolescence, young people often become weaker in these skills compared to when they were pre-pubescent and in comparison to adults of the same intelligence (Blakemore and Chaudhury, 2006).

Studies in fMRI investigated the neural mechanisms that might account for the differences between adolescents and adults in decision making through one-line scenarios (such as 'swimming with sharks'), where subjects were asked to press a button to indicate whether this was a 'good idea' or 'not a good idea' (Baird et al., 2005). It was found that adolescents took significantly longer than adults to indicate that it was not a good idea to swim with sharks, which suggested that, compared with adults, they make less efficient responses.

Risk-taking

Teenagers generally are not strong in exercising **inhibition control** and are prone to engage in risky behaviour (Geldard, 2009), such as experimenting with drugs, sexual encounters and driving fast cars, often encouraged by peers – a phenomenon which illustrates the interplay of brain chemistry and environment.

Adolescent Risk-taking

Tom's behaviour was a mystery to his mother. He was frequently forgetting to do his homework and received regular detentions, even though he was keen not to fail in school. His typical response was, 'I just forgot'. He even forgot to ask his mother if his uncle could get him a brand new BMX bike, which he was keen to have as a birthday gift, and which, arguably, would have been in his *interests* to have remembered. When in time he received the bike, he was reckless, performing stunt after stunt with such excessive risk–taking that he eventually fell from a ramp and broke his wrist. Even after being in plaster for six months, this did not stop him carrying on the same feat again – he appeared to have no fear.

Perspective Taking and Multi-tasking

Perspective memory develops through adolescence as frontal lobe functioning takes over from the amygdala (Ellis, 1996). Perspective memory is the ability to hold in mind an intention to carry something out in the future. Adults may have to accept, therefore, that an adolescent forgetting to carry out a task may not necessarily be a wilful decision but a case of deficit brain functioning. Brain chemistry might enlighten our understanding of why it is that teenagers appear not to see the logic of cautionary restraint (often delivered by protective adults) over risk-taking behaviour like experimenting with harmful drugs, internet flirtation and unprotected sex.

The school counsellor has a vital role in aiding the young client to develop the brain circuitry of neuron connections to encourage wise judgement over impulsive, thrill-seeking behaviour.

The social world of the developing teenager leaves its imprint on the pruning process (Blakemore and Chaudhury, 2006). Accumulating new **social experiences**, such as entering a new school, will also affect the pruning process. Learning the social skills of self-assertion, performing before an audience and asking someone on a date, etc., will also shape the pruning process. In addition, there is the ability to take another person's perspective and this is crucial for social communication. The developing adolescent acquires the skills and understanding to see the world through the eyes of another, to step into their friend's 'mental shoes' and to take a different perspective on an issue than their own.

Perspective taking is related to first-order theory of mind in that it involves surmising what another person is thinking or feeling (Blakemore and Chaudhury, 2006). Perspective taking includes awareness of one's own subjective mental states and the ability to ascribe mental states to another person, and, although the mechanisms for this functioning are not as yet fully understood, there is little doubt that such abilities involve the frontal lobes becoming more developed and brain circuitry strengthened. **Multi-tasking** is believed to be a test of perspective memory as it requires participants to remember to perform a number of different tasks to engage in everyday life.

For the school counsellor to attempt the type of techniques commonly employed in Gestalt therapy, such as the empty chair technique, or in family therapy, such as reflexive circular questioning, it is essential to carry out such cognitive tasks only when it is known that the young client has reached this stage of development. The counsellor may aid this process through careful matching of interventions with an understanding of brain development.

Anger and the Maturing Brain

Teenagers often misread facial expression, particularly with emotions of fear and anger (see Chapter 9). There is an unaccountable dip in cognitive performance. With fearful expressions, those under 14 often see sadness, confusion or anger, but older adolescents perceive correctly as the frontal lobes take over amygdala activity (Yurgelun-Todd, 2002). Misreading is more acute in boys than in girls, who by comparison show a decrease in amygdala activity compared with dorsolateral prefrontal activation (McGivern et al., 2002).

A range of experiments has been carried out with children aged 10 to 17 and young adults aged 18 to 22 to ascertain the various levels of amygdala and frontal lobe activation. Volunteers were shown pictures of faces bearing particular emotional expressions (such as happy, sad, angry), sometimes matching pictures with words, to test out a hypothesis that such a condition places high demands on frontal lobe circuitry, requiring working memory and decision making. The results revealed that at the age of puberty onset, at 11 to 12 years, there was a decline in performance in the 'matching face to word' task compared with the younger group of pre-pubescent children. There was a 10–20 per cent increase in reaction time of the match-to-sample task, a response which levelled out and then improved in later adolescence (McGivern et al., 2002).

If the school counsellor engages with young clients utilising anger-management programmes, it is necessary that the effects of an overactive amygdala are understood.

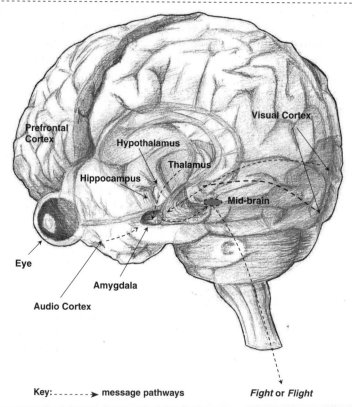

Key: - - - - - ➤ message pathways   *Fight* or *Flight*

Figure 5.1   Parts of the brain regulating the *fight* or *flight* response (sketched by student Charlotte Hessey)

In spite of the highly significant findings of neuroscience, it is important to exercise caution over the combined results of MRI brain mapping and cognitive neuroscience, since research is at an early stage and deductions made from adolescent brain research are still speculative. The supporting evidence of cognitive experiments is not without criticism. Some have questioned adolescent reaction time to facial image experiments and have asked whether an angry face correlates with the real-life situation of meeting an angry person, arguing that there are a lot of interpretive steps in the logic (Sercombe, 2010). There is no full agreement over the effect of inhibition of synaptic pruning for boys (testosterone) compared with girls, and recent MRI studies indicate that the time at which the brain reaches maturity may be later than the end of adolescence (Blakemore and Chaudhury, 2006). However, there is no doubting the temporary deficit in decision making where teenagers are prone to make poor decisions and take risks. In this respect, counselling in school has a significant role to play.

Implications for Counselling

Psycho-education

It has been suggested that teenagers may actually be able to control how their own brains are wired and sculpted, and that the school counsellor can assist clients in exercising their brains by learning to order thoughts, to form abstract concepts and to control personal impulses, and by so doing lay the neural foundations that will serve them for the rest of their lives (Giedd et al., 1999). This may be the case for those pupils who become impulsively angry and 'out of control' through poor adult modelling. The counsellor can assist the teenager by showing them a diagram of their brain and teaching them how an over-sensitive amygdala can be regulated by the prefrontal cortex through relaxation exercises, anger management and self-coaching (see Chapter 9).

Strengthening Strategic Planning

The school counsellor recognises that puberty is a period of synaptic reorganisation and that the teenager's brain will be more sensitive to experimental input; it will be weaker in exercising executive function and social cognition than at any other time. Adolescence may, therefore, offer the greatest opportunity to bring about more lasting change than at any other period of development (Sercombe, 2010). If teenagers are more self-aware and more self-reflective than pre-pubescent children, then the therapist may assist the young person to develop the capacity to hold in mind multidimensional concepts in order to think in a more strategic manner (Blakemore and Chaudhury, 2006).

Managing Risky Behaviour

Preventing young people from taking risks may be self-defeating, particularly if delivered by fear-driven, over-protective adults. Managing risky behaviour is a skill that requires patience and understanding. Some mid-to-late adolescents display behaviour 'designed to shock' – to say something without words (Geldard and

Geldard, 2010). It is a means of assertion, of breaking free of family ties. When condemning smoking, drinking, drug experimentation and sexual relations, by over-moralising about the physical and social threats to well-being, adults are feeding into a condition that has powerful appeal. Responsible decision making is the preferred approach and it is here that counselling is targeted (McGuiness, 1998).

Maturity occurs through taking risks, and, paradoxically, not taking risks may lead to extended periods of infantile behaviour. As Sercombe has said (2010: 24), 'eliminating risk is risky'. In this respect, the school counsellor who assists young clients in exploring options is inadvertently refraining from moralising and censoring guidance in place of permitting them a choice of the possibility of engaging in risky behaviour; in a sense, the therapist is providing a paradoxical intervention.

By contrast, with alcohol misuse, current research suggests that adolescents are more vulnerable than adults to the effects of alcohol in relation to learning and memory (Brown et al., 2000; White and Swartzwelder, 2005), and this suggests that alcoholism among the young should be taken more seriously than risky behaviour.

Selective Memory

If neuroscience has taught us anything, it is that teenagers do not process information in the same way as adults do – what is assumed to be disobedience may merely be different mental functioning. Adult conversations with adolescents may take place on different wavelengths. An instruction that puts pressure on a teenager may be misheard.

Suppose one morning a carer tells her teenage son to 'wash your breakfast dish, get ready for school and pick up your PE kit', and then finds him slouched on the sofa, watching the television, dish on the floor and unprepared for the day. The initial response is to judge that he's being difficult or confrontational and not wanting to do as he's told. This may indeed be the case, but, on the other hand, findings from neuroscience suggest that a lot of the time teenagers are not fully able to pay attention – either they heard the instruction but didn't really register it, or they heard it and they thought it was okay to do it later, or they heard it but whatever came on television seemed more important.

They somehow have reorganised information, so they are not really trying to disappoint or frustrate the parent or carer – it is just that they are on a different wavelength (Yurgelun-Todd, 2002). A similar case is when students appear to deliberately defy their teacher's instructions. In both cases, resultant conflicts through miscommunication regularly bring pupils forward for counselling.

The Role of Parents and Carers

Gibran's poem, which opened the chapter, eloquently expresses an insight of non-possessive parenting. There is an anomaly about quality parenting within modern society, for many experience difficulty because of the lack of preparation given to this exacting task. It is assumed that parenting is an instinctive skill, when it is clear that most adopt a style that is only a slight modification of their own parented experience. Parents and carers will not be perfect, but may be 'good enough', yet will have to develop a range of flexible childrearing skills to facilitate growth.

Exercise, Diet and Boundaries

During adolescent growth spurts, the parent must encourage **exercise** and provide a **balanced diet** of minerals, protein and carbohydrates (Thomas, 1990). There will be undue tension for adolescents living in homes at the two extremes of **monitoring**: where conditions are lax or too regimental. Insecurity and delinquency are inevitable in a family where there are no rules, yet rebellion is the risk where rules are inflexible. While authoritarian parenting is harmful (Biddulph, 1996), a strict upbringing with plenty of love is not in itself as much a problem as one having fuzzy boundaries. Suitable parenting is a question of balance, but is tilted towards firmness.

Psychological necessities for the parent to help develop a positive self-concept include affection, protection, realistic expectations and a predictable environment (Thomas, 1990). Obsessive neurosis can occur where a person feels compelled to do certain things through an excessive **fear of disapproval** as a result of past failures. There will be a lack of confidence about launching into independence. The child will be out of control and will fear that unbridled instincts and impulses might land them in trouble. There will be a felt need to keep checking routines and personal hygiene fastidiously through fear of criticism, leading to disconnected feelings and a compulsion to live out parental wishes – some attempt to channel their children to live out their own aspirations by 'programming' them early.

Encouraging Friendships

Fostering good friendships is important and the wise parent or carer will facilitate social growth by adopting a positive and encouraging stance towards their son or daughter's friends. Some view peer group allegiance as a gesture of personal rejection, but a supportive peer group is essential for the teenager to identify with the experiences of those undergoing the same development (Conger, 1975). 'Good enough' parenting recognises the nature of group membership, the fierce loyalty that can at times be fanatical and the need not to lose face publicly. Disaffected boys can form strong bonds with teachers and youth leaders who become suitable role models in place of older offenders in the street (Biddulph, 2008). Girls and boys can have stronger bonds with grandparents than parents if attachment issues were prevalent when very young.

Some parents encourage regressive behaviours and induce guilt, which limits the horizon of autonomy. Anger may be expressed disproportionately when youngsters arrive late after being out with friends. There will be undue reward for regressive behaviour, such as tears, cuddling and the like – all in order to keep the adolescent ever the child. These are *counter-separation manoeuvres*. The guilt-inducing behaviour is normally displayed covertly by parents whose relationship is likely to be dysfunctional. Often, they have no friends and little social life outside a closeted family of dependents – such parents long for earlier days when a faulty relationship could be hidden behind 'needed' parental roles (Berkowitz, 1987).

Letting Teenagers Go

Letting go of the grown-up child is not easy. Breaking parent–daughter bonds, particularly, can be traumatic for some parents when boyfriends come on the scene. As their adolescent daughter stays more away from home, some parents become over-controlling and often go to extreme measures to halt the process. Adolescents of strongly *enmeshed* families have a difficult time in establishing their independence. Berkowitz (1987) suggests that parents who stand in the way of this separation process may run the risk of pathological behaviour. Many borderline adolescents exhibit guilt, depression and suicidal anomie, in protest against excessive control.

Parents will rationalise their own resistance with the argument that the world is hostile in comparison to safety within the family. Danger outside – rapists, murderers, sex-abusers and drug-pushers – is exaggerated to impede individuation. The hazards are there, but adolescents need to develop social skills to survive such a world, not retreat from living. An unreasonable avoidance creates phobia in face of such risks, with disproportionate fearfulness. Cautious parents point to their off-spring's mistakes along the way to justify over-zealous restrictions.

When a daughter becomes sexually curious, or sexually active, a mother may wish to 'chain her up' or 'vet the boyfriend', while a father may tacitly collude in keeping her bound within the home. There is a compulsion to hold the child close, to possess the outreaching adolescent and to restrict independence. In reality, the child has no problem, but is following a natural inclination to escape a claustrophobic environment. It is the parent's neurosis that is the problem. So, rather than welcoming the fact that their daughter is fleeing the nest, they refuse to see her as the centre of her own initiative.

'Good enough' parents will not see their child's expanding world as a threat but as a resource. Such censoring attitudes may be problematic for strictly religious groups who view 'letting go' as losing their child to a world of immorality and vice, a world that is disrespectful of traditional values, and this can create tension that divides communities and bring many clients to counselling.

Conclusion

Adolescence is a multidimensional process. This chapter has presented adolescence as a search for identity through meeting a series of tasks, but it has acknowledged that other accounts are equally tenable. While it may be true for some that personal autonomy and independence is the goal to which the individual strives, for others the adolescent rite of passage is successful integration within the community. The two are not mutually exclusive, and are likely to be socially constructed paradigms which may change in time and within different cultures – they are not universal commentaries of being.

Perhaps the most significant feature of adolescence for the school counsellor centres on the nature of attachment relationships and how these are played out in school among peers, in pupil–teacher relationships and within the therapeutic relationship. The school counsellor also needs to take special note of the findings of neuroscience regarding the development of the teenage brain. Throughout this book, brief school counselling will often be presented as a means of assisting pupils to meet particular tasks and goals. In every case, it is imperative to be aware of the difference between what a student can achieve and what is achievable – in this respect, discoveries in neuroscience have much to inform the therapist.

The chapter closed by examining how parents and carers can support their off-spring to come through adolescence by avoiding the pitfalls of inflexibility, permissiveness or enmeshment, and any tendency to foist unconsciously their own psychological difficulties onto their children in place of helping them to celebrate this as an exciting stage of growth.

Reflective Exercise

1. Take a moment to reflect on your own adolescence:
   a. What form of consciousness can you recall?
   b. What were the particular pressures you had to face?
   c. What support did you depend on, and what other influences helped you come through this period?

2. Share your reflections with a friend in whom you trust who has carried out the same exercise, and compare your findings. Consider now a teenage client and contrast your experiences to those of your client. (The point is not to compare generational differences, but to examine what counter-transference issues might arise for you when counselling teenagers.)

3. Does the Eriksonian model of adolescent development make sense according to your experience of working with young people? Is the aim in counselling to help teenagers become autonomous and independent, or is it to assist them in becoming more integrated and to recognise the mutual interdependence of living in a community? Discuss.

4. What impact has the presented information on the 'teenage brain' and neuroscience made upon you? Outline how it may affect your work when counselling:
   a. Pre-pubescent children.
   b. Mid-adolescents, i.e. those from age 12 to 14.
   c. Late adolescents, i.e. those from age 15 to 18.

5. 'By not following instructions (as intended), teenagers may not necessarily be choosing to disobey but be processing information differently.' Discuss this view in light of your own experience of teenagers.

6. Through a teenage case study, highlight any attachment issues underlying the presenting problem, and show how *attachment* needs might have a

(Continued)

(Continued)

bearing on classroom situations that teachers have reported, or that have resulted in peer disputes.

7. Some students often complain that teachers single them out personally in classroom altercations, saying that they are 'always picking on me', or that they 'never listen to what I say'. Explore with them their previous childhood experience of living in the family among siblings, and ascertain whether or not family experience, attachment needs or sibling rivalry are being repeated in the context of the classroom. What does this teach us about 'learned' and 'generalised' behaviour patterns?

Key Points

- Adolescence can be an exciting and yet troublesome transition from child to adult, and the school counsellor should synchronise therapeutic interventions according to developmental needs.
- Psychosexual effects of puberty create tensions among teenagers in school who are preoccupied with conforming to perceived standards of 'normality'.
- Teenagers are developing emotionally, and changes will not only be affected by biology but by altering expectations of parents, teachers, peers and even themselves.
- Many pupils will have grown up with *secure attachments*, which are transferred into their peer and adult relationships. But there are others whose attachment is *insecure* or *ambivalent*, and these are likely to present themselves for counselling – *attachment* needs have implications for the counselling relationship.
- Erikson's model views adolescence as a stage where the self undergoes an 'identity crisis', which is resolved when meeting particular tasks. Such an account views the goal as to achieve 'individuation' and independence, but other narratives of adolescence place higher value on community responsibilities like *integration* and *interdependence*.
- Cognitive development to 'formal operational thought' gives adolescents the apparatus to engage in abstract thinking, to see the needs of others and to reflect on how they may be perceived from others' standpoints – the counsellor utilises these abilities in therapy.
- Discoveries in neuroscience of the teenage brain suggest that adolescents will process information in different ways to adults and pre-pubescent children. At the onset of puberty, there occurs a proliferation of synapses followed by selective pruning, and this biological process results in temporary *deficits* in cognitive and emotional functioning. Teenagers become temporarily weak in exercising *inhibition control* and *reading emotional reactions*.
- In mid- to late-adolescence, *perspective functionality* and *multi-tasking* improves, and this offers more possibilities for therapeutic change.
- Parents and carers assist teenagers in development by providing exercise and a healthy diet, encouragement, a structure with boundaries, firmness and love, by accepting their child's friendships and by 'letting go' at the appropriate time.

6 Low Self-esteem: Depression, Anxiety and Reaction to Abuse

This chapter covers:

- Research on depression, stress and low self-esteem
- Counselling depressed young people
- Counselling young people with anxiety to raise self-esteem
- Counselling the sexually abused

Introduction

In spite of the fact that teenagers in school may claim to be depressed, 'clinically depressed' young people are not likely to have survived in mainstream education without notice. That is not to say that students will not on occasion become stressed or exhibit depressive states and a lowering in self-esteem. This chapter illustrates a range of brief therapeutic approaches for lifting pupils from temporary depressive states and for raising self-esteem.

Research on depression and the causes of stress are first considered, along with the physical and psychological symptoms that occur when youngsters become subjected to low mood states. The means of getting pupils to relax are outlined before brief integrative interventions are applied to three categories of clients suffering from low self-esteem: those claiming to be depressed, those who are anxious and those affected through being a victim of sexual abuse.

Research on Depression, Stress and Low Self-esteem

Depression

Research shows that up to one-third of people visiting their doctor are having some form of psychological difficulty, with anxiety disorders and depression being the most common (Sanders and Wills, 2003: 12). According to the DSM-IV manual, 'Major Depressive Episode' is defined by change to five or more symptoms, including 'depressed mood' (feeling overly sad, irritability in children and adolescents), 'diminished interest', 'weight loss', 'insomnia', 'psychomotor agitation', 'fatigue', 'feeling of worthlessness', 'inability to concentrate', 'recurrent thoughts of death', etc., for most of the day and every day within a two-week period. Figures suggest that depression rises after the age of 12 and is almost twice as common in girls as in boys (Lewinsohn et al., 1993).

Costello et al. (2004), reviewing seriously depressed young people in 18 epidemiological studies, found prevalence rates for under 18-year-olds of between 0.2 to 12.9 per cent, the median being 4.7 per cent. Recovery rates through treatment programmes are summarised by Carr (2009a), and the observation that depressed young people are at greater risk of suicide than other disorders is recognised by NICE (2004).

Environmental changes interacting with genetic factors leave some vulnerable to depressive episode (Carr, 2009a), but character traits like intelligence, coping and problem-solving skills, capacities for self-reflection, mastery, an internal locus of control and positive social support networks render individuals less prone to depression (Shortt and Spence, 2006).

Meta-analysis of RCTs on assessment and treatment programmes illustrated improvement for 60–70 per cent of depressed young people through CBT (Harrington et al., 1998; Lewinsohn and Clarke, 1999; Reinecke et al., 1998), 75 per cent of a group of clients improved through brief psychodynamic combined with family therapy (Trowell et al., 2007) and the same figure through interpersonal therapy (Mufson et al., 2004). Similarly high figures for family therapy exist (Carr, 2009a). Not every study showed improvement levels in long-term follow-up, however.

Carr (2009a) concludes that the combined evidence suggests that family-based interventions – which include family psycho-education – linked with individual therapy using behavioural techniques and problem-solving skills should be applied in clinical practice and in school for less severe cases.

'Clinical depression' in young people is likely to have been first diagnosed by a psychiatrist and addressed at off-site clinics through medication and CBT. Although young people get stressed at times (say, before performing a task like a piano solo or giving a presentation), it is the 'continued stress', which leads to anxiety and a prolonged state of being overwhelmed with no conceivable way out, that is the real cause of concern.

Aetiology and Causes of Stress and Anxiety

Although self-esteem is difficult to measure, altered mood states and an uncharacteristic lowering in energy and productivity of young people are obvious to all primary carers. Heightened stress underlies a change in mood states. Research on the continuum from low self-esteem to depressive and suicidal thoughts has revealed some helpful insights on the aetiology and management of stress. From an evolutionary point of view, response to stress through *fight* or *flight* has been an advantage to humans in coping with threatening environments (Lines, 2008; McGuiness, 1998).

Research on anxiety has identified the complex cycle of symptom and rumination, and the triggers that set it off (Sanders and Wills, 2003). Paradoxically, research also suggests that depressed people see the world *more clearly*, though more pessimistically, than those who are 'well', as though humans have developed adaptive filtering systems that disguise life's harsh realities (Alloy and Abramson, 1982). However, depressed people cannot function socially, and are low in energy and productiveness. When youngsters experience being loved and supported, and are in harmony with their social and natural environment, they become less stressed and more energised.

> When under stress, three 'stress chemicals' come into play. As with a cornered animal under attack, human beings may *fight* using anger in order to survive, and this highly charged state causes increased levels of noradrenaline and adrenaline. Alternatively, the instinctive response when afraid is to *escape*. Under such stress, increased levels of adrenaline, noradrenaline and cortisol come into play. Adrenaline and noradrenaline put the body into a state of high alert: *fighting* or *escaping* requires much oxygen, so breathing becomes deeper and faster – under stress, we feel unduly exhausted.
>
> Cortisol, by contrast, induces depressive moods, in which a *submissive stance* of rolling over helplessly and handing over control to others occurs. Cortisol mobilises our glucose and fat stores, sensitises the immune system and reduces inflammatory reactions (Gregson and Looker, 1994). All three chemicals decrease when human beings are relaxed.

Symptoms of Stress

Symptoms of high stress include increased heartbeat, palpitations, shallow breathing, a dry mouth, heartburn, queasy stomach, diarrhoea, constipation, muscular tension in the neck and shoulders, aches, pains, cramps, hyperactivity, finger-drumming, foot-tapping, nail-biting, trembling hands, fatigue, exhaustion, disturbed sleep patterns, feeling faint or dizzy, sweatiness, raised levels of smoking and alcohol intake, and decreased sexual activity. As McGuiness says, 'We are living highly stressed lives, and while the symptoms above can be the result of other life factors, they are identified by Gregson and Looker (1994) as indicators of stress' (1998: 113).

Psychological factors produce low self-esteem and depression, particularly when an individual becomes overwhelmed by a loss of personal control. Many become stressed with change, particularly over loss and bereavement, but adolescents have the added factor of hormonal activity during puberty.

Adams' (1976) patterns of high stress include *immobilisation* (where clients shut down in a self-protective way) and *depression* (where anger, despair, helplessness and hopelessness are shown by lashing out, swearing, verbal aggression or lethargy). Persistent high stress and subjectivity lead to a sense of *learned helplessness* where the person develops a submissive posture of defencelessness (Seligman and Peterson, 1986). A depressed youngster may demonstrate behaviour at both extremes, from social withdrawal to impulsive over-reaction, often making the behavioural objective unclear.

Relaxation Techniques

Stressed clients can learn how to relax through relaxation and brief therapy. Relaxation techniques and meditation can help to bring clients down from high tension to lower mood states before integrative techniques come into play.

Clients can be de-stressed through relaxation exercises, yoga, meditation, guided imagery and the use of Gestalt techniques to develop tranquillity and serenity (Oaklander, 1978). Often, clients say that they 'can't relax' when what they mean, according to CBT, is that they are 'choosing not to relax'. Breathing exercises through specific techniques (Kilty and Bond, 1991) combined with regular exercise are effective, and caffeine intake should be reduced under conditions of high stress.

Relaxation exercises follow the method of 'progressive muscular relaxation' (Jacobson, 1938) – tensing and relaxing – with breathing exercises from deep to shallow inhaling and exhaling, together with a visualisation exercise. Clients usually choose the visualising scene, in which they recall a situation of their younger days where they have felt particularly at ease with themselves and at peace with their relational world. Failing that, I find the most evocative visualising location to be the beach, though I check first whether clients have had a negative experience on holiday:

The scene is imaginatively described as though by the youngster (donkeys, ice cream, ball games, sandcastles, and so on). I then lead them on to view themselves running towards the shoreline and taking off into flight, lifting to the sky like a seagull, higher and higher and way above the clouds until they imagine themselves floating over the land below them. After this dreamy phase of detachment has continued for a spell in silence, I talk them down again, step by step towards the cold reality of banal existence – the detachment is reminiscent of *Jonathan Livingston Seagull* (Bach with Munson, 2006 [1970]).

Therapy for Depression

'Over the past 20 years depression among adolescents has received recognition as a serious psychiatric condition that warrants timely intervention' (Peterson et al., 1993: 155). Cognitive therapy is the classic approach for dealing with 'clinical depression' (Beck et al., 1979), but clients whose lowering in self-esteem borders closely on depression can also be lifted in spirit by utilising features of Beck's work. Person-centred therapy has also been influential as an approach for building self-esteem (Mearns and Thorne, 2010; Prever, 2010a).

Beck (Beck et al., 1979) speaks of the damaging effects of negative thinking and commends that clients in therapy should 'refocus themselves from negative thoughts'. Cognitive therapy is an active, directive, time-limited and structured procedure based on the assumption that feelings and behaviour are largely determined by the way people structure their worlds. The therapeutic method of change is through interview and cognitive-behavioural techniques. However, interviewing depressed people is not easy because of their lethargy and indecisiveness, and in order to change learned patterns cognitive-behavioural techniques require a more controlled setting and more time than is often available in school.

The person-centred contention that the counselling relationship is the fundamental factor for change and for raising self-esteem has sound empirical support (Brammer and Shostrum, 1982; Carkhuff and Berenson, 1977; Norcross and Grencavage, 1989; Rogers, 1967; Truax and Carkhuff, 1967). Mearns and Cooper (2005) confirm this and cite the massive research project undertaken by the American Psychological Association in 2002 (Steering Committee, 2002).

Techniques of 'questioning, of identifying illogical thinking, of ascertaining the rules according to which the patient reorganises reality' (Beck et al., 1979: 142) can work in conjunction with Nelson-Jones' (1996) effective thinking skills.

Two further techniques I find effective with overly sad young people are 'diversion' techniques, and a judicious use of humour and irony (Beck et al., 1979). Diversions encourage the client to re-focus from a whirlpool of sadness through activities that require exercise and movement (particularly when accompanied by sensory experiencing). Humour discharges tension and heightens well-being.

One troubled client I see intermittently enjoys the sharing of jokes to lighten his low spirit. When he enters my room to protest about a minor hardship, with a frown that says, in effect, 'You'd better take this seriously', I look at him in a certain way that makes him smile and this settles him, and enables him to cope with the matter more productively.

Time-limited and goal-centred counselling, which recognises the relationship of 'cognition' to 'anxiety', can prove effective in school for youngsters suffering from depressive thoughts and low self-esteem. The following cases apply brief pluralistic counselling utilising features of narrative therapy, cognitive-humanistic counselling and SFT.

Counselling Depressed Young People

Alterations in mood are not uncommon during adolescence with hormonal activity, as discussed in Chapter 5, but rapid decline towards depressive states is likely to have been caused by environmental factors – such as personal loss, experiences of failure, communal trauma, bullying, illness and injury, moving house or getting into trouble (Carr, 2009a; McGuiness, 1998). There is an optimum amount of stress for each individual, and once that point has been reached the negative effects begin to kick in (Yerkes and Dodson, 1993). The counsellor must *be alert* to the danger signals and *take action.*

All young people, like adults, become stressed at times, but a minority of pupils in school can on occasion consider themselves to be 'depressed', or be classified non-clinically by others as being 'depressed', which indicates a need for brief, less intensive, techniques without medication. It is essential that practitioners make use of brief techniques in time-limited and integrated models of counselling, not merely to lift the spirits of young clients but also to get them back on track. 'Externalising' techniques of narrative therapy can prove useful for young people in temporary states of depression.

The Case of Ann-Marie

Ann-Marie entered secondary school having to manage severe eczema all over her body. So severe was her skin condition – clearly visible on her face – that she visited the nurse during the day to cream her skin to prevent irritation. She said that her condition was worse when she was tense. Through Year 7, she coped quite well, but part way through her next year peer pressure over her complexion through name-calling began to have an effect on her self-esteem. By the Easter term, she had ceased attending school for reasons, claimed the educational social worker, 'of depression'.

Ann-Marie first came to my attention at a Filter Group meeting where she, along with others, was raised due to her non-school attendance and 'depressive state'. It was learnt that there had previously been a CAF meeting on the family, which raised concerns on the *enmeshed* relationships existing between mother and daughters during a stormy period of domestic violence. Some professionals felt that Ann-Marie's mother had foisted her emotional anxieties onto her daughters, kept them shackled within the family home and denied them opportunities to mix with friends, thus thwarting their social development. I was given a task at that meeting to engage with the family.

I first met Anne-Marie's mother and asked how *she viewed* her daughter's absence. She became visibly distressed and said that she did not know where to turn. She said that Ann-Marie had refused to leave the house and was 'permanently depressed'. I asked her what had been happening during Year 7 that was successful but which did not appear to be working now. Her mother was thrown by the solution-focused form of the question (O'Connell, 2005) and paused for a while before saying, 'I suppose school has become more difficult'. She seemed anxious and protective, but agreed to persuade her daughter to try working with me to get over the barrier of getting back to school, since, I continued, 'Many pupils find transition to senior school difficult at first, but Ann-Marie strode over the first difficult hurdle and fell later on'. She brought her daughter in the next day.

As they sat together, arm in arm, with Ann-Marie snuggled up to her mother's shoulder, I began to wonder whether a mother–daughter attachment might have become a little too enmeshed, whether each *needed the problem* to solve other interpersonal relations, and whether stress and fear of failure from one was ricocheting onto the other. Ann-Marie did not answer for herself until I posed a direct NLP-styled question: 'Ann-Marie, what do you want to happen?' After claiming that she wanted to get back to school, I asked her if she would work with me to help bring that about. She said she would because she was bored of being at home. Ann-Marie then said, 'I am sinking under depression'. She was clearly dislocated from friends, imprisoned in the home and socially isolated. The aim, therefore, was to engage her in a larger social world and 'distract' her from a preoccupation with 'depression' and the cocooned existence of home.

She was polite and subservient, and appeared intrigued to engage with me in collaborative goal setting. There was optimism from Ann-Marie and myself about a positive outcome, but her mother remained uncertain. I asked the mother politely if she minded leaving, at which Ann-Marie immediately interjected, 'I'll be all right, mum. You do the shopping. I'll come home with Simon'. It has often proved profitable in school to separate mother from child in cases of enmeshed relationships (Berkowitz, 1987), since collective anxiety tends to be greater than the product of two anxious persons – both parties feed off each other, and the triggers are not always clear.

Ann-Marie was asked how she understood her condition. She explained that she got so depressed she didn't know what to do.

Dennis: How do you understand depression?
Ann-Marie: I think it's feeling so fed up you don't want to go on, but want to give up.
Dennis: What do you mean by 'You don't want to go on'?

Ann-Marie: I don't mean committing suicide or anything like that. I mean giving up. It's all too much.

Dennis: What makes you feel depressed?

Ann-Marie: By having to cream up … putting up with insults … and … going home angry.

Dennis: Do you get angry at home?

Ann-Marie: Yes, quite often.

Dennis: Although anger and depression are similar, I wonder which of the two is setting you back at the moment.

Ann-Marie: Depression, I'd say.

Dennis: I wonder if we could consider seeing depression a little differently. People speak of being 'depressed', or of 'becoming depressed', as though depression is part of them, in the same way as people describe so and so as 'jolly' or 'outgoing', by which they see 'outgoing-ness' and 'jolly-ness' as what we call a character trait, which is another way of saying that they, as a person, are 'jolly' or 'outgoing'. Do you follow me so far?

Ann-Marie: Yes, I think so.

Dennis: But we can all be 'jolly' and 'outgoing' at times, and at other times be 'sad' and 'fed up'.

Ann-Marie: Yea, I know.

Dennis: Now, being 'jolly' and 'outgoing' are positive characteristics, whereas being 'depressed' is considered a negative trait. I would like us to view 'depression' with a capital 'D', as a 'thing' that stands outside of you, like a bully in the swimming baths trying to pull you under [the selected metaphor was drawn from the client's sentiment: 'I am sinking under depression']. You have floats tied to your arms, but Depression is tugging you downward. I would like you to consider seeing how you might do battle with enemy Depression so you can keep his grip from you and remain afloat. I would like you to try and re-find that part of yourself that worked in Year 7 but which has slipped away from you without you noticing and left you unarmed to fight against Depression/boredom at home. Depression attacks you wearing different masks: 'Name-calling at school' comes to assist him by forcing you to stay at home where Depression has you all to himself. 'Hassle in creaming up each day' is another mate that Depression uses because he knows how to 'stress you out' and get your skin all enflamed to get you to take the easy way out and remain away.

The empowering effects of 'externalising language' were elaborated in greater detail.

'Externalising the problem' has been developed as a linguistic tool to help clients to separate a problem from the personality (White, 1995; White and Epston, 1990). The intention is to enable the client to see 'the problem' as a depersonalised entity aside from the self in order to summon inner resources for combat. Externalising language avoids what White refers to as 'problem-saturated' descriptions and perspectives, and 'opens up new possibilities for persons to take action to retrieve their lives and relationships from the problem and its influence' (White and Epston, 1990: 39).

There are disadvantages in using externalising language (Payne, 2006), particularly in school where the overriding cultural ethos is to make pupils responsible and accountable for their behaviour, and where labelling is not uncommon. But the counsellor is using metaphorical language for empowerment and improvement, and some authors have demonstrated the power of this tool for more socially troublesome behaviours than depression – behaviours such as stealing, disruption, abusive behaviour and truancy (Winslade and Monk, 1999). When problems are identified as a product of the self, clients experience a sense of debilitating fatigue that causes them to give up. The counsellor needs to be imaginative in the use of externalising language but must also use the metaphors that are owned by their clients.

We looked for sub-plots (Payne, 2006) in Ann-Marie's narrative of sinking under the weight of depression – events and experiences in her brief life which kept her from being weighed down and sinking further and further into the abyss. After a few moments of reflection, Ann-Marie recounted two sub-plots where she had bravely stood up to a group of teasing boys and had come out on top. She also remembered incidents with her brother and cousin where she had become assertive in challenging them when they poked fun at her because of her complexion. I was gaining the impression that she was keen to get going with in-vivo trials, to be in school and engage with peers.

This optimism was realised one week after our third session. Although her success was not plain sailing, the general trend was improvement, and when she again found the courage she had lost to keep her afloat from **Depression's** attempts to pull her down, her eczema improved remarkably. The point was to *distract* her from obsessive self-focusing and *redirect* her energies for peer engagement through being in school. To reinforce the gains made, I linked her with a skilled peer counsellor who suggested practical strategies she could use to deflect occasional name-calling and taunting (see the training manual at www.geldard.com.au). She acted as a 'buddy' figure to her and met her throughout the day during unmonitored occasions, such as at breaks and lunchtimes.

After a few weeks of school attendance and experiencing positive friendship building, I asked her mother to come into school to reinforce her gains and to serve as what White describes as an 'outsider witness' (Payne, 2006). Ideally, 'outsider witnesses' serve 'not to diminish or take from the person's account, but to reinforce it by resonances from their own lives' (Payne, 2006: 16). Her mother did not turn up, however, in spite of telling me how pleased she had been with her daughter's recovery. Nevertheless, therapy had enabled Ann-Marie to view herself not as a helpless victim to **Depression**, but as a leader for her mother to follow, and in consequence to escape from her own well of anxiety.

Counselling Young People with Anxiety to Raise Self-Esteem

If a school counsellor is viewed positively by the school community – pupils, parents and staff – then a youngster's spirits will be uplifted by the very act of being offered one-to-one interaction with *this person* at *this time*. Self-esteem therefore rises almost before a word has been spoken. In brief counselling, the interpretative–explanatory dimension is not as important as the pluralistic approach of *what can be done* for *this person* suffering *this problem* in *this context*.

In managing anxiety to raise a pupil's self-esteem, I have found it possible to integrate all that is beneficial in the person-centred approach with the fast-moving styles of cognitive therapy, particularly cognitive-humanistic counselling (Nelson-Jones, 1999b). The aim of the humanistic element is to help the client gain access to material in his person, material that is hurting, diminishing and reducing effectiveness. Sometimes painful material is within the defence system. The idea that clients will accidentally set free a monster if unpleasant experience is aired, does not take into account the powerful psychological mechanisms of suppressing unpleasant experiences.

The Case of Mitchell

Mitchell was referred for counselling by staff for being withdrawn and socially isolated. Pastoral teachers commented on how supportive they had found his mother, who was devastated to discover that he had truanted for three weeks. Local residents had seen him sitting alone and looking glum in the park. Mitchell was very unhappy. His mother was in a new relationship after splitting up with his father, and was planning for the family (he and his younger brother) to move into her new partner's house after marriage, much against Mitchell's wishes. Being 16, and in his final year, his social circle was restricted to the area where he had been brought up, and he was adamant that if his mother moved he was staying. He was confident that his friends' parents would look after him, and asserted that he would run away when the time came. This was not his greatest worry, however.

His father was 'addicted' to drugs, and occasionally took heroin. He felt that he would get no sympathetic audience from his mother in voicing his fears to

(Continued)

(Continued)

her, after all 'that's why I left him', she said, along with the 'drinking and getting knocked about'. Although Mitchell acknowledged this, he still worried about him and couldn't get him out of his mind, especially with Christmas coming. He had visions of 'seeing him in an alleyway, stoned', and 'out of his mind'.

Mitchell recounted his last two visits to his father, both of which were weekend stays. He felt rejected by his father, because he showed no pleasure in seeing him or in taking him out. He was not treated as special. Instead, Mitchell was left with his paternal grandmother while his father went out 'with his mates'. What hurt him most was seeing syringe marks on his father's lower arm. 'What's the use of going over? It does my head in! I can't handle this,' he said, while breaking down in tears. Crying in front of a male counsellor does not come easy for boys, but he sobbed in my presence. On his last visit, his father returned home drunk, and when Mitchell challenged him, he became violent and ordered him to: 'Get back to your mother!' From that moment, he vowed never to see him again, and stopped going on alternate weekends, but this did not stop the worrying.

After a week, however, he regretted his decision, but his mother, in order to protect his feelings, put her foot down this time and stopped him seeing his father for the time being. It was his mother's action that had caused Mitchell to be sad, and in session he was visibly very low indeed.

Mitchell's teachers had recognised his low self-esteem, lack of motivation and disinclination to engage in schoolwork. His tutor said that in form he had always been jocular and carefree, but had been downcast in recent weeks. His feelings of rejection by his father were facilitated by the core conditions and active listening skills. The brief integrative-cognitive elements of therapy are elaborated in further detail.

In addressing Mitchell's problem, it appeared that there were two elements that had resulted in sadness and low self-esteem. One was his thinking and the other his behaving.

Counselling Goal 1: Cease Worrying about Dad

Mitchell identified two relationship difficulties: one was his relationship with his father, the other his relationship with himself. Through collaborative conversation over goal setting, he selected the latter first. His goal was to be free of worry about his dad.

The pictures of 'seeing my dad injecting' and 'seeing him huddled up in a doorway on a cold wintry night' were not pleasant images. The first task we carried out was *reality testing* dialogue (Nelson-Jones, 1996) through a series of questions aimed at establishing the likelihood of each scenario:

- How often does dad shoot heroin?
- Is there evidence of him managing heroin rather than being managed by it?
- Does dad have a supportive network of friends to suggest that it would not be likely that he would be left abandoned in a doorway?

Of particular benefit to youngsters who get stuck are the mind skills methods of creating 'self-talk' and 'visual-imaging' (Nelson-Jones, 1996): 'What are you saying to yourself, Mitchell?' and 'What are you seeing?' These techniques address the thinking behind feelings. When Mitchell answered these questions with *reality testing*, his heavy spirit lightened.

The next task addressed the negative image of the time he last saw his father. The destructive dismissal – 'Get back to your mother!' – burnt deep into his sensitive mind like a branding iron. It is very common for the last words spoken by an enraged parent to remain indelibly imprinted in the memory of a youngster. My role was to help him reconstruct a more positive mental image: 'What occasion has been the most pleasant time you have spent with your father?' Mitchell spoke of a time he had 'gone to dad's and went fishing', when, on the last night, they had a barbecue and discussed future plans together. He was asked to practise a mental switch from the indelible words 'Get back to your mother!' to 'Well, that's the end of our holiday, son. It's time to get back to your mother'. This was practised by rote till he felt able to make the switch unconsciously. I would look at him, nod my head, and he would rehearse the modified script.

While he recognised his limited responsibility in his parents' decision to separate, he had *owned too much* responsibility for his feelings over the subsequent parting from his father. 'The life skills counselling approach' (Nelson-Jones, 1997) was adapted to empower Mitchell to develop his humanity through appropriate owning and disowning of areas of responsibility. He was encouraged through brief counselling to explore where the responsibility lay in his father's condition and lifestyle, his mother's attitude over the divorce and his own part in the process (Beck et al., 1979).

Counselling Goal 2: Reunite with Dad

Change had begun with Mitchell's modified outlook. O'Connell (2005) presents the SFT credo of *fixing only that which is broken*, and more particularly the notion that *small change brings about bigger change*, through a co-constructed engagement of client and therapist. Davis and Osborn (2000) similarly speak of the 'ripple', or the 'domino', effect, where a small change in the client's thinking or behaving can produce an exponential rate of improvement. The authors also illustrate the value of 'instead talk', which I find particularly effective with young people.

In attempting to encourage further change and avoid Mitchell indulging in 'problem-saturated' talk, we agreed *not to fix that which was not broken*, which he identified as his relationship with his mother, but rather to set a goal for restoring his relationship with his father. In setting practical goals, it was important to set a goal that was achievable. In British education, pupils are encouraged to set SMART targets, which means they must be Specific, Measurable, Achievable, Relevant and Time-limited. Similarly, in SFT, goals must be Specific, Concrete and Measurable, for 'goal formulation establishes and maintains a focus for counselling', and serves as 'a road trip with a specific destination in mind' (Davis and Osborn, 2000: 64–5).

A range of tasks was brainstormed collaboratively, which included:

- Do I ignore mum and after making contact go over to see dad at the weekend?
- Should I text dad or contact him by phone?
- Should I forget about dad for the time being and wait for him to contact me?

Teenagers need support in goal- and task-setting, which, though collaboratively discussed, needs a little steering with pupils whose condition borders on depression (Beck et al., 1979). Adolescents may take uncalculated risks if the tasks they have constructed are ambitious and not thought through. With task 1, there was the delicate issue of 'ignoring mum' and, recalling the principle of *not fixing something that isn't broken*, Mitchell evaluated the short- and long-term effects of this. He was reminded of mum's dormant feelings over her ex-husband, which had stirred after his father heartlessly sent him home. Feelings and behaviours are not difficult to change, but attitudes are another question.

Occasionally, with similar cases in which young clients wish to behave in a manner which challenges deeply ingrained attitudes and prejudices, I suggest they try the 'drip test', the change that occurs over time like the wear in soft rock with regular falls of water droplets. Challenging head-on entrenched attitudes, like a bull at a gate, causes people to remain fixed behind impregnable fortresses of stubbornness, but letting parents know what is *deeply felt* over something, a little at a time, regularly and consistently, like a drip, drip, drip, proves more effective in softening hardened wills.

The more Mitchell thought this through, the more he felt it would not work. He selected instead task 2 through the strategy/method of sending a text to his father. The closing sessions of brief pluralistic counselling were given over to helping him compose a text message to his father. His first draft text was altered after collaborative work through the technique of 'instead talk' (Davis and Osborn, 2000).

Hi Dad,

Sorry we fell out last time but it wasn't my fault. You know it scares me when you get into drugs. Mum is angry and won't let me come. I was going to come last week. Can I come this weekend?

Love Mitch

xxx

Dennis:	Though it's your text, Mitchell, and it's a good idea to write, I wonder if I could make some suggestions.
Mitchell:	OK. [Mitchell was content for this to happen.]
Dennis:	Instead of 'it wasn't my fault', could we think of a phrase that would not apportion blame?
Mitchell:	Mm, could we say something like, 'Perhaps we both lost our tempers'.
Dennis:	That seems better. I wonder if it is wise to bring up past battles between mum and dad. What can be put instead of mentioning mum's anger? How about, 'Mum doesn't understand how much you mean to me'.
Mitchell:	Yea.
Dennis:	Could we soften the request by recalling the good time you had 'when you went fishing', I wonder?

His final text was sent and this closed our brief work with the satisfactory outcome of him regularly visiting his father on alternate weekends:

Hi Dad,

Sorry we fell out last time. Perhaps we both lost our tempers. You know it scares me when you don't look after yourself. I miss you so much. Mum doesn't understand how much you mean to me. I remember the great time we had together when we went fishing, we got on so well, and I would love to come over as soon as you can spare the time. I can be free any week-end. Be in touch.

Love Mitch

xxx

Counselling the Sexually Abused

The debate over false-memory syndrome of sexual abuse in childhood has largely become frozen, with some taking an affirmative stance on the validity of 'recovered memories' of suppressed material (Sanderson, 1995) and others taking a critical position (Pendergrast, 1996).

The prevalence of reported incidents of child sexual abuse is difficult to ascertain due to variations in classification of what constitutes unwanted sexual behaviour as 'abuse', variations in assessment methods and inconsistent methodological sampling (Fergusson and Mullen, 1999).

Meta-analysis gives figures for the prevalence of child sexual abuse as ranging from 3 to 30 per cent for males and from 6 to 62 per cent for females, which of course is meaningless (Fergusson and Mullen, 1999: 14). In those studies, where the criterion is sexual penetration, or intercourse, rather than indecent exposure by a male family member, 1.3 to 28.7 per cent of females and 3 to 29 per cent of males are classified as having been abused.

Although there is at present no yardstick for measuring child sexual abuse, 5 to 10 per cent of children are exposed to serious sexual assault (1999: 32), not only by family members but also by acquaintances known to the victim – and not always men (1999: 50–1; Lines, 2008). As Fergusson and Mullen (1999) note, this means that in every class of 30 pupils there may be at least one pupil that has suffered serious sexual abuse and who might never disclose the incident.

According to NSPCC research (2010), of those children reporting sexual abuse, 11 per cent was by a non-family member known to them, 5 per cent by an adult they had just met, 3 per cent by a relative when they were a child and 1 per cent by a parent or carer (www.nspcc.org.uk/news-and-views). Other studies indicate the prevalence of abuse on children as occurring between 8 and 12 years (Harris and Pattison, 2004).

There are two counselling approaches for children suffering sexual abuse. These are the preventative (Elliott, 1990) and the responsive (Courtois, 1988; Maher, 1990), the former being criticised (Adams, 1990) for assuming that victims have more control than they often have.

A central counselling task with abused victims is to help them explore the feeling that, though logically they know they are blameless, they still feel that they have contributed in some way to what has happened. The unconscious temptation in counselling is to rescue victims and protect them from further harm. The client's self-analysis may be unclear. Knowing in her head that she was not to blame, there is often a feeling deep inside that she was. It is inconceivable that a child could feel responsible for being raped, but it is known from adult therapy that victims sometimes say that, despite all logic, they have the terrifying experience of feeling partly to blame (Murgatroyd and Woolf, 1982). Abused children may misinterpret innocent gestures of well-meaning adults, like 'giving money' or 'keeping secrets', as 'grooming' and 'complicity' (McGuiness, 1998) from past experience of trickery, but it is best for them to be wary nevertheless.

The confusion of loving the perpetrator and hating the experience makes counselling a challenge, but must not be avoided if suppressed feelings are not to find expression in more destructive symptoms. The counsellor will need to accompany the child as she confronts the ultimate betrayal, the total insult of being raped by the person entrusted to protect her from harm. There is terror and rage in realising that the centre of security in a youngster's universe is in reality a source of pain and hurt.

McGuiness (1998) recognises that counselling young victims of sexual abuse is 'deep work', 'powerful and scary', and this makes demands on counsellors to connect with their own sexuality. He suggests that effective therapy needs to reach the violated inner core of personal being, for sexual abuse threatens the self-system. For this reason, therapy must address in depth the sense of betrayal, terror, rage and longing that has been affected by abuse. Seriously affected pupils will need referring to outside specialists because therapy may not always be appropriate in a school setting where containment is problematic.

William O'Hanlon (1992) has presented a different and briefer model which he calls collaborative solution-oriented therapy. The author recognises the limitations of traditional approaches that work through recollection and catharsis. Therapists cannot help but influence the 'life of the problem' through attending to remembered details and sordid events. By encouraging clients to re-feel and express repressed feelings, there is a tendency to dwell too long on problem-saturated talk. By contrast, collaborative solution-oriented therapy aims to 'co-create the problem that is to be focused on in therapy' (O'Hanlon and Wilk, 1987). Treating the after-effects of sexual abuse involves 'moving the client on' and focusing their attention on the *present* and *future*. Through collaborative conversation, the aim is to move away from pathology towards co-constructed goals that are solvable, and which utilise the client's resources, strengths and capabilities (O'Hanlon, 1992).

The Case of Shane

Shane, a Year 9 pupil, aged 14, came for counselling after a telephone call his father made to my office. His parents had split up and there was much rivalry between them. They couldn't speak with each other, even by phone. A man named Ralph, who lived in the neighbourhood of his mother's home, had sexually abused Shane, and, although his mother had brought him up, the authorities insisted that Shane should be removed from the area to live with his father because of pending legal action and to keep him safe. For Shane's father, this incident became a further opportunity for point scoring: 'If she'd have done her job this wouldn't have happened.' What made matters worse for Shane was that his mother didn't believe his story – she discounted the material in his written statement.

The accused man was known to Shane's mother and was regarded as her 'friend', and as a person of 'social conscience', a 'do-gooder'. For Shane, this made matters worse – not only had he been duped by a person whom he thought

(Continued)

(Continued)

was a 'nice guy', but also his mother would never believe him. The abuser had lured Shane into a friendship, taken him back to his flat for coffee and become a father-figure for him. He took him for driving practice in a local park, and invited him to sit on his lap. While he steered the vehicle slowly around the grounds, he took advantage of Shane and began fondling him.

The abuse took place over a period and led to much more serious abuse in the bedroom. 'He did everything to me', he said. 'I had to do things to him.' Precise details were not drawn from him, but he appeared relieved to have given an outline in counselling. Further, he was suffering flashbacks of particular sexual events that had occurred in the car and the abuser's home, flashbacks which were occasionally triggered by sequences in films at home, material covered in sex lessons, and when sitting in the front seat of his father's car – the smell of car mats triggered his recollection of what had happened.

The introductory session was spent covering briefly his narrative, the legal proceedings and the consequences in respect of leaving his mother to live with his father. As he spoke, he related ambivalent feelings. The ambiguity was that, while he was contented living with his father, he was sad that this involved a temporary break from seeing his mother at his grandmother's home – owing to the fact that 'Shane was lying about the abuse'. The feeling I had when listening to what had happened from his father was that Shane would not have made up the story. This left me curious as to why his mother took sides with Ralph against her son.

There was also ambivalence over his feelings for Ralph. There was a suggestion of being 'loved' when being hugged and touched by Ralph, which only became hurt when things went too far. In consequence, he felt he could never trust a man again.

Dennis: But you are speaking with me, a man, as your counsellor.
Shane: You're all right. I feel safe with you.
Dennis: Are you sure? I can arrange for you to speak with a female teacher who has counselling skills, if you'd prefer.
Shane: No, I think I'd rather speak with you; it'll help me get confidence in speaking to a man.

During a collaborative assessment of Shane's thoughts and feelings, there emerged two goals of future orientation.

The first goal was to reduce the flashbacks he was experiencing: when travelling in his father's car each morning to school, and when watching sex scenes on television. Of available tasks, we selected visual re-imaging work (Nelson-Jones, 1996) and desensitisation of behaviour therapy to practise in session to reduce flashbacks. Not all young people are gifted with imagination, but most are – they dream in vivid images, like adults do, they fanaticise and can produce surreal artwork and poetry. Shane certainly was imaginative.

I asked him to describe the inside of Ralph's car, the colour and smell of the carpets, but then asked him to desensitise the potency of what had happened by reconfiguring events in his mind, by having his abuser humiliated publicly – say, by having him exposed through a news item or harassed by neighbours as a paedophile. He then described his father's car mats, which while resembling those in Ralph's car for smell, matched more by colour the carpet in the home of his childhood.

We applied the strategy of modifying his narrative of abuse through mental rehearsal, without being voiced – he later said that he had re-viewed his father's car mats from being 'the floor of the abuser's car' to being 'the carpet in our first house when mum and dad were together, laughing, and playing monopoly on the floor'. After two weeks, Shane reported that the flashbacks were less severe and less frequent.

The second goal became our next focus of work. Shane felt confused by the series of events that had led to the abuse. He spoke of being really fond of Ralph at first: his goal then was to understand the past abuse and to put an end to self-castigation.

Shane:　He was a good guy. He took interest in me. Took me places, spent money on me. Then he … [the pain came visibly to his face] I liked him at first. He was OK. He used to hug me and make me feel special, and then …

Dennis:　So what's a goal we could work on?

Shane:　I'd like to understand why I was fooled by him, why he …? Why he did it, and why … It didn't feel too bad at first … Why didn't I tell anyone, and why I went back. Why I …?

Dennis:　Why you liked his company? [Tentatively]

Shane:　Yea, I think so.

With Shane having found the courage to say what he felt, the therapeutic task now was to 'move on' from 'problem-saturated' material. After acknowledging briefly his pain through person-centred listening skills, it was necessary to keep the possibilities for change open by using the *past* tense for his 'old self' – as a person vulnerable to abuse – and the *present* and *future* tenses for the 'new self' – as one more guarded and self-protecting (O'Hanlon, 1992).

In order to centre counselling on Shane's resources and to stress the solution-focused nature of therapy, I asked him, 'Shane, how will you know when you no longer need support in counselling?' He replied, 'When I have understood why he fooled me and did it'. Much of the counselling method consisted of teaching Shane about generalised 'grooming behaviour' by sex abusers (hypothetical cases, removed from his own experience), to help him become more aware of manipulative pseudo-friendships.

Through conversations, he was able to see himself as one unconsciously seeking a father-figure attachment, and as one who innocently found in Ralph a person who regarded him as very special. Unlike in other forms of SFT, it is the effect of the *conversation* that becomes the process of change. The purpose of giving the youngster the 'abuser grand narrative' was to help him locate alternative sub-plots to his 'being tricked' narrative. He identified occasions where he could not easily be fooled, and we spent proportionally more time generalising these self-skills than on his narrative of abuse.

Finally, we addressed the issue of his sexuality as being naturally confused by what had happened. He was taught that at his stage of sexual development many young people become confused, that living with confusion was OK and quite normal. He later said in his questionnaire that he had found this reassuring. Young people tend to see sex as exclusively the act of sexual intercourse, and the final session was spent in widening his understanding.

Dennis: We are sexual beings by nature, and we differently enjoy physical contact in many other ways than sexual intercourse, from hugging to play wrestling, with adults and peers, and with both boys and girls. When rules of decency are broken by adults, however, such as forced and unwanted contact, or through trickery, then we need to see the red flag and say, 'something is not right here – time to go'.

Conclusion

Many pupils in school will on occasion become down and upset; it is a common fact of life. At a time when hormones create volatile mood states, events in life can temporarily knock a student off course. Since many teenagers are becoming autonomous, and cease to share their inner feelings with parents and carers, it is invaluable to have a school counsellor at hand to share narratives of despair and heartache. In this chapter, attention has been drawn to the social, psychological and physiological symptoms of low self-esteem; the debilitating effects of continued anxiety that result in fractious peer relations and a decline in performance.

Brief school counselling has illustrated how cognitive-humanistic counselling combined with features of narrative therapy and SFT applied imaginatively can assist pupils to manage their anxiety and deal with stress. Narrative therapy can be instrumental in assisting depressed youngsters to disassociate a temporary feeling from a personality trait, and thereby help them rise above negative reinforcement.

Finally, in raising the mood state of a sexually violated young person, a particular application of brief collaborative SFT, integrated with features of narrative therapy, can aid a client to rebuild shaken confidence from a betrayal of trust. In our example, a teenager needed to reassess potentially threatening situations, but at the same time restore confidence in the company of men, to acquire a balanced view of human sexuality and to come to terms with a mother's lack of support.

Reflective Exercise

1. With the three cases presented above, what models would you have used in therapy?

2. Do the applications of relaxation exercises, mental re-imaging and self-talk coaching skills constitute counselling in essence, or are they the application of psychological life skills?

3. Discuss whether this is true and whether it matters so long as it works.

4. Many school counsellors will have utilised elements of person-centred and cognitive therapy in the treatment of low self-esteem and depressive moods. If this has been your practice, are there any benefits in incorporating cognitive-humanistic counselling or other brief approaches in your work, such as SFT or narrative therapy?

5. What problems would you envisage occurring for a young client, in terms of reality testing, through such externalising language as illustrated above?

6. Collaborative dialogue between therapist and client occurred in the second case presented above, where the counsellor encouraged the initial text to be modified so as to avoid potential misunderstandings. Where is the border to be drawn between facilitating client choice, and directive steering? Discuss.

7. The final case vignette featured a victim of sexual abuse perpetrated by a known acquaintance of his mother:

    a. Is discussing an outline of the abusive occasion by definition 'abusive'?
    b. Can it be justified as a means of avoiding a charade – setting up an incongruent pretence of 'knowing' – or serve as a therapeutic technique to assist in 'voicing' for the client the pain of abuse in order for healing to occur?
    c. The gender of the therapist, after checking with the client, was significant in this case. How important is gender in cases of counselling either male or female sexually abused clients? Discuss.

Key Points

- ⊙ The school counsellor can provide therapy for those suffering low self-esteem, or those having symptoms of depression, but school is not the ideal setting for therapy with 'clinically depressed' youngsters.

- Human beings have evolved means of avoiding threat through *fight* or *flight* responses, and therapy will work from the pragmatic possibilities of these options.

- Depressive and low-mood states are evident through various physiological and psychological symptoms, which are exasperated by hormonal changes during puberty, but the brief counsellor can utilise relaxation exercises and meditation techniques to help calm the teenager before pluralistic therapy is undertaken.

- Beck's cognitive therapy has been the classic approach for depression, but a brief pluralistic approach that integrates features of narrative therapy with mind skills work is quicker and less programmatic in raising self-esteem for depressed and anxious clients in school.

- Victims of sexual abuse who wish to move on can benefit from various integrative SFT approaches that utilise re-imaging techniques and therapeutic coaching to help them cope with the present and make sense of the past, leaving them better able to recognise grooming intentions and more able to protect themselves from further harm.

7 Self-harm and Suicide Ideation

This chapter covers:

- Research on self-harm
- Research on anorexia and bulimia
- Research on suicidal thoughts and actions
- Managing enuresis and encopresis in school
- Counselling clients who self-harm
- Counselling young people with dietary problems
- Counselling students with thoughts of suicide

Introduction

This chapter considers brief therapeutic approaches for addressing a range of self-harming and self-punishing behaviour attributed to psychological causes, including cutting, scratching and rubbing, plucking hair and eyelashes, dietary disorders like anorexia nervosa and bulimia nervosa, along with suicide ideation. Conditions of enuresis and encopresis are also covered.

Self-harm may be understood as an act of aggression *turned in on self*, as illustrated in the self-cutting of arms, legs and upper torso with razor blades or sharp implements, in anorexia and bulimia, and, perhaps, in less severe refusals to eat healthily, but other conditions, like neglect, poor hygiene, enuresis and encopresis may result from learned, or unlearned, behaviour, poor adult modelling, low expectations or poor economic conditions. Some of these difficulties may require treatment in specialist centres, while less severe cases may be addressed with brief therapy in school.

Research on Self-harm

Research has indicated that 50 per cent of women disclose sexual abuse as one of the causes of self-injury, as well as physical and emotional abuse and neglect (Arnold, 1997), but for adolescents there are other factors. Recent findings in the UK show an increase in self-cutting among young people to cope with stress over issues like examination pressures, arguments at home and problems among peers in regard to self-image. Self-harm affects one in 10 young people (Mental Health Foundation/Camelot Foundation, 2006), and psychiatrists are calling for effective school-based initiatives that help tackle what has become a pressing health issue for teenagers (Hawton et al., 2006b) – training materials are available (Sellen, 2006).

Studies show that girls are four times more likely than boys to harm themselves. The majority say it is impulsive rather than something they had planned beforehand, and some social networking sites give advice on how to cut. Clearly, copycat factors are at play. Cutting is the most common form of abuse (65 per cent), followed by overdosing (31 per cent), particularly for pupils who have been bullied (Hawton et al., 2010). For both sexes, deliberate self-harm is correlated with smoking, alcohol and drug use.

According to a large study of self-harm among 15–16-year-olds, one in 10 teenagers self-harm (Hawton et al., 2006a). This research took place in 41 schools across Oxfordshire, Northamptonshire and Birmingham in 2000 and 2001, and surveyed 6000 teenagers. Pupil questionnaires to explore issues surrounding self-harm and suicidal thoughts, along with other problems, showed that 11 per cent of girls and 3 per cent of boys had self-harmed in the last year. Thirteen per cent of the self-harming incidents resulted in hospitalisation, and some reasons given included 'wanting relief from a terrible state of mind', 'wanting to punish oneself' and 'wanting to die'.

Further, 3500 15–16-year-olds from Northern Ireland were asked how they found out about self-harming. The top number said it was 'from friends' but the second (20 per cent) said it was 'from the internet' – 10 per cent claimed they had swapped videos of their own cuts or of their own scarring (O'Connor, 2010).

Research on Anorexia and Bulimia

Eating disorders like anorexia nervosa (wilful self-starvation) and bulimia nervosa (binging and self-purging) among adolescents are to be taken as a serious psychiatric illness (Hoste and le Grange, 2009). Both conditions can lead to electrolyte imbalances, cardiac and gastrointestinal complications, cognitive impairment, infertility, psychosocial difficulties and even death (Powers and Bannon, 2004). It is widely recognised that eating disorders emerge at puberty (Hoste and le Grange, 2009), particularly for girls, and the causal factors include genetic predisposition, low self-worth and family dysfunctionality. While female bulimic patients tend to have friends and boyfriends to support them, anorexics commonly have enmeshed parental relationships that hinder personal development (Pointon, 2005). The wish to strive for the western ideal of beauty affects girls negatively (through the widening of hips and fat accumulation), but boys positively (through broadening shoulders and muscular bulk). Girls often care more about the 'way they look' than the 'way they are' (Pointon, 2005: 7).

Two, empirically supported, treatment programmes have been adopted for each respective eating disorder:

- for anorexic patients, the family-based *Maudsley approach* (Maudsley Hospital, London)
- for bulimic patients, individual CBT (Le Grange et al., 2007) and CBT combined with family-based treatments.

Earlier studies suggested that common familial dysfunctionality corresponded with eating disorders:

- anorexic young people tended to have enmeshed family relationships, where rigid rules and an overprotective management structure offered few skills of conflict resolution (Minuchin et al., 1975; Pointon, 2005)
- bulimics were brought up in chaotic families with few boundaries (Root et al., 1986).

Recent research has generally supported these conclusions (Vidovic et al., 2005). Research points to the interplay of attachment and genetics, and attitudes of mothers towards their daughters can have a negative effect (Pike and Rodin, 1991). It is considered that through continual 'ideal image' bombardment, the influence of the media is not so much the amount of exposure but the effects of internalising a social ideal as the desired norm (Hoste and le Grange, 2009).

Family-based treatments have proved effective with sustained gains after five years (Eisler et al., 1997; Russell et al., 1987) for anorexic teenagers. The treatment involves parents and carers taking full control of their child's calorific intake and weight restoration (Hoste and le Grange, 2009: 173). Later treatment involves handing over more control to the patient to be autonomous in an age-appropriate manner.

For bulimic patients, RCTs have shown a number of effective treatments using CBT, and a combination of CBT and family-based treatment – largely through cognitive restructuring and a behavioural programme that modifies a sequence of 'binging–purging–binging etc.' – but such studies have largely been carried out with adults as opposed to teenagers (Fairburn et al., 1993; Hoste and le Grange, 2009).

Research on Suicidal Thoughts and Actions

There can be nothing more daunting for a parent or carer to hear that their child has contemplated taking their life. Suicidal behaviour can be understood on a continuum from ideation at one end to completion at the other, and the knowledge that a teenager has thoughts of suicide can be as traumatic as the deed to have carried it out. Fatalities of suicide increase from childhood (World Health Organisation, 2002) due to increased capabilities involved in planning, independence from the family, skill in avoiding detection and access to a means of carrying it out, but rates and means will vary from country to country, and according to age, gender and personality.

Generally, attempted suicide through methods like overdosing and wrist cutting is more common among females than males (Bridge et al., 2006), with the latter carrying out higher successful execution rates, such as through hanging, shooting themselves or jumping from heights. Young men who are impulsive, aggressive or under the influence of drugs are more successful in taking their lives when stressed (Shaffer and Gutstein, 2002). Although females may have a long history of mood anxiety and eating disorders to deal with stress, they generally engage in less lethal self-harming practices (Carr, 2009b).

In an extensive systematic review of suicide prevention strategies, involving international researchers, Mann et al. (2005) concluded that there were two effective methods of reducing suicide rates for the population at large:

- training practitioners to recognise and treat depression and suicidal thoughts
- restricting access to lethal methods of committing suicide.

For Carr (2009b), clinical assessment is essential to alleviate the risk of suicide, followed by crisis intervention and controlled management. Psychotherapy for young people can be enhanced by facilitating verbal agreements between clients and their parents or carers to attend the sessions, to conduct follow-up telephone interviews for critical periods while family and individual therapy help to address the thoughts and feelings underlying suicidal ideation.

A number of studies have examined the risk and protective factors associated with successful suicide (cited in Carr, 2009b).

Risk factors include:

- previous attempts with notes left of an intention
- availability of lethal forms of taking one's life
- precipitating events, such as loss or bereavement of a loved one, parent or romantic attachment, along with a diagnosis of serious illness, interpersonal conflict, failing an exam, and imitation of influential peers (Evans et al., 2004).

Protective factors include:

- *a verbal or written contract during a suicide risk assessment*, along with greater vigilance of parents or carers to monitor the young person concerned (Gould, 2003)
- removal of such items as guns or highly toxic substances from reach of the volatile young person.

(Continued)

(Continued)

Carr (2009b) identifies a number of psychological motivations for suicide, including a need to be cared for, and a wish to be sacrificed from a fantasy that it may serve some greater good. Suicidal young people tend to be inflexible in their coping styles and have a limited repertoire of strategies to draw on; they commonly have associated psychological disorders or borderline personality disorder, or come from a family with related difficulties, such as depression, and alcohol and drug misuse (Carr, 2009b).

Education programmes to increase knowledge of suicidal inclinations can be profitable (Gould, 2003; Hickey and Carr, 2002), but what proves most effective for Carr (2002, 2006) are strictly run and manually led preventative programmes that reduce risk for targeted individuals. An assessment of risk is followed by an examination of the client's social network of possible support – in the absence of support, hospitalisation or residential placement may be necessary. Such programmes have been linked with psychotherapy and telephone contacts (Donaldson et al., 1997). Multi-systemic therapy integrating intensive family therapy with individual skills training, normally home-based, has also proved effective (Huey et al., 2004).

Collaborative counselling may be focused on highly destructive and hopeless parts of the self, with little leverage in terms of possibilities for positive change. The school counsellor may have to take control and intervene, and this will have an impact upon the emotions of the therapist. Research shows that keeping clients in therapy – by keeping them talking – reduces the risk of suicide (Cooper and McLeod, 2011: 86–7). There are a number of methods that have proved valuable in relation to responding to suicidal crisis, some of which may be of use to young people:

- suicide helplines and websites
- crisis response plans and a commitment to treatment statements in place of suicide contracts
- outreach work and sending caring letters
- self-help reading.

Managing Enuresis and Encopresis in School

Poor hygiene, self-neglect or self-abuse during adolescence may be a reaction to sexual abuse, or a symptom of need for maternal attention, particularly in cases of enuresis (nocturnal release of urine) and encopresis (involuntary bowel movements). Bell-and-pad conditioning is a more cost-effective method of training than drug treatments to regulate the sphincters, even though it is under-utilised in clinical practice (Mikkelsen, 2001).

Involuntary enuresis and encopresis are more common in boys than in girls, and are normally the result of developmental delay. Often, the pattern of delayed toilet training exists in secondary-aged children only in dysfunctional families. Psychodynamic theorists believe that nocturnal bed-wetting and soiling disorders are due to fixated development through poor attachments or unresolved childhood tensions, but behaviourists contend that they result from inadequate parenting and poor teaching.

Normally, keen observation and assessment by medical professionals, working with a therapist, will indicate what needs to be done, and done very quickly, since, as emphasised in Chapter 5, peer acceptance is crucial for adolescent development – being called 'a tramp' or 'smelly' are labels that stick in school, regrettably. Secondary onset of the problem might be an indication of unresolved tension or current stress that counselling could address.

The Case of Joshua

Joshua's mother approached the school because her son had a relapse of enuresis and had occasionally smeared faeces on his mattress and around his bedroom, which at 13 was holding him back socially. A CAF meeting was called to address a number of family needs. A referral was made for a specialist agency to work with parents in the home on 'retraining' routines. I was asked to offer therapy for Joshua's mother on possible underlying psychological issues. Once the meaning and significance of his *inward crying for mum to be more available* – to pamper him, in close, physical contact, like back when being cleaned up as a child – was realised, the smearing ceased immediately and Joshua was able to sleep dry within two weeks.

Counselling Clients who Self-harm

According to ChildLine, over 50 per cent of their calls are to do with self-harming, which only reflects the number of children who decide to tell someone (Brooks and Silva, 2010). The very nature of self-harm is that it is a covert and hidden phenomenon. NICE guidelines recommend a variety of options to become available for young people who self-harm.

Self-cutting has become a frequent concern in secondary school among (largely) girls, and cases I have worked with have proved effective on joint programmes of cognitive-humanistic therapy (Nelson-Jones, 1999a), techniques drawn from SFT and Gestalt therapy combined with close adult monitoring of carers, pastoral staff and the nurse, within a pluralistic perspective. I have known clients who have cut themselves so extensively that the whole of their upper and lower arms have old and new marks covering every available area of skin. If asked the reason why they do this (a largely redundant question, in my opinion), students invariably say they do not know but add that after cutting themselves they feel relief from anxiety.

In nearly every case I have worked on, anger lies at the root (reinforced by copy-cat principles), and therapy therefore involves *exploring the anger*, anger which is often displaced from a significant person and directed towards the self. Below, a brief case is outlined before a more extensive case follows.

The Case of Darren

Darren's twin brother was also a pupil in Year 9, aged 14, but in many ways the contrasts in personality could not be so stark. He described his brother as being 'sly, crafty, quiet at school, but nasty at home to mum', whereas he saw himself as being 'open and honest', and 'close to mum, but not as close as my brother to dad'. The parents had split up eight months previous to our meeting, and it appeared as though their mother was not finding it easy to manage the twins, often calling on their father to speak with one of them on the phone or to come over to the house to 'sort them out'. But Darren believed his dad always took his brother's side. If this had been exclusively a disciplinary issue, in managing two teenagers who were at loggerheads with each other, there may never have been a counselling role.

Darren's 'openness' was certainly evident in school. When truanting, he would walk past a window where he could be seen, blatantly defying school rules. His Head of College put him on report, but it was the recurrent self-harming that had brought him to counselling.

Initially, he cut his arms with the blade removed from a pencil sharpener. They were not deep but covered both his lower arms. Before we first met, he was found to have tugged large clumps of hair from his head, visible even at a distance, and this brought mockery and ridicule from his peers, which only exacerbated his problem. The school nurse attended to his injuries, while I addressed the anger issues, largely centred on his brother for abusing his mother – 'he takes money from her, argues all the time and even swears at mum for trying to ground him for coming in late ... Tells her to "fuck off" when she won't give him money for fags!'

There were copycat principles over the cutting, since his girlfriend had done the same, and he, like many of his friends, put pictures of his arms on Facebook, almost to compete on a victimisation scale. But there appeared a psychological need to 'sacrifice himself', almost vicariously, in a powerful struggle to protect his mother in a situation where he had no control – *maybe if I suffer, then mum will not suffer at my brother's hands.*

Cognitive-humanistic counselling centred, firstly, on addressing the pain he felt when seeing his mother being 'bullied', in perceiving his father as not understanding the central issue, and, secondly, on examining cognitively his personal constructs. Knowing that he looked a 'geek', as he termed it – and a laughing stock to peers – for cutting his arms, and particularly for tugging out large clumps of hair, I felt sure he would not do this again. I secured from him a pledge that he would share his hurt in the counselling room, not in his bedroom through self-injury. His mother reinforced his pledge (in an unwritten contract), and I asked her to come in to share with me 'her perceptions' of managing the twins.

She made light of her other son's rebellion, so graphically portrayed by Darren in therapy, to such an extent that I had wondered whose account was the most reliable. Had Darren been thinking 'catastrophically' (Ellis, 1994) over his dilemma, for an ulterior motive?

Counselling is not an interrogation for the truth, however; what is important is how Darren viewed the situation and the feelings that had arisen from it. The cognitive element was to centre on his *ownership* of undue responsibility. With peer influence becoming the lever for motivation, his goal in brief counselling was to address his belief system and constructs:

From a personal construct of 'undue ownership', we worked collaboratively to form one which 'released him from the responsibility of his brother's behaviour'.

Darren's construct:	My brother pisses me off when he has a go at mum, and I have to stop it happening, if not telling him to do as mum says, then by forcing him to change by hurting myself.
This he altered to:	It's not my responsibility to correct my brother, it's mum's and dad's. The world's not falling apart when tempers arise. Whatever happens, I'm not going to make an ass of myself when things get out of hand – in the end it doesn't make things better, even mum gets upset when I cut myself.

Change came in terms of self-harming from the new insight; there was no need to engage parents in family therapy in this instance.

The Case of Erica

Erica was a fostered child from the age of 3, to the same parents as her younger sister (her biological mother had died giving birth and her father was shortly to be released from prison). She was attractive and flirted with the boys by regularly throwing her arms around them. Being new to the school in Year 9, this made her unpopular with some of the girls. Before coming for counselling, I had become aware of her situation through pastoral staff who had voiced concern in one of our Filter meetings. It was known that she had been testing her foster mother (whom she addressed as 'mum'). Though generally conforming in school, she was challenging at home.

Both parents were practising Jews, dedicated to their fostered children. Apart from worrying about her father, she had become resentful of her synagogue affiliation and the requirement that she should attend worship every week with the family. In short, she was rebelling, and had regularly voiced to her 'mother', her

(Continued)

(Continued)

social worker and various staff in school, a wish to go into care. In the first session, she could not give a plausible reason why she had become disenchanted with home, but it seemed as though she felt there was more to be gained by being released of any emotional attachment that had grown over the last 10 years.

She was referred for counselling after cuts were seen on her lower left arm. She had begun to publicise this, not only to the school nurse but to various peers in her learning groups. Many pupils were upset to see the depth of cuts to her skin. The academy welfare manager also supported her and the family as she was a 'looked after child'.

Erica sat in the first session attentively, with good posture and eye contact. She was keen to speak frankly about her feelings, about her past and about her living situation. She was a powerful character, but was clearly *angry*, angry over her father going into prison, and angry about her foster mother *trying to control her*. She resented her mum for not allowing her to visit her father in prison. It was as though they were both locked in combat.

At times, she told me of fierce battles in the family home. I was beginning to feel the family was being pulled apart. She delighted, she said, in embarrassing her mum amidst her Jewish friends. Her foster mother spent a week with her sister in respite after Erica had run away for two days and would not disclose where she had been or the boy she had been with. Pastoral teachers felt her excessive flirting left her vulnerable to sexual exploitation in the community. There were strong indications for family therapy, but Erica refused, and waiting lists were long.

Erica freely outlined the narrative of her life in the early sessions: family disruption, lack of knowledge of her extended family, inner struggle over an identity within a clash of cultures and the developmental trials of her adolescence. I therefore met with her regularly. Below is presented a selection of transcript relevant to the residual anger underlying her self-harm.

Dennis:	I m wondering, Erica, what you want from this family?
Erica:	I don't know, but I know I don't want to live with them.
Dennis:	You're telling me what you don't want, but I'm not clear what *you do want*.
Erica:	I just want to get out, I want to go into care, but **she** won't let me.
Dennis:	I'm not so sure 'she' has a choice. It seems to me that you'll get there if you keep pushing as hard as you appear to be doing. Many young people in care long to be fostered or adopted. Are you not afraid of losing what you have?
Erica:	No, I wouldn't mind. I want to be free of **her**.
Dennis:	Free … in a children's home? [She looked up to the right – see Chapter 2].
Erica:	That would be better than what I've got.
Dennis:	Did your mum ever hug you as a child; did you ever feel close to her?
Erica:	Yes, but that was long ago. **She** tries to hold me now but I don't let **her**.
Dennis:	What's the barrier between you and your mum, Erica?

In the fourth session, I asked whether she was still self-cutting, and she said occasionally but not much now. I asked how it had felt when she had cut herself: 'It feels good. I feel relieved.'

Dennis:	Do you mean during cutting your arms or hands?
Erica:	Yea, during and afterwards.
Dennis:	On a scale of 1 to 10 – where 1 represents slight comfort and 10 represents feeling really great and revived – what number would you give to represent the pleasure you felt during and shortly after cutting yourself?
Erica:	[reflecting, eyes down to right] I suppose I would say 6, no, maybe 7.
Dennis:	But how do you feel now, about the idea of having cut yourself?
Erica:	Oh, I hate it.

During these sessions, at no point did I ask to see her cuts by rolling up her sleeves, for very good reason. While others were upset by such a visible expression of stress, I did not want to show interest in, and give undue weight to, the behaviour as opposed to the anxiety underlying it. It was at a feelings level that I wished to communicate with this assertive young student. (Should her carers, or pastoral staff, not have known of the cutting, and supposing the counsellor was the first to become aware, she might have had to ask to inspect the injuries and take an inventory of when they had occurred and what precipitating concerns had led to self-harm, in light of UK safeguarding protocols.)

Before the next session, her foster mother rang me at school to update me on a recent incident. Her father had been released from prison and, during a celebratory party, had become drunk, slapped his younger daughter and stormed out after Erica had stabbed her own hand with a smashed glass – the pattern of self-injury had become her only strategy for dealing with stress. Her foster mother said the girls hated one another and said, 'Erica thinks I always favour Jess over her'. She expressed gratitude that I was seeing Erica and did not want to compromise our confidential agreement.

I asked Erica how she felt generally about her younger sister. At first, she said that she hated her, but then modified her comments somewhat and said: 'My sister doesn't say very much; she's the quiet one.' 'That's your mum's concern', I replied. I elected to carry out empty chair work with her to explore how she thought her sister might view her, and this became a powerful medium in therapy.

Dennis:	Erica, I would like you to leave your bag on that chair and come and sit over here [I pointed to the chair across the room]. Would you become Jess? [She obliged, with a grin, as though we were about to play a game]. Could we relive that moment when you had an argument with dad and stabbed your hand with a glass. In our first session, you said you loved your dad, and, by comparison, you shared with me that you're not very fond of your sister … But then you became very angry with your father after he had hit Jess, as though you felt a need to *protect her*.
Erica:	Yea.
Dennis:	Was she hurt badly?
Erica:	She was battered, bruises on her face and body. Dad had been drinking.

Dennis:	But you felt unable to get back at him and could only target your anger towards a drunken man with words, not blows, and, then, to endorse what you felt, you took a glass and stabbed *your own* hand. Tell me, as though you are Jess, how you felt when being beaten by your father?
Erica:	It was horrible!
Dennis:	Jess, tell me how you feel generally about Erica.
Erica:	[She fully entered into role] She gets on my nerves most of the time, because she always plays up to get her own way.
Dennis:	Do you have a way of getting back at her?
Erica:	Oh yeah [she grins]. I squeal, and mum always comes to protect me; is always on my side. Erica gets shouted at, or grounded, or sent to her room.
Dennis:	It seems to me that you have power over Erica.
Erica:	Oh yeah, I know exactly how to play her game [a surprised look of enlightenment, she looks downward to the left].
Dennis:	Do you think Erica likes your dad more than you?
Erica:	Oh my dad, certainly!
Dennis:	But then, that must have been confusing for you at the time, when Erica *stuck up for you*, remonstrated with your dad for being drunk, and in anger was prepared to hurt *herself* to demonstrate how much she had been hurt by your injuries? [Erica looks forward to the right, processing. There was no need to say more.]

I let a few minutes pass and then asked her to stand up and shake her body to unclothe herself of her sister's personality. I asked her to move back into her previous chair before inviting her to share what she felt about the experience.

Erica:	Amazing, weird but amazing. I've not seen my sister like that before.
Dennis:	Your mum would like me to speak with your sister, Jess, but I'm not sure I should direct that, unless you had a conversation with her and you both would like to meet with me together.

The formal contract with Erica over her self-harming was closed at that point. I spent some sessions working with the two sisters together but there was no longer any emphasis on the self-harming aspects of her behaviour. She was finding alternative ways to vent her frustration.

Counselling Young People with Dietary Problems

Eating disorders are a form of self-harm (Favazza, 1996). *Therapy Today* (BACP, 2005) presented a series of articles on dietary disorders (see also CCYP, 2005) and the recommended treatment programmes ranged from CBT to art therapy (through music and dance) and somatic therapy (through touch and massage). Adapted play therapy within a multimodal framework has also proved effective with adolescents (Rogers and Pickett, 2005). CBT techniques in brief individual and group therapy can benefit students having bulimic patterns of behaviour, but for those with anorexic disorders the work may require counsellor-facilitated parental monitoring for younger pupils, which is paradoxical in light of research that suggests that 'enmeshment' is the cause and 'parental tight control' is the treatment. But safeguarding must take precedence in school. For older students who are moving towards autonomy, educational goals may need to be temporarily suspended in order for the client to return to a pre-morbid state through a programme of 'emotional coaching' (Buckroyd, 2005).

The decision of whether to respond with brief counselling in school for dietary disorders will depend upon the extent of the problem (i.e. whether referral to a specialist clinic is not judged as necessary) and the skills and experience of the therapist. Practitioners will recognise that *anger turned in on self* is a common feature of self-abusive behaviour, and how *internalised* media projections of body image and relational dynamics often result in eating disorders. For anorexic young people, there will be an emphasis on attending to the possibility of an over-constricting parental hold at an age-inappropriate time – where family therapy or couple work may be indicated. For those having a condition of bulimia, there will be an emphasis on predominant cultural messages and peer dynamics – where integrated narrative therapy with CBT will be indicated.

With the duty to safeguard young people in education, therapy in school may have limited scope for serious cases of anorexia and bulimia which require the sort of contracted intervention outlined by Carr (2009b) above, but for short interludes of starvation or bulimia brought on by intermittent psychological pressures, brief therapy may be appropriate. As with other cases of self-harm, it is not uncommon for clients to 'publicise' to their peers a psychological problem through external behavioural indicators, as though the behaviour is a disguised *plea for help*.

The Case of Charna

It was noticed by pastoral staff and Charna's father that she had ceased eating at home and at school. She felt very close to her brother who was currently in prison for offences of burglary and car theft. She regularly insisted she was never hungry, and all coerced means of getting her to eat proved futile. She was taken to her GP on the advice of the school nurse to check on her medically, but he contacted the school to say the problems were more psychological. I was asked to offer her an appointment after her pastoral support manager had learnt from her father that she had lost much weight.

The school nurse recorded her as worryingly underweight. Person-centred counselling – through core counselling skills – addressed her worries over her brother, and by the third session it became apparent that there were other stressors in her life. She was close to her cousin, whom she judged to be very pretty: 'She's fit, she is; all the boys fancy her. I could never get a boyfriend – I'm too fat!' It was then that she disclosed her self-purging ritual.

Charna shared with me that she was fond of a boy in her maths group, 'but he would never see anything in me'. She later admitted half way into the third session that the little her father made her eat at home she got rid of.

Dennis:	What do you mean exactly, 'you got rid of'?
Charna:	I go to the bathroom and make myself sick.
Dennis:	You're able to make yourself sick … without your dad knowing?
Charna:	Yea, I can do it easily. I used to do it to bunk school.
Dennis:	You don't find it unpleasant, having to heave and wretch to make yourself sick?
Charna:	You get used to it; it's practice, really.

She described her typical binging/self-purging ritual after teatime, but we didn't focus on this for long. Should this have been a serious case of bulimia nervosa, I would have engaged her father in a joint programme, or had the matter re-referred to her GP for a specialist clinic. However, Charna had shared with me that she had only just begun doing this; it was a temporary phase that from her perspective had a rational purpose. It was a learned behaviour from a friend last year for quite a different reason – this behaviour had a new meaning.

Following a NLP-questioning format, I asked her what she wanted to happen most of all. She outlined two things: first, was her brother to come out of prison, and second, she said with a chuckle, was to date a boy in her maths group. Of these goals, she had no power over the first and only limited control over the second – *her goal* was not to cease self-purging! Therapy, therefore, following an Egan framework – or any goal-centred approach, including SFT – would have yielded limited results in this case, but integrative narrative therapy offered more scope.

I asked her to bring in a range of teenage magazines, and printouts from her favourite social networking sites of feminine images she found appealing. We explored together the 'grand narrative' of the westernised feminine form, and the exploitation of sex so subtly disguised (and overtly exposed) in the 'manufactured image' of her everyday media. She then said, surprisingly, that she did not want to be like that.

Dennis:	What do you want to be like then, Charna?
Charna:	I don't know, really, pretty, I suppose, like all the others …
Dennis:	The others …?
Charna:	There's this girl in our maths group I'm jealous of, if I'm honest. She's 'fit', thin, not like me. She fancies Connor, and I think he likes her more than me.
Dennis:	And it's Connor you like?
Charna:	Yea.
Dennis:	How do you know Connor fancies her?
Charna:	He talks to her all the time, but, then … he does speak to me sometimes, but it's different somehow …

Dennis:	How will you know whether Connor likes her or you? How can you tell whether his 'different somehow' way of speaking isn't embarrassment, a sense of being coy … of finding a moment to pop the question?
Charna:	Do you think he might … like me?
Dennis:	I really have no idea. That's what makes fancying someone, and falling in love, so exciting, and at the same time so scary … But the real question is: 'How can you tell whether you are likeable *just as you are* instead of trying to make yourself different – more slim, like your cousin?
Charna:	I don't know … By asking friends, I suppose …
Dennis:	Who shall we ask?

The closing sessions were centred upon reviewing what her friends had said in a brief peer-group session I had called at her request. They all said that they thought she was mad, losing so much weight, 'that it wouldn't make Connor like you any more'. When it was pointed out to her that Connor had gone out with a girl previously twice as large as Charna, it was as though a penny had dropped. She began eating normally again and ceased her self-purging ritual, accepting herself as she was and eating sensibly. She never went out with Connor – her interests were drawn in a different direction.

Counselling Students with Thoughts of Suicide

A Year 9 pupil from a neighbouring school hanged himself in his garden by a rope from a birch tree. The reason, as alleged, was for bullying at school. This event had a profound effect upon many youngsters in the community. What raised anxieties further, however, was that his elder brother also took his life by the same method barely three months later, and then a peer acquaintance did the same in a nearby wood. To stem the tide of such 'copycat' behaviour, and in light of regular chat-line publicity, the local authority sent a circular to all local schools instructing them to respond to 'all threats of suicide', by having youngsters admitted to accident and emergency departments of the local hospital.

It is recognised that some adolescents occasionally experience suicidal thoughts. These nihilistic impulses are rarely reasoned, but are articulated to friends or are written on scraps of paper for significant adults to 'discover'. They are *cries for help*. Nevertheless, they are real feelings that need addressing, and addressing promptly. In general, youngsters who talk about suicide seldom take their lives, but it would be irresponsible not to take action merely on the basis of outcome generalities. The practitioner must consider how best to support young clients who, on occasion, entertain suicidal thoughts. It is important to distinguish between planned attempts at suicide (where teenagers are clearly at risk) and suicidal thoughts (bearing I mind, as said above, that continual suicide ideation is a serious risk factor).

For a school counsellor working for the local authority in the UK, a pupil's thoughts and intentions of suicide cannot be kept confidential. As discussed in

Chapter 4, the therapist has a 'duty of care' (McGinnis and Jenkins, 2009) and, in most US states, counsellors are required to breach confidentiality and report all clients' suicidal intentions (Bond, 2010). For students in the UK over the age of 18, in sixth form or at college, there is a difficult balance between the 'duty of care' and a client's rights to 'autonomy', as recognised in the BACP *Ethical Framework* (BACP, 2002: 14). Each case has to be carefully considered, applying the guidelines outlined in Chapter 4, which centre on the *degree of risk* and *a realistic means of prevention*.

Suicidal states are as much to do with 'nihilistic life-meaning' constructs and the lack of future promise as with major loss events or psychological anomie. Spiritual counselling, psychodynamic counselling, Jungian analytical therapy and other transpersonal models, are the traditional approaches for death-wish conditions (Lines, 2006a), but they are time-consuming in bringing about healing, require extensive counselling skills and resources (West, 2000, 2004) and are too elaborate for young people going through temporary depressive states.

From a pluralistic perspective, suicide is recognised as a complex phenomenon, where there are multiple pathways and types of suicidal person. Alternative ways of making sense of suicide have been developed within different schools of therapy, including:

- the notion of destructive inner voices
- the interpersonal theory that the person sees themselves as a burden to others
- the cognitive-behavioural concept of finding reasons for living
- medical risk assessments (Cooper and McLeod, 2011: 86–7).

In the case presented, the third category appeared to offer the most leverage, not through CBT but by a technique stemming from narrative therapy.

The Case of Matthew

Matthew in Year 10 had frequently drifted into the counselling room during breaks for no apparent reason than to avoid mixing. He was not bullied but had elected to be mute every time peers spoke to him. Many pupils attempted to befriend him, but he spurned them. On one occasion, pastoral teachers bought him a fashionable T-shirt and persuaded him to go on a school trip and 'enjoy himself'. This temporarily lifted his spirit.

His routine duties, which he carried out assiduously, included picking up his younger brother after school. He would be seen sauntering home with him in tow, head down as though abandoned. Matthew had lost his mother when he was 7 and the family had never come to terms with the fact that she had taken her life and left her partner to bring up the boys when in his sixties and unwell.

He was encouraged in Year 8 to engage in group therapy sessions (Chapter 11) to help 'normalise' his loss and to articulate within a 'safe group' what the loss

(Continued)

(Continued)

had meant for him, but unlike the others he benefited only marginally from group therapy (Lines, 1999b). He was referred for individual counselling after the educational social worker escorted him into school, having discovered that he had spent two weeks locked away in his bedroom. The previous day, he had written a note saying that he no longer wanted to live. This was not the first time he had written such a note.

Counselling pupils and students who contemplate suicide or who want to die takes counsellor and client to the heart of their existential situations. Nelson-Jones (1996) speaks of a need for greater 'existential awareness' of our finite nature and mortality in a world that is preoccupied with youthfulness and sexual attractiveness. Many view death as something that *cannot happen* to them and therefore *postpone* the notion of non-being (Nelson-Jones, 1996). Matthew had given up on life. He was clearly 'stuck' in his development, and as such was resisting his biological clock – he was physically small in build, looked drab in appearance, never smiled and rarely spoke, following instructions like an automaton, wholly out of touch with feelings and wishes. But as Nelson-Jones would say, Matthew was *choosing* to think and to be this way. In fact, his socialising and energy were absorbed in grieving and overdue longing.

In view of my 'duty of care' (McGinnis and Jenkins, 2009) under current safe-guarding requirements (Chapter 4), I consulted his pastoral support manager, who contacted home and the family GP, not that that action altered Matthew's psycho-logical state. The case was also brought up in supervision. It was necessary to 'hold' him psychologically and build a therapeutic relationship to initially get him to 'speak' with words rather than through 'downcast demeanour'. He was known to be vocal at home, but at school he became frozen. There were long silences in early sessions till he dropped his elected mutism for sporadic conversation.

Narrative therapy has been used with clients who are contemplating suicide, par-ticularly two techniques that are termed 'taking it back' and 're-membering conver-sations' (Speedy, 2000). These dual techniques register how the client's material has affected the counsellor in re-viewing her own narrative, then sharing this with the client. The point is not to go for 'depth' (as in humanistic counselling) but for 'thicker' stories, that is, expanding the qualities of other people and exploring dif-ferent ways of seeing things:

They are contributions to conversations from counsellors who are aware of the two-way benefits of therapeutic conversations and who feel ethically account-able to their clients to take back the ways in which these exchanges have made a difference to their own lives. (2000: 629)

Conversations from significant and influential relationships (with people who may be dead or alive) are described as 're-membered' conversations that have therapeutic import. Speedy (2000) used her experience of personal bereavement to link in with her client's story of his uncle's suicide. The counsellor shared her own re-membered experience of a loss event to thicken the narrative of her client's life. John McLeod has also used this technique (Cooper and McLeod, 2011: 94).

While it is true that no one can have the experience of another (how do you empathise with a young boy losing his mother?), it is also true that bridges can be built through similar experiences. If the counsellor has experienced existential loss, then she has the personal resources to help her clients. I spoke to Matthew of a boy who had contributed to my life, how he helped me to walk but sadly was tragically 'taken away' through a car accident: 'I still imagine his presence alongside me as I walk, just in case I stumble.' My aim in re-membering was not to compete with Matthew on an artificial victimisation scale, but rather to give him permission to begin visualising the contribution of other people to his life.

Reluctantly at first, Matthew began to speak positively of his mother's contribution to his life in place of being angry that she had 'left him', and once the words began to flow I could not hold him back. Beginning from the last holiday the family had spent together, event after event rolled from his lips, his head lifted, his face lit up and his hunched pose uncoiled, to which I sensitively drew his attention. Matthew also brought up a long-distant friend who had taught him to cook, an uncle who had migrated to Canada who once showed him how to fix engines, and others too, to re-join the 'club of his life' (Payne, 2006). He began more freely to recount, by contrast, the flip side of his life (when left powerless to resuscitate his mother), and I felt for him – a parental counter-transference, which I took to supervision. My supervisor felt I should track his mental state over the next few weeks and collaborate with his pastoral staff and his father.

The healing had slowly begun. He had confidence now in articulating the depth of anger underlying his loss, as though he now had permission to grieve and let go. We had formed a therapeutic bond from which future counselling capitalised. Matthew began to redirect energy towards more positive things than overdue grieving.

Conclusion

A significant minority of pupils have resorted to cutting their arms to relieve stress with blades and other sharp implements in modern times. The evidence would suggest copycat principles are influential. It has been suggested that the therapist should not draw attention to the behaviour so much as focus upon the *underlying anger* which the behaviour is attempting to communicate.

With the exception of toileting difficulties, which may be more directly related to early *attachment* issues, self-harming behaviours are an external demonstration of internal stress or current relational conflict. The scope of offering brief counselling in school will be a crucial question in light of research presented where treatment is customarily offered in specialist offsite clinics. Some schools and colleges may have prescriptive procedures for self-harming and dietary disorders in line with their safeguarding policies. The research has shown that, in extreme cases, more overt parental control may be required than is normally considered appropriate in school counselling, particularly for younger pupils.

Students who contemplate suicide have to be taken seriously in school or college under the duty to safeguard young people. In making an assessment, it is imperative to consider the risk factors, and the youngster's potential for carrying out the act, as well as the underlying tensions that are affecting the individual. Only then can it be decided whether brief counselling is indicated, or whether the therapist must inform other parties who have the statutory duty to protect the student. It has been illustrated that non-typical episodes of self-injury, features of less serious dietary conditions and temporary states of suicide ideation can be suitably addressed in school with brief pluralistic therapy.

Reflective Exercise

1. Suppose a Year 9 pupil is brought to you for counselling by her physical education teacher after she had noticed fresh but deep cut marks to both her lower arms. She tells you she does not want to speak about it, and neither does she want her parents to know. How would you address the problem?

2. An anxious mother of a Year 11 pupil requests that you might offer therapy for her anorexic daughter.
   a. What factors would inform you on whether to work solely with the individual, or in combination with the parent?
   b. What would be your customary approach for such a dietary disorder?
   c. How might the research and integrative approaches presented above influence you to try out different models or approaches with this type of client?

3. A Year 12 student of 17 years approaches you for counselling after learning that his friend took his life the previous evening. His friend was popular and the incident and sordid details were publicised on the internet. You learn through the second session that your client has seriously considered taking his own life. Discuss with a colleague where the boundaries are to be drawn between:
   - An individual's autonomy.
   - The expectations of the educational establishment.
   - A duty to the parent or carer.
   - Your own personal beliefs about suicide.

(Continued)

(Continued)

- Your publicised code of confidentiality.
- The BACP Ethical Framework.
- Safeguarding legislation.

4. The case of Matthew presented above illustrated an approach termed 'remembering' to help when suffering from delayed shock and grieving after his mother had committed suicide. He, in turn, contemplates taking his own life, but the seriousness of his intention is not clear. What are the merits and potential psychological hazards in encouraging such troubled youngsters, who are suffering from loss or bereavement, to consider 'contributions' to their past of persons who are now unavailable to them?

Key Points

- Self-harming behaviour can be regarded as a continuum from self-inflicted cutting to suicide ideation.

- Self-injury and self-harming can be viewed as an outward expression of anger and stress arising from relationship difficulties, which will be prominent during adolescence. Therapy should attend to the *anger* underlying the symptoms and the *relationship difficulties* rather than the behaviour itself.

- There may be limited scope for the brief school counsellor to address enuresis and encopresis, unless the practitioner works in conjunction with a nurse or GP.

- Early research suggested that anorexia nervosa could be caused by overly stringent parenting, and that bulimia nervosa commonly results from peer relationship conflicts influenced by western media projections of the ideal body form. Therapy for the former may need to be centred, paradoxically, on a strict regime of parental control with CBT and family therapy, but for the latter integrative narrative therapy may be indicated to challenge the predominant social perspectives of beauty.

- Counselling approaches have been adopted to address suicide ideation, but in school the therapist has to consider the ethical situation and safeguarding practice. A novel approach to consider with suicidal clients who feel they have no purpose in life after losing someone special, is a narrative intervention known as 're-membering', an approach which encourages a recollection of contributions that significant people had made to a person's life.

8 School Bullying

This chapter covers:

- Research on bullying
- Assessing whom to counsel
- Counselling victims of physical bullying
- Counselling provocative victims
- Managing cyber-bullying
- Counselling groups of bullies
- Counselling individual bullies

A gang leader knifes a boy on a run-down council estate for reporting bullying at school.

A girl overdoses in her bedroom after repeated threats from peers in her year group.

Introduction

Rarely does a week go by without a further calamity being reported in the media. These tragedies leave a sense of perplexity about how to check school bullying. In this chapter, the particular role of the counselling practitioner, as distinct from the pastoral teacher exercising a disciplinary role, is examined indirectly through a range of brief counselling interventions that have proved effective. Various approaches are illustrated from a pluralistic perspective, which include techniques used in family therapy, social skills training, Circle Time and CBT.

After reviewing the research, victims of physical bullying are supported with brief therapy and a systemic approach is presented to assist provocative victims gain insight into, and control of, repetitive teasing. Interventions to encourage bullies as individuals and in groups to examine and modify threatening behaviour through a form of restorative justice closes, with a more extreme case being presented in the following chapter.

Research on Bullying

A wealth of material now exists on the nature, causation and effects of bullying in school. From the early research of Olweus (1978, 1991, 1992, 1993) in Scandinavia, school bullying has gained an international focus (James, 2010; Lines, 1999a; Moore et al., 2008). A number of studies reveal an almost universal picture. Although estimates vary slightly (Stassen Berger, 2007), studies show that, on average, for every five pupils one has been a victim of bullying, and that one in ten young people have admitted in anonymous questionnaires to have bullied others, with cyber-bullying becoming increasingly significant (Moore et al., 2008; Smith et al., 2008). Boys tend to bully more physically and girls more covertly (James, 2010; Moore et al., 2008).

Reducing Bullying

Research shows that while bullying occasionally comes into school because of community unrest, schools themselves as institutions create a climate where bullying either thrives or is checked (Samdal and Dur, 2002). The very nature of competition for results creates a climate of 'winners and losers', where bullying, in the form of 'dominance and subjection', can thrive (Lines, 2008). Although most schools have anti-bullying policies now in place, research shows that some are more successful than others with similar socio-economic and ability-level pupils – schools can indeed make a difference.

Much research exists on bullying patterns and appropriate interventions for reduction. Bullying can be reduced (from 30–70 per cent, claimed Olweus, 1993[2]) with a range of imaginative interventions that keep the profile high. Measuring bullying reduction is problematic due to different definitions of what constitutes 'bullying', consistently effective reporting, public campaigns and media reporting (Moore et al., 2008).

Interpretation of Bullying Behaviour

Bullying and oppression have been understood and interpreted as a political paradigm (Marxism), as a natural means of survival (Darwinism), as a legitimate course of national control (Fascism), as forms of power (Nietzsche) and as a narrative of social construction (Foucault, Gergen). Ken Rigby's (2002) comprehensive analysis includes 'intention' as well as 'behaviour', and his own definition reflects a Darwinian 'survival of the fittest'. My own treatment of bullying draws attention to the systemic nature of bully–victim behaviour, suggesting there may be a *payoff* for both parties in the relationship (Lines, 2008).

Bullying Policy

Whole-school anti-bullying policies drawn up and collectively owned by members of the whole school populace are considered essential for bullying reduction (Cowie and Sharp, 1996; Olweus, 1993; Smith and Sharp, 1994), but the 'Plan Report' (2008) of OECD countries has claimed that 'bullying has not been effectively eliminated *anywhere*', and may actually be 'worsening in some countries' (Moore et al., 2008: 12).

(Continued)

(Continued)

Monitoring

Unmonitored periods of the school day, such as at breaks and lunchtimes, are recognised as being occasions of anxiety for victims (Patterson, 1982), where unsupervised adolescents find opportunity for anti-social behaviour – a situation soon rectified with more rigorous surveillance (Klonsky, 2002; Patterson and Stouthamer-Loeber, 1984).

Interventions

The Sheffield project was launched in 1990 (Whitney and Smith, 1993) through Gulbenkian Foundation funding. This surveyed the largest sample in the UK (over 6000 pupils). It applied a methodology that isolated such factors as year differences, gender differences, types and locations of bullying behaviour and reporting.

This work expanded on previous research to investigate a number of strategies, such as, for example, self-assertion, designed to empower pupils in responding to victimisation in ways that were different from those they instinctively deployed, so as to produce a more favourable long-term outcome (Smith and Sharp, 1994).

Playground environments were redesigned to stimulate bored pupils who might otherwise revert to bullying. 'Bully Help Lines' and 'Bully Courts' were set up, peer support was tried, and approaches such as the 'No blame' approach and 'Circle Time' were tested to good effect. Peer support was further researched as a proactive means to reduce bullying (Carr, 1994; Cowie, 1998; Cowie and Sharp, 1996; Naylor and Cowie, 1999).

Influential anti-bullying programmes include the 'Olweus Bullying Prevention Program' (Olweus, 1993), and UK-based awareness and preventative resources include the NSPCC's 'Full Stop Anti-Bullying Campaign' and 'Once is too Often' (Moore et al., 2008): there is an online reporting site which can be customised for any school, academy or college (www.thesharpsystem.com).

Definitions of Bullying

'Bullying involves a desire to hurt + hurtful action + a power imbalance + repetition + an unjust use of power + evident enjoyment by the aggressor and generally a sense of being oppressed on the part of the victim' (Rigby, 2002: 51).

'Bullying behaviour is continual physical, psychological, social, verbal or emotional methods of intimidation by an individual or group. Bullying is any action such as hitting or name-calling that makes you feel angry, hurt or upset' (Lines, 2008: 19).

Name-calling

Although research into verbal bullying is limited, sufficient work has now been done to raise a number of concerns. Several authors have pointed to the psychological effects of name-calling that leave youngsters open to public ridicule (Rigby, 2002), and to the common terms of abuse which are targeted at vulnerable individuals (Lines, 1999a). Even strictly managed anti-bullying policies cannot always dissuade large groups of pupils from daily engaging in what they would regard as trivial teasing, and who see name-calling largely as play and as just 'messing about'.

> Research shows that particular children become subjected to name-calling, that name-calling results in stereotypical racial classifications (Lines, 1999a), that many older adolescents find physical abuse easier to deal with than racial taunting (Cohn, 1987) and that name-calling is more difficult to spot and check than physical bullying (Besag, 1989).
>
> Reporting patterns of name-calling are influenced by previous experience of reporting outcomes in primary school, parental advice and the perceived motives of the main instigators (Lines, 1999a). A number of theoretical interpretations of name-calling exist in the literature (summarised in Lines, 1996).
>
> Slander on the internet and mobile phones is difficult to detect when teenagers release their passwords and personal numbers. The desire for popularity is strong and poor judgements (see Chapter 5) leave many teenagers vulnerable through a wish to have many contacts (Lines, 2008).

Terms of verbal abuse that infuriate young people include, among racial and idiosyncratic terms, names which denigrate the family, such as 'your mum is a ...' (often

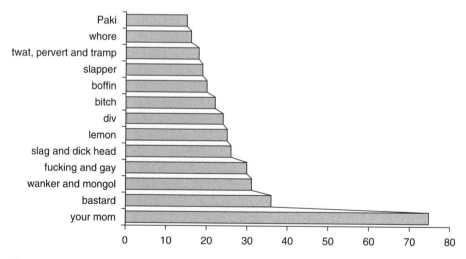

Figure 8.1   Percentage rates of terms used in name-calling by one year-group of 241 year 7 pupils

abbreviated to just 'your mum!') especially in neighbourhoods that have high single-parent (normally mother) families, particular sexual terms like 'wanker', 'slag' and 'fucking', together with those that ridicule achievement, such as 'boffin!', or non-achievement, such as 'mongol', as indicated in my small-scale research (Lines, 1999a) and reproduced in Figure 8.1.

The cognitive changes occurring in children who have been subjected to continual name-calling may cause a belief that they deserve the derogatory names they have been called – they must indeed be 'ugly', 'a pervert', 'a wimp' or 'an idiot', for otherwise they would have been able to cope. Their inability to cope 'proves' *for them* that they are inferior (Payne, 2006), resulting in a gradual but pervasive erosion in self-esteem (Seligman and Peterson, 1986).

'Provocative Victims'

It is the emotional reaction to a given label by the targeted person that is the crucial factor in whether or not the label will stick; it is a process of social reaction and interaction (Besag, 1989). Some victims react so explosively and impulsively that their ineffective defensiveness becomes in itself amusing and a source of 'entertainment' for group witnesses (Lines, 2008). Often, such pupils have poor social skills, low status and, in turn, unintentionally perpetuate (or aggravate) the problem. They are known as 'provocative victims' (Pikas, 1989) or 'victim-perpetrators' (Moore et al., 2008).

> Pikas (1989) distinguished between 'classic' or ordinary victims and others he described as 'provocative victims', and although many of these pupils may suffer with communication-behaviour disabilities like ADHD and cognitive disorders along the Autistic spectrum, there are others who appear to bring on bullying themselves by their poor interpersonal communications.

Cyber-bullying

Cyber-bullying is a particularly nasty form of bullying where individuals spread vicious messages and images rapidly to a big audience at any time (Ortega-Ruiz et al., 2007). It is extremely powerful, is not easy to detect and commonly occurs outside of school, where bullies often rely on a supposition that since PCs, mobile phones and equipment to access the internet are personal property they are not culpable (Dehue et al., 2008; Ybarra and Mitchell, 2005). Cyber-bullying is becoming increasingly significant in school and is currently a major source of conflict that takes up much pastoral time (James, 2010; Smith et al., 2008).

Peer Group Influence

Victims of bullying have low status among the peer group, but this can change with maturation. The tendency for bullies to wind up volatile youngsters and humiliate them publicly lessens in the closing period of secondary education (Arora and

Thompson, 1987), but in the early years the environment can be very hostile, competitive and non-accepting of social and cultural difference. Small groups will encourage bullying behaviour and lure some to fight and taunt the weak, but, conversely, 'bystanders', and even gang participants who are not the main protagonists, will display empathy when viewing victims being beaten or humiliated.

> Strategies for bullying reduction can draw on natural feelings of pity for the victim (Salmivalli et al., 1996). In addition, studies in criminology support the findings of Davies (1986) and Elliott (1986) in illustrating that trauma is experienced by those who witness attacks on the defenceless. Attention has been drawn to the group effect ('mobbing') of bullying behaviour and resulting levels of empathy (Pikas, 1975).

Victims of Physical Bullying

Overall research shows that those having developed strategies of self-assertion and temper control have far fewer difficulties in dealing with physical abuse. School pupils often believe that by ignoring tormentors the problem will go away. It is a forlorn hope that is not modified with past experience, and suggests that a victim has become increasingly frustrated and overwhelmed: *What else can I do to get them off my back?* They repeat ineffective defensive behaviour (like ignoring the bully, or calling names back) in spite of it not working, and are known to suffer rejection, loneliness, low self-esteem and have a tendency to become depressed and anxious (James, 2010). Conventional counselling by pastoral staff and therapists supports victims (Harris and Pattison, 2004), though is not always effective in helping the situation to change (Lines, 2008).

> It is known that victims lack confidence and have low self-esteem, even in later life (Cowen et al., 1973). It is also known that passive spectators as well as victims are affected by bullying (Davies, 1986; Elliott, 1986).
>
> The literature would indicate that victims often show a submissive posture to a perpetrator just prior to attack (Besag, 1989; Schafer, 1977). Thus, a stage exists in secondary school for power-seeking individuals to exhibit their prowess and control over those who are unable to withstand it or fight back.

Assessing Whom to Counsel

To make a general point, it has to be acknowledged that attitudes vary considerably over bullying, and in consequence perceptions and beliefs on what to change, and how to change what needs to change, will not be the same among pastoral teachers and school counsellors. One controversial issue in a society that holds per se that bullying is wrong is to work with bullies, as opposed to their victims, and in some cases bullying behaviour is viewed ambiguously as a projected form of amusement as well as disgrace. While most

Figure 8.2 Popular western cartoon characters – clockwise from top left: Popeye, Road Runner, Tom and Jerry – that surreptitiously endorse bullying behaviour

regard extreme provocation and aggression against an individual as unequivocally wrong, many laugh at the slapstick comedy of someone's misfortune, and cartoon figures that beat and injure their largely innocent characters. Look at the cartoon characters in Figure 8.2 of recognised western culture and consider at what point hurt becomes a spectacle of comedy.

Certainly, in schools, teacher's attitudes towards bullying will reflect those of society:

- Should we punish outright every aspect of bullying and harassment?
- Should we stand up for the victim in all cases, or strengthen their resolve to stick up for themselves and become more resilient?

When reviewing the referral data, the counsellor must first make a choice of whether to work with the victim, the bully, the friends of either, parents of either, supervising teachers or the 'observing group' – either with the victim or in their absence. The counsellor will apply different models when working with the bully than with their victim.

Some pupils receive continual verbal taunting from different groups and within different contexts, which suggests that their responses (conscious or otherwise) provoke attacks against them (Lines, 1985). It is as though they carry the label of victim pasted on their foreheads. They are provocative victims (Lines, 2008; Pikas, 1989) who are often the most difficult to support. Effective treatment programmes are those centred on the victim changing their behaviour, rather than the many exercising self-constraint over verbal intimidation, a controversial approach which is not without criticism (Payne, 2006).

Counselling Victims of Physical Bullying

Research on effective counselling approaches to reduce school bullying is limited and ranges from person-centred, CBT and problem-solving counselling (Harris and Pattison, 2004). Apart from therapeutic support for low self-esteem and depressive states (see Chapter 6), strategies that have been tried in school to support those who are bullied physically include self-assertion exercises to engender confidence (Smith and Sharp, 1994) and teaching self-defence. In my experience, such strategies can go wrong in situations where adults are not present, and can in certain circumstances be misused when, for example, a victim becomes a bully from acquired confidence. Other strategies centre upon general social skills training (Lindsay, 1987), the reasoning being that when an adolescent becomes self-confident and adept in social relations, taunting will have less effect. Overall, studies using RCTs illustrate that no single-level intervention to combat bullying works as well as a combination of strategies (Moore et al., 2008: 14).

Under a social construction interpretation of bullying (Thornberg, 2010), adults (through anti-bullying policies, punishment regimes, etc.) and most pupils (perceptions of justice) endorse a condemnatory narrative of meaning, but there can sometimes be an undetectable *payoff* for some victims of physical maltreatment (Lines, 2008). Either way, something needs to change that avoids punishment and the apportioning of blame, and which thereby militates against possible reprisal.

Self-assertive role play is effective for those victims of bullying who regularly have their dinner money and bus fare extorted by power-abusing peers. They are challenged at the school gates or in secluded areas to turn out their pockets and pay money under threat of being beaten up. When they comply, it is often in the hope that the intimidation is a one-off experience, but they unfortunately become a tagged person through offering no resistance, and so the pattern continues.

Some feel that by yielding they gain popularity among tough peers, perhaps even protection, but these are pseudo, highly manipulative friendships. Because of fear of revenge, such victims rarely report the theft to those responsible for discipline, and so their self-esteem is lowered and the extortion continues unabated. Self-assertion training is often the only means of dealing with such bullying.

Coaching Andrew to be Assertive

Money was taken daily from Andrew at break when trapped in the dining room foyer. Through role play, Andrew was taught to look Curtis in the eye, non-provocatively, and say, 'I don't give my money away, thanks!' We practised this in front of a mirror before in vivo testing. Although trying this required confidence that Andrew generally lacked, he eventually plucked up courage and gave it a try when the time was right, and this checked the habit almost immediately.

Counselling Provocative Victims

Payne (2006) argues that the practice of giving victims strategies for social survival fails in recognising the true culprits of bullying behaviour. He believes that the work should be focused upon the bullies rather than their victims (who merely need support) and that school systems should continually confront bullying head on, since its prevalence is a reflection of unchallenged societal attitudes of abusive power and exploitation. While not fully denying this, if bullying and its social roles and meanings are understood as social constructions (Thornberg, 2010), it can be counterargued that provocative victims (Pikas, 1989) often elicit hostile and fun-poking responses from their tormentors by their reactions.

Blame is not the point here, neither is it to prescribe a pragmatic course with no regard to justice. The following strategy is aimed at making the provocative victim aware of the patterns and effects of their interelating with others, and to reduce tormenting by sharing the responsibility for change so as to make school life a positive experience for all.

I have found less submissive strategies that make use of humour to be highly effective with provocative victims suffering repeated verbal abuse. These victims, who are volatile yet who may have heightened imaginative capabilities, can become susceptible to being called names and to other covert bullying because of the emotional effect that derogatory images have on the mind. Less mature adolescents may imagine an audience that scrutinises their appearance and actions, and that assumes huge and irrational significance when under pressure of ridicule. When called names, an anxious pupil will stand out in a group more in imagination than in fact. The following strategy aims at minimising the effect of this.

A novel way of dealing with victims suffering from repeated name-calling, then, is through a particular form of self-assertion combined with a reframing, or re-storying, technique (Epston et al., 1992; White and Epston, 1990) that I call image replacement and narrative adoption. 'Reframing' is a cognitive restructuring technique derived from family therapy, which uses those very same imaginative abilities that are attacking the self (Burnham, 1986; Watzlawick et al., 1974). The approach involves a co-constructed modification of a victim's narrative (McNamee and Gergen, 1992), combined with a non-aggressive challenge. Through altering images and thinking in an atmosphere of humour, the incidence of name-calling is reduced and the victim is left feeling more under control and less at risk of intimidation (Lines, 2001).

Reframing

The pupil is encouraged first to reframe her situation. In place of believing that **she is hated** because she is called names, she is encouraged to view herself as the *object of entertainment*, which is perhaps just as harrowing but far less debasing. Teasing occurs not because of what **she is**, but because of what *she is allowing to happen* to her.

The self-assertive response involves displaying confidence and acting in a way least expected. For instance, those of a different country or county are encouraged to try an experiment. Rather than attempting to disguise their accent and feel ashamed of their dialect over the jibes when they speak, they may try to exaggerate it and see what happens.

> ## Reframing Personal Constructs
>
> Terry, a Welsh boy, was new to the school and would instantly react to name-calling. Firm disciplinary action was taken with those who called him a 'sheep-shagger', and resulting from this a small group sought reprisal by sniggering every time he spoke in class. He self-referred out of frustration, and tried in vain to erase his identity, but when it was suggested that he might exaggerate his accent, not only did he laugh but his peers laughed too. Inevitably, the taunting ceased and he became friends with the group.

Other victims may be targeted for reasons of looks, physique or mannerism, such as the way they walk fitting a stereotypical caricature of stigmatised groups, particularly gays and lesbians.

Image Replacement

By replacing an image, or images, in the mind of the youngster, the victim begins to take control of the game by regulating his own affective state. I have a string puppet hanging in the counselling room, and this is often shown to victims to indicate how powerful characters within contained group settings can be in pulling strings that control the actions of puppet-like characters. I explain to my clients that the strategies I wish them to use are designed so that they metaphorically take hold of the strings from their (perceived) adversaries and begin to control the show.

> ## Reconfiguring Mental Images
>
> Chris was given a counselling appointment after exclusion, and in the introduction he related frequent episodes of losing his temper through rising to the bait of name-calling. He was taunted by being called 'queer', 'gay' and 'bent', which is a dilemma that many boys find difficult to counteract and ward off. In a report to Chris's parents excluding him for reasons of 'abusive behaviour towards a member of staff', an accompanying report stated:
>
> > Chris was asked to leave the room for swearing. I allowed him back into the room when he promised to get on with his work. However, an argument ensued between Chris and Levi with repeated name-calling. I again asked Chris to leave the room but he refused, saying I should tell Levi to leave …
>
> *(Continued)*

(Continued)

This report illustrates an occasional occurrence in class where order breaks down through anger fuelled by unchecked name-calling. It is not that teachers turn a blind eye to such taunting, but that with some unruly groups name-calling, though beginning low-key, can become difficult to control.

I explored what lay behind his anger and what his beliefs and feelings were about people who were gay, lesbian or bisexual. His reply was that he had no strong feelings against those of a different sexual orientation, but although he was not gay himself (he asserted), he found name-calling offensive. It would be tempting to apply the principles outlined above and encourage this client to exaggerate what he imagined to be gay mannerisms so as to show the group that he was unaffected by their taunts. But there is a problem with this particular taunt that does not apply as much to other sexual labelling – it reinforces stereotypical attitudes of homophobia in school. Instead, I asked him to look at those who ridiculed him and wink at them in a self-assured manner when they called out gay terms of abuse. We practised this in front of the mirror until I felt he was comfortable with winking expressively. Then he tried the proactive response in situ. After two weeks, he reported a distinct decline in teasing, which was confirmed by his confident demeanour.

Underlying these strategies is the notion that bullying is often not over-malicious or power-abusive, but designed to prompt the subject to overreact in such a manner as to amuse an audience of fun-seeking peers, which in fact comprises the majority of name-calling incidents in school (Lines, 1996, 1999a).

Narrative Adoption

The idea of reframing situations is one of adopting a slightly modified narrative that has been co-constructed by the counsellor and client from the material of which the person makes sense of personal experience (Anderson and Goolishian, 1988).

Reconstructing a Script of Self

Cormac became increasingly agitated when his friends derided him by calling out 'granddad', to the point of explosive outburst (his granddad had died three years earlier and he found it a tragic loss). He remonstrated with the teacher for not challenging the tormentors, and stormed out of the classroom, occasionally shouting and disregarding classroom protocol and order. Cormac became aggressive when teased. He was depressed at having been manipulated by peers, some of whom were his 'best friends'. They had not known why he would overreact, but they could predict that he would. 'Granddad' meant much more to him than they could imagine.

The problem was resolved for Cormac through the technique of image replacement. On being asked what 'granddad' media figure made him laugh the most, he chose the character in *Only Fools and Horses*. The narrative adoption technique involved Cormac recalling a scene that he had found particularly amusing. He tried with success the strategy of mentally focusing upon that person in that clip whenever he heard the taunts of 'granddad'. It worked: he smiled when they taunted him. They were surprised and confused, and when pulling the strings no longer had the predicted response they ceased to torment him.

> ## Humour in Warding off Insults
>
> Rudi reacted negatively to the suggestion that her mother was a prostitute by looking down and pretending not to have heard the ridicule. The more she continued her 'hard-of-hearing' pretence, the more the players intensified their mockery.
>
> Being called a 'midget' irritated Trevor in Year 7, and caused him to lose his temper. Time and again, he got into trouble for shouting out in frustration. 'They do it because I'm small', he said.

Rudi found that scoffing ceased when she humiliated her opponent amidst group laughter with the assertive rejoinder: 'Well, me mum went off with your dad last night but he wasn't very good.' Here, from feeling miserable in the belief that her mother was debased, she modified the narrative to put down her tormentors in quick-fired wit.

I asked Trevor what came to mind when he thought of something small and deadly (I was thinking of a virus). He said, 'a bullet'. We rehearsed a saying that he used to positive effect in stopping name-calling and in monitoring his anger: 'Midgets are small, but so are bullets!' An extended case of this dual technique has been written elsewhere (Lines, 2001).

Therapists must exercise caution when using these techniques for those provocative victims who are devoid of social skills and imagination, and those suffering from borderline Asperger's syndrome (a topic I have discussed in previous editions of this book; see Lines, 2006b).

Managing Cyber-bullying

Managing incidents of cyber-bullying in school calls for a collegiate response from all practitioners. Customarily, it is parents who approach the school because their son or daughter has become devastated with the notion that something private has been published on the internet or a mobile phone, and left their child refusing to attend school. Other pupils, particularly girls, get drawn into group feuds where targeted individuals are turned on with a particularly hostile gang mentality, spreading gossip and slanderous messages and images to all and sundry in their address book.

Internet Abuse – Freddie's Poor Judgement

Freddie was brought up in our fortnightly Filter meeting for non-school attendance, and after an attendance worker approached the home, it was learned that he had foolishly exposed his genitals on a webcam to a girl he was fond of, and she in turn passed it around a group of friends on Facebook. They, in turn, passed it on further afield, to such an extent that Freddie had supposed that 'everyone' in school had viewed him naked. Naturally, he was embarrassed to go anywhere near the school.

Social services were contacted by the DST, the school community policeman was brought in to speak with the group of girls and to state that they had committed a criminal offence of harassment, the IT manager spoke with his mother to assist her to put tighter controls on Freddie's internet site access, and the pastoral teacher advised his mother on how to support Freddie, while I offered him cognitive-humanistic counselling (Nelson-Jones, 1997, 1999a).

Dennis:	Freddie, I guess you must feel exposed at the moment and highly embarrassed over what you did [he sat attentive, noting that I had registered his feelings].
Freddie:	I was stupid, man. I don't know what got into me.
Dennis:	Many of us make poor judgements when young, but what is important is that you learn something from it.
Freddie:	I have, man. I'm bloody stupid I am.
Dennis:	Don't be too heavy on yourself, Freddie. Let's see how we can survive the next few days without it becoming a topic of gossip and ridicule. You could deny what you did, but I suppose since many know that seems pretty pointless. I don't know whether you agree?
Freddie:	That wouldn't work.
Dennis:	Do you think these girls are very influential in school?
Freddie:	Well, the girl I showed myself to doesn't attend this school; the rest not very.
Dennis:	That's helpful in a way, but for those that do know I would like you to try some self-talk, and say within your mind: 'Whatever …', leave the question open and focus your mind on something totally different, something you are looking forward to doing after school.
Freddie:	That's easy. I'm going with my dad go-karting tonight.
Dennis:	Fine, stick with that thought and switch off to the words the girls may be saying. Let's see how we get on.

In time, the whispers and slander died down and Freddie was able to attend school regularly and hold his head high as though the incident had never happened.

Counselling Groups of Bullies

One effective strategy to consider is to speak with the group of tormentors, or significant leaders, with the victim absent, in an aim to show how the individual has been left feeling, thus enlisting their empathy and goodwill (Pikas, 1975; Salmivalli et al., 1996). Circle Time is a therapeutic exercise of encouraging each person of a group to voice their feelings, but the running and management of Circle Time is not easy with adolescents in the latter years of school, unless pupils have consistently practised it and have valued it since primary school. This is largely because of the self-conscious nature of youngsters going through middle adolescence and the powerful dynamics of peer-group pressure.

Handled sensitively, with smaller and 'safer' groups, Circle Time can resolve many misunderstandings and overreactions arising from poor communications and ignorance of how intolerant and spiteful behaviour can hurt other people. Protagonists largely act in ignorance of the effects of their verbal abuse, and individuals of the group are able to gain insight into the sensitivities of those who are singled out. Such a strategy has limits, however, within the changing learning environments of large schools where consistent control and regulation are difficult to ensure. It also runs the risk of an over-dependence of the victim on their manager.

It is ineffective for pastoral teachers and managers merely to admonish, humiliate or exclude a perpetrator of name-calling, or physical bullying, without any sensitivity of the possible outcome for the victim who has reported the matter. When threats are made for 'grassing', the belief is reinforced that telling teachers about bullies inevitably makes matters worse – in some cases of lax management, it actually does (Smith and Sharp, 1994; Whitney and Smith, 1993). Creating a win–win culture in solving group feuds in conflict resolution is a more effective treatment than admonishing the 'supposed' guilty parties. Causes of feuds that go back for months, particularly if they have originated in the community, are often difficult to trace. In practice, therefore, partisan alliances, or miscalculated judgements, will lead to grievances about injustice and to further disturbance.

Bringing selected individuals together in group therapy has advantages, particularly where hostile feelings are still fermenting. The counsellor's aim in group therapy is to create a fair and neutral stance in the hope of achieving a win–win solution (Smith and Sharp, 1994). The technique of 'reflexive circular questioning' (Tomm, 1985), where the aggressors are invited to voice a victim's feelings from the victim's frame of reference rather than their own, can be a very powerful means of achieving shared insight. Each involved front player is asked to voice what they feel 'as though the victim', by adopting their personality and name as they speak (Lines, 2000).

Karen was asked to voice how she thought Jackie had felt when 'everyone' turned on her when Delroy asked her out. 'I suppose she thought she was two-timing Steve, her ex-boyfriend', she replied.

Dennis:	No, Karen, speak as though you are Jackie and say what you think you would feel in her situation as you see everyone turn on you for something somebody else has done when asking you out.

After fresh attempts, what she came up with was the cause of insight not only for her, but also for the group:

Karen:	I feel you're all being unfair. Delroy asked me out, I didn't ask him, and Steve dumped me last week. What am I supposed to do? You're all against me, and I thought we were all mates!

Restorative justice programmes bringing bully and victim together have proved effective in Australia (Morrison, 2002) and in my regular practice. In non-malicious, no less tormenting, cases, where aggression is shown merely to see a fellow upset, narrative techniques which draw on the power of the written document may prove effective (Epston et al., 1992; White and Epston, 1990).

Group Harassment of Jenson

Jenson came for counselling in tears during the lunch break saying that Carl and Scott in science kept name-calling, picking on him and digging him in the back when queuing outside the room. Jenson said that he did not want the boys to 'get into trouble' and felt that the 'no-blame' approach of restorative justice might better resolve the conflict than reporting the matter to his pastoral manager.

In Jenson's case, an introductory session was held to offer Carl and Scott support and to enlist their commitment to work on their aggressive inclinations. Awareness-raising over how they were viewed by peers other than those of the neighbourhood was by use of a counsellor-composed narrative. The following written assessment of Jenson's statements and those of witnesses was given to Carl and Scott to read:

Carl and Scott were whispering names about me in the queue. Carl said, 'Jenson, come here you twat!' I knew what would happen so I moved away. They followed me and began calling me names again and digging me in the back. Scott grabbed my coat and called me a 'beanpole', 'cause I'm thin. Carl tried to trip me, but I hung on the door handle to stop being dragged in the sixth-form room.

Carl and Scott keep bullying Jenson **to make him look stupid**. They **do it for a laugh**. Scott isn't as bad as Carl. He **thinks he's good** in front of the girls. Scott's **trying to get Jenson wound up** because he knows he's on his last chance. **Carl hates Jenson** because **he thinks** his brother grassed Carl's brother for nicking cars.

Carl read this narrative and was invited to comment and modify the text, especially the bold type that I had emphasised which expresses opinions and suppositions rather than facts. Scott did the same exercise separately. This was a powerful means of getting both boys to reflect on their identities as perceived not by moralising pastoral staff but by observing peers.

Within a 'no-blame' counsellor stance of restorative justice, both boys began to analyse their respective aggressive identities, and to think about where their reflexive behaviours may have originated and where their behaviour was leading. They were invited to modify the narrative, which was honestly done and which became the means of altering their humiliating tomfoolery and aggressive manner. Given the high exclusion rates of violent pupils, particularly those from some ethnic and social groups, where physical correction is a norm, such remedial therapies are an effective means of avoiding an escalation in physical maltreatment.

Counselling Individual Bullies

Research shows that violent bullying can have as damaging an effect upon bullies as upon their victims (Forero et al., 1999). Such research indicates that some bullies suffer depression through uncontrollable aggression, which indicates that they, along with their victims, deserve counselling support. Counselling approaches based on the notion of 'insight brings change' (psychodynamic and humanistic) can prove useful for those unaware of how their aggressive behaviour is perceived by the peer group generally. Trading on what makes a person popular can be effective in the developmental process of identity formation and individuation (Erikson, 1968).

Apart from bullying due to role modelling (see Chapter 9), other cases reveal that clients often have not dealt with bereavement or parental attachment issues, which have left them feeling as though a cauldron of fury is about to boil over. With these pupils, the aggressive tendencies are initially managed with CBT techniques that draw the person's anger arousal to his attention, say by wearing a rubber band around the wrist, while counselling addresses those primary factors.

Triggers of Anger Management for Paddy

Paddy found the rubber band helpful in reminding him of his volatility in situations where the counsellor was not present. Pulling and releasing the band

(Continued)

(Continued)

signalled to him that he was getting angry, a technique of which those around him were unaware. The band was the signal to rising temper and the need to exercise self-calming talk in anger management. It served to connect mentally with his counsellor and the relaxation sessions in which we had become engaged to desensitise his anger. The technique is a form of containment at a distance.

Having held Paddy's anger to avoid exclusion, humanistic therapy addressed his sense of loss when his father rejected him and showed affection to a younger son of a new relationship.

Some pupils require a short-term pass and an escape route when becoming impulsively angry, while mind-control therapy (see Chapter 2) and brief loss therapy (see Chapter 11) through cognitive-humanistic counselling (Nelson-Jones, 1997, 1999a) begin to develop an internal locus of control.

Planning an Escape to Manage Larry's Outbursts

Larry never came to terms with his father running off with another woman and leaving him. He would explode with extreme violence on every occasion that teachers corrected him for playing up, or when friends teased him. I needed to organise an escape route for him to withdraw from the situation and come to the counselling room to calm down before brief therapy addressed his underlying concerns, firstly through coaching skills of self-control and finally through narrative therapy.

Dennis:	Larry, let's practise a method whereby you can control your anger without me being present. We have learnt how to relax when you become tense, to breathe properly and to conduct self-calming talk. When your teachers correct you, it is not because you are disliked but because they wish to preserve order in the classroom. But I would like you to think about how you are viewed by peers in school when you become aggressive. How do you think others see you when you become aggressive?
Larry:	Tough, I suppose, like my mates on the square. They look up to me when I fight; yes, I feel good they see me like this.
Dennis:	Mm … The problem, Larry, is you have to exist and survive in a school institution that will not permit aggressive means of sorting out problems, and which sees school as a preparation for working life. Do you think you would survive in a work environment by fighting your way out of trouble?

> *Larry:*　Not really.
>
> *Dennis:*　What might work on the street will not work in the workplace, and you have to decide where you want your future to be – having a job and earning money in work, or living on the street, hanging around with nothing to do, being drawn towards drugs and trouble from boredom?

An extended case illustrating these techniques is presented in the following chapter.

Conclusion

Although research on the effectiveness of therapy for bullying problems is limited, there is considerable information on the statistics and patterns of school bullying, its causation and remedy, to give practitioners a clear direction on what to do and how to support and help minimise bullying behaviour. More subtle forms of cyber-bullying, which increasingly affects pupils in schools, are more difficult to manage.

This chapter has illustrated brief counselling approaches and techniques of 'self-assertion', 'reframing' and 'reflexive circular questioning' during Circle Time exercises to support victims of physical bullying, particularly 'provocative victims'. There has been an emphasis on behavioural interventions that examine the 'triggers' of anger and that reduce incidents through 'self-calming talk' for volatile students as an indirect approach to support their victims.

Reflective Exercise

1. Examine your own experience of power dynamics operating in school during your time as a student:
   a. Did you tease or humiliate others?
   b. Were you a victim of bullying in any way?
   c. Does your experience of being a pupil at school affect the way you address bullying behaviour in your work?

2. Discuss whether the hierarchal structure of educational institutions, and the imbalances of power among staff, affects the pecking order and status of students at a subliminal level?

3. Look again at the cartoon characters in Figure 8.2 and consider your own attitude towards minor abuses of power among pupils in school, particularly

(Continued)

(Continued)

in regard to name-calling. Would you admit to finding slapstick drama funny and minor misfortune presented as comedy entertaining to a degree, even at someone else's expense?

4. Suppose, over a term, a significant number of pupils reported to you that they were being bullied by one particular Year 8 pupil. Would you feel compelled to report this to a pastoral teacher – with the possible risk of reprisal if the case were not managed well – or would you send for the identified bully and work with him/her yourself? Discuss with reference to some known or hypothetical cases where either action would be appropriate.

5. As we have seen, some academics view bullying as socially constructed, suggesting that it is a social act which has meaning for the perpetrator and victim. Think for a moment of victims you have worked with and reflect on particular *payoffs* or 'benefits' they may have had from being a victim in school.

6. How would you address a consistent bullying problem for your victim-client if:

   a. She received regular harassment through an internet social networking site, and yet had a communication disorder that left her weak at interpreting body language and innuendo?
   b. She was known to regularly taunt others on the same site?

Key Points

- No school professing to provide a caring and supportive ethos for learning will take bullying lightly; they will have regularly reviewed anti-bullying policies in place.
- Collective research suggests that one in five pupils is bullied in school, and one in ten confess to bullying, but name-calling applies to a much higher proportion.
- An early therapeutic decision is whether to counsel victims, bullies or other parties in mediation work.
- Brief counselling for 'provocative victims' of bullying is challenging, but styles that combine 'reframing the problem', 'narrative adoption' and 'image replacement' can be beneficial in reducing recidivism for such pupils.

- Groups who perpetuate or instigate tormenting a weaker individual are encouraged to change with 'reflexive circular questioning'.

- Since one school bully may be responsible for harassing a number of victims, it makes sense to support bullies with counselling, particularly if being a bully is as much a problem to the person concerned as to their victims.

- School bullies can be assisted with brief counselling using styles that challenge the 'dominant-macho' grand narrative, to aid them to 'see' their behaviour in a broader social context than that which occurs on the street.

9 Anger, Aggression and Violence

This chapter covers:

- Violence and aggression – a social problem
- Research on anger, aggression and violence in youth
- Fighting in school
- Assessment for therapy
- Counselling angry, violent and aggressive pupils

Introduction

Violent pupils have, on occasion, injured, maimed and even killed other teenagers in school. Although murder/manslaughter in school is exceptionally rare in the UK, violence has become a rising concern in some schools. Areas where there is a lack of social cohesion, ethnic and racial tension, and an ingrained drugs culture are particularly prone to violence. But schools generally are ordered institutions and the vast majority of pupils are not violent.

There are some violent students, however, who stand apart where punishment and exclusion have little effect. Significant numbers of pupils become angry in school, which occasionally spills into fights, and root causes for both categories appear to be due to adult modelling and negative peer-group approval. In this chapter, brief therapy is presented for a student who was frequently angry and violent in school (and the community) through a brief counselling programme of insight and behaviour change.

Violence and Aggression – A Social Problem

Murders and shootings in US schools have revealed a dark side of teenage psychology, and have prompted such novels as Lionel Shriver's (2003) *We Need to Talk About Kevin*. The murder of 2-year-old James Bulger by Robert Thompson and Jon Venables (both aged 10) in 1990 shook public confidence in the innocence of youth, and the killings of Stephen Lawrence in 1993 and Rhys Jones in 2007 illustrated the rising use of weapons and the subversive nature of rival groups in some communities in the UK.

When Mitchell Johnson (aged 13) and Andrew Golden (aged 11) of Jonesboro, Arkansas, killed six children and one teacher by randomly firing 134 shells in a school in 1998, questions were asked as to how children could kill so cold-bloodedly – how, indeed, teenagers could so easily get hold of Magnum rifles and Smith and Wesson pistols (Kellerman, 1999)! Such senseless killings of children, teachers and parents by adolescents 'who hadn't even nudged puberty' (1999: 4) often leaves society searching for explanations. How can those be helped who show no remorse?

School murders by children stabbing their peers and teachers have occurred in Europe and Australasia, indicating that the problem is in no way confined to Anglo-American societies (Foderaro, 2007). There is also evidence of rising violence against parents by teenagers who have a predisposition to be aggressive, and who are in control of their carers through having no boundaries in childhood (Brown, 2010).

Remedial steps to curb teenage violence have not been very imaginative. Some American states have responded to violent youth by what is termed 'zero-tolerance' policing, while in the UK the government has attempted to check it with anti-social behaviour orders (ASBOs) under the Criminal and Justice Act (2003) – due to be reviewed. The thinking underlying such action is a lack of confidence in sentencing to correct anti-social behaviour and a felt need to make visible reparation to victims of crime. Programmes of restorative justice have been tried, but as yet have not been fully evaluated.

Research on Anger, Aggression and Violence in Youth

Although anger is a biological reaction for the species to survive (Lines, 2008), there are good grounds for also seeing it as a 'culturally situated performance' (Gergen, 2001: 89). Violence is an international problem (Moore et al., 2008). Conflicts in Northern Ireland and Palestine bear evidence of violence involving young people, along with some Muslim states (Manji, 2004), where youths are drawn to revolt because of religious–political dissatisfaction, but these are triggered by collective causes rather than by interpersonal quarrels.

Victims of aggression and violent assault – in the family, school or the street – suffer a range of symptoms (as discussed in Chapter 8). Anger is often the precursor to aggression and a loss of control, which many regret and find hard to check. Not every teenager has an anger-management problem, however, and of those that have, not everyone turns to violence – many injure themselves (see Chapter 7). Research into impulsive aggression falls on both sides of the nature/nurture divide, and it is likely that reasons are a combination of both factors (Kellerman, 1999: 52–7). It is important to note also that the stereotype of boys always being aggressive and girls exercising covert hostility is not as polarised as is often conceived. The proportion of girls involved in violent street fighting has been underestimated in official statistics (Ness, 2004; Stassen Berger, 2007), and research identifies the mother as having an integral role in a daughter's level of violence (Ness, 2004).

The aetiology of violent and aggressive behaviour of young people is complex, but research appears to favour the effect of witnessing violence and aggression in the home or on the street (Moore et al., 2008) through role-modelling principles and patriarchal attitudes (Seymour, 1998). Although many young people regularly feast on images of aggression and violence displayed in films and video computer games (Kellerman, 1999), there is no direct evidence linking 'viewing' with 'behaving' (Black and Newman, 1995), or of poverty being a sole determinant of violence (Aber, 1994).

There is considerable evidence that youngsters exposed to violence are at risk of a range of psychosocial problems, including reduced academic perform-ance (Moore et al., 2008; Saigh et al., 1997), substance abuse (Kilpatrick et al., 2000), developmental disturbance (Pynoos et al., 1995) and impaired moral development (Bandura, 1986; Thornberry, 1998).

In spite of reports of increased violence by pupils against teachers in Scottish LEA schools (Sorensen, 2002), and reports by UK teacher associations, interna-tional RCT studies of OECD countries in Europe, Australasia and North America reveal no clear picture of rates of violence – its prevalence or reduction – or of the most effective means of curbing it, owing to no consensus of definitions of what constitutes violence or assessment of reduction (Moore et al., 2008).

One study (Winstok et al., 2004) suggested that young boys (1014 subjects, aged 13–18) who had witnessed domestic violence by their father on their mother develop an incoherent image of family structure. Where mild aggres-sion is witnessed, boys identify with their fathers, but where severe aggression is experienced, they align themselves with their mothers. The implications of this hardly need spelling out.

While scapegoats are often found in television viewing, social deprivation and black urban hardship, research has identified the predominant factors as witnessing and being subjected to domestic maltreatment (Campbell and Schwartz, 1996) and corporal punishment (Straus, 1996), where an ethic of *might is right* is unconsciously modelled. There is no substantial evidence that race alone determines aggressive pathology, in spite of the proportionately higher numbers of black boys being prosecuted for assaults in some commu-nities (Kellerman, 1999).

Extreme Violence and Neuroscience

Neuroscientist, Jim Fallon, has studied PET scans of psychopathic killers and has found common damage to the orbital cortex, that part of the brain behind the eyes responsible for executive function, decision-making and conscience – such charac-ters commonly have flat affective states and have a tendency to exercise low-impul-sivity control. He also studied the genetic makeup of interned killers and discovered that they each carry a gene associated with violence carried on the X chromosome (MAO-A, or 'warrior gene' because it regulates serotonin), due to saturation of too much serotonin in the uterus during development, a gene which is more likely to be passed on from mother to son (Hagerty, 2011).

Psychopathology has been linked with a further common factor, which is having been subjected to abuse, whether physical, emotional or psychological, particularly having been exposed to regular violence or a very traumatic event. Bouts of extreme violence and impulsive aggression occur where these three conditions exist to form a predisposition for unpredictable, reactive behaviour.

> Jim Fallon's mother informed her son one day that their family history had a pedigree from the seventh century onwards of psychopathic killers – including 7 notorious murderers (one case of matricide). After examining his own brain pattern and genetic character he made a disturbing discovery; he had a pre-disposition to be a violent person. Yet he wasn't violent, the reason being – arguing for nurture over nature – was that he had not been exposed to any abuse, but on the contrary had been brought up in a close-knit and nurturing family, with plenty on love and care around (Hagerty, 2011).

Therapy for Extreme Violence

Kellerman (1999: 26–8) claims that the evidence shows that exceptionally violent young people do not respond to psychotherapy or rehabilitation if the problem is left late into adolescence, particularly for those he describes as 'psychopathic killers' (1999: 109–13). Fortunately, many aggressive youngsters in school do not exhibit such a level of violence, and are indeed receptive to psychotherapy and counselling.

> Sukhodolsky and Ruchkin (2004) compared male juvenile offenders (361 sub-jects, aged 14–18) with high school students (a control group of 206) in Russia to highlight the influence of the *belief system* on aggressive behaviour, sug-gesting that CBT may be indicated for violent conduct disorders and anti-social behaviour (Herbert, 1978).
>
> School-based, preventative programmes designed to help pupils to become less aggressive through problem-solving and relationship-enhancing skills have proven effective. Smokowski et al. (2004) contrasted 51 third-grade pupils with 50 of a control group to show that those who engaged in programmes of making choices had significantly higher scores on social contact and concen-tration, and less overt aggression.

Fighting in School

Aggressive and violent primary school pupils are soon noticed in secondary school through bullying, assaults and fights, as new pecking orders are established.

With regard to fights and staff responsibilities to break them up, policies tend to fluctuate with different political administrations, ranging from taking positive action to allowing a fight to finish, thus avoiding a personal injury. Teachers' views on reporting minor skirmishes also vary from self-remedial management to requiring a pastoral teacher to exclude all involved parties. Fights will always occur when tempers are lost, but as long as pupils are monitored there is normally no serious injury.

The frequency of aggression and fighting in school is related to the effectiveness of senior personnel and the leadership team, as recognised by Ofsted. Psychologists have addressed aggression indirectly in the learning context through classroom strategies (Rogers, 2000, 2002). The school counsellor may become involved in supporting a pupil after a fight if there is an anger-management issue (through pastoral teacher referral) or a trend towards violent behaviour in the community (through police or parental request).

Assessment for Therapy

As pointed out above, a range of studies have demonstrated how violent and aggressive behaviour is the result of poor role-modelling influences of family members or idealised figures of the street (Campbell and Schwartz, 1996; Kellerman, 1999; Margolin and Gordis, 2004). These studies attribute cause to influential factors of nurture and aggressive rewarding stimuli within the home environment.

Anger Management

A number of referrals for counselling are about issues to do with anger management and temper control. Some students become enraged at the smallest provocation, and there are diagnostic tools to screen the problem and treatment programmes available to address it (Goldstein, 2004). I have developed my own assessment tool (Appendix IV), since I feel that many referrals for anger management in school are inappropriate, in that referrers do not distinguish sufficiently enough between instrumental anger (serving an ulterior purpose), which may be controllable, and impulsive anger, which may be instinctive – due to high levels of adrenalin and an oversensitive amygdala. Anger-management programmes have been created from a behaviourist paradigm (Pegasus NLP, *Mind-Body Health*, undated) – my own is presented below.

Tailoring Interventions

In assessment, the school counsellor may adopt a range of integrative approaches depending upon the particular cause of losing control or the character make-up of the individual client. Factors that cause pupils to lose self-control include:

1. A young person may suppress anger from loss or bereavement, or family conflict, which is discharged through violence.
2. A youngster may have poor communication abilities and a low tolerance threshold, which leaves them vulnerable to intimidation and teasing. With few effective strategies to cope with frustration, they fire up quickly.
3. A teenager may have developed a dominant and aggressive persona from a significant family member or idealised figure of the street.

With the first category, the issues of loss and bereavement will need addressing with pluralistic counselling (Cooper and McLeod, 2011) through integrative approaches which assist young people to manage personal loss within an altered situation (see Chapter 10). With the second, the therapist may engage the client in social skills training, such as that outlined in Chapter 8, or as used in rational emotive behaviour therapy (REBT) (Wu, 1987). But with the third, a client needs to understand where internalised attitudes are leading.

Psycho-education

There are occasions when the counsellor may have a role in teaching the client common features of human behaviour. With aggressive teenagers, I often show them a diagram of the brain (similar to that presented on page 82) and teach them how mental processes function, particularly the role of the amygdala. Studies in neuroscience, as discussed in Chapter 5, show the adolescent brain to be different from that of the adult or pre-pubescent child. The relevance of attachment theory and research mapping of the teenage brain becomes evident when the behaviour of particular adolescents exposed to domestic violence or community unrest is examined.

Through discourse, the client will have related episodes of domestic abuse, or street violence, and the counsellor may offer for understanding plausible accounts of what such a victim might generally feel. Avoiding stereotyping, such accounts are shared with the client in collaborative discourse to see if they register with what is thought and felt, and whether a hypothesis matches personal experience. So what do we know about attachment theory and brain study that has relevance to adolescent aggression?

Violence through an Oversensitive Amygdala

It is broadly acknowledged that the amygdala is associated with emotion processing (Dolan, 2002; Phillips et al., 2003). It is also known that time tends to slow down during a traumatic event, not 'real time' but *perceptual time*, which means that detailed recollections are not reliable. Being in a state of fear, the amygdala kicks into gear; it is essentially an emergency control centre. It lays down memories on a secondary memory track that is completely separate from normal memory, and during playback an event appears to take a very long time. The more energy the brain spends in representing an event, the longer it seems to last. Some parts of recollection will be exaggerated, others forgotten, but all is filtered through a prism of current understanding. Frequent recapitulation tends to generate new meaning (Lines, 2008).

When under threat, the instinctive response of *fight* or *flight* centres on the emotional mind, which is precognitive and which evolved first. It develops earlier, long before the thinking brain, the neocortex, develops. The hippocampus and the amygdala are the two key parts of the primitive 'nose brain' that, in evolution, gave rise to the cortex and then the neocortex. Research has shown that sensory signals from eye or ear travel first in the brain to the thalamus, and then to the amygdala. A second signal from the thalamus is routed to the neocortex – the thinking brain. This branching allows the amygdala to begin to respond before the neocortex, which assesses information through several levels of brain circuits before it fully perceives and finally initiates its more finely tailored response (Goleman, 2006: 17).

The emergency route from eye or ear to thalamus to amygdala is crucial because it saves time in an emergency when an immediate response is required – say a teen is cornered and has to decide whether to escape or attack (both give rise to adrenalin and an increased heartbeat to supply more oxygen to muscles for rapid action). This direct route is reckoned in thousandths of a second. The longer route through the neocortex allows the emotional manager to calculate the better response. Impulsively aggressive teenagers have a hypersensitive amygdala and an undeveloped neocortex, and the counsellor's role through teaching and therapy is to reverse this process.

The work of Jonathan Kellerman (1999), cited earlier, represents the furthest end of the teenage aggression spectrum, and the highly commendable work of Camilla Batmanghelidjh (2006), at Kid's Company, demonstrates what can be done for those almost beyond reach. In a recent article (2009), she brings together new findings in neuroscience with observations of street behaviour among gangs and the psychological effects on those in search of attachment figures (Perry, 2009). If a teenager has an undeveloped neocortex as well as unfulfilled attachment needs, the experience of traumatic events relating to those needs will compound their troubles at and beyond puberty.

Effects of Poor Childhood Attachments

During healthy development, a mother and child communicate with loving exchanges in such a way that neurons in the neocortex – thought to be responsible for calming down, empathy, planning, anticipating the consequences of one's actions and imagining oneself in the future – are activated (Gerhardt, 2004). Close facial proximity and use of the eyes stimulates brain regions in these areas. This early interaction, known as 'attunement' or 'mindful reverie', helps the child to cope with temporary distress, for example when left alone. A child deprived of such early interaction is likely to have attachment needs. If a secure attachment (see Chapter 5) has been ruptured or, worse still, has never existed, such as a primary carer having mental health problems or being drug dependent, or being subjected to domestic violence, the child will experience abandonment, which in turn creates anxiety and the release of stress chemicals. They will have no resilience, will despair quickly and will become hyper-agitated.

They will have experienced humiliation for not being able to intervene in previous violent episodes, and memorise their position as being submissive, recalling the terror they felt from someone being very powerful – the sense of being frozen when time stands still. During adolescence, some learn to 'fight back', and become aggressive through the constant release of *fight* and *flight* hormones from the adrenal glands above the kidneys. They become used to living with high levels of adrenalin and learn to survive on their wits. Even an innocent glance is perceived as a threat.

Both victim and victim-become-aggressor see themselves as not worthy of being saved, and the disrespect they experienced is internalised into self-disgust. Memories of abuse and neglect are stored deep in the emotional centre of the brain. The violent teenager lives in a state of emergency and has to deal with flashbacks and night terror. Being in a state of hyper-agitation, they have to become powerful. Some 'select victims of their own in a repetitious circle and in need to complete the abuser/abused narrative by shifting positions or by taking revenge through harming others … In the beginning, the young-people-turned-abusers see reflections of themselves as small children, pleading for help and not being saved. The image brings up unbearable feelings' (Batmanghelidjh, 2009: 14).

Both sets of children – the initiators and the imitators of violence – seek attachments to defend against assaults, and these can be found in the form of gangs. The gang leader or drugs dealer recruits trapped teenagers, offering them a solution by becoming the new attachment figure. Violent teenagers become stuck with these pseudo-attachment figures. At the street level, they do not use their attachments to each other in an internalised form. They mistrust their peers but are desperately in need of them – affiliations are needed for safety but are not enriching. The counsellor may consider (within obvious limitations) how and whether there may be a role in becoming a suitable role model for such a client.

Role Modelling Aggression

Counselling aggressively–inclined boys over a period of 30 years has reinforced my view that there is a correlation between aggressive solutions to perceived threat and the influence of violent siblings and parents (Seymour, 1998; Winstok et al., 2004) or prestigious characters known to be aggressive in the neighbourhood (Moore et al., 2008).

There is status to be gained through *violence* and *fighting* (Kellerman, 1999), and there is a ready-made audience in school to glamorise and reinforce aggressive behaviour. In my experience, *punishment* and *cost-response* programmes do little to dissuade some from fighting, have little positive effect in offsetting the powerful reinforcing forces of criminal role modelling (Bandura, 1977) and actually add to the kudos of those who wish others to see them as tough. If overt control is limited, then internal control becomes the better course, and if therapy is to be successful then one feature of counselling may be a need to present alternative role-modelling behaviour. This requirement for change may present a challenge for conventional school counsellors.

Counselling Angry, Violent and Aggressive Pupils

A tendency for teenagers to flare up quickly and become angry through an overactive amygdala and undeveloped neocortex was discussed above and in Chapter 5. In the case that follows, we examine the implications of this process in terms of behaviour and self-management, and how a pupil can be helped to prevent exclusion by harnessing impulsive reactions.

As with fighting, there are a range of causal factors to account for why an individual may become angry and out of control. There has been much debate about the value of catharsis with young people. Some feel that through the counselling process an invitation provides an opportunity to vent frustration in a contained setting, and many clients testify that this results in a release of tension. Others counter-argue that validating anger merely repeats, and therefore reinforces, maladaptive behaviour that generally is self-defeating – why practise a behaviour one wishes to eliminate? I favour approaches that help clients examine the antecedents of their anger and the particular triggers that set it off (Goldstein, 2004).

The case presented illustrates a method of assessment and a counselling programme designed to divert an aggressive Year 8 boy from a violent lifestyle. The problem was not merely persistent fighting in school, but an observation that suggested that he used anger instrumentally and appeared to see it as part of his identity.

The Case of Stefan

Stefan was a Year 8 pupil of African ethnicity who had recently moved to the academy after being permanently excluded from his previous school – he struck the headteacher. His father and four older brothers had each served time in prison for violence and physical assault in the neighbourhood. Stefan was at risk of further permanent exclusion after three serious fights within his first half term (one which I had witnessed). He was regarded by teachers as a boy of above-average ability and as a pupil who 'thinks he can get away with things' by being forceful and dominant.

Although I was initially unsure about how he would view me, Stefan was committed to therapy, to exploring how he might avoid getting excluded again and following the course of his older brothers. We were working collaboratively using the Egan

(1990) three-stage model in brief therapy, in which we had identified clear specific goals around an agenda which was both realistic and within his capabilities. Simply put, Stefan's chief goal was to stop fighting. He had witnessed and become engaged in violence throughout his childhood:

Stefan:	I was at this motocross trials with me dad and this man called me names and he hit me just there [Stefan points to his chin]. I told me dad and me dad decked him to the floor, and said, 'Don't you ever hit my Stef!' And I booted his head in. And crowds come round and I got a buzz from it ... like when I have a scrap with mates. My nextdoor neighbours used to fight and do drugs a lot, but that didn't bother me because I was in my own house. It was funny, but if I was one of them kids in the house I wouldn't like it.
Dennis:	So drugs were not used in your home?
Stefan:	They were when I was little, but not so much now ... My brother went to our neighbour and got angry and stabbed him with a knife, telling him where to go. There was blood all over the place, but it didn't seem to bother him; he just laughed. It was horrible.
Dennis:	How does seeing something horrible fit in with what you said earlier about getting a buzz from fighting?

Anger Management

Apart from violence modelled within Stefan's family, there was an underlying anger which emerged just prior to fighting – when being admonished by a teacher, and when intimidated by peers he considered were weaker than him. My initial task was to explore whether this was instrumental anger or impulsive anger, what control he might have and what he was prepared to alter. Teachers and fellow pupils informed me that Stefan would 'see red mist', would 'switch' into rage when confronted, and we needed to understand what fuelled his anger. Stefan completed two diagnostic anger-management assessments, and his responses were interesting.

Anger Management Assessment 1

✓ Are you always able to choose your behaviour when you feel angry?
  When angry, can you still be aware of how others are feeling?
  Do you express yourself clearly and quickly when something upsets you?
✓ Are you aware of the hurt and/or fear that is causing anger?
✓ Do you feel powerful without yelling?
  Are you aware of the body sensations that come with anger?

(Continued)

(Continued)

✓ Do you have a specific plan for when you feel anger coming on?

✓ Have you sorted out upsetting issues of the past so that they don't affect you today?

✓ Are you very clear about how your anger affects others?

Are you able to find the positives in any situation?

(Adapted from Pegasus NLP, *Mind-Body Health*, undated)

Anger Management Assessment 2

Describe two incidents which leave you feeling angry.

A   *When Jason was in the dining room he told Kerry and Suzanne I was a pussy. He's been dissing my mum for ages, and telling kids he can beat me up.*

B   *Mr Osborne had a go at me and told me to move. I said 'why?' He said, 'I don't like your attitude, get out!' I said, 'I don't like yours', and walked off.*

On a scale of 1–10, how angry were you left feeling?

A   *10*
B   *8*

What were you thinking when angry?

A   *I've got to kill him.*
B   *He's a twat!*

What did you do when you were angry?

A   *I smashed his face in, and he's dead after school.*
B   *I stayed under the stairwell til the bell went for next lesson.*

What do you have to do to calm down?

A   *Fight.*
B   *Get away.*

Do you follow anyone in the family in regard to anger?

My mum says I'm like my brother ... and my dad, I suppose – especially when he's drunk.

Underline which applies:

• <u>When angry I swear</u> and don't care what I say.
• <u>I strike out at someone.</u>

(Continued)

(Continued)

- I smash things up.
- I feel bad afterwards/guilty/sad/hateful of others/hateful of myself.
- I know I lose self-control.

Being aware of personal hurt and how Stefan's anger was affecting others was interesting, but I was not sure of his ability to choose his behaviour. The two incidents described have similarities and differences, which may be accounted for by the perceived power Stefan had in either situation. The customary response to threat to self through *fight or flight* were evident and, although I could not be certain how self-aware Stefan was over his abilities of self-control, I was interested in his disclosures of feeling *bad*, *guilty* and *sad* after the event, so much so that I felt this might be the lever by which I could enlist Stefan's motivation.

Not always being self-reflective, I used the angry images chart (Figure 9.1) to help Stefan identify how he felt by likening his feelings to one of the figures, and he selected the bull. I then asked him which of the prompts caused him to become like *angry bull*, and he underlined 'putting me down', 'being shouted at', 'telling me off' and 'putting my family or friends down'.

A feeling of being 'put down' speaks of Stefan's self-image, which was examined later, but in order to help him control personal anger when being corrected and, particularly, 'shouted at', I had to encourage him to replace the mental image of his

Figure 9.1 Angry images chart

threatened state. This 'self-coaching' technique (Nelson-Jones, 1996) I call 'image replacement' (Chapter 8; Lines, 2001). None of us likes being shouted at, but for some youngsters a shout is a prelude to being struck by an adult and, although this shouldn't happen in school, we have to remember that youngsters sometimes react on a primitive level of consciousness.

Dennis:	Stefan, when a teacher shouts at you, I would like you to try not to personalise what is going on, as though your teacher doesn't like you, but see him or her as doing a difficult job of managing your group. Sometimes teachers are acting being angry, but on other occasions they may get angry. They wouldn't hit you. I would like you to keep looking at your teacher when they shout at you, but think in your mind and talk to yourself. Try saying: 'I know I'm OK and lots of people like me, especially Dennis. I'll just sit this out and try not to become angry and say anything that'll make matters worse.' Take deep breaths and remain calm, saying nothing but doing exactly as told.

This was practised in session, and Stefan soon mastered it in lesson.

Anger Triggers and Cognitive Restructuring

When working with pupils like Stefan over impulsive anger, clients are asked to log events which cause them to become very angry. They are then asked in counselling to try to identify the triggers that prompt their loss of control. I ask clients to take an A4 sheet of paper and draw a line from top to bottom. On the left, they list the triggers, and on the right, we attempt to identify what hidden beliefs and assumptions may account for their impulsive anger stemming from those identified triggers, following a CBT methodology. Three of Stefan's unconscious assumptions were:

Antecedent trigger	Underlying assumption
1. Kids in class cuss me.	1. Kids put me down, making out I'm stupid.
2. I get told off.	2. The teacher thinks I'm no good.
3. A kid stares at me.	3. The kid thinks he's hard and wants a fight.

These negative irrational beliefs, or negative unconscious assumptions, were disputed in therapy, and more realistic ones were superimposed on Stefan's first constructs:

1. The first assumption was rephrased as: *Pupils might cuss me because they are playing a game of winding me up to over-react, just as I do with other kids. It doesn't mean they think I'm stupid.*
2. The second was reframed as: *The teacher thinks I could improve and so takes the trouble to correct me. If he thought I was no good, he would let me do as I liked.*
3. The third assumption was altered to: *The kid may be scared of me and may stare because he is nervous that I might beat him up. There's no obvious connection between staring and wanting a fight.*

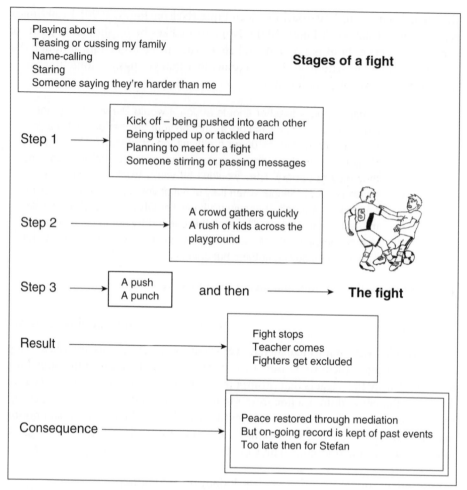

Stages of a fight

> Playing about
> Teasing or cussing my family
> Name-calling
> Staring
> Someone saying they're harder than me

Step 1 ⟶
> Kick off – being pushed into each other
> Being tripped up or tackled hard
> Planning to meet for a fight
> Someone stirring or passing messages

Step 2 ⟶
> A crowd gathers quickly
> A rush of kids across the playground

Step 3 ⟶
> A push
> A punch

and then ⟶ **The fight**

Result ⟶
> Fight stops
> Teacher comes
> Fighters get excluded

Consequence ⟶
> Peace restored through mediation
> But on-going record is kept of past events
> Too late then for Stefan

Figure 9.2 Antecedent stages leading to a fight

With the second negative assumption, I could not rule out the possibility that Stefan might experience low self-esteem and a sense of 'having to prove something' amidst significantly powerful adults; therapy could have explored this possibility under a person-centred model. But the more urgent need was to arrest the frequency of fighting, and so therapy had to address this concern first (see Figure 9.2). Underlying Stefan's violent outbursts were powerful role-modelling influences and unconscious expectations of him within his social environment, and altering reinforced beliefs and attitudes is a larger and more difficult task.

Stefan began to understand that when events moved to Step 3, even to Step 2 and 1, it was then too late – when peers could sense a fight was about to happen, expectations were high and the jostling crowd would give him no outlet to back down and withdraw. A fight (and all that that might cost) was sure to occur. We needed to arrest the process prior to Step 1, since I felt that Stefan was powerless to work on consequential contingent factors at his stage of development.

Modelling Calm, Self-controlled Behaviour

There were occasions where Stefan observed my calm response to stress: I was asked to drive him home on one occasion after he had lost his temper, and an impatient driver drove close to my boot, blasting his horn, at which point I pulled over, allowing him to pass. Similar self-controlled calmness by Stefan's friends served as effective role-modelling behaviour: one pupil made light of serious intimidating and modelled being unperturbed, using humour to desensitise tension, and since Stefan had a sense of humour we drew on this in therapy as a technique he could utilise to good effect.

Further therapy involved working on how he felt when corrected by teachers, and what he was saying to himself when threatened. We planned escape routes of humour, 'self-coaching' skills and 'self-talk' to help him remain calm (Nelson-Jones, 1996). At the slightest hint of a fight brewing, he was instructed to remove himself from the situation and come and sit in the counselling waiting room to practise what we had rehearsed in session. He was given a pass for teachers to excuse him. It was essential for Stefan to keep checking at base after every failure and success in order to fine-tune his responses to new situations.

A New Narrative of Being

The tight monitoring programme was helping Stefan to manage those occasions where impulsive anger might trigger a fight, but why did Stefan sometimes *want to fight* without apparent provocation and in spite of declaring that such action would get him permanently excluded, an outcome he said was not what he had wanted? In the short term, how could I help him cease fighting *intentionally*, and in the long term aid him to explore alternative means of behaving that would lead to more positive relationships? Causal factors for Stefan's aggression were not as significant as why he needed to maintain the 'tough guy' persona. We could not now avoid examining the attitudes and beliefs he had been brought up with and which had been regularly reinforced in his social milieu (Seymour, 1998).

The counselling revealed a sub-plot (Payne, 2006) in his general narrative of *might is right*, and I was keen to explore this ambivalence.

Dennis:	How do you feel when you see adults fight?	
Stefan:	My heart flutters [Stefan taps his chest with his hand]. I don't expect them to fight.	
Dennis:	You mean it's OK for kids to fight, but not for adults?	
Stefan:	Don't expect adults to fight. I don't think they should fight.	
Dennis:	I went on a trip to Blackpool once and my father became angry with the coach driver because he would not wait for his friend before starting home. He got up and squared up to the driver, ordering him to stop the coach and step outside for a fight. I was worried; I didn't want to see my dad fight.	
Stefan:	No, I don't like it ...	

An element of self-disclosure was felt necessary to help match our varied experiences, but what followed was an unprompted revelation:

Stefan: When I was younger I watched old people struggling with shopping and digging the gardens. I used to help them but my mum didn't always like it.

Dennis: Really?

Stefan: Yeah. There's this man next door to nan's, an old man, and he struggles a lot, but me mum lets me go and help him. His name is Joe. I do his gardening sometimes, and help him wash his car. Me mate sometimes takes the mick, but I ain't bothered.

Dennis: I guess, Stefan, this shows me a different side to your personality. I wonder whether the need to fight and come over as tough is just for you not to feel small. I wonder whether when you're grown up you want to be another 'tough guy', or to become a caring, sensitive human being ...

There appeared to be a caring side to Stefan's customary persona of a fighter, and this sub-plot was highlighted. In one sense, there were clear indications that Stefan was a sensitive boy with genuine altruistic tendencies, and in another there were other indications of a need to develop a self-concept to survive in his social world by becoming exceptionally aggressive, almost to live up to the expectations of his older brothers and father.

Dennis: What have you learned over these sessions?

Stefan: That fighting isn't worth it. You only get into trouble.

Dennis: Is that the only reason why you might stop fighting, just to keep out of trouble?

Stefan: I don't know, to stop getting kicked out of school.

Dennis: Is there any other reason to stop fighting that might have something to do with the way you want to see yourself? Or be seen by others? I mean, do you want to see yourself as a scrapper, growing up as an adult fighter?

Stefan: No, not really.

Dennis: Let me broaden this out. Do you want to become an adult who has people as friends just because they're afraid of him, or because he's a great guy to be with?

Stefan: The second one. I don't want kids to like me because they're afraid of me.

Dennis: Is that because you want me to see you that way?

Stefan: Yea [Stefan laughs].

His response to change in order to please me, the counsellor, indicates the growing bond that was developing between therapist and client, and reinforces the view (Thorne, 1984, 2002) that the client must *feel the therapist is alongside of him* in an imaginary sense, *willing him* to try life within a new narrative – in the day-to-day trials of perceived threat – if he is to make real progress. Therapy became effective when we engaged in future imaginary projections of particular personas and their likely outcomes.

> Dennis: If I can share this with you, to be a fighter might bring you some popularity when you're younger, but not for the reasons you think. As you pass through the school, kids will be more confident, not so scared of you, and will want you as their friend or otherwise because of your personality, not because they need your protection. You must decide whether you want a genuine friendship or whether you want kids to be outwardly friendly just to be on the right side of you [Stefan kept his eyes fixed on me as though transfixed in thought].

My narrative of persona popularity could not be enforced as 'the truth'; it could only be offered as a suggestion for trial (Cooper and McLeod, 2011). Stefan began to experiment with the new narrative of 'calm and friendliness bringing popularity' and found almost instant positive results, which in turn reinforced the *non-aggressive persona* as the way 'to be', in replacing the learned *might is right* narrative of his social milieu.

As time went on, Stefan came for brief sessions less and less, and within the next 12 months there were no further fights reported in school. Stefan had learned, and not just to please me but through life experience, that by dropping his aggressive demeanour he became a more attractive personality and so likeable that peers could feel relaxed in his presence and jostle and tease him, as boys do in play, without fear that by pushing him too far they would end up being punched or beaten up. In Year 9, he joined the team to become an effective peer counsellor.

Conclusion

Fights occasionally occur in school through misunderstandings, rumours, accidental brushes and collisions, rumours or challenges to pride, but this chapter has focused primarily on brief therapeutic interventions for a particular category of pupils who are excessively violent as a result of aggressive role-modelling influences. Most pupil vignettes presented in this book are composite characters, which represent the nature of my work in school, but in the case of Stefan he was a client (though pseudonym) which involved a range of approaches – anger-management and cognitive-narrative therapy – to divert him from a future where his only means of resolving external and inner conflict was through violence.

The chapter examined the social implications surrounding a pupil's impulsive (undeveloped neocortex) and instrumental (belief system) aggression, and the subtle effects of inadequate role modelling. Some cited research covered the far end of the violence spectrum, where specialists tend to be sceptical of the value of counselling support. But in cases which commonly occur in school, brief therapy can have a marked effect, so long as practitioners are prepared to consider engaging in opportunities for role modelling calmness when under stress, a radical suggestion which challenges much conventional theory and practice of counselling and psychotherapy, but which for some therapists having other roles in school might be considered entirely appropriate and fitting (see Chapter 3).

Reflective Exercise

1. Consider the following two statements, and discuss the therapeutic implications if statement i. or statement ii. is judged by you to be correct:

    i. For a humanistic-inclined therapist, the 'true nature' of Stefan should not be considered as 'aggressive scrapper', but as 'caring person', who, through environmental forces and adult expectations, has found it necessary to develop a violent persona to survive within a social milieu where an ethic of 'might is right' predominates.

    ii. For a brief therapist, informed by social construction theory, Stefan has a broad range of selves to live by and narratives to explore for life relevance. Both client and therapist have more space for manoeuvre if constructs are more flexible and creative than if they are fixed.

2. Discuss the relevance of such statements in relation to the question:

    Should practice be theory led, or should practice lead in forming theory?

3. Do you agree that excessively violent adolescents are beyond therapeutic support? If you are optimistic that such can be helped, what particular approach or model would you consider the most effective for those who use violence instrumentally to establish a *tough persona*?

4. Do you consider anger-management training and monitoring the role and responsibility of a school counsellor? Discuss how your answer argues the cases for collaborative practice and clearly defined roles of different personnel in an educational setting.

5. Give typical examples of where you think the border should be drawn between therapeutic support and instilling discipline.

6. Role modelling calm behaviour during a stressful occasion for particular youngsters who may be aggressively inclined requires social interaction that is generally beyond the remit of the counsellor and the counselling context; it is more likely to occur when pastoral staff engage with pupils in out-of-school, and often residential, situations. But, as pointed out in Chapter 3, some school counsellors may have a broader role than therapy per se. Discuss the possible boundary and personal implications if the headteacher asked you to consider a broader involvement which included taking part in a school disco once every term.

Key Points

- Skirmishes between pupils sometimes spill into fights and aggressive conflict, but few incidents generally require counselling in school, unless there is an unresolved issue.

- Research on violent young people suggests that significant family members and street role models have a profound influence on them.

- Youngsters brought up in homes where violence is prevalent will have limited non-aggressive strategies to resolve their disputes, and the school counsellor can assist such pupils in a teaching role.

- Anger management has become a common requirement of counselling referrals in school, and an accurate assessment of why a particular client becomes angry – such as bereavement, unresolved issues or having a *tough guy* persona – will direct therapy.

- Habitually aggressive youngsters can be helped in therapy through integrative cognitive-narrative styles that emphasise that such behaviour can lead to exclusion from school, domestic violence and future imprisonment.

- Some high-risk youngsters may need more than a talking cure; they may need the influence of lived experience among role models who resolve their own tensions through non-aggressive means. Such a requirement may stretch the remit of most youth counsellors beyond their normal method of working.

10 Loss and Bereavement

Introduction

Traditional approaches have proved effective in supporting bereaved clients in school, but the limitations of time and lack of a suitable counselling arena of containment may not allow the processes of healing to take place completely. Even brief models of psychodynamic, person-centred or existential therapy may not realise their potential in a setting where non-interruption cannot be guaranteed. This chapter examines both individual and group therapeutic means of helping pupils and students deal with their losses through brief integrative models. Therapy needs to be geared to the setting and to the developmental transfer of adolescents from parental dependency to peer-group allegiance.

In this chapter, loss and bereavement as they affect pre-pubescent and adolescent pupils within western society are first examined, particularly as they impact within school. The theoretical insights of how bereavement affects young people through transitional stages are then reviewed, with a particular emphasis upon adjustment to loss.

The Effects of Bereavement on Development

Many young people of secular families are not emotionally equipped to deal with death and dying compared with those in eastern religiously-centred cultures. An eastern Buddhist story teaches the universality of death:

A mother who is bereaved of her daughter is given the impossible task of entering a village to collect mustard seeds, but only from those houses where no one had died – none could be found! In every home death had left its mark. (cited by Farrell, 1999)

The clinical administration of modern-day funeral rites, and the continual viewing of manufactured images of killing and death in the media, immunises young people from the cold reality of non-existence. Three factors account for the excessive anxiety in teenagers experiencing unexpected death:

- Children in the West are not encouraged to take spiritual development seriously.
- Children may be shielded from visible grief expressed at funeral services.
- Children are fed on a diet of cosmetic scenes of killing in films and computer games.

All this leaves pre-pubescent children and adolescents wholly unprepared to face the stark reality of the death of a loved one.

Adjustment to Loss

The tasks and challenges of adolescence – increased autonomy, sexual maturation, risk taking, experimenting in alcohol, drugs and sex – were discussed in Chapter 5, together with the accumulating evidence of teenage brain neuroscience (Cicchetti, 2009), which accounts for observable characteristics of sensitivity, jumpiness and emotional volatility. Bereavement, however, is an added pressure. Some theorists view adolescence itself as a period of mourning for an irretrievably lost childhood (Noonan, 1983). Impulsive reactivity may be necessary for 'ego-identity' (Erikson, 1956) and to break away from parental over-control towards autonomy (Berkowitz, 1987), but death can halt, or at least seriously hinder, development through shifting the platform upon which a teenager stands.

Refugees and asylum seekers may have witnessed their parents and extended family being slaughtered, and will have also lost their culture and way of life. Bereavement will be compounded if they have not had space or opportunity to grieve, if they have not found a sympathetic ear to understand their cultural ceremonies for letting loved ones go, or if they experience marginalisation and further persecution and disadvantage. Entering school in a secular western culture – where death has little religious significance – can be overwhelming for those from traditional families.

Emotional Effects

Adolescence is not a good time to lose a parent (Smith, 1999). According to psychoanalytical theory, the Oedipus myth accounts for the process of individuation (Jacobs, 1993). While not beyond criticism (Howard, 2000), the story explains adolescent experience (at least for males [sic.]) as needing metaphorically to 'kill' the parent in order to find true self, to push the boundaries of control and containment en route to adulthood.

If, however, the process is thwarted, by an untimely parental death, there is no authority against which the adolescent can revolt for self-differentiation – the teenager is not only robbed of the agent of support and nurture, but of the very mechanism of personal self-development. For settled immigrant pupils, news of the death of a loved one overseas will be doubly catastrophic, since the practicalities of expense and distance will deny them an opportunity to take part in funeral rites, and thus prolong the bereavement process.

The 'highs' and 'lows' of hormonal activity throughout puberty intensify the emotional responses of adolescents, and the developmental psychosocial changes 'put young people particularly at risk of the multiple impacts of loss experiences' (Rowling, 1996). The loss of a parent through bereavement has therefore a twofold effect:

- security is disturbed because the concept of 'the family' is shattered, and
- the adolescent's world is less stable and far less predictable.

Cognitive Effects

Teenagers bereaved of their carers unconsciously seek out substitute authorities – alternative parents, older friends or moralistic ideologies, such as those found in religion, politics, humanitarian or environmental concerns (Lines, 1999b). With cognitive development, young people acquire the faculties to challenge the received world views of their upbringing (Jacobs, 1993), a process of moving from literal to figurative views of the universe – a process which is not static and which accounts for the 'idealism of youth'.

Literal views, such as 'God provides for those who love him', may be retained if supported by authorities, such as the 'inspired holy text' (Lines, 1995b), the religious leader or the sacred community, but the general trend is towards symbolic accounts of experience, metaphor and paradox (Lines, 2006a). 'Formal operational thought' occurs between the ages of 12 and 16 (Inhelder and Piaget, 1958), and is the capacity to think abstractly and to form hypotheses of future scenarios (see Chapter 5), of life beyond conceptions, or to deduce nihilistic meaning from available evidence.

Cognitive development is highly significant in the mourning process and in coming to terms with loss by forming a convincing rationale to account for what is felt. Religious belief, or lack of religious belief, becomes paramount, with no guaranteed outcomes that all will be well: some gain greater faith, some lose faith and others begin to face radical doubts they have fostered secretly and which have lain dormant for some time. Although the nature and content of religious belief are culturally determined, it is nevertheless for many a time of spiritual growth or a move towards nihilism. Spiritual questions rise to the surface after bereavement (Lines, 1999b), and paranormal accounts may become credible (Lines, 2006b).

Social Effects

Bereavement is a time when human mortality is brought into question. It is a time for radical re-evaluation and reorganisation of the self, but adolescents who are already going through a transitional phase will be left temporarily disorientated. Some will become seriously depressed, detached and unreachable, even by those familial fellow sufferers who have the capacity to give emotional support. They need strong supportive adults around them to carry them through. Counselling is helpful, particularly for those where support is not available and where friends don't have the capacity to become an emotional crutch.

Teenagers with weak social and friendship-building skills are likely to withdraw into themselves and become isolated. Irritability and unprovoked anger displayed by grieving youngsters make them unattractive to peers, who often feel their sympathy and concern has been spurned. Children generally have little awareness of how other people think and feel, but during adolescence innate empathic capabilities are developing and need nurturing (Rowe, 1996). Increased socialisation helps in the process, but there is the need to facilitate personal sharing of experience through communication in aiding adolescents to develop a higher sense of human 'connectedness' with other people (Lines, 2000, 2002b, 2006a).

Social Darwinism, for some theologians, points to human commonality and cooperation in order to survive (Wright, 2009); all breathe the same breath (spirit) of God according to the Genesis/Koranic narrative. Any means of drawing attention to human interconnections – comradeship, collective ritual, team spirit, intimacy, the counselling relationship – will foster empathy (Lines, 2006a; Mearns and Cooper, 2005; Rowe, 1996).

The counsellor's personal resources and empathy are a prerequisite in helping bereaved students to cope and make the necessary adjustment to loss.

Managing Bereavement in School

In spite of its debilitating effects, teachers generally are not comfortable talking about death with young people in school for reasons of their own experience of loss, a wish to preserve the 'innocence of youth' and a belief that the issue is too deep and complex (Rowling, 1996). But the curriculum provides regular stimuli on death and dying that may trigger flashbacks of suppressed grief from pupil's earlier losses, catching them off-guard and causing them to breakdown in class. This is more likely to be the case for those who sweep death under the carpet (Nelson-Jones, 1996). On-hand counselling provision can be invaluable in such cases.

Schools are large cross-cultural communities and have sometimes had to face their own tragedies of a teacher's, or a pupil's, unexpected death. Education authorities have provided guidance and strategies for major disasters, and there is also a demand for proactive curriculum input on death and dying to be given as a matter of course.

> Rowling (1996) studied Year 11 pupils in two schools of mixed cultural and rural/urban catchments in Sydney, Australia, to emphasise the value of teaching about loss in school. His research showed what could be achieved by teachers 'being human' and by sharing in a frank manner their own experiences of loss and grieving.
>
> Major disasters (school trip tragedies in England, shootings at Dunblane and in USA schools – see Chapter 9) have left school communities devastated (McGuiness, 1998), and in the UK have prompted materials to manage critical incidents (Yule and Gold, 1993). There is, in the USA and Australia, a growing recognition of the need to deal more directly with loss issues in the curriculum in the aftermath of school shootings, bus crashes and natural disasters, such as hurricanes and bush fires. Rowling (1996) summarises the materials that have been produced, and an excellent teaching module is now available in the UK (English, 2006).

Loss for children and adolescents that has to be managed is not just about bereavement of relatives and friends, but about the death of pets, and the separation of parents or carers (see Chapter 11). Other loss situations include:

- a change of schools or neighbourhood
- migration to a new country
- loss of health through illness or accident
- loss of expectation, such as failing to make a team
- loss of self-esteem through rejection by a friend or a failure in school
- a break-up with a first girlfriend or boyfriend
- passage from one life stage to another (Rowling, 1996).

Bereavement Counselling

There are counselling agencies (such as Cruse Bereavement Care in the UK) that are dedicated to bereavement work with adults and youngsters. Short-term counselling may also be offered from hospice resources to particular family members who cannot cope, either before or in the aftermath of the decease of a loved one. Counselling in school is not intended to replace such provision but to supplement it, since many pupils feel a greater need to be strong in the family home than in school.

Counselling for the bereaved is demanding, and requires practitioners who can handle deep feelings and who have resolved their own bereavement issues (McGuiness, 1998). Bereavement counselling attends to the grief experience and the maladaptive behaviour resulting from a client's loss. Theoretically, it is directed towards the recognition of patterns or stages through which bereft individuals pass following a death, towards assisting clients to deal with grief and to develop adaptive responses (Parkes, 1986; Worden, 1984). The ground-breaking work of Kübler-Ross (1982) has formed the basis of bereavement work.

Farrell (1999) addresses the need to challenge an unconscious *denial of intrinsic human impermanence* that leaves the bereaved feeling powerless. The inability to accept human mortality is recognised by many counselling theorists (Ellis, 1987; Jacobs, 1993; Nelson-Jones, 1996).

Kübler-Ross (1982) suggested that practitioners must avoid dealing with bereavement and loss by *denial* if they wish to prevent their patients from doing the same. There is a fundamental need to confront the aftermath of death at any one or more of seven significant stages which the bereaved go through:

1. A sense of 'numbness'
2. Denial and isolation
3. Anger
4. Bargaining
5. Depression
6. Acceptance
7. A sense of hope (Kübler-Ross, 1982).

These stages are common but not watertight or predictable states occurring in a natural sequence. There is much overlap and some stages will hardly be discernible in some people. The timing and period of each stage is equally variable. Parkes (1986) questions the 'fixed stages of grief' model and thinks such stages are more fluid and fluctuating.

Loss necessitates the completion of a range of tasks from experiencing grief to reinvesting energy into former or different activities (Worden, 1984). Elmore (1986) felt the fixed stage model of loss applied as much to the experience of parental separation (see Chapter 11) as to bereavement, where children clearly react negatively (Longfellow, 1979).

Brief Individual Bereavement Counselling

Judging when a young person may require bereavement counselling is not easy, and some boys in western society are not 'permitted' to show grief publicly. This was the case with Jamail, a Year 7 African boy, whose father had drowned in a lake.

Distant Bereavement for Jamail

Jamail's father was drowned in his vehicle as it submerged beneath the water. Onlookers stared powerlessly as the roof disappeared from view. Jamail's mother had sufficient funds to take him to the African village for the funeral, yet he found the journey a harrowing experience. On returning to school a month later, his behaviour was sullen and withdrawn, indicating he was not coping. He spurned every offer of help, until a fight with his best friend prompted his pastoral support manager to bring him for counselling. This being an involuntary referral, Jamail sat downcast and refused to talk.

I used a diversionary tactic (Beck et al., 1979) and asked if he would kindly make a cup of tea and water the flowers, in order to withdraw him from a 'counselling-seated' pose where he was 'expected' to articulate his feelings. He was still at the stages of *numbness* and *anger* (Kübler-Ross, 1982), but in carrying out these little tasks he loosened up and began chatting about his father's interest in classic cars (a mutual interest sparked by pictures on my wall), which began to sow seeds of a workable relationship. I have on occasion taken pupils around the school to ease the tension of 'therapeutic-talk' expectations. This was not necessary for Jamail, however, since he began to speak through the 'scribble' technique.

The 'continuous line', or 'scribble' technique, has been used to positive effect with bereaved young people who struggle to communicate (Le Count, 2000). The technique involves clients drawing freehand with their non-dominant hand, with eyes closed, for 30 seconds, after which they are asked to identify with a little added detail two animals or human shapes within the line. It is hoped that images are thereby released from the unconscious to act as prompts for speaking about feelings. Feelings of anger are articulated through the drawing and verbalising of what is 'seen' and interpreted.

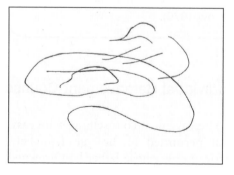 

Figure 10.1 Jamail's scribbles

From his scribble, Jamail drew a dove taking flight from a lake, signifying for him *his belief* that his dad had 'taken off' to heaven from still waters (Figure 10.1). The technique loosened his tongue to articulate ambivalent feelings when in Africa: his picturesque homeland now tainted by sad memories; his father's face 'at rest' compared with his handsome features in photos; his greeting back home contrasted with his reception in England.

Kirsty's Bereavement

Kirsty was excluded for regularly swearing at teachers. During the post-exclusion interview, her mother said that Kirsty was very angry after her grandmother's death. On an earlier occasion, she was offered bereavement counselling but she declined, saying, 'It upsets me too much, I can't handle it'. The loss of her grandmother took a heavy toll, not only on herself, but also on her mother. Kirsty was brought up by her grandmother, and before her death had frequently visited after school, since she lived only two doors away. After the funeral, she daily visited her grandfather and would fetch her mother if he was low.

The family routinely visited the grave where flowers were placed every Sunday morning. Since this was three years after the death, the family appeared 'stuck' and unable to move on. Family therapy was not available, but individual counselling was offered at her mother's request.

Kirsty was 'brought' to me by her mother to be 'cured', and initially she declined to speak, being at the *bargaining* stage – 'Give me back my grandmother and I'll cooperate!' (Kübler-Ross, 1982). An initial diversionary tactic from the loss event enabled us to begin to converse, however. Kirsty's grandmother had loved the music of Bryan Adams and kept a scrapbook of photos and magazine articles on him. I asked if she would mind bringing it to the second session.

She not only complied but also brought her grandmother's favourite track, which she played in session. The music, and particularly the lyrics, *Everything I do, I do it for you*, reduced her to tears, and I also felt a depth of sadness that touched me too. As I pondered the sentiments and imagined her sitting at her grandmother's bedside in those last dying days, in tears, and looking into her eyes, I again was touched deeply: *Look into my eyes* [and] *you will see what you mean to me … I'd die for you … Everything I do, I do it for you.*

This was the beginning of a therapeutic bonding that had healing potential, in that the song became the key to unlock feelings of loss. Time and again, she visited me during those six months after our four-session brief therapy contract to thank me for 'being with her during that difficult time'. The song became the link between us and we explored, through phrase after phrase, the hopes and wishes of her grandmother for Kirsty to have a fulfilled life in the strength of their relationship – without her in body but with her in spirit. Five years after working with Kirsty, I am still unable to hear that song without becoming 'connected' to the memory of Kirsty's sadness.

Carina's Sibling Bereavement

Carina was in Year 9 and was 'stuck'. In her case, a different integrative approach was used to get therapy moving towards goal-centred work. She had lost her brother Darren to leukaemia, and at her insistence his bedroom and belongings had not been touched since the day of his death.

She suffered from insomnia, and often cried herself to sleep just thinking about her brother. Past friends were cut off and she refused to go out. She had no motivation for school work as the future held no promise. She said that her depressive state was due to seeing her mother and grandmother broken in spirit and constantly tearful.

The counselling, therefore, apart from validating her sense of loss through a person-centred approach, was primarily focused upon setting goals to help her move on, to shape a future, to improve her sleeping pattern, and finally to consider how she might deal with the distress of her mother and grandmother.

Carina was keen to bring to my attention two paranormal events, which, although not frightening, were intriguing. She said that on many occasions her bedroom radio came on by itself and that the CD player, which rarely worked, had come on a couple of times. She was convinced that Darren had done this, and her mother claimed that she had seen Darren on a few occasions. Carina said that she had never seen him herself, but would have dearly loved to have done so.

I rarely give credence to paranormal experiences or rate them high on the therapeutic agenda, since these experiences right themselves and become integrated into the person's belief system once emotional and social healing has taken place. I have spoken elsewhere (Lines, 1999b) of the need for young people undergoing bereavement therapy to hold on to a belief system. It is important not to crush these beliefs, no matter how tentatively they are held, since they serve as cognitive support mechanisms to help deal with loss. Consequently, I make use of paranormal beliefs as metaphors of meaning (Lines, 2006a). I asked Carina what she thought Darren wanted of her, and this gave 'permission' for her to develop a future-centred perspective and sense of *hope* (Kübler-Ross, 1982).

We became solution-focused for three sessions. On electing not to remain 'stuck', we moved on towards an imagined future scenario. Her 'stuckness' was the *decision* to hold the hands of the clock still at the point at which Darren had died, as though time had become frozen. It seemed painful for her to live without Darren, and an approach which registered *that pain* within a goal-centred programme was required.

Such an approach has been constructed by Dunkley (2001), and represents the pain barrier diagrammatically in order to assess the state of 'being stuck' within movement towards a preferred scenario. The model in Figure 10.2 has four columns and brings together motivational interviewing (see Chapter 2), the Cycle of Change (see Chapter 13) and bereavement coping within the Egan three-stage framework (1990).

The diagram provides a self-explanatory task, and in Carina's situation it served to move her on more rapidly by 'seeing' in print the painful obstacles that she needed to overcome in order to reach her desired goal of *acceptance*. Like most goal-centred models, options are collaboratively constructed with no prescription, and the emphasis is on future orientation.

At A, Carina had registered progress and renewed optimism after the second session; she felt better after seeing her situation diagrammatically and after sharing her feelings in counselling. She reflected on the oscillating stage at B, the frustration of an intolerable present and a future that could only be enjoyed through passing the pain barrier, and she recognised her current scenario as being 'stuck'. The option to go back (C) or to remain in the pain zone (D) was unimaginable, but to push through the pain barrier (E) was felt by her to be the only viable course for a future of friendships, independence and autonomy. The line at B helps to replicate the meandering experience of actions driven by feelings, and the division of the pain barrier into 'beginning, middle and end' (D) creates the real experience of the process of overcoming resistance for long-term benefit, a process that is different for everyone. The diagram does not

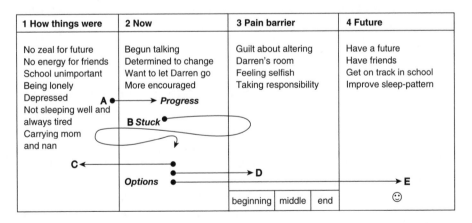

Figure 10.2 The pain barrier diagram

Source: This diagram format was first published in 'The pain barrier diagram' by Christine Dunkley, which appeared in the February 2001 issue of the journal *Counselling and Psychotherapy*, published by the British Association for Counselling and Psychotherapy. This diagram is reproduced with the kind permission of the author and publisher.

provide therapy, but, as Dunkley (2001) says, serves as a therapeutic tool. I have found the technique to be beneficial with young people.

Although meeting the goal in full was not achieved in the four pre-planned sessions, she had begun the process through the method of moving out some of Darren's belongings. To find energy for social integration, she needed to attend to a second goal, which was to address *insomnia*.

I asked her how often and for how long she lay awake before falling asleep. She said, 'most nights' and for up to 'three hours'. I asked her if she had pictures of Darren in her bedroom. She replied that she had, and that she had often looked at them before falling asleep. I said that I thought this was a positive thing to do, but that when looking at the picture she should recall the *good times* they had spent together rather than thinking about what was lost, to *celebrate his life* in place of over-mourning his decease. I asked her further to consider a sleep strategy different from the one she had been using.

Dennis: Rather than lying for hours trying to will yourself to sleep, try getting up and doing something different: remove your quilt, sit up or on the edge of your bed and read a page of a magazine, or listen to music on your iPod. Alternatively, you might find it helpful to go downstairs and make a drink. This often helps by taking your mind off negative thinking, and somehow helps your exhausted body to overcome your active mind and allow you to slip into sleep.

Frankl (1959: 127) calls such a technique a 'paradoxical intention', a process of replacing hypertension which prevents sleep with hypertension to stay awake. Carina found this helpful in giving energy to complete the remaining tasks, which later follow-up sessions confirmed were completed, including ceasing to take undue responsibility for family grief.

Brief Group Bereavement Counselling

Group bereavement counselling provides the opportunity for adolescents to confront their losses together with those who can experience the same, and to explore in a spirit of inquiry what might result from shared dialogue (Gergen and Kaye, 1992).

Four boys had received individual counselling before I decided to bring them together in three group sessions, the last being recorded without me being present. The group sessions were not the culmination but the mid-point of each client's programme. The goal was to 'normalise' the varied experiences of four bereaved boys through collaborative discourse, and this involved the task of bringing them together for a group session to assist in the healing process by finding answers to critical personal questions (Rowling, 1996).

Group Bereavement – James, Phillip, Matthew and Clint

James had received two sessions of person-centred counselling before engaging in group therapy, Phil five sessions and Matthew three. Clint had received five sessions of counselling – three person-centred in form and two of CBT.

James was in Year 9, aged 14, and, although he had self-referred for relationship difficulties, he had much to offer as a 'buddy figure'. Phil, Matthew and Clint were in Year 7 (aged 11–12) and were referred by pastoral teachers for behavioural reasons.

Phil was difficult to manage: he refused to come to school, threw tantrums in corridors, would be found sitting and crying on stairwells, and had often spurned teachers inappropriately with comments like, 'You don't care!', when they were trying to settle him.

Matthew refused bluntly to do PE, claiming that he should not be made to carry out physical exercise after having lost his mother. He wrote a note to his PE teacher during a non-activity lesson: 'My mum was a PE teacher and she's the only one to teach me PE.' He also wrote on his progress statement that he hated life and wished he were dead.

All the boys were emotionally scarred by their bereavements, and the development of each was held in check by their various losses.

Clint was the most articulate of the group. He was confrontational towards teachers at times, challenging when corrected, but was normally reduced to tears after the crisis was over. It was claimed that he was sometimes difficult to satisfy.

The sessions prior to group therapy involved the sharing of narratives, beliefs and measures of loss through the completion of loss diagrams. James' loss diagram shown in Figure 10.3 is presented as an example.

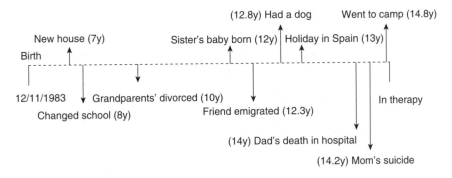

Figure 10.3   James' loss diagram

Loss diagrams are a powerful means of helping the bereaved to place their loss in a broad context of life experience. Naturally, this is not easy for adolescents and young children. Clients are asked to draw a line representing their lifespan from birth to present. Each of the clients has to draw bisecting lines at time intervals upward and downward to represent a life event which they would regard as a gain or loss – bereavement, separation of parents, move of house, births of siblings, and so on. The length of bisections (say, from 1–10 mm) is the measure of how an episode has affected the individual – it represents the degree of gain or loss. In this way, bereaved clients are encouraged to develop a perspective of *relative* gain and loss. In some instances, losses can be *re-viewed* as gains in the sense of growing independence, or the end of family violence.

Narratives of Bereavement

The discourse begins with accounts of each participant's bereavement, and then moves on to present fascinating records of how each individual was making sense of his loss in accordance with his current *belief system* and cognitive ability. Finally, and curiously, the discourse closes on a spiritual theme of a speculative post-death existence, a theme I have discussed elsewhere (Lines, 1999b, 2006b).

It was evident how James took up the leading role in the interview throughout. He assumed this for himself, possibly because he was senior. James lost both parents quite recently, while Matthew's mother had died seven years previous to therapy. The group was content for James to lead the discussion and to take responsibility for the interview. He became the 'expert', though at times he found it difficult:

James: I lost my parents last year. I lost my dad first after he went into hospital with stomach ulcers and it caused a disease that destroyed his liver and kidneys. Several weeks later my mum died of an accidental overdose on paracetamol: my dad died in February, my mum died in April ... You never get over it but you learn to carry on.

Phil: I lost my brother about two years ago. He died of a heart problem, 'cause I was in junior school, and my mum's friends came and told me that my brother died in the afternoon. I started crying and I went home and saw my family crying. I didn't want to sleep upstairs at bedtime, 'cause we were scared just in case we saw a ghost of him.

Clint: I lost my dad not so long ago when we broke up for two weeks. I was told on the day we broke up that he'd died. He was actually in hospital at the time, and he died of a blood clot on his lung. Even though on the day he died he was diagnosed as having cancer, he died of a different thing. We had, sort of had ... good times when he was alive. [Voice breaks up, chokingly] Seems a bit boring [he breaks down] ... now that he's dead. I sometimes come to see Mr Lines. And, sometimes, I talk to my mum and stuff.

Matthew: I lost my mother in 1992 ... She died of a heart problem ... Well, every time I try and talk to my dad about it he starts being upset as well.

Each participant gave a much fuller account when the second opportunity presented itself. In spite of competitive interjections and interruptions, each appeared very keen to hold the floor and amplify his narrative on loss. It seemed to be cathartic to tell the story, and tell it fully. The discourses of two respondents illustrate the two extremes of coping.

While James' introduction is comprehensive, his second account of a further 27 words is more elaborate, and is a poignant development that bears more than a hint of guilt – 'in a way I still blame myself because she called out to me at 6 o'clock in the morning but I was groggy and I didn't know what was wrong with her … I was half-asleep. So I went back to sleep'. His third account is more than doubled in length (252 words), and contains an amusing anecdote – 'at first the doctor said part of the next 12 hours was crucial … They said, "He's got about 12 hours to live". He had to be awkward, he lasted 18' (*the group laugh*).

Matthew's second account is treble the length of the first, and covers how he found his mother in the morning – 'I went upstairs to say "good morning" to my mum and when I opened the door of the bedroom I saw everyone crying. I walked over to my mum's side and saw her lying face down on the floor'.

Our selected method involved asking the respondents to prepare questions to ask of the others prior to the recorded session, and though I had not seen them, it was not difficult to guess what they were after studying the transcript. The questions were significant and marked new themes in the discourse.

- James repeatedly asked, 'How do you think you're coping?'
- Matthew asked, 'What things do you have in common with your parents?'
- Phil asked, 'Where do you reckon heaven is?'
- Clint asked, 'Do you think it was, like, better … to find out when you were at home with all your family [than at school with friends] …?'

Clint's question was more tentative; he needed a means of coming to terms with the shock announcement *at school* that his father had died – Phil infers he was also told at school.

The session allowed each participant in turn to explore the answers of the group to their most pressing questions, which in itself was a window of the stage they had each reached (Kübler-Ross, 1982), and which arguably was assisting in the healing process. From pre-planned questions, therefore, the group used the session to resolve individual dilemmas:

- James: to know how better to cope
- Matthew: to press for identity with his mother, since this was the only thing he had left
- Phil: to explore where his brother might be now, and
- Clint: to assess whether school was the best place in which to hear his father had died.

Group therapy provided an opportunity to voice concerns in search for answers as part of the *acceptance* process. There was evidence, then, that such an approach facilitated a confrontation of each pupil's loss at a significant point in healing, but can such novices in experience handle the deeper feelings that bereavement inevitably brings out?

Empathy and Handling Deep Feelings

There were indicators of varying degrees of *acceptance* of what had happened, particularly the use of stark terminology, such as the term 'dead' to replace the introduced term 'lost'. James took the lead and gave the group the clause 'I lost my ...', which each respondent borrowed. The term 'lost' was first replaced by the term 'died' by James ('My mum died'), then was repeated by each respondent in turn – Phil: 'He died'; Clint: 'He died', 'He's dead'; Matthew: 'She died'. Death and dying did not imply non-existence, however (Lines, 1999b).

There was evidence that James was carrying guilt over his mother's call for help and his lack of response – 'And in a way I still blame myself because she called out to me ...' – which he later contradicted – 'You should never blame someone, especially yourself, 'cause it's no one's fault'. This was entirely consistent with his philosophy of 'You never get over it', but you 'learn to carry on'.

Rationalising Loss

James felt he should provide all the answers. Like a mini-philosopher (Parkes, 1986), he had discovered patterns in each of their experiences:

> *James:* So, there is a connection between you two. His mother died with a heart problem and your brother died with a heart problem ... The thing we all have in common is we all carried on; we don't loaf around. I think you get some people who just loaf around after death [mimicking, altered voice] 'Oh that's so unfair. Why did they have to take him?'

Although this was an assumption made by James, prompted by a need to find commonality in their varied experiences, it was of much assistance to Matthew and Clint in restructuring their thinking and behaviour to face loss and to get on with the business of living. James offered a pragmatic explanation for death:

> *James:* My dad always said to me 'When it's time to die it's time to die'. You can't stop it. So I just think, well, that's it, they're gone, can't do anything to change it. And they wouldn't want me moping around for the rest of my life. So I try and do the best I can, not just for me but for them as well.

He had an answer for everything, offering sound practical advice: 'I work hard. Enjoy life while you can. Any chances you get grab them 'cause you won't get a second one.' He felt that he should take bullying on the chin and not blame others for insensitivity and mockery, since, 'The good times will always run over the bad'. One should be content with few material possessions – he only wanted a bag for Christmas.

There was little evidence of any respondent feeling for the pain of the others, then, but the emphasis, as dictated by James, was not upon 'feeling' but upon 'saving' group members by giving advice on how to cope: 'It's no good grieving', 'Moping around is not going to help', 'Work hard …', and so on.

Phil was quite egocentric (as they all were at their transitional stage). He showed more than a passing interest in astronomy in a forlorn hope that he might see his brother in some distant star or something – he did not specify. He described the effects of his loss as, first, being scared at night in case he saw his brother's ghost and, second, having a sense of *numbness*: 'I felt I was dreaming.' His primary interest, however, was in seeing his brother again: 'Er, James, where do you reckon heaven is?'

It was interesting to see how concise and direct Matthew's deliberations were once prompted. Seven years had separated the interview from the bereavement event, but for Matthew it was as if it were yesterday. His diversionary tactic to manage was to focus on a 'sad son/deceased mother' identity assurance:

> Mat.   To my mum, I've got the same colour eyes, the same colour hair, the same hearing problem [*James and others laugh*] and the same heart problem.

Coping Strategies

Most of the coping strategies were philosophical in directing thoughts towards attitudes and beliefs that were accepting and getting on with the business of living. No one (James included) was able to resolve Clint's lethargy – 'It's [*life's*] a bit boring now that he's dead' – but, nevertheless, he could still offer some practical coping strategies. These involved:

- *voluntary counselling* – 'I sometimes come to see Mr Lines …'
- *talking* – 'I talk to my mum …'
- *looking at photos to remember the good times* – 'I look at photos, I think that helps …'
- *crying*.

> James: Crying forever, moping around is not going to help.
> Clint.   It's not like that for me though. It's, like, one day I can be fine, but then the next day something could happen.

Matthew was the most reserved and offered little in terms of support for the others. It was evident how current conditions were more influential in fuelling his nihilistic attitude towards life and his resistance to do PE. This was evident in the interview when he indicated that his father was not coping and was unable to talk about his mother's death: 'Every time I try and talk to my dad about it he starts being upset.' Matthew was thereby having to parent his father (and younger siblings – picking them up after school, cooking their teas) when, perhaps, what he yearned for psychologically was to be cuddled and nurtured by a mother who had been snatched away.

Although the boys had not the resources to handle each other's bereavement feelings in depth, their coping strategies and basic pragmatism appeared mutually effective for the giver and the given. In spite of little empathy on the part of each of the boys, there was evidence in follow-up individual counselling that the process of narrative sharing and the phenomenological sense of group 'connectedness' had fostered a deeper level of 'feeling for others outside of the self' than was evident before (Rowling, 1996).

The Outcome of the Group Session

The four boys illustrated different degrees of *numbness, denial, anger* and *depression* as they struggled to accept and cope with their losses (Kübler-Ross, 1982). Clint carried the most overt *anger* (targeted against his mother for telling him at school) and slight *depression* (moving towards *acceptance*), while Matthew appeared to direct his *anger* inwardly and towards his PE teacher who served as a displacement. With Phil, there was marginal evidence of *numbness* and *denial*. He oscillated between these and *anger*, but was a long way from *acceptance* – and still dreaming (Parkes, 1986). James, on the surface, was accepting but was also *angry* (though not depressed); at one brief moment, there was catharsis as he vented his *anger* over divine injustice, but generally he maintained a stoic demeanour that appeared to be detached from true feeling. Their *hope* lay in literal conceptions of a post-death continuance (Lines, 1999b):

- Phil: 'If I look through the telescope I'm going to see my brother.'
- James: '[the dead] sort of float around watching over us, a bit like angels but not with those stupid wings.'
- Clint: 'I think he [my dad] is where he wanted to be … in a dream place.'

Three of the boys continued in brief individual counselling after this session and focused on many of the themes on the tape. James worked on issues of guilt. His older sister parented him and his peer relations improved. He accepted an invitation to go on a camp that had been organised by an outside agency voluntary care group.

Matthew was bitter over his loss and had suffered long-overdue effects, as demonstrated through his anger and resistance to do PE. In this respect, James' stoic advice proved helpful – in fact, he took up PE voluntarily after this interview.

Clint had a few brushes with peers, but became more conciliatory towards teachers managing him. He left for a grammar school at the close of Year 8, but not before coming to the counselling room to shake my hand in gratitude for all the support he felt he had received.

Phil attempted to break free of his mother's constraints by wandering from home to play. His mother had another baby. The family accepted family therapy with the aim of establishing some emotional space in the 'mother–son enmeshed' relationship, and to help his mother see the tenuous connection of loss and risk of further loss through Phil dying in the same manner as his brother had done, a neurosis hindering Phil from growing up. Having built stronger friendships with peers, Phil became more content in himself and better able to *accept* his loss and face the future. He also shared more sensitive material later in individual work, including that his father had committed suicide when Phil was only a baby.

Client Self-evaluation

Each of the boys was asked to speak on the benefits of the group session and to say whether it had helped:

- James: 'I felt less isolated, as though I was not the only person who had gone through losing my parents.'
- Clint: 'I found it helpful, yea.'
- Phil: 'It was OK. I wasn't the only one going through it.'
- Matthew [smiling]: 'Yea, it was good … You've got to get on with life.'

Matthew was much more outspoken in following sessions of individual work and revealed information not previously disclosed, including that his mother had taken her life (a heart problem was his earlier account, perhaps influenced by Phil), and that the family had (deliberately) never been away – his mother died just after a family holiday. Matthew came again for counselling (see Chapter 7) to help build better peer relations and to learn 'to be happy' (Nelson-Jones, 1996).

Conclusion

Evidence presented in this and the following chapter highlights the serious effects of death and loss for pre-pubescent and adolescent young people. Many teenagers are ill-prepared for an event like death that shatters their sense of permanence and security, and there is a call for the subject to be covered more adequately in the curriculum.

Bereavement counselling draws on the reserves of the therapist; it is heavy work that may have implications for practitioners and put them in touch with their own personal experience of bereavement, hence the importance of supervision. Schools may, at times, have to manage the death of a pupil or teacher, or a collective tragedy occurring on a school trip, and this will undoubtedly affect the whole school and draw on the therapist to carry the community through.

This chapter has acknowledged the appropriateness of conventional approaches of therapy to support youngsters in school, but has also considered brief integrative styles that utilise a range of interventions, such as 'the scribble' technique and 'the pain barrier diagram', for those clients who have become stuck. A more extensive study of a pre-recorded session of four boys undergoing bereavement therapy concluded the chapter, and illustrated how a collaborative sharing of each other's narratives helped in some way to normalise their experience within their own individual belief systems and cognitive abilities.

Reflective Exercise

1. A family having many relatives in school suffered two bereavements within a month – one, an older brother killed on a motorcycle, the other, an uncle who had had an unexpected heart attack. What would you consider to be the effects for a teenager who had had *secure attachments* in early life of multiple losses in such a brief time?

2. Suppose you had groups of three or four pupils arriving at your door for counselling because their friend had been killed in a car crash. Since each requires permission for absence from lessons, would you manage this by offering group therapy or individual sessions later on by pre-planned appointments? Give reasons for your answer.

3. Suppose you had been telephoned by the headteacher one evening informing you that there had been a minibus tragedy over the weekend, where nine pupils had been killed, and that you should prepare yourself for a high number of pupils arriving at your door, traumatised. How would you manage such large numbers of pupils coming in the next day?

4. What particular approaches and techniques have you found the most effective in dealing with teenagers who have been bereaved of family loved ones or friends?

   a. What particular elements of your chosen model do you think best suit bereavement for adolescents?

   b. What particular techniques and interventions illustrated above would you consider utilising in your own work?

5. Examine critically the various discourses of the four boys engaged in group bereavement therapy presented above. What are your views on the conclusions drawn as a result of putting these boys together in one recorded session?

6. Suppose a client in Year 11 (aged 16), whom you had previously engaged in bereavement therapy a year ago when her father died, approached you, appearing quite relieved, and told you that she had visited a spiritualist medium who had shared with her information about the deceased she 'could never have known'. She tells you the medium said that her father was now at rest, but that her sister would soon lose her job and her mother would have a breakdown.

   a. How would you engage this client now in therapy?

   b. What place might religious beliefs or views of paranormal activity have in your work?

   c. Should your own views on such matters be shared in counselling or be brought to supervision?

Key Points

- Cultural groups have different ways of understanding and coping with death, but in western industrialised countries, where there has been a gradual erosion of religion, there has tended to be a denial and sanitisation of death and dying.

- There are indications that youngsters require death and dying to be covered in the curriculum, following Australian research, so as to better prepare them for future loss.

- Bereavement of a loved one will have serious social, emotional and behavioural effects on pre-pubescent and adolescent young people, and a feeling to be 'strong' in the family may cause some to break down in class.

- For refugee and asylum-seeking young people, this may mean not only a personal loss of a family member back home, but the loss of culture and of an opportunity to deal with death through familiar ceremony and ritual.

- Under psychodynamic interpretations of development, the death of a parent is not merely the loss of a youngster's nurturing and economic support but the removal of a psychological means of moving towards autonomy and independence.

- Conventional psychodynamic, person-centred and existential approaches have proved effective when dealing with loss, but brief styles that utilise therapeutic tools like the 'scribble' technique, recollection objects of the deceased, 'the pain barrier diagram' and loss diagrams, can open communication channels in individual work.

- Conventional bereavement therapy assists clients variously at one or other of the stages of mourning – the sense of feeling *numb,* of being in *denial* and *isolated,* of becoming *angry,* of wishing to *bargain,* of becoming *depressed,* towards an eventual *acceptance* and a development of *hope* for the future.

- 'Buddy' figures can offer support for bereaved youngsters, and group therapy can be a powerful means of helping isolated pupils to 'normalise' their experience through shared narratives, even though participants are not likely to have the capacity to manage deeply expressed feelings.

11 Parental Separation and Step-parent Conflict

> This chapter covers:
>
> - Research on parental separation
> - Managing parental separation
> - Counselling teenagers facing parental separation
> - Counselling after separation
> - Counselling students in conflict with step-parents

Introduction

Many youngsters experiencing parental separation come forward for counselling, for this can be an anxious time. In this chapter, I use the term 'parental' separation instead of 'divorce' in order to be inclusive, and I view young persons' adult monitors and providers as their 'parents', rather than 'carers', for this is how youngsters generally see them even if they do not address them as 'mum' or 'dad'. I thereby imply no detriment to carers who, in many instances, may be a better parent to the child than their biological parent has been.

So common is the single-mother family in some areas of the UK that the traditional 'nuclear family' is becoming the norm only for those of ethnic communities. In fact, as many of my white clients of non-professional families come forward for counselling appointments, only half of them live at home with both biological parents, and nearly one third are brought up by a single mother (see Appendix I).

After recording the statistics of family make-up within the UK, the chapter outlines brief integrative approaches that can be applied to three groups of young people: those experiencing trauma at the beginning of parental separation; those suffering loss of self-esteem after parental separation; and those experiencing conflict with a step-parent. The first group needs support in facing the consequential tensions arising at home, and the other two experience readjustment difficulties when a parent leaves the family home.

Research on Parental Separation

The Marriage Guidance Council was established in 1938 in response to the meteoric rise in divorce rates. It was renamed *Relate* and operated as a mediation counselling agency in London. *Relate* served over 8000 couples in 1983–88, but in the jubilee year of the organisation numbers increased to nearly a quarter of a million (Litvinoff, 1991).

Many modern marriages and partnerships are entered into with the belief that they can be terminated if they fail. Change in family structure results from the liberalisation of public attitude over parental separation, the effects of feminists challenging traditional gender roles, and social and political factors. In many modern households, the male is taking over child-rearing duties quite ably.

Cohabitation, as a preferred 'family' model, may result in instability for those children who have experienced repeated changes and a diminishing network of support, but can be beneficial for those who formerly experienced domestic violence (Smith, 1999). Violence can exist within families, both before parental separation and during post-separation contact (Wolfe et al., 1986). Concentration is affected by anxiety and feelings of low self-worth, by living in a hostile atmosphere, and by being exposed to adults who continually cheat and lie to one another (Smith, 1999). Parental modelling of dishonesty undermines a child's sense of truth.

Statistics on Parental Breakdown in the UK

The 'nuclear family' is no longer the norm in some communities (Pechereck, 1996). At the turn of the millennium, there were as many as 900,000 step-families living in the UK (Webb, 1994) and 200,000 children living with only one biological parent (Holland, 2000). The provisional number of marriages registered in England and Wales in 2008 was the lowest since 1895: around 37 per cent of all marriages were remarriages for one or both parties, but this was a drop of 4 per cent from 1998. Since 1992, there have been more civil ceremonies in England and Wales than religious ceremonies, accounting in 2008 for 67 per cent of all ceremonies (OfNS, 2008a).

The number of dependent children living with cohabiting couples and lone parents both increased by 0.6 and 0.1 million respectively between 1998 and 2008. The proportion of dependent children living with cohabiting couples rose from 8 to 13 per cent, and the proportion of dependent children living in lone-parent families rose from 22 to 23 per cent (OfNS, 2008b). Asians are least likely to live in lone-parent households. Only 10 per cent of Indian households and 13 per cent of both Pakistani and Bangladeshi households with dependent children contained a lone parent in 2008. In contrast, around half of Black Caribbean (48 per cent) and Other Black (52 per cent) households with dependent children were headed by a lone parent. The percentage for the White British group was 22 per cent. Just one fifth (19 per cent) of Black Caribbean households contained a married couple, which was the lowest proportion of any ethnic group. Asian households were also the least likely to contain a cohabiting couple (OfNS, 2008c).

> Of those children calling ChildLine from April 2008 to March 2009 to express a 'concern' about parental drugs and alcohol misuse, the 'main problem' was identified as 'physical abuse' within the family (35 per cent), followed by 'family relationship problems' (20 per cent), then by 'sexual abuse' (10 per cent) and 'neglect' (4 per cent) within the family – 6 per cent reported being lonely (NSPCC, 2010).

Social and Cultural Factors Affecting Family Relationships

In 2008, 68 per cent of women in the UK with dependent children were reported to be working mothers, a rise of 20 per cent within the last 50 years (OfNS, 2008d). Women are increasingly attaining high professional qualifications and many are seeking more in their lives than motherhood.

It is not uncommon for unions to break down while the woman is pregnant, or during the early months of an infant's life, for these periods test relationships to a considerable degree (Smith, 1999). Increased teenage pregnancy is a cause for concern in the UK, not least because unprepared young parents are commonly living in inadequate conditions for child rearing.

When couples 'fall out of love', or become 'sexually incompatible', there is no longer a social stigma in putting their own wants and life fulfilment above the ethic of 'staying together for the sake of the children' (Litvinoff, 1991). The industrial shift from manual work has left many men confused over their masculinity, and fathers may experience a dilemma when dealing with family conflict in ways that are largely out of step with modern societal attitudes.

The subtle erosion of religious principles that underpin marriage vows has lessened feelings of guilt when couples choose to part against the wishes of their children, and for some ethnic groups who hold traditional religious or cultural beliefs about arranged marriages and non-permissible divorce there are added tensions when their teenage children adopt contrary views to their own, unions which are permitted in British law – such as cohabiting, gay and lesbian relationships and civil partnerships. Conversely, children of devoutly religious families may suffer community rejection if their parents split up.

The Effects of Parental Splits

Research has been carried out to compare the common features of bereaved youngsters in school (see Chapter 10) with those whose parents have separated, and has linked loss experience with a range of physiological disorders, emotional vulnerability and behavioural disturbance, with delinquency and anti-social behaviour, with clinging, neuroticism, childhood depression and psychiatric disturbance (Holland, 2000).

Although children under 5 are thought to be especially vulnerable to family change (Dominian et al., 1991; Elliot and Richards, 1991), adolescents are similarly a high-risk group, particularly those experiencing a second separation of parents or step-parents. Young children may respond by 'freezing emotionally' and will regress, but adolescents (especially girls) are likely to become depressed and lose enthusiasm for living (Smith, 1999).

There is evidence that children involved in parental conflict may not do as well as they could at school (Smith, 1999). School refusal, disruptive behaviour and learning problems have been associated with parental separation (Holland, 2000).

The Effects of Domestic Violence

The prevalence of domestic violence is a cause of parental separation (Lines, 2008), since women are, these days, less likely to stay in relationships with abusive partners. It is alleged that those who grow up in violent families may become violent adults (see Chapter 9) or, conversely, victims of violence, through life and may go on to abuse their own children. Since the research for this later finding is based upon what adults remember of their childhood, it cannot wholly be reliable (Smith, 1999).

In the UK, the Department of Health annually receives around 120 notifications of child deaths caused by physical assaults by parents or step-parents. A large proportion of these are fathers or stepfathers with an earlier history of violence towards female partners as well as children (Smith, 1999). One third of children who call ChildLine about alcohol-related family conflict say the 'main problem' is to do with physical assault (NSPCC, 2010).

A review of research suggests that 40–60 per cent of children are physically abused in families where there has been violence against women partners (Smith, 1999), and ChildLine confirms these figures. Nearly all children in one North American study could give details of violence from one parent (Smith, 1999). Since children are adept at 'crying silently', the level of abuse is not always detected.

Evidence is inconclusive, however, in correlating violent upbringing and parental separation with violent behaviour in adulthood. Canadian research found that about one-quarter of children raised in an atmosphere of domestic violence were unaffected, and further that two-thirds of the boys and four-fifths of the girls functioned within 'normal' limits (Wolfe et al., 1985).

Researchers find that the recovery rates for all children are high if violence ceases and if support is promptly available – hence, the importance of counselling in school.

Managing Parental Separation

Society expects divorce and separation to have terrible consequences for children (Humphreys and Stanley, 2006), but this assumption is rarely tested. One study, which listened to young people themselves, concluded that, in spite of initial trauma, children can feel secure and settled in time if separation is managed well (Smith, 1999).

Lewis (1992) found that many children find in school a safe haven from parental conflict and separation, with teachers generally being more able to support them with this than with bereavement. Raphael (1984) suggested that bereaved pupils and those suffering parental separation were able, as Holland (2000) says, to 'mark time' until the teacher was free to attend to their distress. Loss is only problematic 'when it overwhelms the individual' (Holland, 2000).

It is an open question whether boys suffer more significantly from parental separation than girls, since the research is contradictory (Smith, 1999). According to ChildLine, boys who live with depressed fathers who drink a lot have greater difficulty in coping with the situation than boys living with their mothers. In answering the question of what makes for a good parental separation, Smith (1999), writing from a mother-centred perspective, outlines three factors:

1. Children need to see their father and have his support, approval and loving care – to feel very special. This means not just seeing him, but experiencing genuine interest and encouragement in place of unsympathetic discipline.

2. Children want their mother to get back to some form of normality after separation, to be warm towards them and respecting of their feelings for their father.

3. Children want to be told things, and have information honestly shared with them. They do not like having to keep secrets and want to cease being the go-between in parental feuds. Parents need to be honest and open, and know that children can handle deep feelings. Perhaps information about infidelity should be kept from children, but, in other respects, lying to children is not helpful and continual lying by both parents models poor behaviour.

At the time of separation, all children without exception want hostility to end, but there does not appear to be any direct relationship between parental separation per se and the child's subsequent well-being (Rodgers and Pryor, 1998). Entering new family compositions where step-parents become involved may be another matter.

Counselling Teenagers Facing Parental Separation

When counselling teenagers in school who have been traumatised by changes in the family, the work may have an effect upon the therapist who, consciously or unconsciously, will see parallels or connections with their own loss experience. In such circumstances, it is taken as read that if the engagement involves issues of counter-transference then this must be taken up in supervision.

A second point that may have an effect upon the therapist relates to the politics of the altering composition of family life in the UK. As noted earlier, the rise in feminism, the altering nature of cohabitation and the economical landscape of Britain, have resulted in a situation where many women may have to combine the dual role of mothering and working to earn a living, resulting in men sometimes having to take on non-traditional family roles and some mothers not having as much time for their children as would have been formerly the case. In what follows, these professional and political issues are side-stepped in favour of the therapist exercising the core condition of *unconditional positive regard*. The case examples show how brief pluralistic therapy can support victims of family change.

Research cited above indicated that parental separation may not be injurious to the child or teenager if managed well, but for those who experience their base of support shifting, brief counselling in school may have a crucial role in aiding their adjustment.

Parental Separation for Angela

Angela, aged 14 years, came for counselling initially over theft of school property from a stockroom. Her pastoral manager referred her because he wondered whether or not she was caught up in a criminal fraternity. An early analysis, however, established that this was not the case and that the theft was a one-off event from which she had learned her lesson. Later, Angela approached me about another matter since she had found the earlier experience of counselling helpful. She was worried that her parents were not getting on and that a split was imminent.

There were frequent arguments each evening, and one fight in which her father had hit her mother with a kitchen pan. This resulted in him leaving home to live with his parents. The last occasion her father stayed away was for over a month. Finances, rather than extra-marital relationships, were regarded as the source of conflict, but they no longer loved one another and had slept in separate beds.

Angela was very close to her mother, who had confided in her that she had not really loved her husband for over a year. Angela's father had had his own business, which meant that the parental split would have economic consequences. Unable to continue mortgage payments, Angela's mother felt she would have to sell the house even though her husband had agreed that she should stay with the children in the family home.

Counselling for Angela consisted of supporting her for a future that looked bleak, and over altered family conditions that would bring hardship. Her request for counselling followed a discussion in the home the previous night in which both parents called the children together to tell them of their plan to separate. Each of the children could choose with whom they would like to live. Both parents were keen to maintain frequent contact.

Nelson-Jones (1996) speaks of clients being able to *predict and create their own futures* with effective thinking skills and a sense of optimism: 'You have no facts about the future since it has not happened' (1996: 113). One way of looking at the future, he says, is to view it as a 'mental construction based on your subjective as contrasted with objective reality. It is the words and pictures in your head about what is to come' (1996: 113).

After a short session of facilitating her feelings of loss and disappointment around imagining an unpromising future, Angela found the means of contemplating an altered world more optimistically with effective thinking skills. Pupils in school facing the prospect of their parents' separating often have a pessimistic view of the outcome, and this has to be handled sensitively.

But predictions of the future often contain perceptual distortions. Clients who have experienced parental separation, although suffering trauma at the time, often view the separation as a positive and more beneficial outcome in the longer term, but for those at the beginning of this process and without the benefit of hindsight this can be a very daunting prospect – not too dissimilar to bereavement, as research above has shown. Clients will often underestimate the good and overestimate the bad consequences of their parents ceasing to live together.

Obviously, fear of change is unsettling and young clients need to feel supported during this delicate phase. The fear of failure also weighs heavily and often has an effect on peer relationships. Clients often *catastrophise* their situations and make absolutist demands on themselves (Ellis, 1994). Pupils also *misattribute* (Nelson-Jones, 1996) the cause of the split to their own behaviour, and increase thereby the tendency for self-fulfilled prophecies. Since they cannot change their behaviour overnight, they *must be responsible for their parents continuing to fight*, and such reasoning shifts blame and makes splitting up 'legitimised'.

Scaling can be a useful method of assisting a client to weigh up the advantages and disadvantages of their parents parting, and this technique was used to help Angela see that all was not lost with her parents choosing to separate. 'Can you scale from 1–10 (high number to represent gains) the advantages in terms of a reduction in hostility, shouting, mistrust and violence that would result when your parents part? Can you similarly scale the disadvantages?' Her scores and reflections are illustrated in Figure 11.1.

Advantages	Disadvantages
8 – No shouting, no fighting, no mistrust	Not much money coming in – 7
6 – I can concentrate on school	Mom or dad may get lonely – 5
4 – I can bring friends back to an argument-free household	Friends ask embarrassing questions – 4
18 – In total	In total – 16

Figure 11.1   Scale chart

From her imagined predictions, Angela was encouraged to conduct *reality testing* on whether the future would be as catastrophic as she had imagined once her parents had parted. Nelson-Jones (1996) suggests four stages in setting personal goals for reality testing:

- authorship of your life
- clarity of focus
- increased meaning
- increased motivation.

Claiming *authorship of your life* meant, for Angela, that her future prospects were not wholly dependent on her parents' happiness, and that energy spent in fruitless longing was distracting her from personal goals. *Increased motivation* derives from *increased meaning* and *clear goals from clarity of focus*, and this became the focal point of therapy.

Through the 'miracle question' (de Shazer, 1988), Angela was encouraged to imagine awaking one morning with the world being very different (Lines, 2000). Her parents were no longer together; she lived with her mother and visited her father at weekends. What would the world look like? As she began to speculate more positively, she began to realise that her social world as a teenager of 14 would not alter that much. Yes, there would be an initial sense of lost-ness, and less money for designer-label clothes and for going out. But, then, her visits to her father over the weekends might present other social opportunities and, possibly, pocket money to continue her pursuits with different friends.

We needed in the final stages of therapy to set a goal to help her think positively about *accepting* what had happened, and to operate in a *doing* rather than a *being* mode. Adolescents speak the language of activity, and this can give impetus and an optimistic outlook in 'reality testing'. Through brainstorming, we explored a range of tasks within a pluralistic process of Egan's framework of preferred scenario:

1   To spend more time out of the house with friends.
2   To behave neutrally over her parents' decision and be mature in accepting that this was 'their choice'.
3   To voice her disgust and protest about how her parents' future plans had left her feeling terribly disheartened.

Task 1 was selected, with task 2 being a secondary and subsidiary task. This gave her not only a more settled feeling about her parents splitting up, but also a clearer understanding of adult responsible decision making and a more realistic perspective that the outcome – with two parents apart – would not be the end of the world.

Counselling after Separation

Children in individual counselling for parental separation are not to be seen as patients in need of in-depth therapy, but as clients in need of short-term support.

Managing Parental Separation for Luke

Luke, aged 14 years, was referred for counselling because of challenging behaviour. He was disruptive in lessons, attention-seeking and easily angered when peers provoked him. His teacher was particularly skilled in observing misbehaviour that was not simply wilful nonconformity. While Mitchell, Luke's older brother, had left the family home to live with his grandmother, Luke and his young sister (known as 'Princess') had been left to cope in an unsettled home with two parents with severe alcohol dependence. This continued for a year until their aunt took over their care and allowed access for both children to see their parents (who by now were separated) on a weekly basis.

During the introductory counselling session, Luke said that although Mitchell was valued by his grandmother and Princess was dad's favourite, he didn't feel close to anyone. Luke was keen to receive counselling, for there were unresolved issues in his relationship with his father. He knew he could never compete with Princess, but, nevertheless, his father was still special. A recent crisis, however, brought matters to a head.

He had gone along with his brother to a Premier League football match, where his father sold football programmes. He considered himself fortunate to receive a free ticket from one of his brother's friends, since Mitchell regularly attended the matches. After the game, the family went to the pub. While drinking lemonade, his sister slipped from a stool and accused Luke of messing about. By this time, Luke's father was 'merry' with drink, and though he was not drunk he began to remonstrate with Luke after Princess had accused him of pushing her off the stool. Dad shouted aggressively, told him to 'fuck off' and, when Luke protested and stormed off to the toilet, his father followed.

Fortunately, the men in the group, being aware of the volatility of Luke's father, followed him into the toilet. Luke's father had attacked Luke, punched him in the ribs and kicked him while on the floor – it took three of them to pull him off. Apart from suffering bruises, Luke was traumatised by the assault and vowed never to see his father again. Luke's grandfather admonished his son and social services were contacted to monitor the situation temporarily. Under child protection regulations, a Child Protection (CP) Care Plan was drawn up. Therapy occurred after CP procedures had ceased and social services had closed the file.

For children who are still traumatised by family violence, person-centred counselling is often indicated, and where children have been separated from parents and are mildly depressed, humanistic counselling and short-term psychodynamic therapy have often proven beneficial (Cooper, 2008; Leichsenring, 2001; Lines, 2000). These approaches can be time-consuming, however. The advantage of brief cognitive-humanistic therapy is that there is within the approach the useful integration of humanistic counselling, aimed primarily at validating a client's feelings of loss and sense of being let down, with cognitive styles (research validated for anxiety: Cooper, 2008) that combine thinking skills with time-limited problem solution.

Nelson-Jones speaks of 'mind skills', and of the ability to think about resolution through open choices in solving personal dilemmas (Nelson-Jones, 1996).

Our collaboratively discussed goal was to repair his relationship with his father. The humanistic element of counselling tasks was centred upon Luke's ambivalent feelings for his father, combined with the practical consideration of how he might deal with visits to stay with him over future weekends. This was particularly important after Luke's father had apologised and was beginning to speak with him by phone.

After person-centred counselling, Luke was asked how he saw the future. In session, he brought up three issues. One was whether he could ever trust his father again after the pub incident: Luke said that he was not afraid of him being drunk, that he had learnt to cope with that many times before, but that the assault had left him very upset. It added to his sense of loss that his mother, who was in a new relationship, was (according to rumour) currently pregnant. The third issue was that, unlike Mitchell and Princess, Luke had no parent with whom to *attach* and *model* himself for future adulthood. These three issues were written down to form our tasks:

1   How could I deal with the possible risks of dad's aggression when drunk on future weekend stays?
2   What does it mean to me that my mother is pregnant by another man, that she wants a 'replacement child' to me and my sister?
3   What does it mean to me that I no longer live with either mum or dad?

In the next session, I asked Luke what he could remember that stood out from our previous meeting. It was a combination of the second and third issues. Luke clearly had a good relationship with his auntie, but he could not resolve his sense of loss of both parents through alcohol misuse, a loss that was reinforced by the assault and by the fact that his mother was going to have another child.

The underlying issue in counselling was to ascertain to what degree these experiences of loss were being generalised and were affecting his behaviour with peers. There was the question of the emotional, social and behavioural consequences that could result from 'thinking' that *neither mum nor dad live with me and consider me of unique worth* (McGuiness, 1998).

Through mind skills work, we looked at what he might be telling himself from very real feelings of rejection. The counselling relationship was fundamental in raising his self-esteem (Chapter 1), yet counselling needed to move on from validating his sense of loss to giving him a strong sense of self for independence. The very act of selecting *him* and giving *him* time and an arena for *special attention* was in itself the beginning of a process, but counselling needed to address termination issues and to enable Luke, even as a minor, to function self-sufficiently.

Nelson-Jones reminds us that 'one way of viewing personal problems is that they are difficulties that challenge you to find solutions' (1996: 3). But how can a child persuade a parent that he or she is worthy of love? In the majority of cases, children do not have to. For those benefiting from a *secure attachment* from childhood (see Chapter 5), parents tend to have a biological predisposition to love their children, just as children are predisposed to be loved and nurtured by parents, and unconsciously project messages to that effect. In Luke's case, the goal had no practical task but was one of positive thinking, in spite of received messages to the contrary, messages that shouted out, 'You're not important, bugger off, I've got better things to do than bother with you!'

How did Luke think of himself among friends – who at the very least lived with one biological parent – when he was living with neither? Nelson-Jones (1996) suggests that we cannot cease but to think, and when we think we *choose* what we think, and, by self-control, choose *what not to think*. He also speaks of an existential awareness of our finite existence and the need to take responsibility for *my life* in *this period* in which I occupy *my place* on the earth. People who have suffered accidents (Lines, 1995a), or who have come close to death with cancer (Eva in Yalom, 1990), or who have survived national tragedies like the Holocaust (Frankl, 1959), often feel as though they are living a second life on borrowed time. There is an outlook, a philosophical stance, so to speak, that does not dwell on past losses and bitter regrets, on wishing life had been other than it is, but which *re-focuses on that which is, on taking responsibility for one's own existence with regard to those opportunities for growth that come along.*

It may appear ridiculous to suggest that a 14-year-old such as Luke should *re-view* his situation, of loss of both parents to drink, in a more favourable light, but this is what Luke needed to do to move on and get the most from life. Apportioning blame rarely helps parties move on. His parents had so many problems that they could barely look after themselves, let alone their children. Luke was beginning the process of individuation, and engaging in a peer group would be the direction in which to steer him.

Effective thinking skills to fulfil Luke's task required reframing his situation of loss. Against those approaches which encourage catharsis to discharge strong feelings, Nelson-Jones says, 'Feelings tend to be the parents of choices. You can decide whether to develop them, to regulate them or to treat them as unimportant' (1996: 36). Choosing what to think involves listening to your body; and assuming responsibility for what you think involves listening to your 'inner-valuing processes' (Mearns and Thorne, 2010).

Luke was fully aware that he had been poorly parented, that his mother and father, in different ways, had failed as parents, and that their drinking had had effects on his well-being – the early work covered this – but this effect did not need to be permanent, nor his situation impossible.

In carefully phrased questions, I persistently asked Luke whether he thought these early life experiences would always hold him back. Assertively, he said no, and this assertion was beginning to give birth to a more determined spirit that said, in effect, *I won't let this beat me, but will rise above it.* Empowerment for Luke meant thinking of opportunities which living with his auntie might offer him. I asked Luke to spell out the social advantages of living with his aunt:

> Luke: I've formed a friendship with Jason and Michael, and hang round with them. We go bowling on Wednesdays …, swimming with aunt and her kids on Sunday mornings …, and rollerblading down the park most nights.

Once *freed* from the responsibility and daily worry of parenting his parents, Luke was beginning to engage in a renewed social world.

Counter-transference issues of unconsciously 'wishing to parent' clients can get in the way of client empowerment, particularly for those in homes where alcohol is misused.

The counsellor must find ways of helping clients move on through the individuation process, *because of*, not in spite of, early familial impoverishment. Effective thinking skills offer the integrationist counselling practitioner a means of bringing about this end.

Pupils will be reminded occasionally of their losses through material delivered in the curriculum. Through peer boasting of good times had in wholesome families, they will feel deprived and sad, and may have memories of violent and social unrest by comparison. In order to counteract these disabling images cognitively, the client needs a perspective that is enabling. Luke was able to progress from an environment of little hope and promise to another that was nurturing. From a negative self-frame, he formed through brief counselling a new mental construct that said: *This is my life. I will make the most of it. I don't have to let my fucked-up childhood hold me back. I can move forward through positive thinking.*

Counselling Students in Conflict with Step-parents

Living with a step-parent can be a positive replacement for some pupils, and adjusting to new partners of a separated parent can also work out, but there are cases when children are not accepted by the parent's new partner or step-siblings. Where domestic violence has caused a break up, young people often hope things will change with the abusive parent.

Step-parent Conflict for Abeer

Abeer (aged 13) and her older brother Saeed (aged 15) spent most of their memorable childhood living with their mother and her white partner – with whom they had a good relationship. At weekends, however, they had an over-night stay with their father and his new partner. At times, Abeer was left in the company of her father's partner and her baby, Chisti, yet she was becoming concerned about the way he was treated. Knowing that her parents had sepa-rated because of domestic violence, and that her father still had a tendency to be aggressive, she was perturbed to see Chisti being maltreated. She became increasingly worried after every weekend, but told no one, not even her mother.

At school a pastoral teacher, noticing she was overly anxious and distant, per-sistently asked questions and eventually drew out from her a disclosure. A child protection referral was made, and when the authorities asked searching ques-tions of Chisti's parents, they deflected the enquiry by claiming that Abeer had been abused by her own mother, but was frightened to report it. When the (unfounded) enquiry centred on her own family, there was much upset and ill feeling, with the result that Abeer 'acted out' her frustrations within the family, not least to test her mother's feelings towards her – whether indeed she had been 'forgiven' for 'saying something' that had unintended consequences.

Individual sessions were planned with Saeed and Abeer: Saeed for aggression towards Abeer, and Abeer for excessive screaming and shouting in an age-inappropriate manner, almost tantrum-like. I then engaged them in a game of Jenga[3] to note their interactive behaviour and communicating manner, and this revealed volumes about their relationship with each other.

They then took part in an exercise of 'reflexive-circular questioning' (Tomm, 1985). This was a powerful means by which each could learn something of the other. Although they could both enter the mindset and feelings fairly accurately of their sibling, the critical issues about what each had thought and felt about past episodes in the family were not understood or acknowledged by either of them. Abeer had learnt that when Saeed became aggressive, and eventually brought to tears on top of the stairs (uncommon for a 15-year-old boy), he was afraid he might turn out like his father – a grown-up male who batters women!

Saeed had learnt how much the 'forced' disclosure had affected his younger sister, about the sense of betrayal she had felt and the resulting rejection by her father. Saeed had also learned that these necessary procedures had built a wall between his sister and their mother. Abeer had felt she had betrayed her mother by saying something that brought the authorities to the front door, and that whatever she tried to do she could never be as close to her mother as her brother was – that, indeed, the testing had become a redundant means of winning her mother's approval, and had fulfilled the script composed *within her mind* that she was not worthy of a mother's love.

Dennis: Do you feel that Saeed gets pleasure from hitting you, Abeer, when you've wound him up by shouting and screaming?

Abeer: Yea. He does it all the time. He loves to push me about; it doesn't bother him at all.

Saeed: **No, I don't**. I hate it when you push me so far [Abeer looks puzzled, eyes raised to the left] … it, it makes me think I'm no better than dad [she fixes her eyes on him].

Dennis: Saeed, you said earlier that you'd witnessed most domestic violence against your mother, that your sister had seen virtually nothing, and that she was not affected by it.

Saeed: Yea, that's right.

Abeer: **No it isn't**. You've got no idea what I saw. I might have been young then, but I saw lots when you were at nan's [Saeed looks up right, aghast, then left in contemplation].

Dennis: And what about the time social services came knocking on the door. How do you think that affected Abeer?

Saeed: It didn't really. She had to go in the back room while they questioned me and mum.

Dennis: And what about the many hours she cried on her bed for the trouble she felt she had caused, when only doing what was right to protect Chisti?

Saeed: I don't know. It couldn't have affected her as much as me and mum, being asked if mum knocked me about and that.

Abeer: **That's just it, Saeed. You just don't know**. You think it only affected you, not me. **I didn't want this to happen**; I was just saying that I didn't like the way Tahira was treating Chisti … [both begin to cry].

It was then clear where each had needed therapeutic support.

For cases where young people experience step-parent conflict when having to move into a new home, the therapist can offer support with coping and coaching self-talk (Nelson-Jones, 1996).

Readjustment for Karl after Parental Separation

Karl's parents had split up three years before self-referring. His form tutor had asked him, months earlier, to attend counselling to seek support over his temper and to receive anger-management training. In spite of three exclusions for fighting, and two visits by his mother to his pastoral manager to speak of his violence towards her and his explosive temper in the family generally, he failed to heed the advice to come for therapy until the family moved in with Jack, his mother's new partner.

When his mother began this new relationship with Jack, Karl vocally protested. He said that his mother was 'just looking after herself and planning for the time us kids had left'. When they were to move into Jack's house, there was a violent scene that prompted Karl to run away and live for a week at his girl-friend's home. Karl eventually succumbed to his mother's wishes and moved into the new house.

Tension rose almost daily, as his feelings for Jack turned to hate. Karl was to reach his 16th birthday in two months' time, after which he was off! His request for counselling was to help him cope and see time through. A further reason was to explore whether to stay and make his mother see 'how much she was being taken in by Jack' and get her to leave. The night before approaching me, Jack had chased Karl from the house after a heated argument – he raced after him by car, slammed on the brakes and squared up to him. They were braced face to face, but neither would throw the first punch.

Selecting a short-term goal for Karl was through collaborative counselling during a mini-crisis. Managing aggression was important for Karl because it was being manifested in other contexts that would affect future socialising with peers. His behaviour may have been an unconscious manoeuvre to get Jack out, behaviour which might prove counterproductive and which would involve him in investing too much energy to too little effect, and at the expense of his individuation (see Chapter 5). Although he felt for his father being 'down' after the separation, the dominant issue was how he could live for a brief time with a step-parent that his younger brother and sister had appeared to accept.

Person-centred counselling facilitated his growing sense of loss at seeing his mother besotted by a man other than his father, but Nelson-Jones' effective thinking skills of 'coping self-talk', 'coaching self-talk' and 'doing as well as I can' helped Karl maintain self-control (1996: 46–56).

Coping self-talk helps manage stress, anger and impulsivity (Meichenbaum, 1983, 1986). Negative self-talk focuses on the possible *outcomes*, which for Karl meant wishing to be rid of Jack, but positive self-talk focuses on the *processes* of survival, which for Karl meant 'coaching himself through' his final stage of adolescence before 'moving on', given the probability that his mother might remain with Jack. Negative self-talk for Karl involved him *catastrophising* (Ellis, 1987) a life for his mother living with Jack as being unbearable and inconceivable.

The tasks involved self-talking skills in combination with relaxation techniques. I felt it would be helpful to teach Karl how to relax, since his agitation was as much thought-induced while sitting in his room as incident-induced. Relaxation exercises were conducted in session following the customary method of 'progressive muscular relaxation' (Jacobson, 1938) and breathing exercises from deep to shallow inhaling, together with visualisation to help calm his situational stress (see Chapter 6).

Elements of Nelson-Jones' (1996: 136) structured approach were made use of as a framework for counselling:

- Get yourself relaxed.
- Emphasise coping rather than mastery.
- Strive for a clear image. Verbalise the contents of the image.
- Take a step-by-step approach. Visualise the less anxiety-evoking scenes before moving on to the more anxiety-evoking scenes.
- Use coping self-talk, with its coaching and calming dimensions.

When Karl visualised the worst possibility, or worse-case scenario, of his mother being happy 'in the arms of Jack', he became angry in session, since he felt powerless to alter his mother's feelings for Jack. He was even angrier when he recalled the street incident. However, once Karl had begun to focus on his mother 'being happy', as opposed to 'being depressed' as she had been before meeting Jack, his expression was more of regret than of anger. Redirected visualising was a start. 'Calming self-talk' and 'coping self-talk' serve to reduce hostile feelings in situations that cannot be altered. Karl had no *power* or *responsibility* to change his mother's feelings for her new partner, and it would have been unproductive to think otherwise. But Karl could alter *his own feelings* through effective thinking skills about how he allowed his mother's preferences to affect him. The point was to help divert his thinking from 'self-oppression' to 'self-support'. This was the major focus of the next few sessions.

It required little work to enable him to accept that this must happen, that his negativity was affecting his peer relationships adversely and that his resentment was worsening his relationship with his mother. 'Calming self-talk' was rehearsed in session with Karl saying to himself:

I can remain calm and relaxed. I wish things could have been happier with dad and mum together, but it's not the end of the world; she's obviously in love with Jack and I can't alter that. I'm glad she's no longer depressed.

'Coping self-talk' was also rehearsed:

We have to move on. I have my girlfriend and we're happy, and I'll be out of here when I'm 16. I won't let this get to me. I can put up with it for a few more months 'til after my exams.

In addition to 'self-talking' and positive visualising of 'mum being happy' rather than 'mum being depressed', other coping management skills to defuse enflamed anger were offered to Karl in case of a further heated exchange with Jack. Youngsters often resent being corrected by step-parents, and although most cohabitees recognise this, it occasionally results in arguments when outspoken adolescents challenge authority. In Karl's case, this had already happened. Karl was encouraged to create positive images of himself being powerful, not over Jack but over his own affective state, and the techniques of thought-stopping and vacuuming the negative thoughts and images from his mind were taught as an emergency aid in moments of crisis (Nelson-Jones, 1996).

The counselling contract closed after 'coaching self-talking' skill work had been completed in anticipation of a probable confrontation with Jack. Karl described what led up to a typical altercation – usually Jack correcting Karl for being rude to his mother when telling him off for coming in late:

When Jack steps in to protect mum, I must see where this may lead and back off for mum's sake. I have to look away, take a sharp intake of breath and relax my shoulders.

We rehearsed what he might say in 'coaching self-talk':

I will say, 'Sorry', even if I don't mean it. I will let Jack have the last word even though he has no right to butt in, again for mum's sake. I will slip away from him upstairs to my room and carry out relaxation exercises.

This self-talk coaching was learned by rote and was practised in session a few times to help Karl generalise the principles that could be applied in other possible scenarios.

Conclusion

This chapter has considered the effects of parental separation as a form of bereavement with all the psychological effects that are normally associated with the death of a loved one. Although humanistic counselling is commonly applied with such clients, the three presented categories – imminent parental separation, parental separation and adjustment to altered family circumstances – have illustrated the therapeutic support of elements of SFT integrated with effective thinking skills of 'self-coping' and 'self-coaching'.

In each of the three cases, the sense of loss has involved the student feeling a sense of powerlessness, which is where person-centred and other humanistic therapies appear most appropriate over CBT, but within the time constraints of an educational setting the cognitive elements of cognitive-humanistic therapy can be beneficial not to alter family matters, but to modify *the client's perspectives and attitudes* about what has happened.

Reflective Exercise

1. The research presented in this chapter has largely covered statistics of the altering nature of family life in the UK, attempting to avoid taking a political position.

   a. Is this realistic?
   b. Suppose parents approached you to announce they were separating and were concerned about the effects on their teenage children. In supporting the two affected teenage clients, how would the politics of parental rights to separate affect your work if the material suggests that the separating parents had prioritised their own happiness over the well-being of their children?

2. Compose your own Genogram (family diagram – see www.SmartDraw. com for software) and highlight the significant persons in your family who have affected, or been affected by, parental separation or cohabitation of new partners. Take a moment to reflect upon the costs or benefits of these changes from hindsight.

   a. Now examine a particular client of yours and your own counter-transference feelings during therapy.
   b. Make a list of significant comments of your young client and any transitional stages during the process of therapy, and describe how these affected your own feelings at the time and afterwards. Share these experiences with a colleague whom you trust.

3. The interventions in each of the three cases have largely centred upon social skills training, the exercise of coping skills and reframing techniques customarily applied in REBT – albeit following a humanistic stance of empathising with the client's feeling of loss.

   a. Discuss a possible tendency for counselling interventions to become preoccupied with mental reframing at a cost of effecting change through catharsis, or the counselling relationship.

(Continued)

(Continued)

   b. What are the strengths and limitations of coaching and coping skills with such clients as presented above, and in light of research cited in Chapters 1 and 2?

4. The second case of Luke featured a student having no parental ally. What change would you consider could be brought about through the person-centred contention of a quality therapeutic relationship without any cognitive interventions?

Key Points

- In spite of an increase in cohabiting family compositions comprising western multicultural society and divorce and separation becoming more common, youngsters facing the prospect of their parents separating can still have a traumatic experience.

- The occasion of a parent leaving home is similar to that of being bereaved for many young people.

- Research suggests that, although parental separation leaves children devastated initially, in time they can accept what has happened so long as both parents communicate with each other, remain happy and personally fulfilled and don't expect their children to be the go-between in keeping and divulging secrets.

- The school counsellor can support youngsters of separating parents with brief interventions of cognitive-humanistic counselling.

- Clients having to contemplate a new future without one parent around may attribute the separation to being *their fault*. In such cases, therapy can help them re-examine the changed conditions through scaling the pros and cons of altered circumstances.

- Contact and overnight stays with a separated parent might produce tension from new family compositions. Effective thinking skills assist adolescents in reframing situations and re-directing energy from overdue longing towards improved social engagements with friends.

12 Smoking, Drugs and Alcohol Misuse

This chapter covers:

- The use of drugs in western society
- Research on addictive behaviour and therapy
- Insights for therapy
- Responsible decision making for targeted groups
- Counselling smokers
- Counselling for drug and alcohol problems

Introduction

This chapter presents brief integrative interventions for adolescents who have begun smoking, drinking alcohol or experimenting with drugs, those who wish to cease or regulate a behaviour that has become for them a regrettable habit. The chapter also provides insights into addictive behaviour to support pre-pubescent children of drug-dependent parents.

In what follows, pluralistic therapy with children and adolescents centres on helping them to manage their own addiction through brief motivational interviewing integrated with features of narrative therapy. Counselling young people in school for smoking, drugs and alcohol misuse involves raising awareness of the subtle influences of addictive behaviour, giving information for responsible decision making, regulating intake and maintaining sobriety.

The Use of Drugs in Western Society

Western culture is no different from many other cultures in recognising the pleasures and hazards of chemical substances for altering mood and mind-states, and in setting codes for regulation for personal or collective good. For some cultures, drug intoxication is not merely desirable, it is a prerequisite for initiation and active social engagement, but in industrialised countries there are paradoxes and mixed messages about drunkenness and drug misuse.

It is illegal in the UK for young people under the age of 16 to purchase cigarettes, and they have to be 18 to purchase alcohol. Unclassified volatile substances that can be inhaled have few statutory regulations other than controlling sales for the purpose of sniffing – where this can be proved. Drug-taking and 'trafficking' are offences that are met with various penalties depending on how serious the drug is rated. The 'decriminalisation' of cannabis (marijuana) is regularly the topic of political debate.

Parental attitudes to alcohol are ambivalent in western society, 'abuse' being defined by the degree of consumption, or by the company kept when drinking. For example, for young people to drink wine at lunch, or spirits and lager at parties – where parents are present – is not generally perceived as a problem, but street drinking in gangs may be regarded as a 'social problem'. While some pupils smoke in school during non-contact time, and may even be found under the influence of alcohol, drugs policies in many institutions appear overtly censorious and inflexible over the use and traffic of controlled substances.

Both subtle and explicit societal messages may encourage chemical misuse. Pre-pubescent girls are bombarded with images and messages about the 'perfect body' – messages that suggest that the way they are is not good enough. Social drinking for emancipated females represents a shedding of stereotypical taboos as well as abandoned attempts to diet.

Teenage boys may suffer from neglect, be short of suitable role models (Biddulph, 2008) or long for physical affection from adults that cultural attitudes largely view as suspicious. Chemicals can provide a psychological substitute for attachment needs (see Chapter 5) and the lack of safe touch that many boys experience in their lives. Substance misuse can be a way of putting distance between young people and the pejorative messages they receive about themselves from the media.

Research on Addictive Behaviour and Therapy

Cooper (2008: 41) claims that 'psychological therapies have been found to be moderately effective in the treatment of substance abuse problems, though relapse rates are relatively high, with no clear indications of superiority for any one orientation (Roth and Fonagy, 2005)'. In my judgement, counselling students who regularly smoke and drink *willingly* largely fails to curb their habit. This is due to misconceptions about addiction and addictive behaviour. One misconception is to view the cigarette, the joint, the pill or the drink as the 'central problem'. A further misconception is to see the motivating factors for change as being merely those issues related to health, and to financial and social hardship.

A decisive question for researchers is why some, rather than others with an equivalent genetic predisposition for addictive behaviour, fall prey to alcoholism. Although there may be different causes for young people who misuse substances, there are common factors, the major two being the nature of parental support, and the availability of the substance.

Researchers have recognised that professionals 'are losing the war on drugs' (Diamond, 2000). Addicts giving up one addiction often fall prey to another (Knapp, 1996). In light of such a tendency, adult drinkers adopt a bargaining approach to therapy, not aiming for complete sobriety but controlled drinking and regulated consumption.

Cannabis reduction has been treated with CBT and motivational enhancement therapy with moderate success (Denis et al., 2004; Emmelkemp, 2004). Cocaine- and opiate-related problems have been addressed with a range of combined programmes of psychological therapy, again with moderate success (Crits-Christoph and Gibbons, 1999; Linehan et.al., 2002; Roth and Fonagy, 2005), but there is no substantial evidence of efficacy for psychological interventions alone (Mayet et al., 2004[2010]).

Short-term psychodynamic therapy has proved effective with opiate abuse but not cocaine (Fonagy et al., 2005). Brief therapy for alcohol problems has proven effective (Moyer et al., 2002), along with aspects of CBT and motivational interviewing (MI) (Ball et al., 2007; Cooper, 2008).

The double paradox of craving for the same chemical that is controlling the person, and suffering hangovers when wanting relief, is rarely registered by substance addicts.

Causal Factors of Misuse

DNA evidence indicates that biology and cultural factors have a mutual influence upon each other (Diamond, 2000). Research suggests that all addictions are driven by the 'addiction of control' and the 'management of mood-states' (Knapp, 1996). The addicted have become tired of 'playing by the rules', of complying with social conventions, and seek perpetual pleasure and freedom from pain.

Smoking *may* result from modelling behaviour of adults or significant peers in the first instance (Chapter 5), but addiction to drugs and alcohol could also be symptoms of family disruption and internal pain and confusion. Drugs and alcohol can be a way for adolescents to block memories of sexual abuse by anaesthetising themselves from depression and suicidal feelings (see Chapters 6 and 7). Similarly, young gay and lesbian clients can use drugs to blunt fears of rejection when considering 'coming out' (see Chapter 13). Drugs *may* also serve to disguise same-sex desires for those who are struggling to acknowledge their sexuality.

Risk-taking in Adolescence

Drugs feed into the sensation-seeking and risk-taking tendencies of adolescents. Geldard and Geldard (2010) review the research on risk-taking behaviour of adolescents involved in smoking, drinking alcohol, sniffing solvents and taking drugs: marijuana, a variety of pills such as amphetamines, psychotropic substances such as 'magic mushrooms' and LSD, and hard drugs such as cocaine and heroin. They argue that it is misleading to link habit-forming addiction with the experimental behaviour of youngsters and, although adolescence represents the transition from non-smoker to smoker (Geldard and Geldard, 2010), there is growing evidence that young people, particularly girls, begin smoking before the stress-related transfer to secondary school (OfNS, 1998).

Peer-group Influence

Research shows that the dominant factor for the increase in drug taking and drinking is the introduction of substances by friends (Geldard and Geldard, 2010). There are two reasons for this:

- The socialising tendencies of young people can put them in touch with suppliers.
- The need to be accepted 'by the group' leaves some feeling isolated if they choose not to become initiated through what the group view as important.

But peer-group influence generally yields inconsistent research evidence – not all teenagers are led into addiction by friends.

> Although addiction tends to pass from generation to generation, according to Diamond (2000) peer-group influence is persuasive. The modelling effects of significant friends are strong in taking up smoking (Hu et al., 1995; Wang et al., 1997), in spite of adolescents recognising accepting the health risks involved in becoming a regular smoker. But Geldard and Geldard (2010), aware that adolescence is a self-assertive phase towards individuation, contend that some young people are more than capable of making personal decisions within the context of peer pressure.

Naturally, when factors converge, the risk of addiction is strong. When factors of 'families not abusing drugs themselves', 'friends having no interest in drugs and alcohol', 'restricted access to drugs or alcohol' and 'no psychosocial or school-based difficulties' combine, abstention from alcohol, cannabis and other drugs is more likely (McBroom, 1994). Not surprisingly, academic performance is adversely affected by drug misuse (Jenkins, 1996).

Drug- and Alcohol-dependent Parents

Many young addicts experimenting with substances are grieving for the loss of mothering and fathering due to their parents' addiction, for alcohol and drugs offer symbolic substitutes. Parents who emotionally abandon their children leave them in roles of responsibility for which they are not ready, leading them to make pseudo-mature decisions over hazardous things such as early sex and drug taking. These children live in an alcoholic-centred, not a child-centred home, and are expected to parent younger siblings before being ready for parenthood themselves.

Children in therapy sometimes feel burdened by guilt when parents blame them for their addiction. Others have low self-worth, and reason 'if they loved me they would stop drinking'. Many can recount times when they have been embarrassed among friends by their parents' drunken behaviour. If peers or teachers criticise their parents' drunkenness, children begin to internalise a sense of shame – some blame their non-drinking parent and many worry about their health and well-being, about whether accidents may befall them while out or whether they may fall asleep with a cigarette in their hand.

Insights for Therapy

Alcoholics Anonymous (AA) and drug-focused counsellors have begun to recognise the powerful relationships that addicts have with their substances. The medical model aims for total abstinence within a supportive community of 'recovering addicts' (AA and Narcotics Anonymous) or within a treatment centre (NHS), while the education model favours responsible decision making. Both recognise that drugs and alcohol relegate all other concerns and relationships to a very poor second place. Collaboration with supporting agencies and parents is essential in some cases, and local treatment centres and organisations (such as AA) have much experience from which to draw.

The challenge of obtaining the substance is part of the excitement of risk taking that has appeal for adolescents. Studies of volatile substance taking in England, Scotland and the USA (Ives, 1994) highlight the importance of decision-making skills, parental involvement and positive peer influence, for many sniffers who become 'lone sniffers' suffer from low self-esteem (Lines, 1985). The counsellor will need to understand the patterns of individual and group sniffing. Glues and solvents, such as deodorants, butane lighter fuel, 'poppers', cleaning chemicals and the like, are readily available. Glue sniffing has the highest first-use mortality level, though this is more a result of accidents when intoxicated than through suffocation (OfNS, 1998). Incidents of pupils inhaling butane gas through the nose or mouth have resulted in first-use mortality.

Some clients entering therapy have been sent by the courts or by senior staff, which limits their motivation for change, hence the value of motivational interviewing (McNamara and Atkinson, 2010). Lambert's (1992) research, cited in Chapter 2, shows that 15 per cent of therapeutic improvement is due to an instilled 'sense of hope' (O'Hara, 2010) and an 'expectancy of positive change' (Asay and Lambert, 1999), and in light of 'the placebo effect', where patients actually improve through belief in the efficacy of a neutral drug (Cooper, 2008), it seems that a brief approach like MI is likely to yield positive results.

Motivational interviewing (Miller and Rollnick, 1991) addresses addictive behaviour at the point where clients express ambivalent attitudes to habitual behaviour: 'I want to stop, I don't want to stop.' Against therapy that views the client's resistance to give up the habit as pernicious 'denial', MI recognises that ambivalence is at the heart of the problem, and through non-judgemental questioning the MI practitioner aims to elicit the motivation for determined change. In light of the fact that young substance abusers are not likely to have incurred permanent physical or neuropsychological damage, and that they are impulsive and risk taking, conventional MI techniques may need modifying and simplifying (Tober, 1991).

The pluralistic brief counsellor knows that therapy has to acknowledge the 40 per cent factor of powerful environmental influences for change (Asay and Lambert, 1999) – both positive and negative: 'You cannot detox patients and then send them back into deprivation and poverty and expect them to stay free from drugs' (Diamond, 2000: 263).

In *Games People Play*, Berne (1968: 64–70) parodies the alcoholic's lifestyle. From a transactional analysis perspective, he describes the supportive characters of the addict's social world. Time and again, I have found the following to be a common family dynamic:

- Alcoholic's behaviour is reinforced by **Persecutor** – normally the spouse, who serves as 'Parent', and whose role it is to give **Alcoholic** a hard time.
- Alcoholic is supported by **Rescuer** – usually a same-gender friend, or the GP.

The *payoff*, and point of the *game*, is not the binge drinking (this is merely the prelude) but the hangover, for it is within the stage of hangover that players take up their respective roles – 'Feel sorry for me, "parent" me, I am sick "Child"'. In transactional analysis, treatment is through awareness and through getting all parties to stop playing the *game*. Even children and teenagers play supporting roles as 'Child' or 'Adult', and often in their own behaviour display similar manoeuvres: 'See if you can stop me', which involves lying, hiding things, seeking derogatory comments, looking for helpful people, finding a benevolent neighbour who will give free handouts (Berne, 1968: 70). But if such dynamics require a family therapy approach, the school may not be the appropriate location for such work.

Young people's substance-abusing habits and journey through recovery have been understood as a rite of passage (White and Epston, 1990), as a phase where a person loses track of time before becoming socially reincorporated. Ironically, heroin, mescaline and cocaine are shrouded in mystery, ceremony and ritual that mirror the adolescent's rite of passage. A measured understanding of where experimental behaviour can lead is an important insight for the counsellor of young people around 'safer' drugs such as nicotine, cannabis and alcohol.

> The narrative therapist is more interested in knowing *what sort of person has a disease* than what sort of disease affects a person. Diamond (2000) has demonstrated the effectiveness of narrative psychotherapy integrated with the 29-step programme of AA, in which the therapist encourages the client to aim for gradual recovery rather than permanent change. Often, clients are asked to refrain from taking drugs before therapy, to keep a behaviour inventory of their drinking, or to indulge in a less harmful drug after therapy. This is in order to aid self-control rather than therapist control, and to avoid perceptions that suggest an 'all or nothing' remedy (Diamond, 2000). Brief approaches for addicted young people make use of these insights (Moyer et al., 2002).

Responsible Decision Making for Targeted Groups

Anxiety is one of the most powerful triggers of addiction:

> It follows then that one of the most difficult tasks facing therapists treating alcoholism is to *lessen a person's denial* and *encourage increased self-awareness* and disclosure while they're trying to *keep their client's anxiety to a minimum.* (Diamond, 2000: 62 – my emphasis)

Responsible decision making helps to remove anxiety in the short term (Chapter 6), while the source of anxiety is explored through brief counselling.

Drugs policies have tended in recent years to refrain from 'moralising' and to educate young people to make responsible decisions, and, as discussed in Chapter 5, discoveries in neuroscience on the teenage brain suggest that assisting pupils to 'organise their thoughts' is beneficial in reconfiguring the brain. Although the curriculum on drugs within personal, social and moral education programmes of study is not the focus of this book, the counsellor might, at times, take on a teaching role with small groups of targeted individuals. Teaching responsible decision making has been demonstrated recently (Winslade and Monk, 1999) by use of the narrative technique of 'interviewing the problem' (Roth and Epston, 1996). Group members are encouraged to make responsible decisions through an exercise in which they are granted a rare opportunity to interview the targeted *drug* as though it were a person.

Identified Group over Misuse of Cannabis

Acting Role

Two or three members of the group are asked to imagine they are *cannabis spliffs,* that cannabis has through them become personified. They are to illustrate the complexity of the problem by indicating the strong appeal and fun that can be had when under the influence of *Drug Cannabis,* as well as the lows, the depression and the ostracising effects of being addicted. Good acting persuades the group to befriend *Drug Cannabis.* Marketing includes a typical scenario where *Drug Cannabis* has given the group 'a good time' at a party, where all have become 'intoxicated', but finally go home when the host's parents return.

The Pros of Cannabis misuse

The second stage involves a structured reporter's interview during a press conference. Broadening-out questions illustrate the tactics that *Drug Cannabis* typically uses to lure the unguarded into its clutches, such questions as:

- What are your favourite tricks of persuasion?
- What hopes and dreams do you offer those who have no future?
- Do you have different tactics with girls than with boys?
- How do you pull mates in and keep teachers and parents out?

The Cons of Cannabis Misuse

Half way through, the group are asked to change tack. This is investigative journalism, and they are required to put hard questions to *Drug Cannabis,* so as not to let *him* off the hook. Questions come readily to mind as group members become animated through the neutrality of the counsellor. Questions draw attention to the demoralising effects of *Drug Cannabis,* the manner in which addicts give up on life, the crime that inevitably results for serious addiction, the subtle spiralling pessimism and the ensuing fractured relationships that *Drug Cannabis* brings about.

Coming Out of Role and Follow-up Discussion

After the group has observed the benefits and hazards of *Drug Cannabis,* and made notes on the conflicting arguments, the drugs team come out of role by changing seats and shaking off the drug identity; they then re-enter the circle for discussion. As the authors suggest, it is helpful to ask each protagonist to say three things that make them different from *Drug Cannabis,* so as to eliminate a tendency to label individuals (Winslade and Monk, 1999).

The aim is to help the group view people's drug problems from *Drug's* perspective. The re-storying aspects of narrative therapy continue through the closing follow-up work. This highlights the methods that successful addicts in recovery have used to 'frustrate the plans of *Drug Cannabis* to take control of their lives', and the 'devious plans of *Drug Cannabis* to win back a recovering addict'. Failed *Drug Cannabis* might be asked to account for *his* (or *her*) most embarrassing failure, to expound what form of addict resistance had caused *Drug Cannabis* to almost give up, or to recount what is least palatable to hear from young people.

Plenary

In our group, Larry and Rob portrayed *Drug Cannabis* pushing Tom to take a spliff for over an hour with continual jibes of 'being scared'. But this had no effect other than that Larry's girlfriend dropped him for 'being a prat!' saying, 'Is that the only thing you think about?'

Counselling Smokers

While traditional approaches to addictive behaviour have been largely ineffective, Diamond (2000) argues for the efficacy of integrative narrative approaches. Brief motivational interviewing (MI) (Miller and Rollnick, 1991) and the Cycle of Change (CoC) (Prochaska and DiClemente, 1982) have also proved effective with a number of addictive behaviours, including smoking, serious drinking and drug abuse (Cooper, 2008; Devere, 2000), particularly for young people (McNamara, 2009). I have found brief integrative models, which utilise aspects of these, to be effective with adolescent smokers. This integrative model is demonstrated in group and individual work.

Group Therapy for Smokers

Because of a lack of resources, group therapy is more productive than individual counselling for those youngsters whose genuine goal is to stop smoking, particularly for identified groups to offset negative modelling influences (Hu et al., 1995; Wang et al., 1997). From a pluralistic counselling stance, the collaboratively offered task is through the CoC model, and the four offered/negotiated methods are:

- motivational interviewing to address denial and cognitive dissonance
- keeping a log/diary of smoking habit
- planning an individualised change of routine to avoid temptation, and
- meeting once each week for review and feedback.

In the introductory session, the CoC task is described to the group with the diagram shown in Figure 12.1. The introduction gives an optimistic but realistic outline of the model's therapeutic scope for five-session programmes of habit reduction.

I modify the CoC model to the stepping on and off of a playground roundabout having five sectors (Figure 12.2).

Ground rules are clearly stated to allay the natural apprehension of young pupils around confidentiality. While brief weekly group sessions are largely for review, evaluation and encouragement – fine-tuning, renewed action plans following failure, etc. – the methods are individually planned according to each client's social circumstances. The counsellor is aware of how peer-group associations are formed through smoking habits, how clients generally prefer their parents not to know, and the common use of dinner money to purchase cigarettes during the day.

Change takes place by encouraging members of the group as individuals to step on the roundabout of change of their own volition. The roundabout of change

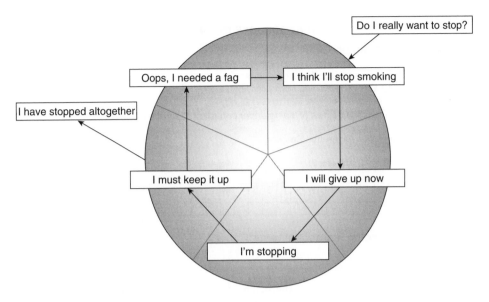

Figure 12.1   Cycle of change with smoking

begins with 'contemplation', where engagement or disengagement is discussed through MI and group Rogerian therapy. During this session, I give candidates a self-learning personal record to complete that is written in externalising language, as shown in Figure 12.3.

During the first group session, each member is asked to describe their smoking habit, the degree and frequency of wishing (not needing) to smoke, the where and when and with whom they elect to smoke, its costs each week, age when starting,

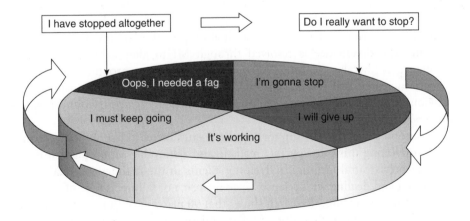

Figure 12.2   The roundabout of change for giving up smoking

SAYING GOODBYE TO TOBACCO

PERSONAL RECORD OF:_____

1. *What is the degree of Cigarette's hold on you?*
2. *What will you lose by departing from your Fag Buddy?*
3. *How will you begin to say 'Get lost' to Fag Buddy?*
4. *When do you wish to be free of 'being under control of Cigarettes'?*

Continuing Progress – Cigarettes Smoked:

Week 1								Week 2								Week 3								Week 4							
M	T	W	T	F	S	S		M	T	W	T	F	S	S		M	T	W	T	F	S	S		M	T	W	T	F	S	S	

Figure 12.3   Keeping a personal record

and the hold smoking has upon them. This information is not judged from a moral perspective, but serves as baseline data to measure progress and success. An undue stress on journal recording becomes de-motivating after about four weeks, as most youngsters cut down in the early stages of drawing their attention to the degree of their habit and its costs, but then find it difficult to maintain the lower smoking rate or give up completely first time round.

The second session focuses primarily on dissonance in a frank and honest manner. 'Cognitive dissonance' is recognised when ambivalence and inconsistency are discussed and when clients acknowledge their irregularities in thinking and behaving (McNamara and Atkinson, 2010). With habitual behaviour, there is often a mismatch between thinking and behaving (see Table 12.1).

Again, they may *alter their belief,* as though in denial, in an attempt to con themselves with shallow arguments like the high numbers of smoking-addicted doctors and nurses in the medical profession, or their elderly relatives smoking well into their eighties, and so on. They may *denigrate themselves* by highlighting their *lack of willpower* and *causal excuses,* like 'examination pressures' or 'my mother driving me mad'. The dissonance is resolved through MI to alter habitual behaviour. Dissonance is thereby weakened through enlightenment around ambivalence, through increased self-esteem, through attributing personal responsibility for behaviour and through increased motivation – I encourage behavioural imaging exercises, as shown below.

The second stage involves supporting the client's belief in her ability to change before converting this into specific, realistic and achievable action plans through cognitive-behavioural techniques. Helping clients in the maintenance stage is by recognising and dealing with relapse, since relapse, not failure, is part of the process for permanent change. Research shows that 90 per cent of those with smoking, alcohol, heroin and crack cocaine problems relapse at some point after treatment (Cooper, 2008; Devere, 2000). After relapse, the client may return at any point and

Table 12.1 Cognitive dissonance

My expressed wish	The reality of my behaviour
Smoking is injurious to my health	*I continue to smoke*
I want good health	*I continue to smoke*
I like to have spare money	*Smoking takes all my cash*
I want to have clean breath	*My breath smells of tobacco*
I want to smell nice	*My clothes stink of smoke*

step on the roundabout as often as the model proves a useful and motivating tool for long-term possibilities.

The advantage of this model for habit-forming behaviour is that it offers an effective means of dealing with relapse (Carroll, 1996). Students can also utilise it beyond the counselling room, and this is important for a therapy that largely takes place in the client's social world. If youngsters fail (as most do at first), then they have a model to which they may return with greater determination later on, rather than one which highlights failure and leaves them feeling permanently dispirited. Prochaska and DiClemente (1982) found that most smokers go round the cycle three to seven times before finally quitting.

Group Therapy for Smokers

Ranjit, Naomi, Denzal, Will and Sharya were asked to spend a moment at the point of lighting up and look at the cigarette and ask:

'Do I really need You right now?'

I ask them, after a few drags, to stare at the smouldering cigarette and ask themselves:

'Are You really helping me?'
'How are You taking a hold over me?'
'Why are You taking over?'
'Do You really make me feel better or am I kidding myself?'

These externalising questions are designed to weaken dissonance and strengthen resolve.

The results of group-session work for pupils wishing to give up smoking can vary, depending upon social and personal factors. With this particular group, Ranjit cut down to one cigarette a day after twice jumping on the roundabout

(Continued)

(Continued)

of change. Naomi hardly modified her behaviour at all, during or after the pro-gramme. Denzal and Will cut down their smoking to one a day during lunch-time, after which they gave up altogether and stepped down from the roundabout, having twice dealt with relapse. Sharya reduced her smoking to three a day, then on re-try gave up altogether after going out with a boy who was a non-smoker.

Therapy is not terminated when a goal is reached, since the model serves to empower the individual for future change. Change is not due to the counsellor but to the client's use of a technique which instils hope and motivation. The timing for change is not restricted to the period of counselling sessions. The advantage of this approach is in its durability and the fact that the roundabout can be imagined and internalised. It serves as a permanent model to which to return at later periods when resolve is increased or when social or personal influencing factors have altered.

Therapy for an Individual Smoker

A second case illustrates the approach applied for an individual where smoking had become the cause of a more serious relationship difficulty.

Erica's Smoking Habit

Erica approached me asking for ideas on how she might give up smoking after a fight with her mother when she was discovered with a cigarette. The key to motivation, however, was not to avoid another fight but another factor.

Erica's wish to stop smoking was not for reasons of health or personal image or because the smell of smoke on breath or clothing sometimes affects an adolescent's sense of personal attractiveness. She needed to save £30 for a puppy, and by not buying cigarettes she could save £4 each week on top of her pocket money. Her smoking habit and its frequency, her social acquaintances, her mother's attitude to smoking and other reinforcing factors were explored.

While she would not smoke in front of her mother, she did not feel too intimidated when her mother reprimanded her in the street for 'having a fag in her hand'. Erica was largely unperturbed by this incident even though it resulted in a public scene that ultimately put her in care for a week for protec-tion. She felt she needed to smoke more during term time than in holiday periods. She smoked alone as much as with friends, and all adults viewed her as a strong individual.

On deciding on a goal for brief integrative counselling, the salient factors appeared to be:

- a resolute desire to stop smoking
- a character with a strong ego
- a clear motive for change
- a realisable goal within four weekly sessions.

When negotiating our tasks, it seemed to me that the narrative approach offered some promise, but two elements would not be appealing to Erica. She had had some considerable contact with social services, and in consequence a method that relied upon written documents might not have worked (she mistrusted authority figures). If she wrote a 'farewell' letter to her smoking 'partner' (as illustrated in Diamond, 2000), she may have become suspicious about its purpose, see it as a gimmick and become wary about what might become of anything put in writing.

When trying to externalise the problem (White, 1989) of smoking – as an invading enemy, or a disease that might creep up and catch her unawares while she is down – it did not prove effective, apart from helping her to see herself as a 'non-smoker'. Erica did not feel herself to be 'addicted' to nicotine or to be powerless or out of control, but on the contrary to be a person very much *in control* of most aspects of her life (Geldard and Geldard, 2010).

An integrative approach using techniques of SFT was therefore attempted. The therapy focused on *changing only that which needed changing* (O'Connell, 2005), and it appeared that scaling would help monitor her progress in ceasing to smoke at school.

Baseline data were collected in the first session and this revealed a pattern of smoking around the back of the sports hall with one friend during lunchtime, and smoking a further cigarette alone at the bus stop on the way home. On both occasions, Erica smoked 'because she wanted to', not because of peer influence or social pressure (Geldard and Geldard, 2010). The counselling aim, therefore, was to further encourage a trait already present in her character by restructuring her social habits and routines.

In the second session, we devised an action plan that involved her offering assistance at lunchtimes in a drama production that was scheduled for a month's time, and opening an account with the school bank in order not to support her habit by having spare money from lunch and bus fares with which to buy cigarettes. The third and closing sessions involved monitoring her progress – the money she had saved for her pet and her withdrawal symptoms after giving up.

Scaling techniques proved successful in self-assessment of the wearing-off effect of 'gasping for a fag!', and in terminating our collaborative work:

- 'On a scale of 1 to 10 – 1 representing "I'm fully able to go it alone" and 10 the sentiment "I am desperate for your support" – what number will you need to have reached before we close counselling?'

She said '2'.

Over the four-week period, her scaling scores of 'gasping for a fag' were 7, 2, 3 and 1, respectively, where high scores represented maximum temptation to smoke. Her scaling scores for withdrawing from therapy were 8, 6, 2 and 1, respectively.

Her saving target was also reached by week four, and a follow-up session two months later revealed that she had completely stopped smoking for other benefits than having a puppy – in fact, she bought a mobile phone instead of a puppy, because her mother would not allow her to have a pet in the house.

Counselling for Drug and Alcohol Problems

'Once an alcoholic, always an alcoholic' is one of the mantras that lead AA and the medical community to aim for regulation and management of addiction, rather than cure. Psychotherapy has largely been unsuccessful with addictive behaviour because of three misconceptions:

> Addicts and alcoholics embrace a lifestyle that *avoids pain* at all costs, *seek immediate gratification,* and tend to *rely on – put their faith in – chemicals more than people.* In other words, for those who are addicted recovery means abandoning the very things that sustain them. (Diamond, 2000: 2 – my emphasis)

Traditional psychotherapy can be a *painful and scary business*, requiring a letting go of control. It often offers *no short-term recovery* but uncomfortable feelings, and is based wholly upon *the person of the therapist* to bring clients through. Hence, for adult drug addicts and alcoholics, the three principles of therapeutic change are jettisoned. I think there is more hope for young people.

The cornerstone of change for Diamond (2000) is the recognition that addicted clients form strong relationships with their addictive substances. Bidding farewell to drug and drink companions through 'externalising language' and 'parting letters' and documents is one process of recovery and reorientation to life without the drug companion. But I have found MI and the CoC, in combination with the language styles of narrative therapy, to be effective with habitual drinking and other drug behaviour for young people.

Miller and Rollnick (1991) speak in terms of clients' *attachments* to addictive behaviours rather than their relationships with substances. The prerequisite of what follows assumes adherence to the BACP *Ethical Framework* (2002) and safeguarding principles. The counsellor will have established whether to work on managing the drug or alcohol intake, or whether to tackle other problems of which chemical dependency is symptomatic.

It is unusual for counselling in school to be offered for very serious drug addicts (heroin and cocaine), since most are likely to have come before the authorities, been excluded to protect other pupils, given a prison sentence or referred to a drying-out clinic. The higher the tariff of the 'drug–dependency–penal outcome' triad, the less likely it is that group work is indicated in place of individual counselling. Schools need to protect

their image as well as their pupils, and group work indirectly reinforces a social accepta-
bility of drug misuse that senior managers are keen to play down. The behaviour of the
serious drug addict is met with greater censure in the current competitive climate than
the casual cigarette smoker or the social drinker of low-proof alcohol.

Nathaniel's Problem Drinking

Nathaniel referred himself for support with a growing problem of alcohol
addiction to spirits and whisky. His parents were highly tolerant of his drinking
and often encouraged him, at 14, to drink when entertaining middle-class
friends, which was often. What they were unaware of was that Nathaniel was
helping himself regularly to a cocktail of spirits each afternoon before his parents arrived home from the family business.

His 'manly [*sic*] prowess' was evident when bragging to his friends, at 16, that
he could 'drink them under the table'. Rather than revelling in this identity, he was
acutely aware of his growing dependence on spirits to 'bury the pressures of the
day'. This was a pertinent observation at the time, since his father was under a
medical consultant for liver malfunction, and his mother was becoming more
and more embarrassing when flirting with his friends after a glass of brandy.

The introductory session scanned for a focus of therapy through Egan's three-stage
model of brainstorming preferred scenarios (Egan, 1990; Mabey and Sorensen,
1995). Nathaniel wished to see himself as a 'non-dominated alcoholic', and though
the MI technique of 'rolling with resistance' (Miller and Rollnick, 1991) helped to
reveal the inner contradiction of Nathaniel's thinking on personal freedom, elements of narrative therapy became the preferred approach in planning therapeutic
tasks to meet his goal of sobriety.

Through 'externalising language', we reframed his ideal self-concept as the 'Nathaniel
who wards off *Devilish Demon Drink*' – the subtle enemy who lures him into thinking
that mild intoxication removes the 'pressures of school life'. His worry and embarrassment over his father's health and his mother's exhibitionism were first validated through
person-centred counselling. Then, through collaborative conversation, Nathaniel
selected the motivational lever of 'keeping *Demon Drink* at bay' through heightening his
personal resolve. Cognitive therapy was not indicated because there was no evidence of
cognitive dissonance: he was fully aware of the health risks through his father's worsening
condition, and he ceased apportioning blame for his drinking on external circumstances.

The second session, through Egan's framework of goal setting and action planning, was wholly dedicated to explaining the CoC model. The processes of change –
'contemplation', 'dedication', 'action', 'maintenance', 'relapse' and on to 'contemplation'
again, and so round the circle till sobriety is reached – were discussed.

His motivation for change was high at this point and this indicated that he was at
the 'dedication' stage. The roundabout analogy that I customarily use was dropped for
the traditional CoC diagram, given Nathaniel's intelligence and ability to register

diagrams. In spite of moving speedily through the first two sectors of contemplation and dedication, the action stage and, particularly, the maintenance stage had become problematic; it was hardly surprising that relapse occurred within four days and binge drinking followed for the next three. This pattern was repeated for each of the next three weeks, and although the binge period was gradually becoming reduced, Nathaniel had become demoralised in that his goal of complete sobriety had not been achieved.

The fifth and closing session addressed the very real problem of dealing with the negative thinking of relapse behaviour. Statistical information was presented to Nathaniel to help give him a sense of 'normalising' his experience of relapse. We reapplied the externalising language of *Demon Drink* and we composed a letter to his subtle enemy on the computer to help personalise the problem and give it greater gravity.

Dear Demon Drink,

You have been my uninvited companion for two and a half years, and I have begun to realise that I am better off without **You**.

You have fooled me for too long now into thinking my school problems will go away with your acquaintance. The next day convinces me **You're** wrong.

You disguise yourself in many ways, and that gets me angry. **Your** velvet feel through sparkling wine, **Your** tempting sharpness through claret red, **Your** enticing fire through burning whisky and **Your** social 'respectability' through crystal clear gin – **Your** various guises fool me no longer.

Look what **You've** done to dad. Look what **You're** doing to mum. I'm sorry, but I've decided that whatever benefit **You've** given me in the past, it's time for **You** to go and trouble someone else instead. I may miss aspects of **Your** friendship, but **You** will trick me no longer.

With no regrets,

Nathaniel

Initially, the letter was collaboratively composed for no other purpose than to heighten his motivation for sobriety, but, in view of its forceful effect on his thinking and resolve for complete abstinence the following week, we decided to share the letter in a closing 'witness-audience' meeting with his parents (Payne, 2006; White and Epston, 1990).

This session was moving. Both parents began to cry, as their modelling influence on their son's acquired habit became apparent and as their son's determination to 'lead the way' became transparent. Follow-up sessions one and three months later confirmed his ongoing sobriety, with only one confessed relapse after which he re-entered the CoC from having internalised the diagram.

Conclusion

Counselling teenagers for smoking and the use and misuse of drugs and alcohol is problematic. Customarily, clients coming for therapy wish to change an aspect of their life, but when young people begin to take substances to relieve anxiety, or to alter their mood, this may not be as much of a 'problem' *to them* as it might be for their parents or teachers, or society at large. Although the law on obtaining and misusing various substances is specific, public attitudes are not so fixed.

While short-term psychodynamic counselling, CBT and, particularly, motivational styles of therapy have claimed moderate success for clients with substance abuse, psychotherapy generally has not been very effective in the treatment of severe alcohol and drug addiction. In this chapter, we have considered the application of motivational interviewing and features of narrative therapy for those teenagers who have expressed a wish to change an aspect of their behaviour centred upon the habits of smoking cigarettes and cannabis and routine habits of drinking alcohol.

It has been shown that brief integrative counselling in an educational setting can be effective for those clients who genuinely wish to curb or change their habit, and that one important ingredient of the programme is to centre on a means of reviving hope for teenagers who inevitably relapse.

Reflective Exercise

1. While it might be true to claim that all counselling and psychotherapy is about assisting clients to change, it is a pertinent question to consider whether change involves teaching (psycho-education), a question which is pressing for non-directive counselling styles. Compose a brief list where your own counselling style for drug-related problems has involved an element of teaching, from pointing out *causal factors, risk factors, inherent dangers with addictive behaviour,* or *the 'gateway' argument,* where addicts tend to pass from less to more severe drug taking.

2. Suppose your teenage client of 16 years approached you and disclosed they were taking heroin, and in the course of your session gave hints of their suppliers. If they had expressly stated that they wished to cease the habit and wanted your support, how would you address the legal issues of your position as a school counsellor? How would you resolve the tension of safeguarding principles and the BACP *Ethical Framework* if your client made it clear that the support they wished you to give them should not involve breaching confidentiality and sharing any information with parents, school staff or the authorities?

3. A senior pastoral teacher approaches you and asks if you would consider engaging in some group work with four girls of 14 who were habitual drinkers and who had begun attending parties with older boys of 17 years and over:

(Continued)

(Continued)

    a. How would you engage the group?

    b. What styles of therapy would you consider most appropriate?

    c. Would you consider it necessary to involve parents? And, if so, what form of engagement would you consider appropriate?

4. A Year 10 pupil, aged 15 years, has been referred for therapy, after having arrived at school in a mildly intoxicated state through drinking gin. Senior teachers have been unable to contact the parents, and the youngster's headache and other hangover symptoms have faded to the point that he is now fully conscious and conversant. How would you engage such a client if he began to disclose that both his parents were alcoholics and that they would not register with undue concern the significance of what had happened that morning?

Key Points

- Although short-term psychodynamic counselling, CBT and motivational therapeutic styles have claimed moderate success, psychotherapy generally has largely been ineffective in treating addictive behaviour.

- Addicts form *powerful relationships* with their substances, relationships which disregard personal loved ones and other concerns.

- Paradoxical messages exist in western society about drugs, which can be aired in session, and while causal explanations of addiction may bring insight for clients, what has more chance of change (reduction or abstinence) is a programme that utilises *personal motivation*.

- Motivational interviewing (MI) and the Cycle of Change (CoC) have proved to be effective treatments with addictive behaviours like smoking, drinking and drug misuse, principally because such programmes offer a means of dealing with relapse.

- Stopping teenagers from smoking occasionally in school is notoriously difficult during non-contact time, largely due to their *dissonant thinking*, but brief MI group therapy for those who *really want to change* can help to curb the habit.

- The MI approach begins by examining *cognitive dissonance*, then youngsters are encouraged to move round the CoC: contemplation to determination, action planning and maintenance, and finally on to manage relapse until eventually they give up their addiction.

- When MI and CoC are combined with elements of narrative therapy and SFT, clients who are 'lone smokers' or 'secluded drinkers' are more motivated to mobilise their own resources in overcoming the craving for chemical substances.

13 Teenage Sexuality

This chapter covers:

- Early adolescent sexual experience
- Research on sexual orientation
- Environmental influences
- Confidentiality and safeguarding practice
- Insights for therapy
- Counselling heterosexual young people
- Counselling gay and lesbian teenagers

Introduction

Two anomalies of early sexual experience leave educationalists unsure of how to support youngsters in school. The first is the fact that the UK has the highest number of school-age pregnancies in Europe at the time of writing, in spite of lessons on sex education in most schools. Second, at a time when young people have become more open and expressive about their sexuality, there is evidence that extreme homophobia still prevails in some quarters.

The professional, legal and ethical position of school counselling was examined in Chapter 4 with reference to the level of confidentiality that can be afforded to pupils in school. In this chapter, the implications of those boundaries with respect to teenage heterosexual, homosexual and bisexual orientation and conduct are explored. Because of the pressures in school arising from homophobia, gay and lesbian sex will be covered in greater detail than heterosexuality.

Early Adolescent Sexual Experience

There is, in the UK, a high frequency of self-reported risk-taking sexual behaviour among adolescents (Downey and Landry, 1997). Rates of teenage births for 15–19-year-olds in the UK during 1998 were five times those of the Netherlands, three times those of France, twice those of Germany, yet still two thirds those of the

USA: 'The United Kingdom has the highest teenage birth rate in Europe' (UNICEF, 2001: 2). The median age of first intercourse among male and female adolescents between 16 and 19 in 2000 was 16, a fall from 17 a decade ago. The proportion of males 'reporting' intercourse before the age of 16 was 30 per cent, 26 per cent for females, figures which have remained consistent in recent years (Wellings et al., 2001). 'First sex before 16 is more common in those from manual social classes, without qualifications, who did not live with both parents up to the age of 16, those leaving school before age 16, and those who do not cite school as their main source of information about sex' (Dennison, 2004: 2), particularly for those whose first occurrence of menstruation occurred before the age of 13.

Research on Sexual Orientation

Earlier theories that suggested that as many as 10 per cent of people were homosexual (McLeod, 1993) have now been discounted in favour of figures as low as 3 per cent of men and a smaller percentage of women. Current research into genetics questions dated views that human sexuality is a choice. Some geneticists believed they could identify a different gene in the homosexual person, and studies in anthropology and sociology, together with observations of sexual arousal from visual images, appeared to confirm the same (Harrison, 1987). They thereby reasoned that sexual orientation was unlikely to be experienced 'as choice', but, while this may be true, the genetic evidence is inconclusive. The argument is particularly relevant for bisexuals.

> Dean Hamer's team (Hamer et al., 1993) found a common genetic marker on the X chromosome associated with the maternal uncles and male cousins of 114 subjects who were gay (Bragg, 1999), but further research questioned this correlation (Rice et al., 1999) – the case remains open.
>
> However, the contention that homosexuality is 'perverted behaviour' capable of 'cure' is wanting in light of other research. One study points to the futility of seeking cause or 'cure' for homosexuality, on the grounds that 'most men [sic] have homosexual and heterosexual fantasies, feelings, or behaviours' (Hall and Fradkin, 1992: 372). It appears that teenagers have an inclination of their sexual orientation before engaging in first sex, suggesting that gay, lesbian and bisexuals do not 'choose' their orientation.

Bisexuals feel an inclination to satisfy both heterosexual and homosexual drives, and are largely to be found in heterosexual relationships (Scher et al., 1987). It is recognised that most bisexuals marry into heterosexual relationships before they exercise their gay inclinations. The rush to enter into heterosexual union is in itself a *denial* of a sexual orientation that would bring with it a measure of social and intra-familial conflict (Matteson, 1987). In light of expected prejudice and homophobia, counsellors must abandon a pathological model of sexual orientation in favour of a gay/lesbian/bisexual affirmative model of psychotherapy (Hitchings, 1994).

Gay and lesbian young people cannot escape the cultural attitudes underlying censorious narratives that stigmatise their sexual preference and will either hate themselves because of their sexuality or have reason to contemplate suicide.

There is a two-fold increased risk of suicidal ideation associated with homosexual and bisexual young people, particularly for young females (Van Heeringen and Vincke, 2000). Other studies in the USA (The Massachusetts Youth Risk Behaviour Survey, 2006) give figures as high as four times the risk of attempted suicide among lesbian, gay and bisexual high school students compared with those who are straight (Malley et al., 2008). Young gay men and lesbians in the UK are at risk of suicide, particularly during the school years where homophobia is prevalent (Bridget, 2006).

A British survey of 4000 lesbians, gays and bisexuals found that 34 per cent of men and 24 per cent of women had experienced violence because of their sexuality. It was noted that 32 per cent had been harassed in the last five years and 73 per cent had been called names in the last five years because of their sexuality (Mind, 2010). According to official statistics reported by the Samaritans (2009), there has been a decline in suicide rates from 1999 to 2008 for all parts of the UK, apart from Northern Ireland, but at least two young people between the ages of 15 and 24 commit suicide every day and many cases are over same-sex issues.

Environmental Influences

Peer Pressure for Early Sexual Intimacy

Dusek (1996) discusses the broad diversity in cultural attitudes towards early sexual behaviour and the anomaly of parental influences being minimal, whether promoting strict abstinence or being laissez-faire over premarital sex. Conversely, there is some evidence to suggest that unprotected sex is less likely when mothers monitor their daughters rigorously. My own experience confirms the findings of Geldard and Geldard (2010: 37), that peer relations are a major influencing factor in opting for early sexual intimacy, and that once sexual intercourse has been experienced it tends to occur 'persistently rather than sporadically' (2010: 46). Teenagers who have sexually active friends, or friends *they believe* to be sexually active, are more likely to be drawn to early first intercourse through pressures of 'normalcy' and of not being left out.

Mid-to-late adolescence is an exciting and yet testing period of sexual urges and rapid mood swings, where the emotions are stirred by internal hormonal and external social factors (see Chapter 5). These sensory and psychological drives coincide with the transfer from parental to friendship bonding. Fierce competition takes place during courtship, and some feel awkward and out of step with the perceived norms.

A Tragedy of First Sex Experience

At 18, Leanne felt pressured by her friends to go out with a man she barely knew. She wanted sex and to lose her virginity, so as to appear 'with it' to her friends and not 'frigid', but her first, unplanned, sexual encounter was a tragedy – she was raped in a field by a man who proved to be older than he had declared. She suffered repetitive nightmares in which she saw herself tangled in long grass before the brutal robbing of her virginity. This left her with no confidence for further intimate relationships. She saw her youth passing away as she witnessed her friends entering long-term engagements.

Counselling for Leanne consisted of restoring her confidence, providing an image-replacement (Chapter 8) strategy to reduce the potency of the nightmare, helping her to decide what she wanted from male relationships and giving her self-protective strategies in risky situations.

Dennis: Leanne, could we try and desensitise the effects of your nightmare, and write a 'new conclusion' to what you see in your dream, and rehearse it before going to sleep? Let's visualise your attacker, say, standing naked in the field, searching for his clothes, with all his friends laughing at him and calling him a 'pervert' and 'child-molester' (Leanne laughs).

Societal Pressure for Gays and Lesbians

No systematic data exist on first sex experience for gay, lesbian and bisexual young people in the UK, apart from Bridget's (2000) small-scale study. For some young adolescents, feelings about sexual preference can become confused with a common need for same-gender friendships. Same-gender siblings may become engaged in sex play when sharing bedrooms/beds, largely through curiosity. This experimental phase seldom lasts long and could hardly be described as homosexual, since a few of them also experiment mutually with their opposite-gender sibling's bodies, even practising imitative sexual intercourse secretly within the home. For others, their same-sex sexual urges are an early indicator of leanings towards same-gender partnerships, which if known about can result in excessive taunting from homophobic peers (Rivers, 1996; Rofes, 1989).

Gay and lesbian young people may experience intense conflicts in their peer and family relations (Anderson, 1993), which result in serious loss of self-esteem, stigmatisation, loneliness, isolation and sometimes depressive symptoms (Radkowski and Siegel, 1997). There is clearly a need for more research on the sexual practices of gay and lesbian teenagers (aged 13–19) in order to devise fact-based programmes of support, particularly for the former group, argue Sussman and Duffy (1996).

A Case of Early Same-sex Experimentation

Two 13-year-old boys, Damian and Clive, camped out in a tent in the back garden, and among acts of petty devilry, engaged in mutual masturbation. They enjoyed the experience and planned to camp out the following week. The next day, however, Damian – through fear that he might earn a pejorative label in the eyes of 'the lads' – began to spread rumours that Clive was gay (a 'dick-sucker') and that he was attacked in the night by Clive trying to force his 'dick' into his mouth.

Damian was in fear of his reputation and felt uneasy that he had enjoyed the sex play. He was anxious about the implications of enjoying what he thought of as gay sex in respect of his own sexual identity. Clive, needless to say, was very angry and felt let down by Damian's disloyalty and dishonesty. As a result, both boys came separately for counselling, but for very different reasons.

Same-gender sexual experiences in early adolescence are not in themselves evidence that either party is gay or lesbian, or bisexual, but are examples of youngsters experimenting with their sexual urges in situations that are mistakenly thought to be safe in a society that is largely homophobic.

At middle-adolescence, such boys and girls may not be wishing for sexual intimacy so much as wanting to come to terms with feelings of having 'fallen in love' with friends of the same gender, and to understand a sensual wish to hug and fondle each other. Fond embracing is not uncommon with adolescents in secondary school, and is not in itself an indicator of sexual designs, though boys are less likely than girls to be seen hugging each other publicly.

Sexual Abuse through the Internet

The internet has opened the door to homophobic bullying any time of day and, as stated in Chapter 8, networking sites have potential for broadcasting abuse to a wide audience and introducing youngsters to undercover paedophiles. Teenagers are generally ill-equipped in spotting potential risks on social and dating sites when devious characters groom them with comments of flattery, and many have webcams in their bedrooms which have been used to publicise their profiles. One Year 9 pupil of the Academy made a poor judgement by masturbating graphically on his webcam to a girl he liked. Rather than luring her to date him, she claimed she was 'disgusted' after her mother had discovered the image on Facebook. This brought him into conflict with senior staff at her mother's request and consequently resulted in a referral to social services and to me for therapy (see Chapter 8).

The Youth Justice Board report said that 1664 children were given police warnings or court orders for sex offences in 2002–3, but by 2005–6 this had risen to 1988. One in 10 of the offences were committed by children aged 12 or under (Triggle, 2007). The NSPCC runs 22 services in England, Wales and Northern Ireland, and the charity treated over 750 youngsters last year – the overwhelming majority being boys – with an average age of 13, though children as young as 5 were seen by NSPCC specialists for sex offences. Children are viewing abusive sexual images on the internet, and pornography is only a few clicks away. The problem, as reported by the NSPCC, is that continual viewing desensitises young people and enables them to tell themselves that what they are seeing and thinking is acceptable (Triggle, 2007).

Confidentiality and Safeguarding Practice

Having due regard to the law (see Chapter 4), to the BACP (2002) *Ethical Framework* and to the principles and procedures of the educational institution, there may still be room for ethical judgements and discretion in cases of teenage sexuality. There is no direct law in the UK that prevents a youth counsellor – who will have similar legal latitude to that of the GP and the school nurse – from becoming involved in counselling a gay or lesbian young person.

In cases where a pupil has not 'come out' to his parents, and yet is engaged in an under-age, consenting, gay or lesbian sexual relationship, any support without parental knowledge will pose professional and ethical difficulties for the counsellor in school (DfEE, 2000). After assessing that the client is 'Gillick competent', the counsellor in an independent agency has greater latitude than a school counsellor when working on areas of a client's sexual conduct, whether heterosexual or homosexual.

As for school-based practitioners (as discussed in Chapters 3 and 4), it is advisable for therapists to consult their line manager or contract of employment so as to anticipate the ethical dilemmas before they arise. In principle, practitioners have expressed confidence in exercising their own judgement on whether to disclose information on sexual conduct or keep matters confidential (see Appendix III). Teachers in school have the status of a 'reasonable parent', but the school counsellor works within a broader framework. Pastoral practitioners using counselling skills under local educational authority contracts and service agreements or Academy codes are pulled between two obligations:

- loyalty to pupil-clients under codes of confidentiality, and
- the legal position of in loco parentis.

Clients in school or college require a higher degree of confidentiality than many current safeguarding requirements in the UK are permitting, which results in tension, since referral to outside counselling agencies is problematic for young gays and lesbians in educational settings (Hitchings, 1994). The issue of appropriate counsellor–client matching in terms of sexual orientation has been regularly discussed in therapy literature, but in school or college this may be a technical question. Re-referral without parental knowledge and consent can leave therapists open to the charge of drawing a youngster into a gay sub-culture. Even directing pupils and students to gay helplines and supportive networks may leave the practitioner open to criticism.

But gay and lesbian adolescents need information. In light of this impasse, it is advisable to direct a pupil to where such information on supportive networks can be found, rather than leave them vulnerable to internet sites (Scher et al., 1987). The school counsellor would do well to clearly set the boundaries of her work at the outset for those pupils contemplating making self-referral for sexual counselling, and to publicise them in the waiting room and the school prospectus.

Insights for Therapy

Psychodynamic theories of homosexuality stem from Oedipal relations (Freud, 1933) and early sex therapists of cognitive schools viewed gay and lesbian sex as 'learned conditions' capable of 'cure' (Ellis, 1965, 1976). Such early understandings tended to view anything other than heterosexuality as pathological illness (Lines, 2002a). The American Psychiatric Association now acknowledges that homosexuality is not a pathological condition. Harrison (1987) points out that there is no correlation between sexual orientation and psychological health and pathology. He showed there to be no single profile of the gay, lesbian or bisexual person, that sexual orientation is established early on in life and that it is not subject to change (Hooker, 1985).

Congruence with Gay and Lesbian Clients

All counsellors should aim to be non-judgemental and accepting of their clients, irrespective of ethnicity, creed, gender or sexuality. They subscribe to the core conditions (Rogers, 1967) and believe that in order to facilitate change – which includes an acceptance of the self – the therapist must openly centre on the feelings and attitudes which are 'flowing in him' in the current counselling situation, without front or façade and without feigning empathy: to engage at a level of 'relational depth' (Mearns and Cooper, 2005).

Congruence is the personal quality of genuineness and it implies that the counsellor is in touch with her own thoughts and feelings. In maintaining congruence with homosexual clients, the importance of supervision cannot be understated. It is in supervision that the counsellor is given an opportunity to explore personal feelings about those clients having a sexual orientation that is different to her own, particularly if strong religious or cultural beliefs are held, whether the practitioner engages in deep or brief work.

The counsellor's role is not to change the client's beliefs to conform to her own, but to help *them to arrive at what is right for them* (McLeod, 1993), and if they are 'offended' by their client's disclosures they should 'stop playing the game' (Masson, 1992: 232) because the therapeutic relationship cannot help but be affected. Gay and lesbian clients may have come to the counsellor for a form of support and understanding they have not found elsewhere.

Counselling Heterosexual Young People

Authors highlight the dominant discourses that underlie abusive behaviour (Payne, 2006; Winslade and Monk, 1999). Chapter 5 examined narratives of adolescents being highly sexual beings from a constructionist perspective. Payne (2006) contends that being over-concerned with counselling a victim of abuse fails to challenge the patriarchal narratives that authorise such behaviour. Winslade and Monk (1999) illustrate narrative questioning interventions that aim at combating abusive behaviour through the work of Alan Jenkins (1990). The problem I find with such approaches is that abusive people are rarely accessible for therapy – it is the victim who arrives at the counsellor's door.

In the following case, counselling boundaries are highlighted with regard to underage consenting heterosexual behaviour. The case illustrates how the practitioner may choose to support the young client in school by supporting her carers in the home. A pluralistic approach with features of narrative therapy, cognitive-humanistic counselling and solution-focused perspectives is illustrated through a goal of opening dialogue between a mother and her daughter (Davis and Osborn, 2000).

Caroline – Initial Meeting for Therapy

Caroline was approaching 13 and had been going out with a boy aged 13 for two months. She came voluntarily for two separate counselling sessions about sexual matters. On the first occasion, she approached me feeling anxious that her mother and stepfather might discover something through her cousin 'grassing her up'. She talked around the issue for some time, and the counselling was getting nowhere. She said that something had happened the night before with her boyfriend, and I guessed that it had something to do with sex. It was fear of what her carers might say that was crucial.

As Caroline sat beside me, she made fixed eye contact, and I felt she wanted me to know but was embarrassed to outline what had happened. I decided to challenge her and asked 'Have you had sex with your boyfriend?' She immediately looked relieved and said that she had. 'Did you take precautions and use a condom?' I asked. She replied that they hadn't.

With her permission, I arranged for her to speak with the school nurse, who organised a pregnancy test. She also engaged her in sexual health counselling and offered her personal contraceptive advice. Counselling practitioners working in UK schools are not permitted to give individual contraceptive advice and, as discussed in Chapter 4, opinion is divided on whether to report to social services such behaviour as consenting teenage sexuality in light of the Sexual Offences Act 2003. For a school nurse, however – with a medical responsibility for her patient – there is no such prohibition. Since this was dual support, involving myself as school counsellor and the school nurse, we discussed the case at length and I further took the matter to supervision.

The Sexual Offences Act 2003 regards a child under 13 to be unable to give consent for sex, but the law is designed to protect children from abuse and exploitation by those of an age of criminal responsibility[4]. After sharing Caroline's reflection that this was a one-off event for which she did not feel ready, we felt there were no immediate risks facing her. Nevertheless, my supervisor's counsel was that I should offer a follow-up session to monitor her progress in dealing with the issue. Over the first incident, then, the school nurse and I decided not to inform Caroline's parents, though this was no easy decision.

Caroline – Second Meeting for Therapy

Having experienced a non-judgemental reception, Caroline approached me a second time, arm in arm with a friend, to announce that she had had sex again, but this time not with a peer but with a young man of 17. I judged this to be more serious. Her first sexual experience might be put down to experimentation, but this time I could not rule out exploitation and the need to consider child protection procedures.

We discussed this fully in session, and I felt it was necessary to explain to her that I considered her welfare was at risk and that we should seriously consider sharing this information with her mother. I was acutely aware of the issue of 'client confidentiality', here in tension with 'respect for autonomy'. My normal practice is to give my client the opportunity to take the initiative, and, in consequence, I asked her if she would speak to her mother that night. Although she said she could 'if the right opportunity presented itself', I was doubtful she would. After putting off the ordeal, I spoke to her mother on her behalf, which initially caused her to worry but in retrospect brought relief.

Her mother was naturally devastated and said that her partner had not been surprised to discover she might be sexually active. 'The signs were there', he said, which made her feel doubly foolish for not picking it up. She saw me regularly to discuss an appropriate course of action.

Apart from my concern over Caroline's welfare, the 'normalising' influence among her girlfriends of losing her virginity so young troubled me; by being facilitative, there is an inadvertent endorsement of her behaviour that I was keen to play down while being neutral in all other respects. Counselling was offered, therefore, to Caroline and her friends in order to place 'normalising' perceptions in a broader context. The counselling work focused primarily on work with Caroline's mother, whom I refer to as Mary.

Mary and I agreed that she and her daughter needed an opportunity to speak openly, and this became our goal in therapy. I reiterated the importance of this by saying that there was no time that Caroline needed her more than at this moment. Mary kept punishing herself with guilt and wept over the realisation that her 'innocent little girl' was no longer a virgin. Her grief was accommodated in person-centred counselling and a

Dominant narrative	Applied narrative	Modified narrative
Adolescents know all about sex these days	My daughter is 'experimenting' *because* she doesn't know all about sex	My daughter will need proper information and advice from me
Girls want sex even when they say no – they're playing 'hard to get'	My daughter may have been hoodwinked by a male sexual predator – I have lost her	We are still close – Caroline needs me now, and *we decide* on whether our relationship is lost
With premarital sex, girls are sluts, boys are studs	Promiscuous girls vaunt their sexuality to vulnerable boys and lose their virginity early and justifiably	My daughter has been exploited by someone who is responsible for a criminal offence of sex with a minor
Emancipated women neglect their children	I've been too busy working to notice my daughter's needs	My generated income improves my children's lives and models an example of industry
Females are responsible for their own sexual protection	A 17-year-old man may not care if my daughter were pregnant; *he should know,* but she'll have to safeguard her own welfare	My daughter needs my experience to better prepare her for such events that border on rape or abuse

Figure 13.1 Mary's narrative chart

collaborative exploration of the dominant narratives which were operating unconsciously on her thinking was undertaken. Overriding cultural narratives were applied to Mary's situation, and were modified (as shown in Figure 13.1) to help Mary support herself and to see her natural feelings of guilt and sadness in a broad social context.

In spite of feeling a little better about the destructive thought of 'if only' (I'd have spent more time with Caroline …, spoken to her more …, given her appropriate sexual information, and so on), Mary was acknowledging that wanting to speak with Caroline was not going to be easy. It is important to recognise how difficult it is to confront those we love and to get it right. An enormous pressure builds up, and well-rehearsed scripts work better in the mind than in practice. Nelson-Jones' (1996) effective thinking skills of 'thinking positively' were applied.

> I often find transferred thought helpful when I am faced with a difficult challenge – for example, when I go to the dentist, I do not ruminate on the needle and drill, but on imagined future situations and on having left the unpleasantness behind me.

I asked Mary, in preparation, to focus mentally on an enriched relationship of closeness and adulthood from sharing information on the most delicate area of sexual relationships. Mary felt confident to relate in counselling her own sexual history, and recalled how she had had a traumatic time in dealing with her own mother's scorn and disapproval. I asked how much of this detail was known to Caroline.

She was not sure what her daughter knew, apart from the fact that she was born when Mary was only 15. She did not want a rift to occur between them as had happened in her own childhood. In consequence, she was keen, albeit nervous, to open dialogue. I was not prescriptive about what personal information Mary should give Caroline, only that she should begin speaking, remain solution-focused and believe that the powerful feelings of love that caused her to regret her daughter's loss of virginity would clearly shine through in creating an opportunity for bridge building, so long as she could remain calm.

In this case, it was Mary not Caroline who became my principal client. The goal for Mary was to set the stage for communication through an initial task of rehearsing *what she would say to Caroline and the tone in which she would say it* to begin the process. Although no follow-up session was planned, Mary thanked me on the phone and Caroline confirmed that our work had brought them closer together.

Counselling Gay and Lesbian Teenagers

For pupils and students who are convinced of their gay and lesbian orientations and who approach the counsellor for support in 'coming out' to their parents and/or friends, CBT, SFT, Egan's three-stage model and cognitive-humanistic counselling, in particular, may prove effective. The therapy is goal-oriented and the aim is to help the client gain confidence and find ways to carry out the specified task with a minimum of personal trauma.

These approaches help confident students to manage the effects of social isolation, labelling and stigma when personal disclosures to friends have become public.

Mark's Decision to 'Come Out'

Mark was a bright Year 13 student, popular with the girls but ostracised from the macho-oriented males of his learning group. In citizenship lessons, his debating skills were exceptional, and in this respect he towered above his peers. He sat alone near the front, and appeared detached from all but two girls with whom he regularly conversed. He had ambitions to enter medical school later on. He came for counselling after school when he knew he could find me alone. He informed me straight away that he was gay: 'I don't know whether you are aware of it, but I'm gay.'

He was in a relationship with a junior doctor in his mid-twenties. His companion had a flat and Mark often stayed over the weekend and had consensual sex – pretending to his mother that he was staying at the home of a friend. The relationship had begun a few months earlier, but had become more intense during his final year at school.

Mark was asked in the introductory session why he wished to disclose to me that he was gay. His reply was that he wanted support in bringing him to the point of 'coming out' to his mother and friends. Egan's (1990) three-stage scheme was adopted within a pluralistic perspective. There were no ethical compromises to consider, and a contract of three sessions was agreed upon with the aim of achieving his goal within two weeks with stage-by-stage tasks. The remaining part of the first session was spent in establishing frank and honest dialogue.

His sexual inclinations and judgements were discussed, at his request, to help him assess whether or not he was being exploited, particularly since he was in a relationship with an older man. His preferred scenario – to have his sexual orientation validated and made known within the family – was explored.

From a legal perspective, as Mark was an intelligent young man approaching 18, his gay relationship was not *his* problem; his concern, and his purpose in coming for counselling, was to enlist my support in 'coming out' to his mother. Counselling consisted of rehearsing how he might do this and what he might say. He confirmed that he and his partner were practising safe sex. He anticipated that his mother would accept him being gay, for there were already gay role models within the family: his two sisters were lesbians. Heterosexual relationships were not the 'norm' for this family. Mark was grateful for my support and therapy terminated when his goal had been accomplished.

In cases like Mark's, where clients are secretly engaged in gay or lesbian relationships, it demands considerable courage within a homophobic society to even approach a counsellor (who is assumed to be straight), let alone share intimate discourse. The client will be anxious about a decision to 'come out', which often comes without prior warning and with little awareness of how it might be received (Hitchings, 1994). Admitting one's same-sex inclinations is an early step towards autonomy, and the school counsellor can help in this process, so long as there is no fear of significant moral or physical risk and so long as the young person is 'Gillick competent'. The counsellor must 'maintain an attitude of respectful, serious attention … no matter how shocking, trivial or ridiculous the patient's productions are' (Frank, 1986: 16).

Jessica's Dilemma – Has She Lesbian Inclinations?

Jessica was a Year 11 pupil, aged 16, who approached me to help resolve an inner conflict. She had been in counselling previously for difficulties in her relationship with her mother. She felt at a disadvantage in social relations through what she described as a 'very strict' upbringing. Her mother appeared to counteract every social engagement she had planned at school – going to the cinema, dating boys and going to parties, and so on – with demanding chores at home and baby-sitting. As time moved on in her final year of school,

(Continued)

(Continued)

her mother relaxed these responsibilities, and the particular problem she presented in the introductory session arose from a party.

She had attended her best friend's 16th birthday party and was allowed to sleep over at her house. Some began leaving at a set time and the clearing up was being done when the sleeping arrangements were discussed. There were not enough beds for the group of girls sleeping over, so Jessica agreed to share the double bed with her friend, Sarah. They changed into nightclothes and talked through the early hours about the party. Slipping into sleep but still conscious, Jessica became aware of Sarah snuggling up to her back, but still she read nothing into it. She then became anxious as Sarah's hand stroked her breast, and after being kissed several times on the neck with the soft words, 'I love you, Jessica', she became confused. She did not know how to respond.

She had suspicions that Sarah had had lesbian relations with a mutual friend, by their exclusive conversations and incessant wish to be with each other all the time, often pushing boys away – but how could she respond to this situation? She felt a little nervous. Should she turn and face Sarah, which might lead to more intimate masturbation than she felt ready for, and that she felt sure Sarah wanted? She had some attraction for Sarah but not in a way she felt she wanted to express sexually. Should she spurn her advances and say, 'I'm sorry, Sarah, but I don't feel the same for you', which would appear rejecting and hurtful? She replied, in a non-committal tone, 'Yes, I know. Goodnight, Sarah'.

They both fell asleep without an escalation of sexual activity, and spoke nothing of the matter the next morning. She came for counselling to help resolve confusion over her sexual inclinations – whether she had heterosexual or lesbian urges, or both – and, in the light of such feelings, to arrive at a decision of whether to encourage or discourage any further sexual encounters with open and frank discussion. She also felt ambivalent about coming between Sarah and their mutual friend.

At the close of the third session of cognitive-humanistic counselling (Nelson-Jones, 1999b), she felt she should put a stop to any gestures that would give an impression of anything other than a platonic friendship. Although she recognised within herself a trace of same-gender attraction and fondness for Sarah, she could not be sure she wanted to express her feelings sexually. She therefore discussed her goal with me and we devised the task of speaking 'directly' to Sarah through role play and 'self-talk' exercises (Nelson-Jones, 1996), practising what she might say and the context within which she would discuss it – all with compassion and understanding.

For those who are struggling with bewildering and powerful sexual feelings, who may even regret their desires for same-gender affiliations, goal-centred therapy may not be indicated. For those tormented by gay and lesbian fantasies and urges – to be hugged, kissed or to engage in more intimate sexual stimulation – and who are in conflict with their value system and social expectations, narrative styles which pay greater attention to 'what we are' within prevailing societal attitudes may be more beneficial.

With sexual mores becoming more relaxed generally but still homophobic, anxiety results for those who are gay, lesbian or bisexual. In the community, and in school and/or college, gay young people are often regarded as 'queer' or 'perverse'. That prejudice and stigma exist in school goes without saying, 'otherwise, adolescents would simply pair off in social activities as they wish and there would be no occasion to comment' (Harrison, 1987: 226).

Michelle's Dilemma – Being Accepted as a Lesbian

Michelle had persistent dreams of engaging in lesbian sex (never heterosexual) with her friends in Year 9, and when her older brother spread a rumour around the school that she was a 'dyke', she felt unable to face people and hold her head high. Her anxiety was heightened with the realisation that her parents would never accept her as a lesbian.

After her brother discovered her secret book of poems on lesbian sex, she found the ridicule at home so unbearable that at one point she contemplated suicide by taking an overdose. Her friends brought her for counselling after seeing her in a 'troubled state'. Her problem was not the acceptance of self, but of being accepted by significant others.

Michelle's dreams and poems may or may not have been an indicator of fixed lesbian inclination at her developmental stage, but the effects of unwisely speaking of such dreams, even among 'unsympathetic' family members, can be disastrous for social integration. The counselling role was first to affirm the validity of her feelings and desires in a non-judgemental way, then to work on the implications with regard to social relations. How could she convince her parents to at least accept her for what she was? It seemed an impossible goal.

After a brief focal psychodynamic session (childhood experience and dream analysis), the pluralistic emphasis (Cooper and McLeod, 2010) involved an integration of narrative and solution-focused techniques. The 'miracle question' (Davis and Osborn, 2000) prompted Michelle to say, 'I want my friends and particularly my mum and brothers to accept me as I am, whatever I find myself to be'. We attempted to 'externalise the problem' (White, 1989), which we selected as the censorious 'homophobic narrative' itself that had infiltrated the minds of her parents and had altered their consciousness like an invading alien, but though the analogies made us laugh, when we thought them through the approach seemed to lack seriousness.

We explored sub-plots to her story (Payne, 2006) of 'not being accepted for who I am', and discovered that her mother had eventually accepted other facets of her personality that she had earlier tried to change, such as her daughter's tastes in music and clothes, preferred foods, friends and places of entertainment, and so on.

From this, we speculated how long it would take for her parents to eventually come round. This proved helpful and increased her optimism that 'someday she'll accept me for who I am, heterosexual or lesbian'. Realistic goals of confronting her brother's attitudes and feelings and entrenched homophobic prejudices were set, and scaling helped her to reach the point where she could confidently terminate counselling (O'Connell, 2005).

Many pupils become confused over whether their same-gender attractions are sexual or merely the longing for stronger friendship bonding.

Male Students with Bisexual Feelings

Two Year 10 boys, Paul and Sean, came independently for counselling, convinced that they were gay, and that they had known it since they were small. Paul had been with a male and a female partner on separate occasions and had strong bisexual urges; Sean felt an irresistible urge to consummate his desires 'when the time was right'. Paul continually, almost obsessively, desired to be in the company of a male friend from another school, yet in the two weeks that followed the session began dating a girl in his year group.

Sean remained resolutely convinced about his inclinations and was in many ways quite brave in warding off occasional insults. His parents were determined to humiliate him and to convince him that he was all mixed up and not really gay at all.

Dominant narrative	Applied narrative	Modified narrative
Homosexual people do dirty sexual things – they are queer	My parents think I am sexually active in ways they think are 'disgusting'	I don't know what I want yet sexually, and my parents have unfounded fantasies about my sexuality; people are ignorant of homosexual lifestyles
Homosexuality is not 'natural'	My parents are ashamed of having given birth to someone who is not straight, like them	I know what my general inclination is by now. It is sad, but I am not responsible for their felt shame
Homosexual inclination in youth is a phase of being mixed up because of hormones	My parents can't face the prospect of me being different from them – it suits them to think I'm confused	I know my wishes and desires in every other respect, why not my sexual preferences?
Homosexuals seek publicity!	My parents think I am attention-seeking and are embarrassed about people finding out	The opposite is true for me. I'm struggling to keep my sexual identity a secret – who on earth wants to be singled out?

Figure 13.2   Sean's narrative chart

In both cases, brief counselling had no goal to work on other than *self-acceptance*. For both Paul and Sean, narrative questioning, as illustrated in Figure 13.2, proved helpful in accepting themselves *as they are,* and in helping them combat homophobic pressure through self-assertion social skills training, as illustrated in Chapter 8.

The combined evidence of youngsters feeling stigmatised and needing to talk, together with high suicide rates, suggests that adolescents in schools are struggling to come to terms with same-gender sexual desires. The professional course has to be one that gives such young people unequivocal support. In a wholly affirmative manner, the school counsellor must help clients *accept themselves*, and plan collaboratively how they may respond effectively to homophobia and prejudice. Above all: 'The ethical counsellor must not become the agent of repression, but rather will help the boy understand himself and responsibly manage his sexuality' (Harrison, 1987: 226).

Conclusion

There are few developmental challenges that confront school counsellors as much as teenage sexuality. Personal judgements and therapeutic engagements are likely to be varied and, perhaps, in some cases, controversial. In light of the statistics of what is known – and what remains unknown – of early sexual behaviour among teenagers and peer pressure to lose one's virginity quickly, or to cope with homophobia in school and the community, practitioners cannot but address the needs in spite of the controversy, and in an affirmative manner. Yet, in spite of the difficulties and likely hazards, practitioners should recognise that exploring human sexuality can be a thrilling adventure and is an important milestone in adolescent development.

This chapter has explored the legal and ethical boundaries centring upon early adolescent sexual behaviour, and has confronted the technical question of genetics and homosexual orientation. While genetic evidence of orientation remains inconclusive, other amassing research would suggest that all counsellors might take an affirmative stance with young gay, lesbian and bisexual students. Ethically, school counsellors should take it as read that the core conditions of unconditional positive regard, empathy and congruence have to extend to teenagers engaging in heterosexual intercourse and gay and lesbian experimentation, all within the 'Gillick principle' and whatever safeguarding principles operate in the particular agency or institution.

Combinations of goal-centred approaches and elements of SFT and narrative therapy have been illustrated within a pluralistic perspective in the various cases presented above. The principal aim is to support youngsters where experimentation has gone wrong and poor judgement has occurred, to encourage gay and lesbian students to *accept themselves* and their newly discovered orientation – all within guidance on practising safer sex. Second, where applicable, the role is to assist clients in finding a way and a manner to 'come out' to friends and family where homophobic fears and prejudices are found to exist. 'Coming out' may present greater hurdles for those gay, lesbian and bisexual young people of some ethnic and strictly religious families.

Reflective Exercise

1. A hypothetical case was presented in Chapter 4 where a young teenager of 12 had entered a sexual relationship with a peer of the same age. This chapter presented one such case, Caroline. This is controversial.

   a. Within the current 'reporting culture' of safeguarding procedures, as you understand them in applying to your own practice, what course of action would you have taken versus reporting the matter after the first occasion to the parent, to a pastoral teacher or to social services? Give reasons for your course of action.

   b. Carry out the same exercise in relation to the case of Mark outlined above, giving reasons for your course of action.

2. Do you think that teenagers can have a strong sense of their sexual orientation while at secondary school? Supposing you had to help a pastoral teacher compose a procedures document with regard to pupils of the school who disclose that they know they are gay or lesbian, what principles would you consider most important from your own therapeutic insight?

3. Do you consider that it is possible to engage in therapy around sexuality with an at-risk student who is known to be sexually active, without it having a bearing on your own sexual history and experience, or the guidance you would give to your teenage son or daughter? Select any one of the above cases, and make a few comments on how the material, or the therapeutic intervention taken, affected you personally.

4. Take a fresh look at the case presented in Chapter 5, where a client of 14 years could hear her mother having sex with numerous partners in a downstairs bedroom during the afternoon. Under role-modelling principles, what psycho-education would you consider appropriate if you knew your client was beginning a sexual relationship with a boy of the same age whom she had dated for six months?

Key Points

- Sexual relations among young people can be an exciting as much as traumatic time; parental attitudes and cultural values determine views on what is normal, what is healthy and what is permissible.

- Adolescent sexual development is varied in the West: for some, their first experience of sexual intercourse and loss of virginity is not always a positive experience; for others, it is an opportunity for testing fantasies and for bolstering self-esteem and sexual prowess.

- School counsellors must consider the boundaries within which they work in relation to teenage sexual behaviour; their principal role is not to teach sex education so much as to work towards positive relationships and responsible decision making, and to always encourage safe sex for all orientations.

- When youngsters become lured towards sexual exploitation, the school counsellor has a responsible role to balance confidentiality with child protection, and to secure the welfare of those who are immature and who will sometimes make naïve decisions.

- Gay and lesbian youngsters can have a traumatic time in *being accepted* by their parents and friends, and in due course in *accepting themselves* because of their sexual preferences and inclinations, particularly within a homophobic culture.

- Brief counselling must take an affirmative view of the whole spectrum of sexuality in light of what is known of sexual orientation and in light of the high suicide risk of those who discover themselves to be gay, lesbian or bisexual – such people do not have *conditions to be cured,* but differences to accept and deal with.

- Goal-centred therapeutic approaches prove helpful for students who are ready to 'come out', or who wish to counter mistaken signals, but, for those who are confused, SFT techniques and narrative therapy charts can help clarify their inclinations within a societal context.

Appendix I

Counselling Report

Academic year 2009/2010

Abstract

94.7 per cent of pupils engaging in brief therapy (on average 3–4 sessions) reported improvement by up to 4 points on a 10-point scale, and 97.3 per cent said they had felt 'better', or 'much better', or were 'fine now', to such a degree that 68.4 per cent of these claimed they had no need of further counselling support. A good number, 84.2 per cent, of clients said that their problem was 'serious', 'quite serious' or 'unbearable'. The major causes that brought them to therapy were issues to do with anger, bereavement, serious arguments with parents and issues within the family, and bullying. There was found to be a tendency for many pupils to overrate their ability level when compared with SATS attainment levels. Finally, factors to do with low potential attainment included 60.5 per cent of families having no adult in full-time work, one in every five pupil-clients, conceivably, having no 'place for private study', and six in every ten coming from families dependent on state benefit.

Method

This report is a triangulation study of anecdotal experience and self-evaluation questionnaires given to pupil-clients engaged in counselling for three sessions or more during the summer of 2010. Every client counselled through the academic year was not reviewed in detail, but 38 were randomly selected to serve as subjects for analysis. The responses of the pupils who benefited from single session interventions (by far the majority) were not asked for and are therefore not reflected in this report.

The first questionnaire required a tick response to a series of six questions, and a numerical rating (1–10) to indicate how students felt *before* in contrast to *after* counselling (41 questionnaires were given out, but three were discarded owing to evident confusion on self-rating scales). The second served as a blind cross-reference, but also contained questions of client demography – family composition, ethnicity, economy – that may have a bearing on learning potential and social mobility. Pupils completed questionnaires anonymously. Because of the sensitive nature of the data, the questionnaire was piloted by four students before arriving at the final form, largely to ascertain the level of intrusiveness of the questions.

Although it was stressed that honesty was paramount – with me not being present during the completion of the questionnaires – the subjective nature of the first questionnaire and parts of the second is accepted. It is acknowledged, particularly in the health service, that self-evaluation questionnaires on the quality of service and management of received healthcare have inherent weaknesses. Patients have a sense of loyalty towards their doctors and nurses, and it is in their personal health interests to overrate performance by exaggerating outcome scores. In the same manner, many pupils will intuitively overrate my performance and anticipate a 'required' response by recording what they think I would like them to say. Owing to the managerial logistics of having others compile and complete such a questionnaire instead of me (job description, available time, etc.), however, it is difficult to see how any alternative could be carried out in school at this time.

Counselling Evaluation Questionnaire: Results (Per cent)

1. Referrals

Self-referred	Other-referral	Staff-referral	Parents/carers	Friends
44.7	55.3	50	0	5.3

Note: pupils who ticked box for 'Staff-referral' and 'Friends', also ticked 'Other-referral'.

2. General nature of the problem

Bullying	Family matters	Loss/Bereavement	Falling out	Other reasons
10.5	47.3	13.2	5.3	23.6

3. Feelings evoked by the problem

Anger	Upset	Illness	Loneliness/Isolation	Other feelings
39.5	36.8	7.9	2.6	13.1

4. Resultant behaviours

Behaving out of character	Behaving aggressively	Becoming negative	Getting into trouble	Behaving in other ways
10.5	21	44.7	15.8	7.9

5. Seriousness of the problem

Minor	Quite serious	Serious	Very serious	Unbearable
15.8	36.9	26.3	13.1	7.9

6. After counselling clients felt

Worse	No difference	A little better	Better	Much better
0	5.2 (new problems)	26.3	34.2	34.2

7. Scored improvement of 1–10

Negative	1 step	2 step	3 step	4 step	5 step	6 step	7 step	8 step	9 step
0	0	0	5.3	21.1	36.8	15.8	10.5	7.9	2.6

Regarding the last question, **all clients felt there was an improvement** on a numerical scale of at least three points, 94.7 per cent felt improved by up to four points, and 73.6 per cent recorded improvements over five points on a self-report scale.

8. Termination of counselling agreements

Matters are fine now	I no longer need counselling	Request for further counselling
15.9	68.4	15.9

Of the 15.9 per cent of pupils reporting that they would like further counselling, none were asked specifically whether it was because the problems were ongoing or whether there were 'new problems' occurring.

Demography Questionnaire: Results (Per cent)

1. Ethnicity – self-described

British	English	Scottish	Welsh	Irish	Asian	Pakistani	African	Chinese
18	14	3	0	0	1	1	1	0
47.3	36.8	7.9	0	0	2.6	2.6	2.6	0

2. Gender and year group composition (Option 2 and 3 on demographic questionnaire)

	Male			Female	
	21			17	
	55.2			44.7	

Year 7	Year 8	Year 9	Year 10	Year 11	Years 12/13
1	11	10	12	4	0
2.6	28.9	26.3	31.5	10.4	0

Regarding Years 12 and 13, four students were counselled but were unavailable for recording.

3. Disparity of ability self-rating compared with English SATS scores (KS2 or KS3, if taken)

'Very bright'	'Above average'	'Slightly above average'	'Average'	'Below average'
3	9	3	18	5
7.9	23.7	7.9	47.3	13.2

It seems that reporting 'average' was safe. Comparing self-assessment with previous KS2/3 results showed that **53 per cent of clients (20) made accurate assessments**, and **47 per cent (18) reported inaccurately** – of these, 15 (83 per cent) overrated and 3 (17 per cent) underrated their ability.

4. Detailed nature of the problem

No.	%	Description
9	24	problems with anger
6	15.8	loss and bereavement
6	15.8	experienced conflict with parents

No.	%	Description
5	13	had been bullied
3	7.9	got into too much trouble
1	2.6	had a fall out with friends
1	2.6	depression
1	2.6	self-harm
1	2.6	impending split of parents
1	2.6	clash with a teacher
1	2.6	unable to control aggression
1	2.6	suffered abuse on an internet site
1	2.6	disappointment over a football trial
1	2.6	confidence building
0	0	worried about health, disability, diet or obesity

5. Number of arranged appointments

3 sessions	4 sessions	5 sessions	6 sessions	7 sessions	8 sessions
16	4	12	2	3	1
42.1	10.4	31.6	5.3	7.9	2.6

6. Feeling of change

Felt the same	Felt better	Felt a little better	Felt much better	Fine now
2.6	2.6	28.9	42	23.7

No clients felt worse and **97.3 per cent of clients said that counselling had helped them feel better.**

7. Siblings living in the family home

Only child	1 sibling	3 siblings	4 siblings	5 siblings	6 siblings	7 siblings	9 siblings	10 siblings
0	11	10	10	2	1	2	1	1
0	28.9	26.3	26.3	5.2	2.6	5.2	2.6	2.6

Correlating the data with reported employment status of parent/s, it may be assumed that 44.7 per cent of pupils (i.e. those living in a family with three siblings) might suffer from crowded conditions in the family home, and that 18 per cent, or **one in five pupils coming for counselling, might find 'a place for private study' very difficult. This has massive implications for learning potential.**

8. Parent/carer from infancy

Mother and father	Mother alone	Father alone	Mother and partner	Adopted	Grandparent/Relative
50	28.9	5.2	10.5	2.6	2.6

One client was brought up initially by grandmother but later by mother and father, two clients by mother and father then by mother alone, three by both parents then by mother and stepfather, two by mother then by father and partner, and three by mother and father then by father alone.

9. Regarding employment

One parent in full-time employment	No parent/carer in work	Parent in training	Parent claiming disability benefit
15	18	1	4
39.4	47.3	2.6	10.5

Overall, **60.53 per cent of families (or 6 in every 10) of a child receiving counselling had no parent or carer employed and therefore were on state benefit.** This matched free meal figures, where 24 (63.10 per cent) clients (or 6 in every 10) had a free meal and 14 (36.8 per cent) clients paid for their own.

10. Plans for the future

I have no idea what to do after leaving school	I plan to carry on in further education	I know exactly what I want to do after reaching the SLA	I want: a family; good grades; a good job; not to turn out like my brother
5	5	22	6
13.2	13.2	57.8	15.8

In sum, **84.2 per cent of students had a clear idea of what they wanted to do after the SLA.** Apart from further education, vocations selected included:

Army (2), author, chef, child carer, dance teacher, doctor, driver, footballer (3), game designer, hairdresser, hypnotherapist, carer for sick children, mechanic (2), musician, nursery nurse, paramedic, policeman, builder.

One reported she 'wanted a career, not like my brother', two said they 'wanted good grades', one 'wanted a family' and two just 'wanted a job'.

Discussion

These results illustrate that those young clients receiving counselling felt that this had been beneficial to them, and it would be interesting to see what other measures could be used to record improvement more objectively ('feeling better' is not 'becoming better'), such as improved attendance figures or raised scholastic attainment. But, as already acknowledged, self-report ratings are notoriously subjective.

Further, identifying the specific factors attributable to client outcome is virtually impossible, as largely recognised in the field of psychotherapy research. It is extremely difficult to isolate counselling intervention from concurrent changes in individuals' lives – such as changing friends, moving forms or learning groups, healing after losses, changes in family circumstances (such as step-parents or elder siblings leaving the family home), a troublesome neighbour being evicted or a change in the family's economic situation, etc. – to be able to state with certainty that counselling alone has brought improvement. It may be that after one counselling session a pupil's attendance improves, but other influences could cause the same to happen, such as a firmer resolve from the parent, a visit from an attendance worker, an absent father taking more control, a warning from the school or the Educational Social Worker (ESW) threatening legal action.

Correlating a counselling intervention (particularly in brief therapy, where sessions may be as short as three or four) with raised academic performance and then making dogmatic assertions is questionable. Counselling is aimed at insight into behavioural patterns or the encouragement (through CBT) of modified behaviour, and, as such, improvement – assessed by individuals and/or their parents – can be relatively quick, albeit subjective, but learning measures through schooling are much more timely, so that claiming that any one has influenced the other is difficult to substantiate.

Conclusions and Observations

A few observations arise from the demography questionnaire. Bearing in mind that the 38 questionnaires were merely a sample of counselling work, and did not include single or double session therapeutic interventions (by far the most), it was judged that there was an even distribution of clientele in terms of ethnicity and gender (compared with on-roll composition), but not, surprisingly, of year groups. Owing to curriculum demands of Years 10 and 11, particularly Year 11, the bulk of longer-term work engaged Years 8, 9 and 10 early on into the year. But Year 7 occupies proportionally a low take-up. I think this is because, in the early secondary years, the form tutor, the nurse, attendance workers and other pastoral staff engage with them quite frequently (and have relatively more parental contact) through conventional care and behaviour correction methods, before the particular skills of the school counsellor are brought in and 'Gillick competency' issues arise.

Although it was clearly 'safe' for pupil-clients to report their ability level as 'average', it surprised me that 83 per cent of the cohort making inaccurate assessments of their ability – when compared with English SATS level attainments – had **overestimated** their ability in comparison to the 17 per cent that had underrated themselves. There may be issues to do with 'false' or 'inflated' beliefs that might delude some low-ability pupils into believing they are more able than they are. While 'high expectation' in psychology is recognised to deliver better attainment results in education and counselling, there may be a need for some accurate 'reality testing' lower down the school earlier on to inform pupils 'where they currently are' and 'where they need to be'.

It was no surprise that 'anger', 'bereavement' and 'conflict with parents or carers', followed by 'bullying victimology' and 'getting into too much trouble', took up most of the therapeutic work.

The 93.7 per cent of clients who had reported that counselling had made them 'feel better' was not surprising, in view of the comments made above, but nevertheless was reassuring.

The data on family composition and employment status was interesting. It was heartening to see how many pupils were brought up from birth to the present by both parents, or still had continual contact with the other parent not living at home. Nevertheless:

The figure of over 60 per cent of families having no parent or carer in full-time work is a major concern in terms of behavioural modelling, and the relative high proportion of families receiving state benefit can leave an impression of 'inevitability' – of 'one's lot – or a preference that such becomes 'a life choice' as opposed to 'bettering oneself' or furthering a career. Considering that two outcome measures of the *Every Child Matters* agenda are to 'make a positive contribution' and 'achieve economic well-being', there are great challenges for any school in this area in terms of curriculum planning and exploring roles in voluntary work.

There are grave consequences of sibling crowdedness in regard to learning potential that will have implications for home-based study. Crowded conditions (confirmed by anecdotal data), which are due to more than three siblings in three-bedroom homes, makes private study space for pupils quite problematic. Coursework set to be completed away from school, which has relative low importance to other family tasks, and where highly motivated adult guidance and leadership may be lacking, may not yield the best results and become a limiting factor for students to become upwardly mobile.

Counselling Evaluation

(Place a tick in the box ✓)

Came to see Mr Lines for counselling	I was asked to see Mr Lines for counselling	I was referred for counselling	My mum or dad asked me to see Mr Lines	My friend said I should see Mr Lines

My problem was about bullying	My problem was to do with family matters	My problem was coping with losing someone close	My problem was falling out with friends	My problem was something else

My problem made me feel angry	My problem upset me	My problem made me feel unwell	My problem made me feel lonely	I felt some other way

My problem caused me to behave strangely	The problem caused me to be aggressive	I began to think negatively	I started to get into trouble	I started to behave in some other way

Before I came for counselling my problem was:

A minor problem	Quite serious	Serious	Very serious	Unbearable

After having counselling I now feel:

Worse than before	No different at all	A little better	Better	Much better

Note a number from 1 to 10, with 1 feeling slightly bad and 10 feeling unbearable

Counselling sessions	Score before counselling	Score after counselling	I need more counselling	I think things are fine now	I need extra help

Name of pupil _____   Form _____

Demographic Questionnaire

Clients Receiving Three Sessions of Counselling or More

Please complete the following:

Please state your ethnic origin, or the group to which you feel you belong socially:

_____ (for example, British, English, Welsh, Scottish, Irish, Asian, African descent, Pakistani, Chinese, or other)

Underline which applies:

1. I am male/female
2. I am in Year 7/Year 8/Year 9/Year 10/Year 11/Year 12/Year 13
3. I consider myself to be below average/about average/slightly above average/very bright
4. In my last English SATS results I achieved level 3/level 4/level 5/level 6
5. I came to counselling myself/my parents asked me to come/my teacher advised that I should come/my friend said I should come/counsellor sent for me/I don't know
6. My problem had something to do with:
   being bullied/being angry/getting into too much trouble/someone dying and being sad/being angry about my parents/being worried about my health/my disability/being obese and needing dietary help/falling out with my friends/feeling low/being depressed/cutting myself/refusing to eat/not seeing my dad or mum/my parents being about to split up/other reasons _____
7. I came for up to three sessions/between four and five sessions/over five sessions
8. I now feel just the same/a little bit better/much better/fine now
9. In my family I have one brother or sister/there are three of us children/four of us/five of us/six of us/or _____ of us
10. I now live with my mother and father/my mother only/my father only/my older brother or sister/my grandmother or grandfather/another relative/a foster parent/my adoptive parent(s)/in a care home/my friend's family home/or other _____
11. For most of my life I was brought up by _____
12. In the family my main carer is in full-time work/has not been able to find employment/is unable to work through disability/has to look after young children/is in training
13. I am currently on free school meals: YES/NO
14. My plans for the future are to: _____

Dennis Lines
3 September 2010

Appendix II

Counselling Referrers

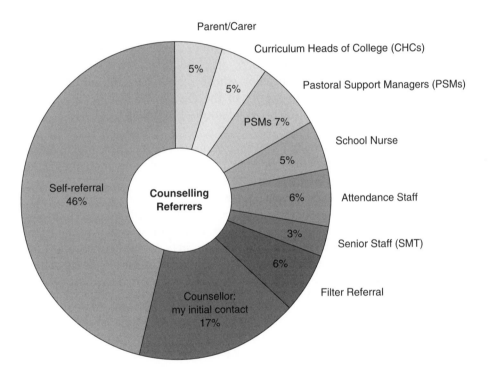

Parent/Carer

Curriculum Heads of College (CHCs)

Pastoral Support Managers (PSMs)

School Nurse

Attendance Staff

Senior Staff (SMT)

Filter Referral

5%

5%

PSMs 7%

5%

6%

3%

6%

Self-referral
46%

Counselling
Referrers

Counsellor:
my initial contact
17%

Figure Appendix 2.1

Appendix III

Counsellor Responses
Mini Survey

School counsellors (as individuals and in groups) were presented with ethical dilemmas, some via email and others after being led in discussion. The latter group were led by a counsellor whose school had announced a new policy of requiring all staff to report to the Designated Senior Teacher for child protection (DST) any student who had disclosed that they were sexually active.

With those counsellors having the benefit of discussing the dilemmas, questions were raised as to whose needs are being met under the 'duty to report'. Are anxious adults reporting to help make themselves feel better?

The *Every Child Matters* agenda and results of serious case reviews have resulted in practitioners on the 'coal face' feeling vulnerable. 'We need to protect ourselves' and, for one group, 'there was a concern expressed that in doing this we are in danger of becoming defensive practitioners. With these cases it often feels we are walking on a tight rope'. The combined results were as follows (Group response in italics: *The Group for Counsellors in Education Settings*, Oxfordshire, 10 January 2011).

Case 1a

A child of 12 years 11 months is known by you to be having sex with a 13-year-old partner. Should this youngster be your client who had disclosed this, would you pass on the information to the child's parent, the Designated Senior Teacher of child protection or to Children's Services as a referral?

Contain the client	Inform parent	Refer to DST	Refer to Children's Services
Individuals = 100%	–	*Group = 100%*	–

Rationale:

To refer would traumatise the child and lead him/her to not trust helping professions. I think/feel that sexual legislation is by its very nature fuzzy as we are dealing with puberty that isn't age-defined (i.e. ages 9–17 by the current evidence). We are in danger of giving credence to an unnatural protestant ethic by sticking strictly to a law that is there for guidance rather than a hard and fast rule. By the time the referral is taken up, the child is nearer to the age of consent. I would need to satisfy myself that precautions were being taken to reduce the chances of pregnancy and STDs. If the child was pregnant/infected, my course of action would be different.

I would not feel compelled to pass on information of this sort – a crime is being committed but there seems to be no power differential here and no abuse. I don't have a legal duty to report crime, and I do have a duty of confidentiality to the client. If I felt there was some element of abuse in the relationship, or the young person was seriously endangered in some way, then I would report it to the Designated Senior Teacher.

This was the most challenging case. If it appeared to be a meaningful relationship and there was no history of other sexual relationships, I would probably contain only.

For the sake of one month? No, I wouldn't think it would be necessary to open a can of worms. However, I would be tentatively exploring issues around staying safe and ensuring that the relationship was not an abusive one.

This would be expected of me in my CP role at school. As a youth counsellor, I would initially contain.

The general consensus was that we would pass the information on to the DST and that it was their duty to decide whether to involve the parents or not.

It was felt the number of incidences of this case will be low – although one member was in a position akin to this and it was clear that one partner was being coerced to do something they were not happy with.

The case requires us to be alert to power dynamics and if we evaluate this case using the dimensions of Age, Size, Power and Understanding, these pupils are vulnerable and we would need to seek advice. We were clear that it is not wise to make a decision based on one dimension only.

In the first instance, we could do a no – names consultation with Social Care.

Case 1b

What difference would your course of action be if your client's partner was known to be 14 or 15, and in your judgement you felt your young client was 'Gillick competent'?

Contain the client	Inform parent	Refer to DST	Refer to Children's Services
Individuals = 60%	–	Individuals = 20%	Individuals = 20%

Rationale:

As above, my main concern would be the protection of the child in respect of infection/pregnancy.

I would treat this situation in exactly the same way with regard to older young people.

Going to sit on the fence a bit with this one because I might feel the client to be Gillick competent. I think I would like to have a 'chat' with the DST (if the DST is not someone who's part of the 'reporting culture' and is a very experienced individual whom I would trust to do the right thing and not because she would be covering her back).

[Refer to Children's Services] Because of the age difference, bearing in mind the girl is under 13.]

Case 2

Suppose your client is a boy of 14 years (quite mature in your judgement and quite able to give consent, again in your judgement) who was engaged in intimate sexual relations with a girl of 17 years at the same school or youth club. Supposing you could determine no power differential, and it was a question of different levels of maturity, would you feel compelled to inform the parent, the Designated Senior Teacher of child protection or Children's Services? (Assuming that the contractual arrangements of the school, youth club or therapy agency permits engagement with young clients without, of necessity, involving the parents or a statutory service.)

Contain the client	Inform parent	Refer to DST	Refer to Children's Services
Individuals = 100% _Group = 100%_	–	–	–

Rationale:

As above, my main concern would be the protection of the child in respect of infection/pregnancy.

This feels more uncomfortable. I find it hard to imagine a 14-year-old with the maturity the scenario describes wanting to relate sexually with a 17-year-old girl, and vice versa. Leaving that aside for a moment, for the reasons given above, I would not report this to anybody, unless I had concerns about the 17-year-old girl. I might wonder what her family culture was like (abusive?) and be on the alert to gain some information regarding this through the counselling process.

Contain only.

First, I would be pleased for him that he felt (due to our therapeutic relationship) he could talk to me about his relationship. I would take the matter to Supervision (he would be aware from our initial session that I access personal supervision and that I might need to 'take him' at some point).

OK at school – only three years difference and no exploitation or abuse issues.

Contain in youth setting.

The focus here would be on curious inquiry regarding the relationship. For example, what impact is this relationship having on the young person?

We would be curious and alert to any wider CP issue that might be present.

We wondered if our responses would be different if it were a 14-year-old girl and a 17-year-old boy. There was a sense that within the decision making, we need to be mindful that we are not sexually discriminating.

Case 3

Two young clients approach you who are involved in a gay or lesbian relationship with each other. They are 14 and 15 years of age and there is no power differential but a fully consenting engagement. They approach you because they are afraid of homophobic taunting from peers in school and also because of what their parents may say should they find out – they have not come out publicly within the family. Would you as a counsellor 'contain' these two young clients or feel compelled to pass on this information to a third party?

Contain the clients	Inform parents	Refer to DST or pastoral teacher	Refer to other parties
Individuals = 100% Group = 100% raise matter with SLT staff	–	–	–

Rationale:

I do not see the point in making their lives more miserable. Most exploratory same-sex acts occur at the ages of 12/13. There are no indications at this age what final sexual assignments are – they may be bisexual or become defined as straight in later years. Why make it harder?

I would have a very strong ethical objection to reporting this scenario to anyone. Doing so would be to treat them differently to a heterosexual couple of the same age and become part of the homophobic dynamics they have come to me to deal with. So I absolutely couldn't do so.

Contain only, but endeavour to obtain consent to refer to a trusted specialist counsellor for gay young people.

They are struggling enough as it is. I would be pleased that they felt they had found a safe place where they felt heard and not bullied/ridiculed. I would like to think that I would be working towards supporting them in moving forward and check out with them possible ways I could support them. If they felt they wanted to tell their parents but did not know how, I would like to think I could help them with this.

No differential based on gender of young people.

Issue here is perhaps more systemic. The problem being presented is homophobic bullying and this is a school-based issue. The issue needs to be taken to senior management and raised as a whole school problem.

Would we pass on relationship details for a heterosexual couple of that age?

In schools where there is more than one counsellor, each pupil would have a separate counsellor. Where there is a sole practitioner, there was some debate as to whether the counsellor would see them together or not. Working together means you could observe any power differentials that may exist between them.

Initially felt important to sit with the ambiguity and 'hold the edge' whilst always being alert to any CP issues.

Case 4

A youth of 14 years shares information about an argument at home the previous evening whereby his stepfather (with whom he had been living with his mother since he was 3) had hit him across the mouth with the back of his hand for 'swearing at his mother' who had challenged him over 'theft of money and drinking alcohol in the park in the evening hours'. He had a red mark showing on his face and he was still angry. He said in counselling that he had never been hit like this before and that his stepfather had no history of being abusive. The pupil was known to be challenging in school.

Contain the client	Inform parent	Refer to DST	Refer to Children's Services
Individuals = 75%	–	*Group = 100%*	Individuals = 25%

Rationale:

I would be interested in working through what was causing the challenging behaviour in school whilst this allows me to keep a close watch on his relationship with his stepdad. There does not appear to be immediate danger to the client, so it is important to take one-off situations in context.

This situation would concern me, and my response would depend in part on the degree to which I trusted the young person to be truthful with me about the stepfather. Domestic violence is a real killer and very difficult to recover from, so if I am sure it's present there is a real threat to client and other family members. That said, I would be inclined to contain this situation, monitoring developments carefully and consulting and discussing my concerns with the client.

Contain only.

Assuming we are in a working and supportive relationship and he was able to bring 'stuff' into session for exploration, I guess I would feel as Yalom states: 'It's all grist for the therapeutic mill'.

No choice at school. In counselling would work towards gaining his agreement to a referral.

Clear that a mark still on the face means it was a hard hit and we cannot ignore it and collude with the child's need to brush it off.

Challenging behaviour and drinking are telling us something is not right. Our role is to try and discover what is going on for this young man.

DST would be informed.

Appendix IV

Anger Management Screening

ANGER MANAGEMENT SCREENING Angry Responses Scale 0–4	Never	Hardly ever	Sometimes	Mostly	All the time	I don't know
Impulsive Responses	0	1	2	3	4	–
The slightest thing can get me very angry						
When I'm angry, I hit out at anyone						
When I'm angry, I smash things up						
When I'm angry, I punch the wall or door						
When I'm angry, I scream and cry and shout						
When I'm angry, I don't know what I'm doing – I see red						
When I'm angry, I swear and don't know what I'm saying						
When I'm angry, I keep things buttoned up inside						
I explode and become violent at the slightest thing						
I don't know in advance when I'm about to blow						

Learned Responses

When I'm angry, I know what I am doing; I have full control						
My anger pattern is similar to someone in my family						
I know I can get what I want by being forceful						
I want to be like grown-ups who show anger to win battles						
We all get angry in my family if things don't go our way						
I can act being angry to avoid being threatened						

State of Being

I am angry with myself and how I am						
I am unhappy with my body, and how I look						
I am angry about something that happened long ago						
When I get angry, I think of killing myself						
I get angry because I don't feel important						
I don't know why I am so angry at the moment – it's not like me						

Resulting Behaviour

When angry, I get hot, breathe heavy and my heart beats fast						
When I'm angry, I cut myself						
When I'm angry, I refuse to eat						
When I'm angry, I smoke						
When I'm angry, I drink alcohol						
I become angry when accused of something I haven't done						
I hate being asked to do the impossible						
My blood boils when people make fun of me						
When I get angry, I have to escape from the situation						
When I get very angry, I want to kill someone						
When angry, I take it out on others						

Describe two incidents that have left you feeling very angry. On a scale of 1–10, score how angry you were left feeling:

Incident in the home   *Score 1–10 (1 = not very angry) =* ▢
Incident in school   *Score 1–10 (1 = not very angry) =* ▢

What has to happen for you to calm down?

Do you follow anyone in the family in regard to anger?

Notes

1. Other meta-analysis indicates more modest figures of 7–17 per cent (Beutler et al., 2004). Other research suggests that while a quality relationship may be *related* to outcome, this does not necessarily mean it is the *cause* of improvement (Cooper, 2010).
2. Such claims have been questioned by some authors (Moore et al., 2008: 13).
3. Jenga, also called a Stress Tower, is a game where each player removes carefully a wooden block from an erected tower and places it on top. It is a game of fine-motor skills where the winner is the one whose re-placed block keeps the tower standing.
4. It is known that 11 per cent of young people under 16 experience penetrative sex, oral sex or attempts at these, 'against their will', by people known but unrelated to them and that 25 per cent of all rape victims are under 16 years of age (Cawson et al., 2000).

References

Abbass, A.A., Hancock, J.T., Henderson, J. and Kisley, S. (2006) Short-term psychodynamic psychotherapies for common mental disorders. *Cochrane Database of Systematic Reviews*, 4: CD004687.

Aber, J.L. (1994) Poverty, violence, and child development. In C.A. Nelson (ed.), *Threats to Optimal Development: Integrating biological, psychological and social factors*. Hillside, NJ: Erlbaum.

Adams, J. (1976) *Understanding and Managing Personal Change*. Oxford: Martin Robertson.

Adams, S. (1990) Child self-protection: concerns about classroom approaches. *Pastoral Care in Education*, 8(3): 3–6.

Ainsworth, M., Blehar, M., Waters, E. and Wall, S. (1978) *Patterns of Attachment: Assessed in the strange situation and at home*. Hillsdale, NJ: Erlbaum.

Ajmal, Y. and Rees, I. (2001) *Solutions in Schools: Creative applications of solution focused brief thinking with young people and adults*. London: BT Press.

Alloy, L.B. and Abramson, L.Y. (1982) Learned helplessness, depression and the illusion of control. *Journal of Personality and Social Psychology*, 42: 1114–26.

Anderson, D.A. (1993) Lesbian and gay adolescents: social and developmental considerations. *High School Journal*, 77: 13–19.

Anderson, H. and Goolishian, H. (1988) Human systems as linguistic systems: evolving ideas about the implications for theory and practice. *Family Process*, 27: 371–93.

Arnold, L. (1997) *Working with People who Self-injure*. Bristol: Bristol Crisis Service for Women.

Arora, C.M.T. and Thompson, D.A. (1987) Defining bullying for a secondary school. *Education and Child Psychology*, 4(3): 110–20.

Asay, T.P. and Lambert, M.J. (1999) The empirical case for the common factors in therapy: quantitative findings. In M. Hubble, B.L. Duncan and S.D. Miller (eds) *The Heart and Soul of Change: What works in therapy*. Washington, DC: American Psychological Association, pp. 33–55.

Bach, R. (illustrated by Munson, R.) (2006 [1970]) *Jonathan Livingston Seagull*. New York: Scribner Books.

Baginsky, W. (2004) School Counselling in England, Wales and Northern Ireland: A review. NSPCC and Keele University. Available at: www.nspcc.org.uk/inform/resourcesforteachers/publications/schoolcounselling_wdf48931.pdf.

Baird, A., Fugel-sang, J. and Bennet, C. (2005) *What were you thinking: an fRMA study of adolescent decision-making*. Paper presented at the Cognitive Neuroscience Society meeting, New York, April.

Ball, S.A., Martino, S., Nich, C., Frankforter, T.L, van Horn, D. and Crits-Christoph, P. (2007) Site matters: multisite randomized trial of motivational enhancement therapy in community drug abuse clinics. *Journal of Consulting and Clinical Psychology*, 75(4): 556–67.

Bancroft, J.H. (2009) *Human Sexuality and its Problems* (3rd edition). London: Elsevier-Churchill Livingstone.

Bandura, A. (1977) *Social Learning Theory*. New York: General Learning Press.

Bandura, A. (1986) *Social Foundations of Thought and Action: A social cognitive theory.* Englewood Cliffs, NJ: Prentice Hall.

Batmanghelidjh, C. (2006) *Shattered Lives: Children who live with courage and dignity.* London: Jessica Kingsley.

Batmanghelidjh, C. (2009) Terrorised and terrorising teenagers: the search for attachment and hope. In A. Perry (ed.) *Teenagers and Attachment: Helping adolescents to engage with life and learning.* London: Worth Publishing, Chapter 7.

Beck, A.T., Rush, A.J., Shaw, B.F. and Emery, G. (1979) *Cognitive Therapy of Depression.* New York: Guilford Press.

Bergin, A.E. and Garfield, S.L. (eds) (2004) *Handbook of Psychotherapy and Behaviour Change* (5th edition). New York: Wiley

Berkowitz, D.A. (1987) Adolescent individuation and family therapy. In J.C. Coleman, *Working with Troubled Adolescents.* London: Academic Press.

Berman, J.S. and Norton, N.C. (1985) Does professional training make a therapist more effective? *Psychological Bulletin,* 98(2): 401–7.

Berne, E. (1968) *Games People Play: The psychology of human relationships.* London: Penguin.

Besa, D. (1994) Evaluating narrative family therapy using single-system research designs. *Research on Social Work Practice,* 4(3): 309–25.

Besag, V. (1989) *Bullies and Victims in Schools.* Milton Keynes: Open University Press.

Beutler, L.E., Malik, M., Alimohamed, S., Harwood, M.T., Talebi, H., Noble, S. et al. (2004) Therapist variables. In M.J. Lambert (ed.) *Bergin and Garfield's Handbook of Psychotherapy and Behavior Change* (5th edition). New York: Wiley, pp. 227–306.

Biddulph, S. (1996) *The Secret of Happy Children.* London: Thorsons.

Biddulph, S. (2008) *Raising Boys: Why boys are different – and how to help them become happy and well-balanced men* (2nd edition). Berkeley, CA: Celestial Arts.

Black, D. and Newman, M. (1995) Television violence and children. *British Medical Journal,* February: 273–4.

Blakemore, S.J and Chaudhury, S. (2006) Development of the adolescent brain: implications for executive function and social cognition. *Journal of Child Psychology and Psychiatry,* 47(3): 296–312.

Blos, P. (1979) *The Adolescent Passage: Developmental issues.* New York: International Universities Press.

Bond, T. (1994) *Counselling, Confidentiality and the Law.* Lutterworth: BACP.

Bond, T. (2010) *Standards and Ethics for Counselling in Action* (3rd edition). London: Sage Publications.

Bor, R., Ebner-Landy, J., Gill, S. and Brace, C. (2002) *Counselling in Schools.* London: Sage Publications.

Bowlby, J. (1952) A two-year-old goes to hospital: a scientific film. *Proceedings of the Royal Society of Medicine,* 46: 425–7.

Bowlby, J. (1969) *Attachment and Loss, 1: Attachment.* London: Hogarth Press.

Bowlby, J. (1973) *Attachment and Loss, 2: Separation: Anxiety and Anger.* London: Hogarth Press.

Bowlby, J. (1980) *Attachment and Loss, 3: Sadness and Depression.* London: Hogarth Press.

Bragg, M. (1999) In Our Time. BBC Radio 4, June. London: BBC Broadcast.

Brammer, L.M. and Shostrum, E.L. (1982) *Therapeutic Psychology* (4th edition). Englewood Cliffs, NJ: Prentice Hall.

Bratton, S.C., Ray, D., Rhine, T. and Jones, L. (2005) The efficacy of play therapy with children: A meta-analytic review of treatment outcomes. *Professional Psychological Research and Practice,* 36(4): 376–90.

Bridge, J., Goldstein, T. and Brent, D. (2006) Adolescent suicide and suicidal behaviour. *Journal of Child Psychology and Psychiatry,* 47: 372–94.

Bridget, J. (2000) Lesbian, Gay, Bisexual Young People and Teenage Pregnancy. Available at: www.lesbianinformationservice.org/pregnancy.rtf

Bridget, J. (2006) *Online Research on Lesbian, Gay and Suicide Research in the USA.* Available at: www.lesbianinformationservice.org/suicide

British Association of Counselling and Psychotherapy (BACP) (2002) *Ethical Framework for Good Practice in Counselling and Psychotherapy.* Lutterworth: BACP.

British Association of Counselling and Psychotherapy (BACP) (2005) *Therapy Today.* Lutterworth: BACP.

Brooks, T. and Silva, A. (2010) No longer taboo. *CCYP,* June: 26–7.

Brown, K. (2010) Living with teenage violence. *Therapy Today,* December, 21(10): 11–15.

Brown, S.A., Tapert, S.F., Granholm, E. and Dellis, D.C. (2000) Neurocognitive functioning of adolescence: effects of protracted alcohol abuse. *Alcoholism: Clinical and Experimental Research,* 24: 164–71.

Buckroyd, J. (2005). In C. Pointon (2005) Eating disorders: our knowledge of how eating disorders develop has changed in recent years. *Therapy Today,* 16(8): 4–7.

Burnham, J.B. (1986) *Family Therapy.* London: Routledge.

Butler, G. and Low, J. (1994) Short-term psychotherapy. In P. Clarkson and M. Pokorny (eds) *The Handbook of Psychotherapy.* London: Routledge.

Campbell, C. and Schwartz, D.F. (1996) Prevalence and impact of exposure to interpersonal violence among suburban and urban middle school students. *Paediatrics,* September: 396–402.

Capey, M. (1998) *Counselling for Pupils and Young Adults: Examples of what LEAs and schools provide.* Berkshire: Education Management Information Exchange.

Carkhuff, R.R. and Berenson, B.G. (1977) *Beyond Counselling and Therapy* (2nd edition). New York: Holt, Rinehart and Winston.

Carr, A. (2002) *Depression and Attempted Suicide in Adolescence.* Oxford: Blackwell.

Carr, A. (2006) *Handbook of Child and Adolescent Clinical Psychology* (2nd edition). London: Blackwell.

Carr, A. (2009a) Combating depression. In K. Geldard (ed.) *Practical Interventions for Young People at Risk.* London: Sage Publications, pp. 45–55.

Carr, A. (2009b) Preventing suicide. In K. Geldard (ed.) *Practical Interventions for Young People at Risk.* London: Sage Publications, pp. 66–78.

Carr, R. (1994) Peer helping in Canada. *Peer Counselling Journal,* 11(1): 6–9.

Carroll, K.M. (1996) Relapse prevention as a psychosocial treatment: a review of controlled clinical trials. *Experimental and Clinical Psychopharmacology,* 4(1): 46–54.

Casemore, R. (1995) *Confidentiality and School Counselling.* Lutterworth: BACP.

Catchpole, S. (2010) Working for positive outcomes. *CCYP,* March: 10–14.

Cawson, P., Wattam, C., Brooker, S. and Kelly, G. (2000) Child maltreatment in the United Kingdom: a study of the prevalence of child abuse and neglect. London: NSPCC ISBN: 1842280066. Available at: www.nspcc.org.uk/Inform/publications/downloads/childmaltreatmentintheukexecsummary_wdf48006.pdf

CCYP (2005) *Counselling for Children and Young People,* autumn. Lutterworth: BACP.

Chatterjee, P., Bailey, D. and Aronoff, N. (2001) Adolescence and old age in twelve communities. *Journal of Sociology and Social Welfare,* December.

Cicchetti, D. (ed.) (2009) *Development and Psychopathology* (special issue) 21(1).

Claiborn, C.D., Goodyear, R.K. and Horner, P.A. (2002) Feedback. In J.C. Norcross (ed.) *Psychotherapy Relationships that Work: Therapist contributions and responsiveness to patients.* New York: Oxford University Press, pp. 217–33.

Cohn, T. (1987) Sticks and stones may break my bones but names will never hurt me. *Multicultural Teaching,* 5(3): 8–11.

Coleman, J.C. (ed.) (1987) *Working with Troubled Adolescents: A handbook.* London: Academic Press.

Conger, J.J. (1975) *Contemporary Issues in Adolescent Development.* London: Harper and Row.

Cooper, M. (2006) Research on counselling in schools. *Therapy Today,* 17(3): 49–50.

Cooper, M. (2008) *Essential Research Findings in Counselling and Psychotherapy.* London: Sage Publications.

Cooper, M. (2009) Counselling in UK secondary schools: a comprehensive review of audit and evaluation data. *CPR,* 9(3): 137–50.

Cooper, M. (2010) The challenge of counselling and psychotherapy research. *Counselling and Psychotherapy Research,* 10(3): 183–91.

Cooper, M. and McLeod, J. (2011) Pluralistic Counselling and Psychotherapy. London: Sage Publications.

Cooper, M. and Richards, K. (eds) (2009) Counselling in Schools. *Counselling and Psychotherapy Research: Special Issue,* Vol. 9(3). BACP: London: Routledge.

Cooper, M., Rowland, N., McArthur, K., Pattison, S., Cromarty, K. and Richards, K. (2010) Randomised control trial of school-based humanistic counselling for emotional distress in young people: feasibility study and preliminary indications of efficacy. *Child and Adolescent Psychiatry and Mental Health,* 4(1): 1–12.

Costello, E., Mustillo, S., Keeler, G. and Angold, A. (2004) Prevalence of psychiatric disorders in childhood and adolescence. In L. Luborsky, J. Petrila and K. Hennessy (eds) *Mental Health Services: A public health perspective.* New York: Oxford University Press, pp. 111–28.

Courtois, C. (1988) *Healing the Incest Wound.* New York: W.W. Norton.

Cowen, E.L., Pederson, A., Babigian, H., Izzo, L.D. and Trost, M.A. (1973) Long-term follow up of early detected vulnerable children. *Journal of Consulting and Clinical Psychology,* 41: 438–46.

Cowie, H. (1998) Perspectives of teachers and pupils on the experience of peer support against bullying. *Educational Research and Evaluation,* 1: 108–25.

Cowie, H. and Sharp, S. (eds) (1996) *Peer Counselling in Schools.* London: David Fulton.

Cox, S. (2010) Defining moments. *Therapy Today,* 21(6): 25–9.

Crits-Christoph, P. and Gibbons, M.B.C. (1999) Relational interpretations. In J.C. Norcross (ed.) *Psychotherapy Relationships that Work: Therapist contributions and responsiveness to patients.* New York: Oxford University Press, pp. 285–300.

Curwen, B., Palmer, S. and Ruddell, P. (2000) *Brief Cognitive Behaviour Therapy.* London: Sage Publications.

Daniels, D. and Jenkins, P. (2000) Reporting child abuse. *Counselling,* 11(9): 551–4.

Davies, G.T. (1986) *A First Year Tutorial Handbook.* Oxford: Blackwell.

Davis, T.E. and Osborn, C.J. (2000) *The Solution-Focused School Counsellor: Shaping professional practice.* Philadelphia, PA: Accelerated Development.

De Shazer, S. (1988) *Clues: Investigating Solutions in Brief Therapy.* New York: W.W. Norton.

Dehue, F., Bolman, C. and Vollink, T. (2008) Cyberbullying: youngsters' experiences and parental perceptions. *CyberPsychology and Behavior,* 11: 217–23.

Denis, C., Lavie, E., Fatséas, M. and Auriacombe, M. (2004) *Psychotherapeutic interventions for cannabis abuse and/or dependence in outpatient settings. Cochrane Database of Systematic Reviews,* 3: CD005336.

Dennison, C. (2004) Teenage Pregnancy: An overview of the research evidence. Wetherby: NHS Health Development Agency.

Devere, M. (2000) New models: the counselling of change. *Counselling,* 11(7): 412–13.

Diamond, J. (2000) *Narrative Means to Sober Ends.* New York: Guilford Press.

Dilk, M.N. and Bond, G.R. (1995) Meta-analytic evaluation of skills training research for individuals with severe mental illness. *Journal of Consulting and Clinical Psychology,* 64(6): 1337–46.

Dolan, R.J. (2002) Emotion, cognition, and behavior. *Science* 298: 1191–4.

Dominian, J., Mansfield, P., Dormor, D. and McAllister, F. (1991) *Marital Breakdown and the Health of the Nation*. London: One Plus One – Marriage and Partnership Research.

Donaldson, D., Spiritio, A., Arrigan, M. and Aspel, J.W. (1997) Structured disposition planning for adolescent suicide attempters in a general hospital: preliminary findings on short-term outcome. *Archives of Suicide Research*, 3: 271–82.

Downey, V.W. and Landry, R.G. (1997) Self reporting sexual behaviours of high school juniors and seniors in North Dakota. *Psychological Reports*, 80: 1357–8.

Dryden, W. (ed.) (2002) *Handbook of Individual Therapy* (4th edition). London: Sage Publications.

Dunkley, C. (2001) The pain barrier diagram. *Counselling and Psychotherapy*, 12(1): 13–15.

Durrant, M. (1993) *Creative Strategies for School Problems*. Epping, NSW: Eastwood Family Therapy Centre.

Dusek, J.B. (1996) *Adolescent Development and Behavior*. Englewood Cliffs, NJ: Prentice Hall.

Egan, G. (1990) *The Skilled Helper* (4th edition). Monterey, Pacific Grove, CA: Brooks/Cole (originally published in 1975).

Eisler, I., Dare, C., Russell, G.F.M., Szmuker, G.I., le Grange, D. and Dodge, E. (1997) Family and individual therapy in anorexia nervosa: a five-year follow-up. *Archives of General Psychiatry*, 54: 1025–30.

Elliot, B.J. and Richards, M.P.M. (1991) Effects of parental divorce on children. *Archives of Disease in Childhood*, 66: 915–16.

Elliott, M. (1986) *Kidscape Project*, unpublished research. London: The Kidscape Primary Kit. Available from: Kidscape, 82 Brock Street, London W1Y 1YP.

Elliott, M. (1990) A response to Steve Adams. *Pastoral Care in Education*, 8(3): 7–9.

Elliott, R. and Zucconi, A. (2010) Organization and conceptual framework for practice-based research on the effectiveness of psychotherapy and psychotherapy training. In M. Barkham, G. Hardy and J. Mellor-Clark (eds) *A Core Approach to Delivering Practice-based Evidence in Counselling and the Psychological Therapies*. Chichester: Wiley, pp. 287–310.

Ellis, A. (1965) *Homosexuality: Its causes and cures*. New York: Lyle Stuart.

Ellis, A. (1976) *Sex and the Liberated Man*. Secacus, NJ: Lyle Stuart.

Ellis, A. (1987) The impossibility of achieving consistently good mental health. *American Psychologist*, 42: 364–75.

Ellis, A. (1994) *Reason and Emotion in Psychotherapy* (revised edition). Secaucus, NJ: Birch Lane.

Ellis, J. (1996) Prospective memory or the realisation of delayed intentions: a conceptual framework for research. In M. Brandimonte, G.O. Einstein and M.A. McDaniel (eds) *Prospective Memory: Theory and applications*. Hillsdale, NJ: Erlbaum, pp. 1–22.

Elmore, L.J. (1986) The teacher and the child of divorce. Paper presented at the 7th Annual Families Alive Conference, Ogden, UT, 10–12 September.

Emmelkemp, P.M.G. (2004) Behavior therapy with adults. In M.J. Lambert (ed.) *Bergin and Garfield's Handbook of Psychotherapy and Behavior Change* (5th edition). New York: Wiley, pp. 393–446.

English, P. (2006) Losing Someone Close. Available at: http://twup.org.uk

Epston, D., White, M. and Murray, K. (1992) A proposal for a re-authoring therapy: Rose's revisioning of her life and a commentary. In S. McNamee and K.J. Gergen (eds) *Therapy as Social Construction*. London: Sage Publications.

Erikson, E.H. (1956) The problem of ego identity. *Journal of the American Psychoanalytic Association*, 4: 56–121.

Erikson, E.H. (1968) *Identity: Youth and Crisis*. New York: W.W. Norton.

Evans, E., Hawton, K. and Rodham, K. (2004) Factors associated with suicidal phenomena in adolescents: a systematic review of population-based studies. *Clinical Psychology Review*, 24: 957–79.

Fairburn, C.G., Marcus, M.D. and Wilson, G.T. (1993) Cognitive behavioural therapy for binge eating and bulimia nervosa: a comprehensive treatment manual. In C.G. Fairburn and G.T. Wilson (eds) *Binge Eating: Nature, assessment, and treatment.* New York: Guilford Press, pp. 361–404.

Fallon, J. (2010) Supervision talk 2. *CCYP,* June: 24–5.

Falzon, R. and Camilleri, S. (2010) Dyslexia and the school counsellor: a Maltese case study. *Counselling and Psychotherapy Research,* December, 10(4): 307–15.

Farrell, P. (1999) The limitations of current theories in understanding bereavement and grief. *Counselling,* 10(2): 143–6.

Favazza, A. (1996) *Bodies under Siege: Self-mutilation and body modification in culture and psychiatry.* Baltimore, MD: Johns Hopkins University Press.

Feltham, C. (1997) *Time-Limited Counselling.* London: Sage Publications.

Fergusson, D.E. and Mullen, P.E. (1999) *Childhood Sexual Abuse: An evidence-based perspective.* London: Sage Publications.

Finkelhor, D. (1980) Sex among siblings: a survey on prevalence, variety, and effects. *Archives of Sexual Behaviour,* 9(3): 171–94.

Finn, S.E. and Tonsager, M.E. (1997) Information-gathering and therapeutic models of assessment: complimentary paradigms. *Psychological Assessment,* 9(4): 374–85.

Foderaro, L.W. (2007) Between teacher and student: the suspicions are growing. The New York Times, 20 June.

Fonagy, P., Roth, A. and Higgit, A. (2005) The outcome of psychodynamic psychotherapy for psychological disorders. *Clinical Neuroscience Research,* 4 (5–6): 367–77.

Forero, R., McLellan, L., Rissell, C. and Bauman, A. (1999) Bullying behaviour and psychological health among school students in New South Wales. *British Medical Journal,* 319: 344–8.

Frank, J. (1986) What is psychotherapy? In S. Bloch (ed.) *An Introduction to the Psychotherapies* (2nd edition). Oxford: Oxford University Press.

Frankl, V.E. (1959) *Man's Search for Meaning.* New York: Washington Square Press.

Freud, S. (1933) *New Introductory Lectures on Psycho-analysis.* London: Penguin.

Freud, S. (1937) *The Ego and the Mechanisms of Defence.* London: Hogarth Press.

Galatzer-Levi, R.M. (2002) Created in others' eyes. *Adolescent Psychiatry: Developmental and Clinical Studies,* 26: 43–72.

Gardner, F. and Coombs, S. (eds) (2009) *Researching, Reflecting and Writing about Work: Guidance on training course assignments and research for psychotherapists and counsellors.* London: Routledge.

Geddes, H. (2006) *Attachment in the Classroom: The links between children's early experience, emotional well-being and performance in school. A practical guide for schools.* London: Worth Publishing.

Geldard, K. (ed.) (2009) *Practical Interventions for Young People at Risk.* London: Sage Publications.

Geldard, K. and Geldard, D. (2010) *Counselling Adolescents: The proactive approach for young people.* London: Sage Publications.

Gergen, J.K. (2001) *Social Construction in Context.* London: Sage Publications.

Gergen, K.J. and Kaye, J. (1992) Beyond narrative in the negotiation of therapeutic meaning. In S. McNamee and K.J. Gergen (eds) *Therapy as Social Construction.* London: Sage Publications.

Gerhardt, S. (2004) *Why Love Matters: How affection shapes a baby's brain.* Hove: Brunner-Routledge.

Gibran, K. (1972 [1923]) *The Prophet.* New York: Alfred A. Knopf.

Gibson-Cline, J. (1996) *Adolescents from Crisis to Coping: A thirteen nation study.* Oxford: Butterworth-Heinemann.

Giedd, J., Blumenthal, J., Jeffries, N., Castellanos, F., Liu, H., Zijdenbos, A., Paus, T., Evans, A. and Rapoport, J. (1999) Brain development during childhood and adolescence: a longitudinal MRI study. *Nature Neuroscience*, 2(10): 861–3.

Gingerich, W.J. and Eisengart, S. (2000) Solution-focused brief therapy: a review of the outcome research. *Family Process*, 34(4): 477–98.

Goldstein, A.P. (2004) *New Perspectives on Aggression Replacement Training*. Chichester: Wiley.

Goleman, D. (2006) *Emotional Intelligence* (10th anniversary edition). New York: Bantam Dell.

Goodyear, R.K. (1990) Research of the effects of test interpretation: a review. *Counselling Psychologist*, 18(2): 240–57.

Gould, M. (2003) Youth suicide risk and preventative interventions: a review of the past 10 years. *Journal of the American Academy of Child and Adolescent Psychiatry*, 42: 386–405.

Gould, R.A., Otta, M.W. and Pollack, M.H. (1995) A meta-analysis of treatment outcome for panic disorder. *Clinical Psychology Review*, 15(8): 819–44.

Gregson, O. and Looker, T. (1994) The biological basis of stress management. *British Journal of Guidance and Counselling*, 22(1): 13–26.

Hagerty, B.B. (2011) 'A Neuroscientist Discovers a Dark Secret'. Available at: www.npr.org/templates/story/story.php?storyId=127888976

Hakuta, K., Bialystok, E. and Wiley, E. (2003) Critical evidence: a test of the critical period hypothesis for second language acquisition. *Psychological Science* (14): 31–8.

Hall, A.S. and Fradkin, H.R. (1992) Affirming gay men's mental health: counselling with a new attitude. *Journal of Mental Health Counselling*, 14(3): 362–74.

Hamer, D., Hu, S., Magnuson, V.L., Hu, N. and Pattatucci, A.M.L. (1993) A linkage between markers on the X chromosome and male sexual orientation. *Science*, July, 261(5119): 321–7.

Hamilton, C. (2004) *Offering Children Confidentiality: Law and guidance*. Colchester: Children's Legal Centre.

Hanley, T. (2010) School-based counselling: what does the research really say? *CCYP*, 1: 21–4.

Harrington, R., Whittaker, J., Shoebridge, P. and Campbell, F. (1998) Systematic review of efficacy of cognitive behaviour therapies in childhood and adolescent depressive disorder. *British Medical Journal*, 316: 1559–63.

Harris, B. and Pattison, S. (2004) *Research on Counselling Children and Young People: A Systematic scoping review*. Lutterworth: BACP.

Harrison, J. (1987) Counselling gay men. In M. Scher, M. Stevens, G. Good and G.A. Eichenfield (eds) *Handbook of Counselling and Psychotherapy with Men*. Newbury Park, CA: Sage Publications.

Hawton, K., Harriss, L. and Zahl, D. (2006a) Deaths from all causes in a long-tem follow-up study of 11583 deliberate self-harm patients. *Psychological Medicine*, 36(3): 397–405.

Hawton, K., Rodham, K. and Evans, E. (2006b) *By Their Own Young Hand: Deliberate self-harm and suicidal ideas in adolescents*. London: Jessica Kingsley.

Hawton, K., Harriss, L. and Rodham, K. (2010) How adolescents who cut themselves differ from those who take overdoses. *European Child and Adolescent Psychiatry*, 19: 513–23.

Herbert, M. (1978) *Conduct Disorders of Childhood and Adolescence*. Chichester: Wiley.

Hickey, D. and Carr, A. (2002) Prevention of suicide in adolescents. In A. Carr (ed.) *Prevention: What works with children and adolescents? A critical review of psychological prevention programmes for children, adolescents and their families*. London: Routledge, pp. 336–58.

Hill, C.E. (1999) *Helping Skills: Facilitating Exploration, Insight and Action* (2nd edition). Washington, DC: American Psychological Association.

Hitchings, P. (1994) Psychotherapy and sexual orientation. In P. Clarkson and M. Pokorny (eds) *The Handbook of Psychotherapy*. London: Routledge.

Holland, J. (2000) Secondary schools and pupil loss by parental bereavement and parental relationship separations. *Pastoral Care in Education*, 11: 33–9.

Holmes, J. (1993) *John Bowlby and Attachment Theory*. London: Routledge.

Hooker, E. (1985) The adjustment of the overt male homosexual. *Journal of Personality Assessment*, 21: 18–23.

Hoste, R.R. and le Grange, D. (2009) Addressing eating problems. In K. Geldard (ed.) *Practical Interventions for Young People at Risk*. London: Sage Publications, pp. 169–79.

Houston, G. (2003) *Brief Gestalt Therapy*. London: Sage Publications.

Howard, A. (2000) *Philosophy for Counselling and Psychotherapy: Pythagoras to postmodernism*. London: Macmillan.

Howard, K.I., Kopta, S.M., Krause, M.S. and Orlinski, D.E. (1986) The close-effect relationship in psychotherapy. *American Psychologist*, 41: 159–64.

Hu, F.B., Flack, B.R., Hedeker, D. and Syddiqui, O. (1995) The influence of friends and parental smoking on adolescent smoking behaviour: the effects of time and prior smoking. *Journal of Applied Social Psychology*, 25: 2018–47.

Huey, S., Henggeler, S., Rowland, M., Halliday-Boykins, C., Cunningham, P. and Pickrel, S. (2004) Multisystemic therapy effects on attempted suicide by youths presenting psychiatric emergencies. *Journal of the American Academy of Child and Adolescent Psychiatry*, 43: 183–90.

Humphreys, C. and Stanley, N. (eds) (2006) *Domestic Violence and Child Protection: Directions for good practice*. London: Jessica Kingsley.

Inhelder, B. and Piaget, J. (1958) *The Growth of Logical Thinking from Childhood to Adolescence*. London: Routledge and Kegan Paul.

Ives, R. (1994) Stop sniffing in the States: approaches to solvent misuse prevention in the USA. *Drugs, Education, Prevention and Policy*, 1: 37–48.

Jacobs, M. (1993) *Living Illusions: A psychology of belief*. London: SPCK.

Jacobs, M. (2010) *Psychodynamic Counselling in Action* (4th edition). London: Sage Publications.

Jacobson, E. (1938) *Progressive Relaxation* (2nd edition). Chicago, IL: University of Chicago Press.

James, A. (2010) *School Bullying*. London: NSPCC. Available at: www.nspcc.org.uk/inform/research/briefings/school_bullying_pdf_wdf73502.pdf

Jayasinghe, M. (2001) *Counselling in Careers Guidance*. Buckingham and Philadelphia, PA: Open University Press.

Jenkins, A. (1990) *Invitations to Responsibility: The therapeutic engagement of men who are violent and abusive*. Adelaide, Australia: Dulwich Centre Publications.

Jenkins, J.E. (1996) The influence of peer affiliation and student activities on adolescent drug involvement. *Adolescence*, 31: 297–306.

Jenkins, P. (2005) Working together: the rise of mandatory child abuse reporting. *CCYP*, autumn: 2–4.

Jenkins, P. (2010) Child protection: the duty to refer. *CCYP*, March: 17–20.

Kellerman, J. (1999) *Savage Spawn: Reflections on violent children*. New York: The Ballantine Publishing Group.

Kilpatrick, D.G., Aciermo, R., Saunders, B., Resnick, H. and Best, C. (2000) Risk factors for adolescent substance abuse and dependence: data from a national sample. *Journal of Counselling and Clinical Psychology*, 65: 1–12.

Kilty, J. and Bond, M. (1991) *Practical Methods of Dealing with Stress*. Guildford: Human Potential Resource Group, University of Surrey.

Klonsky, M. (2002) How smaller schools prevent school violence. *Educational Leadership*, 59(5): 65–9.

Knapp, C. (1996) *Drinking: A Love Story*. New York: Dial Press.

Koss, M.P. and Shiang, J. (1994) Research on brief psychotherapy. In A.E. Bergin and S.L. Garfield (eds) *Handbook of Psychotherapy and Behaviour Change* (4th edition). New York: Wiley, pp. 664–700.

Kübler-Ross, E. (1982) *On Death and Dying.* London: Tavistock.

Kuhl, P.K. (2004) Early language acquisition: cracking the speech code. *Nature Reviews Neuroscience,* 5(11): 831–43.

Lambert, J.L. (1992) Implications of outcome research for psychotherapy integration. In J.C. Norcross and M.R.G. Goldfried (eds) *Handbook of Psychotherapy Integration.* New York: Basic Books.

Lambert, M.J. and Bergin, A.E. (1994) The effectiveness of psychotherapy. In A.E. Bergin and S.L. Garfield (eds) *Handbook of Psychotherapy and Behaviour Change* (4th edition). New York: Wiley, pp. 143–89.

Lambert, M.J. and Ogles, B.M. (2004) The efficacy and effectiveness of psychotherapy. In M.J. Lambert (ed.) *Bergin and Garfield's Handbook of Psychotherapy and Behavior Change* (5th edition). New York: Wiley, pp. 139–93.

Layard, R. (2004) *Mental Health: Britain's biggest social problem.* Available at: http://cep.lse.ac.uk/layard/psych_treatment_centres.pdf

Lazarus, A.A. (1981) *The Practice of Multimodal Therapy.* Baltimore, MD: John Hopkins University Press.

Lazarus, A.A. (1990) Why I am an eclectic (not an integrationist). In W. Dryden and J.C. Norcross (eds) *Eclecticism and Integration in Counselling and Psychotherapy.* Loughton: Gale Centre Publications.

Lazarus, A.A. (2005) Multimodal therapy. In J.C. Norcross and M.R. Goldfried (eds) *Handbook of Psychotherapy Integration.* New York: Oxford University Press.

Le Count, D. (2000) Working with 'difficult' children from the inside out: loss and bereavement and how the creative arts can help. *Counselling,* 18(2): 17–27.

Le Grange, D. and Lock, J. (2007) *Treating Bulimia in Adolescents: A family-based approach.* New York: Guilford Press.

Lees, S. (1993) *Sugar and Spice.* London: Penguin.

Leichsenring, F. (2001) Comparative effects of short-term psychodynamic psychotherapy and cognitive-behavioural therapy in depression: a meta-analytic approach. *Clinical Psychology Review,* 21(3): 401–19.

Lethem, J. (1994) *Moved to Tears, Moved to Action: Solution-focused brief therapy with women and children.* London: Brief Therapy Press.

Lewinsohn, P.M. and Clarke, G.N. (1999) Psychosocial treatments for adolescent depression. *Clinical Psychology Review,* 19(3): 329–42.

Lewinsohn, P.M., Hops, H., Roberts, R.E., Steely, J.R. and Andrews, J.A. (1993) Prevalence and incidence of depression and other DSM-III-R disorders in high school students. *Journal of Abnormal Psychology,* 102: 133–44.

Lewis, J. (1992) Death and divorce: helping students cope in single-parent families. *NASSP Bulletin,* 76(543): 55–60.

Lilliengren, P. and Werbart, A. (2005) A model of therapeutic action grounded in the patients' view of curative and hindering factors in psychoanalytic psychotherapy. *Psychotherapy: Theory, Research, Practice, Training,* 3: 324–99.

Lindsay, W.R. (1987) Social skills training with adolescents. In J. Coleman (ed.) *Working with Troubled Adolescents.* London: Academic Press.

Linehan, M.M., Dimeff, L.A., Reynolds, S.K., Comtois, K.A., Welch, S.S. and Heagerty, P. (2002) Dialectical behavior therapy versus comprehensive validation therapy plus 12-step for the treatment of opioid dependent women meeting criteria for borderline personality disorder. *Drug and Alcohol Dependence,* 67(1): 13–26.

Lines, D. (1985) *Counselling Adolescents in Secondary School.* Unpublished booklet (dennis@schoolcounselling.co.uk).

Lines, D. (1995a) *Coming Through the Tunnel*. Birmingham: published by the author (dennis@schoolcounselling.co.uk).

Lines, D. (1995b) *Christianity is Larger than Fundamentalism*. Durham: Pentland Press.

Lines, D. (1996) Early secondary pupils' experiences of name-calling behaviour through a discourse analysis of differing counselling interviews. Unpublished dissertation, Westhill College, Birmingham (dennis@schoolcounselling.co.uk).

Lines, D. (1999a) Secondary pupils' experiences of name-calling behaviour. *Pastoral Care in Education*, 17(1): 23–31.

Lines, D. (1999b) Bereavement group therapy in school: the role of a belief in a post-death existence within adolescent development for the acceptance process of loss. *Journal of Children's Spirituality*, 4(2): 141–54.

Lines, D. (2000) *Counselling Approaches for Young People in Secondary School: From Traditional Approaches to Eclectic and Integrative Counselling*. Birmingham: published by the author (dennis@schoolcounselling.co.uk).

Lines, D. (2001) An approach with name-calling and verbal taunting. *Pastoral Care in Education*, 18(1): 3–9.

Lines, D. (2002a) *Brief Counselling in School: Working with young people from 11–18* (1st edition). London: Sage Publications.

Lines, D. (2002b) Counselling in the new spiritual paradigm. *Journal of Humanistic Psychology*, 42(3): 102–23.

Lines, D. (2003) Collaborative practice. *Counselling in Education*, winter: 5–10.

Lines, D. (2005) A peer counselling service in a secondary school to combat bullying: issues in planning and ongoing management. *Pastoral Care in Education*, 23(2): 19–27.

Lines, D. (2006a) *Spirituality in Counselling and Psychotherapy*. London: Sage Publications.

Lines, D. (2006b) *Brief Counselling in School: Working with young people from 11–18* (2nd edition). London: Sage Publications.

Lines, D. (2008) *The Bullies: understanding bullies and bullying*. London: Jessica Kingsley Publishers.

Lines, D. (2010) The duty to refer. *CCYP*, June: 30–1.

Lipton, B. (2009) *The Biology of Belief: Part 1*. Northampton: The Healing Trust, pp. 44–6.

Litvinoff, S. (1991) *The Relate Guide to Better Relationships*. London: Vermilion.

Longfellow, C. (1979) Divorce in context: its impact on children. In G. Levinger and O.C. Moles (eds) *Divorce and Separation*. New York: Basic Books.

Luxmoore, N. (2000) *Listening to Young People in School, Youth Work and Counselling*. London: Jessica Kingsley.

Luxmoore, N. (2006) *Working with Anger and Young People*. London: Jessica Kingsley.

Mabey, J. and Sorensen, B. (1995) *Counselling for Young People*. Buckingham: Open University Press.

Maher, P. (1990) Child protection: another view. *Pastoral Care in Education*, 8(3): 9–12.

Malley, E., Posner, N. and Potter, L. et al. (2008) Suicide risk and prevention for lesbian, gay, bisexual, and transgender youth. *Suicide Prevention Resource Centre*. Available at: www.sprc.org/library/SPRC_LGBT_Youth.pdf

Maluccio, A.N. (1979) *Learning from Clients: Interpersonal helping as viewed by clients and social workers*. New York: Macmillan.

Mander, G. (2000) *A Psychodynamic Approach to Brief Therapy*. London: Sage Publications.

Manji, I. (2004) *The Trouble with Islam Today: A wake-up call for honesty and change*. Edinburgh: Mainstream Publishing Company.

Mann, J., Apter, A. and Bertolote, J. (2005) Suicide prevention strategies: a systematic review. *Journal of the American Medical Association*, 294: 2064–74.

Margolin, G. and Gordis, E.B. (2004) Children's exposure to violence in the family and community. *Current Directions in Psychological Science*, 13(4): 152–5.

Masson, J. (1992) *Against Therapy*. London: Harper-Collins.

Matteson, D.R. (1987) Counselling bisexual men. In M. Scher, M. Stevens, G. Good and G.A. Eichenfield (eds) *Handbook of Counselling and Psychotherapy with Men*. Newbury Park, CA: Sage Publications.

Mayet, S., Farrell, M., Ferri, M., Amato, L. and Davoli, M. (2004[2010]) Psychosocial treatment for opiate abuse and dependence. Cochrane Database of Systematic Reviews 4: CD004330.

McBroom, J.R. (1994) Correlates of alcohol and marijuana use among junior high school students: family, peers, school problems, and psychosocial concerns. *Youth and Society*, 26: 54–68.

McDermott, I. (2008a) NLP Toolbox 4: in the right state to make change possible. *CCYP*, December: 16–18.

McDermott, I. (2008b) NLP Toolbox 2: different questions, new futures. *CCYP*, June: 13–14.

McDermott, I. and Jago, W. (2001) *Brief NLP Therapy*. London: Sage Publications.

McGinnis, S. and Jenkins, P. (eds) (2009) *Good Practice Guidance for Counselling in Schools* (4th edition). Lutterworth: BACP.

McGivern, R.F., Andersen, J., Byrd, D., Mutter, K.L. and Reilly, J. (2002) Cognitive efficiency on a match to sample task decreases at the onset of puberty in children. *Brain and Cognition* (50): 73–89.

McGuiness, J. (1998) *Counselling in Schools: New perspectives*. London: Cassell.

McLeod, J. (1993) *An Introduction to Counselling*. Buckingham: Open University Press.

McLeod, J. (1998) *Narrative and Psychotherapy*. London: Sage Publications.

McLeod, J. (2003) *An Introduction to Counselling* (3rd edition). Buckingham: Open University Press.

McLeod, J. (2009) *An Introduction to Counselling* (4th edition). Maidenhead: Open University Press.

McLeod, J. (2010) *Case Study Research in Counselling and Psychotherapy* (2nd edition). London: Sage Publications.

McLeod, J. (2011a) *Doing Counselling Research* (2nd edition). London: Sage Publications.

McLeod, J. (2011b) *Qualitative Research in Counselling and Psychotherapy* (2nd edition). London: Sage Publications.

McNamara, E. (2009) *Motivational Interviewing: Theory, Practice and Applications with Children and Young People*. Ainsdale: Positive Behaviour Management. Available at: www.positivebehaviourmanagement.co.uk

McNamara, E. and Atkinson, C. (2010) Engaging the reluctant with MI. *CCYP*, December: 15–21.

McNamee, S. and Gergen, K.J. (1992) *Therapy as Social Construction*. London: Sage Publications.

Mead, M. (1928) *Coming of Age in Samoa*. Harmondsworth: Penguin.

Mead, M. (1930) *Growing up in New Guinea*. Harmondsworth: Penguin.

Mead, M. (1949) *Male and Female*. Harmondsworth: Penguin.

Mearns, D. and Cooper, M. (2005) *Working at Relational Depth in Counselling and Psychotherapy*. London: Sage Publications.

Mearns, D. and Thorne, B. (2010) *Person-centred Counselling in Action* (3rd edition). London: Sage Publications.

Meichenbaum, D. (1983) *Coping with Stress*. London: Century.

Meichenbaum, D. (1986) Cognitive-behaviour modification. In F.H. Kanfer and A.P. Goldstein (eds) *Helping People Change* (3rd edition). New York: Pergamon.

Mental Health Foundation/Camelot Foundation (2006) *Truth Hurts: Report of the national enquiry into self-harm among young people*. London: Mental Health Foundation.

Mikkelsen, E.J. (2001) Enuresis and encopresis: ten years of progress. *Journal of American Academy of Child and Adolescent Psychiatry*, 40(10): 1146–8.

Miller, S.D., Duncan, B.L. and Hubbie, M.A. (1997) Escape from Babel: Toward a unifying language for psychotherapy practice. New York: W.W. Norton.

Miller, W.R. and Rollnick, S. (1991) *Motivational Interviewing*. New York: Guilford Press.

Milner, P. (1980) *Counselling in Education*. Trowbridge: Redwood Burn.

Mind (2010) Suicide Rates, Risks and Prevention Strategies. Available at: www.mind.org.uk/help/research_and_policy/suicide_rates_risks_and_prevention_strategies#young

Minuchin, S., Baker, B.L., Rosman, B.L., Liebman, R., Milman, L. and Todd, T.C. (1975) A conceptual model on psychosomatic illness in children: family organisation and family therapy. *Archives of General Psychiatry*, 32: 1031–8.

Molnos, A. (1995) *A Question of Time: Essentials of Brief Dynamic Psychotherapy*. London: Karnac.

Moore, K., Jones, N. and Broadbent, E. (2008) School Violence in OCED Countries. Available at: http://plan-international.org/learnwithoutfear/files/school-violence-in-oecd-countries-english

Morrison, B. (2002) Bullying and victimisation in schools: a restorative justice approach. *Trends and Issues in Crime and Criminal Justice*, February, 219. Canberra: Australian Institute of Criminology.

Morrow-Bradley, C. and Elliott, R. (1986) Utilization of psychotherapy research by practicing psychotherapists. *American Psychologist*, 41(2): 188–97.

Mosher, W.D., Chandra, A. and Jones, J. (2005) Sexual behavior and selected health measures: men and women 15–44 years of age, United States, 2002. *Advance Data from Vital and Health Statistics*, no. 362. Hyattsville, MD: National Center for Health Statistics.

Moyer, A., Finney, J.W., Swearingen, C.E. and Vergun, P. (2002) Brief interventions for alcohol problems: a meta-analytic review of controlled investigations in treatment-seeking and non-treatment-seeking populations. *Addiction*, 97(3): 279–92.

Mufson, L., Dorta, K.P., Pollack, K., Moreau, D. and Weissman, M. (2004) *Interpersonal Psychotherapy for Depressed Adolescents* (2nd edition). New York: Guilford Press.

Muncie, J., Wetherell, M., Dallas, R. and Cochrane, A. (eds) (1995) *Understanding the Family*. London: Sage Publications.

Murgatroyd, S. and Woolf, R. (1982) *Coping with Crisis*. London: Harper and Row.

National Institute for Clinical Excellence (NICE) (2004) *Self-harm: The short-term physical and psychological management and secondary prevention of self-harm in primary and secondary care*. London: NICE.

Naylor, P. and Cowie, H. (1999) The effectiveness of peer support systems in challenging school bullying: the perspectives and experiences of teachers and pupils. *Journal of Adolescence*, 22: 467–79.

Nelson-Jones, R. (1996) *Effective Thinking Skills*. London: Cassell.

Nelson-Jones, R. (1997) *Practical Counselling and Helping Skills: Text and Exercises for the Life Skills Counselling Model*. London: Cassell.

Nelson-Jones, R. (1999a) Towards cognitive-humanistic counselling. *Counselling*, 10(1): 49–54.

Nelson-Jones, R. (1999b) *Creating Happy Relationships: A guide to partner skills*. London: Cassell.

Ness, C.D. (2004) Why girls fight: female youth violence in the inner city. *The Annals of the American Academy of Political and Social Science*, 595(1): 32–48.

Noonan, E. (1983) *Counselling Young People*. London: Routledge.

Norcross, J.C. and Grencavage, L. (1989) Eclecticism and integration in counselling and psychotherapy: major themes and obstacles. *British Journal of Guidance and Counselling*, 17(3): 227–47.

NSPCC (2010) Information for journalists: Facts and figures about child abuse: www.nspcc.org.uk/news-and-views.

O'Connell, B. (2005) *Solution-Focused Therapy* (2nd edition). London: Sage Publications.

O'Connor, R. (2010) Adolescent Self-harm in Northern Ireland. Available at: www.cawt.com/Site/11/Documents/Projects/DSH/RoryOConor.pdf

O'Hanlon, B. and Wilk, J. (1987) *Shifting Contexts: The generation of effective psychotherapy.* New York: Guilford Press.

O'Hanlon, W. (1992) History becomes her story: collaborative solution-oriented therapy of the after-effects of sexual abuse. In S. McNamee and K.J. Gergen (eds) *Therapy as Social Construction.* London: Sage Publications.

O'Hara, D. (2010) Hope: the neglected common factor. *Therapy Today,* November, 21(9): 17–19.

Oaklander, V. (1978) *Windows on our Children: A Gestalt therapy approach to children and adolescents.* Moab, UT: Real People Press.

Olweus, D. (1978) *Aggression in the Schools: Bullies and Whipping Boys.* Washington, DC: Hemisphere.

Olweus, D. (1991) Bully/victim problems among school children: basic facts and effects of a school-based intervention. In D. Pepler and K. Rubin (eds) *The Development and Treatment of Childhood Aggression.* Hillsdale, NJ: Erlbaum.

Olweus, D. (1992) Bullying among school children: intervention and prevention. In R.D. Peters, D. McMahon and V.L. Quincy (eds) *Aggression and Violence Throughout the Life Span.* Hillsdale, NJ: Erlbaum.

Olweus, D. (1993) *Bullying at School: What we know and what we can do.* Oxford: Blackwell.

Orlinsky, D.E., Ronnestad, M.H. and Willutzski, U. (2004) Fifty years of psychotherapy process-outcome research: continuity and change. In M. Lambert (ed.) *Bergin and Garfield's Handbook of Psychotherapy and Behavior Change* (5th edition). New York: Wiley, pp. 307–89.

Ortega-Ruiz, R., Mora-Merchan, J.A. and Jäger, T. (eds) (2007) Acting Against School Bullying and Violence: The role of media, local authorities and the internet. Landau: Verlag Empirische Pädagogik. Ebook available at: www.bullying-in-school.info

Parkes, C.M. (1986) *Studies of Grief in Adult Life.* Madison, CT: International Press.

Patterson, G.R. (1982) *Coercive Family Process.* Eugene, OR: Castalia.

Patterson, G.R. and Stouthamer-Loeber, M. (1984) The correlation of family management practice and delinquency. *Child Development,* 55: 1299–307.

Paul, G. (1967) Strategy for outcome research in psychotherapy. *Journal of Consulting Psychology,* 31(2): 109–18.

Payne, M. (2006) *Narrative Therapy: An introduction for counsellors.* London: Sage Publications.

Pechereck, A. (1996) Growing up in non-nuclear families. In A. Sigston, P. Corran, A. Labraun and S. Wolfrendale (eds) *Psychology in Practice with Young People, Families and Schools.* London: David Fulton.

Pegasus NLP (undated) *Mind-Body Health.* Available at: www.pe2000.com

Pendergrast, M. (1996) *Victims of Memory.* London: Harper-Collins.

Perry, A. (ed.) (2009) *Teenagers and Attachment: Helping adolescents to engage with life and learning.* London: Worth Publishing.

Peterson, A. Compas, B. Brooks-Gunn, J., Stemmler, M., Ey, S. and Grant, K. (1993) Depression in adolescence. *American Psychologist,* 48: 155–68.

Phillips, M.L., Drevets, W.C., Rauch, S.L. and Lane, R. (2003) Neurobiology of emotion perception I: the neural basis of normal emotion perception. *Biological Psychiatry,* 54: 504–14.

Pikas, A. (1975) Treatment of mobbing in school: principles for and the results of an anti-mobbing group, *Scandinavian Journal of Educational Research,* 19: 1–12.

Pikas, A. (1989) A pure concept of mobbing gives the best results for treatment. *School Psychology International,* 10: 95–104.

Pike, K.M. and Rodin, J. (1991) Mothers, daughters, and disordered eating. *Journal of Abnormal Psychology,* 100: 198–204.

Pointon, C. (2005) Eating disorders: our knowledge of how eating disorders develop has changed in recent years. *Therapy Today,* 16(8): 4–7.

Powers, P.S. and Bannon, Y. (2004) Medical comorbidity of anorexia nervosa, bulimia nervosa, and binge eating disorder. In T.D. Brewerton (ed.) *Clinical Handbook of Eating Disorders: An integrated approach.* New York: Marcel Dekker, pp. 231–55.

Prever, M. (2010a) *Counselling and Supporting Children and Young People: A person-centred approach.* London: Sage Publications.

Prever, M. (2010b) Needed: your self. *CCYP,* September: 26–30.

Prochaska, J.O. and DiClemente, C.C. (1982) Transtheoretical therapy: toward a more integrative model of change. *Psychotherapy: Theory, Research, and Practice,* 19: 276–88.

Pynoos, R.S., Steinberg, A.M. and Piacentini, J.C. (1995) A developmental model of childhood traumatic stress. In D. Cicchettii and D.J. Cohen (eds) *Developmental Psychology 2: Risk, Disorder and Adaptation.* New York: Wiley.

Radkowski, M. and Siegel, I.J. (1997) The gay adolescent: stresses, adaptations and psychosocial interventions. *Clinical Psychology Review,* 17: 191–216.

Raphael, B. (1984) *Anatomy of Bereavement: A handbook for the caring professions.* London: Hutchinson.

Reid, W. (1996) School counselling: a client-centred perspective. Australia: Kids Help Line (www.kidshelp.com.au/school/report).

Reinecke, M., Ryan, N. and Dubois, D. (1998) Cognitive-behavioural therapy of depression and depressive symptoms during adolescence: a review and meta-analysis. *Journal of the American Academy of Child and Adolescent Psychiatry,* 37(1): 26–34.

Rhodes, J. and Ajmal, Y. (1995) *Solution-Focused Thinking in Schools.* London: Brief Therapy Press.

Rice, G., Anderson, C., Risch, N. and Ebers, G. (1999) Male homosexuality: absence of linkage to microsatellite markers at Xq28. *Science,* 284(5414): 665–7.

Rigby, K. (2002) *New Perspectives on Bullying.* London: Jessica Kingsley.

Rivers, I. (1996) The bullying of lesbian and gay teenagers in school: a hidden issue. Keynote speech given at the NUT Conference, Birmingham, 7 December. (Transcript address: Department of Psychology, University of Luton, Park Square, Luton, Bedfordshire LU 3JU.)

Rodgers, B. and Pryor, J. (1998) *Divorce and Separation: The outcomes for children.* York: Joseph Rowntree Foundation.

Rofes, E. (1989) Opening up the classroom closet: responding to the educational needs of gay and lesbian youth. *Harvard Educational Review,* 59(4): 444–53.

Rogers, B. (2000) *Cracking the Hard Class: Strategies for managing the harder than average class.* London: Sage Publications.

Rogers, B. (2002) *Classroom Behaviour.* London: Sage Publications.

Rogers, C.R. (1961) *On Becoming a Person: A therapist's view of therapy.* London: Constable and Co.

Rogers, C.R. (1967) *On Becoming a Person.* London: Constable and Co.

Rogers, L. and Pickett, H. (2005) Play therapy lends itself to work with adolescents. *Therapy Today,* 16(8): 12–15.

Root, M.P.P., Fallon, P. and Friedrich, W.N. (1986) *Bulimia: A systematic approach to treatment.* New York: W.W. Norton.

Roth, A. and Fonagy, P. (2005) *What Works for Whom? A critical review of psychotherapy research* (2nd edition). New York: Guilford Press.

Roth, S. and Epston, D. (1996) Consulting the problem about the problematic relationship: an exercise for experiencing a relationship with an externalized problem. In M. Hoyt (ed.) *Constructive Therapies II.* New York: Guilford Press.

Rowe, D. (1996) Developing spiritual, moral and social values through a citizenship programme for primary schools. In R. Best (ed.) *Education, Spirituality and the Whole Child.* London: Cassell.

Rowling, L. (1996) Learning about life: teaching about loss. In R. Best (ed.) *Education, Spirituality and the Whole Child*. London: Cassell.

Russell, G.F., Szmukler, G.I., Dare, C. and Eisler, I. (1987) An evaluation of family therapy and anorexia nervosa and bulimia nervosa. *Archives of General Psychiatry*, 44: 1047–56.

Ryle, A. (1990) *Cognitive-Analytic Therapy: Active participation in change*. Chichester: Wiley.

Saigh, P.A., Mrouch, M. and Bremner, J.D. (1997) Scholastic impairments among traumatised adolescents. *Behaviour Research and Therapy*, 35: 436–9.

Salmivalli, C., Lagerspetz, K., Björkqvist, K., Osterman, K. and Kaukianen, A. (1996) Bullying as a group process: participant roles and their relations to social status within the group. *Aggressive Behaviour*, 22(1): 1–15.

Samaritans (2009) Samaritans information resource pack. Available at: www.samaritans.org/ PDF/SamaritansInfoResourcePack2009.pdf

Samdal, O. and Dur, W. (2002) The school environment and health of adolescents. WHO Policy Series: Health Policy for Children and Adolescents, Issue 1. Copenhagen: WHO Regional Office for Europe.

Sanders, D. and Wills, F. (2003) *Counselling for Anxiety Problems* (2nd edition). London: Sage Publications.

Sanderson, C. (1995) *Counselling Adult Survivors of Child Sexual Abuse*. London: Jessica Kingsley.

Schafer, S. (1977) *The Victim and His Criminal*. Reston, VA: Reston Publishing.

Scher, M., Stevens, M., Good, G. and Eichenfield, G.A. (eds) (1987) *Handbook of Counselling and Psychotherapy with Men*. Newbury Park, CA: Sage Publications.

Seligman, S.E.P. and Peterson, C. (1986) A learned helplessness perspective on childhood depression: theory and research. In M. Rutter, C.E. Izard and P.B. Read (eds) *Depression in Young People*. New York: Guilford Press.

Sellen, J. (2006) *See Beyond the Label: Empowering young people who self-harm and those who seek to support them*. London: Young Minds.

Sercombe, H. (2010) Teenage brains. *CCYP*, March: 21–4.

Seymour, A. (1998) Aetiology of the sexuality of children: an extended feminist perspective. *Womens' Studies International Forum*, 21(4): 415–27.

Shaffer, D. and Gutstein, J. (2002) Suicide and attempted suicide. In M. Rutter and D. Taylor (eds) *Child and Adolescent Psychiatry* (4th edition). Oxford: Blackwell, pp. 529–54.

Shapiro, D.A. and Shapiro, D. (1982) Meta-analysis of comparative therapy outcome studies: a replication and refinement. *Psychological Bulletin*, 92(3): 581–604.

Sherratt, E., MacArthur, C., Cheng, K., Bullock, A. and Thomas, H. (1998) *Young Peoples' Lifestyle: Survey 1995–1996 (West Midlands)*. Birmingham: NHS Executive, Birmingham University.

Shortt, A. and Spence, S. (2006) Risk and protective factors for depression in youth. *Behaviour Change*, 23(1): 1–30.

Shriver, L. (2003) *We Need to Talk About Kevin*. New York: Counterpoint.

Smith, H. (1999) *Children, Feelings and Divorce*. London: Free Association Books.

Smith, M.L., Glass, G.V. and Miller, T.L. (1980) *The Benefits of Psychotherapy*. Baltimore, MD: Johns Hopkins University Press.

Smith, P.K. and Sharp, S. (eds) (1994) *School Bullying: Insights and perspectives*. London: Routledge.

Smith, P.K., Mahdavi, J., Carvalho, M., Fisher, S., Russell, S. and Tippett, N. (2008) Cyberbullying: its nature and impact in secondary school pupils. *Journal of Child Psychology and Psychiatry*, April, 49(4): 376–85.

Smokowski, P.R., Fraser, M.W., Day, S.H., Galinsky, M.J. and Bacallao, M.L. (2004) School-based skills training to prevent aggressive behavior and peer rejection in childhood: evaluating the making choices program. *The Journal of Primary Prevention*, 25(2): 233–51.

Sorensen, D. (2002) Statistician, The Scottish Executive Education Department. In D. Lines (2007) Violence in school: what can we do? *Pastoral Care in Education*, 25(2) June, 2007: 14–21.

Speedy, J. (2000) White water rafting in cocktail dresses. *Counselling and Psychotherapy*, 11(10): 628–32.

Stassen Berger, K. (2007) Update on bullying at school: science forgotten? *Developmental Review*, 27(1): 90–126.

Steering Committee (2002) Empirically supported therapy relationships: Conclusions and recommendations on the Division 29 task force. In J.C. Norcross (ed.), *Psychotherapy Relationships That Work: Therapist Contributions and Responsiveness to Patients*. Oxford: Oxford University Press. pp. 441–3.

Straus, M.A. (1996) A spanking and the making of a violent society. *Pediatrics*, October: 837–42.

Street, E. (1994) *Counselling for Family Problems*. London: Sage Publications.

Sukhodolsky, D.G. and Ruchkin, V.V. (2004) Association of normative beliefs and anger with aggression and antisocial behavior in Russian male juvenile offenders and high school students. *Journal of Abnormal Psychology*, 32(2): 225–36.

Sussman, T. and Duffy, M. (1996) Are we forgetting about gay male adolescents in AIDS related research and prevention? *Youth and Society*, 27: 379–93.

Talmon, M. (1990) *Single Session Therapy*. San Francisco, CA: Jossey-Bass.

The Sainsbury Centre for Mental Health (2006) *We Need to Talk: The case for psychological therapy on the NHS*. London: Sainsbury Centre for Mental Health.

The Massachusetts Youth Risk Behaviour Survey (2006). Available at: www.cdc.gov/mmwr/preview/mmwrhtml/ss5505a1.htm

Thomas, R.M. (1990) *Life-Span Stages and Development*. London: Sage Publications.

Thornberg, R. (2010) Victimising of Bullying: A grounded theory (*ECER Programmes*). Available at: www.eera-ecer.eu/ecer-programmes/conference/ecer-2010/contribution/1188-2/?no_cache=1

Thorne, B. (1984) Person-centred therapy. In W. Dryden (ed.) *Individual Therapy in Britain*. London: Harper and Row.

Thorne, B. (1994) Brief companionship. In D. Mearns (ed.) *Developing Person-centred Counselling*. London: Sage Publications.

Thorne, B. (1999) The move towards brief therapy: its dangers and its challenges. *Counselling*, 10(1): 7–11.

Thorne, B. (2002) *The Mystical Power of Person-centred Therapy*. London: Whurr.

Thornberry, T.P. (1998) Membership in youth gangs and involvement in serious violent offending. In R. Loeber and D.P. Farrington (eds) *Serious and Violent Juvenile Offenders: Risk Factors and Successful Interventions*. Thousand Oaks, CA: Sage Publications.

Tober, G. (1991) Motivational interviewing with young people. In W.R. Miller and S. Rollnick (eds) *Motivational Interviewing*. New York: Guilford Press.

Tolan, J. (2003) *Skills in Person-centred Counselling and Psychotherapy*. London: Sage Publications.

Tomm, K. (1985) Circular questioning. In D. Campbell and R. Draper (eds) *Applications of Systemic Family Therapy: The Milan Approach*. London: Academic Press.

Toolkit (2010) (PDF) Available at: www.bacp.co.uk/information/schoolToolkit.php

Treasure, J., Todd, G., Brolly, M., Tiller, J., Nehmed, A. and Denman, F. (1995) A pilot study of a randomised trial of cognitive analytical therapy vs educational behavioral therapy for adult anorexia nervosa. *Behaviour Research and Therapy*, 33(4): 363–7.

Triggle, N. (2007) Warning over children who abuse. News item, BBC News, 2 March. Available at: http://news.bbc.co.uk/1/hi/health/6408837.stm

Trowell, J., Joffe, I., Campbell, J. et al. (2007) Childhood depression: a place for psychotherapy. An outcome study comparing individual psychodynamic psychotherapy and family therapy. *European Child and Adolescent Psychiatry*, 16: 157–67.

Truax, C.B. (1971) Self-disclosure, genuineness and the interpersonal relationship counsellor. *Education and Supervision*, 10(4): 351–4.

Truax, C.B. and Carkhuff, R.R. (1967) *Towards Effective Counselling and Psychotherapy*. Chicago, IL: Aldine.

Tryon, G.S. and Winograd, G. (2002) Goal consensus and collaboration. In J.C. Norcross (ed.) *Psychotherapy Relationships that Work: Therapist contributions and responsiveness to patients*. New York: Oxford University Press, pp. 109–25.

Tudor, K. (2001) *Transactional Analysis Approaches to Brief Therapy*. London: Sage Publications.

UNICEF (2001) *A League Table of Teenage Births in Rich Nations*. Innocenti Report Card No. 3. Florence: UNICEF Innocenti Research Centre. Available at: www.unicef-irc.org/publications/pdf/repcard3e.pdf

Van Heeringen, C. and Vincke, J. (2000) Suicidal acts and ideation in homosexual and bisexual young people: a study of prevalence and risk factors. *Social Psychiatry and Psychiatric Epidemiology*, November, 35(11): 494–9.

Vidovic, V., Juresa, V., Begovac, I., Mahnic, M. and Tocilj, G. (2005) Perceived family cohesion, adaptability and communication in eating disorders. *European Eating Disorders Review*, 13: 19–28.

Wang, M.Q., Fitzheugh, E.C., Eddy, J.M. and Fu, Q. (1997) Social influences on adolescents smoking progress: a longitudinal analysis. *Adolescence*, 21: 111–17.

Waterman, A. (1984) *The Psychology of Individualism*. New York: Praeger.

Watzlawick, P., Weakland, J. and Fisch, R. (1974) *Change: Principles of Problem Formation and Problem Resolution*. New York: W.W. Norton.

Webb, S. (1994) *Troubled and Vulnerable Children: A practical guide for heads*. Kingston-upon-Thames: Cromer.

Wellings, K., Nanchahal, K., Macdowall, W., McManus, S. and Evans, R. et al. (2001) Sexual behaviour in Britain: early heterosexual experience. *Lancet*, 358: 1843–50.

West, W. (2000) *Psychotherapy and Spirituality*. London: Sage Publications.

West, W. (2004) *Spiritual Issues in Therapy*. Hampshire: Palgrave Macmillan.

Whiston, S.C. and Sexton, T.L. (1998) A review of school counseling outcome research: implications for practice. *Journal of Counseling and Development*, 76: 412–26.

White, A. and Swartzwelder, H.S. (2005) Age-related effects of alcohol on memory and memory-related brain function in adolescents and adults. In M. Galanter (ed.) *Recent Developments in Alcohol, 17: Alcohol problems in adolescents and young people*. New York: Springer, pp. 161–76.

White, M. (1989) *Selected Papers*. Adelaide: Dulwich Centre Publications.

White, M. (1995) *Externalising Conversations Exercise*. Adelaide: Dulwich Centre Publications.

White, M. and Epston, D. (1990) *Narrative Means to Therapeutic Ends*. New York: W.W. Norton.

Whitney, I. and Smith, P.K. (1993) A survey of the nature and extent of bullying in junior/middle and secondary schools. *Educational Research*, 35: 13–25.

Wilson, C.J. and Deane, F.P. (2001) Adolescent opinions about reducing help-seeking barriers and increasing appropriate help engagement. *Journal of Educational and Psychological Consultation*, 12(4): 345–64.

Winslade, J. and Monk, G. (1999) *Narrative Counselling in Schools: Powerful and Brief*. Thousand Oaks, CA: Corwin Press.

Winstok, Z., Eisikovits, Z. and Karnieli-Miller, O. (2004) The impact of father-to-mother aggression on the structure and content of adolescents' perceptions of themselves and their parents. *Violence against Women*, 10(9): 1036–55.

Wolberg, L.R. (1968) *Short-term Psychotherapy*. New York: Grune and Stratton.

Wolfe, D.A., Jaffe, P., Wilson, S.K. and Zak, L. (1985) Children of battered women: the relation of child behaviour to family violence and maternal stress. *Journal of Consulting and Clinical Psychology*, 53(5): 657–65.

Wolfe, D.A., Jaffe, P., Wilson, S.K. and Zak, L. (1986) Child witnesses to violence between parents: critical issues in behavioral and social adjustment. *Journal of Abnormal Child Psychology*, 14(1): 95–104.

Worden, W. (1984) *Grief Counselling and Grief Therapy*. London: Tavistock.

World Health Organisation (2002) Suicide Rates and Absolute Numbers of Suicide by Country. Available at: www.who.int/mental_health/prevention/suicide-country-reports/en/index.html

Wright, R. (2009) *The Evolution of God: The Origins of Our Beliefs.* London: Little, Brown Book Group.

Wu, L. (1987) The effects of a rational-emotive group on rational thinking, social anxiety and self-acceptance of college students. *Bulletin of Educational Psychology*, 20: 183–203.

Yalom, I.D. (1990) *Existential Psychotherapy.* New York: Basic Books.

Ybarra, M.L. and Mitchell, K.J. (2005) Exposure to internet pornography among children and adolescents: a national survey. *CyberPsychology and Behavior*, 8(5): 473–86.

Yerkes, R.M. and Dodson, J.D. (1993) The relation of strength of stimulus to rapidity of habit-formation. *Journal of Neurological Psychology*, 18: 459–82.

Youdell, D. (2003) Identity traps or how black students fail: interactions between biographical, sub-cultural, and learner identities. *British Journal of Sociology of Education*, 24(1): 3–18.

Yule, W. and Gold, A. (1993) *Wise Before the Event: Coping with Crisis in School.* London: Calouste Gulbenkian Foundation.

Yurgelun-Todd, D. (2002) Inside the Teenage Brain. Frontline Interviews Fact Sheet. Available at: www.pbs.org/wgbh/pages/frontline/shows/teenbrain/interviews/todd.html

Legal and Government Documents

Axon v. Secretary of State for Health [2006]: Sue Axon's attempt to sidestep the Gillick ruling, as established in the case of *Gillick v. West Norfolk & Wisbech Health Authority* [1986] AC 112 that it is contrary to the rights of parents to respect for their family life under Article 8 of the European Convention on Human Rights.

Children Act (1989) and (2004). London: HMSO.

Data Protection Act 1998. London: HMSO.

DfEE (2000) *Sex and Relationship Educational Guidance.* London: DfEE 0116/2000.

DfES (2001) *Promoting Children's Mental Health within Early Years and School Settings.* Available at: www.dfes.gov.uk/mentalhealth

DfES (2004) *Every Child Matters: Change for Children.* London: DfES 1110–2004. Available at: www.publications.parliament.uk/pa/cm200405/cmselect/cmeduski/40/40.pdf

Gillick v. *West Norfolk Wisbech Area Health Authority* [1986] AC 112, [1985] 3 All ER 402, HL.

Human Rights Act (1998). London: HMSO.

Office of National Statistics (OfNS) (1998) *Young Teenage Smoking in 1998: A Report on the Key Findings from the Teenage Smoking Attitudes.* London: OfNS.

OfNS (2008a) www.statistics.gov.uk/cci/nugget.asp?id=322

OfNS (2008b) www.statistics.gov.uk/cci/nugget.asp?id=2193

OfNS (2008c) www.statistics.gov.uk/cci/nugget.asp?id=458

OfNS (2008d) www.statistics.gov.uk/cci/nugget.asp?id=1655

Police and Criminal Evidence Act (PACE) (1984). London: HMSO.

Prevention of Terrorism Act (2005) www.legislation.gov.uk/ukpga/2005/2/contents

Safeguarding Vulnerable Groups Act (2006). Available at: www.legislation.gov.uk/ukpga/2006/47/contents

Safe Network (2011). Available at: www.safenetwork.org.uk/getting_started/Pages/Why_does_safeguarding_matter.aspx

Sexual Offences Act (2003). London: HMSO.

Working Together to Safeguard Children: A guide to inter-agency working to safeguard and promote the welfare of children (2010). *Department of children, schools and families.* Available at: www.education.gov.uk/publications/eOrderingDownload/00305-2010DOM-EN.pdf

Index

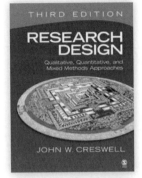

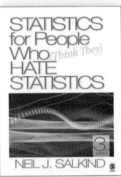

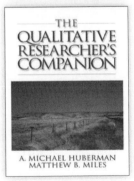